EXPLORING ZECHARIAH,

VOLUME 2

ANCIENT NEAR EAST MONOGRAPHS

Editors
Alan Lenzi
Juan Manuel Tebes

Editorial Board
Reinhard Achenbach
C. L. Crouch
Esther J. Hamori
Chistopher B. Hays
René Krüger
Graciela Gestoso Singer
Bruce Wells

Number 17

EXPLORING ZECHARIAH,

VOLUME 2

The Development and Role of Biblical Traditions in Zechariah

by
Mark J. Boda

SBL PRESS

Atlanta

Copyright © 2017 by SBL Press

All rights reserved. No part of this work may be reproduced or transmitted in any form or by any means, electronic or mechanical, including photocopying and recording, or by means of any information storage or retrieval system, except as may be expressly permitted by the 1976 Copyright Act or in writing from the publisher. Requests for permission should be addressed in writing to the Rights and Permissions Office, SBL Press, 825 Houston Mill Road, Atlanta, GA 30329 USA.

Library of Congress Cataloging in Publication Control Number: 2016961865

Printed on acid-free paper.

Ad majorem Dei gloriam

For Michael H. Floyd

Contents

Preface	ix
Abbreviations	xiii
1. Reading between the Lines: Inner Biblical Allusion and Zechariah	1
2. Terrifying the Horns: Persia and Babylon in Zechariah 1:7–6:15	17
3. *Hoy, Hoy*: The Prophetic Origins of the Babylonian Tradition in Zechariah 2:10–17	39
4. Oil, Crowns, and Thrones: Prophet, Priest, and King in Zechariah 1:7–6:15	59
5. Writing the Vision: Zechariah within the Visionary Traditions of the Hebrew Bible	83
6. Zechariah: Master Mason or Penitential Prophet?	101
7. When God's Voice Breaks Through: Shifts in Revelatory Rhetoric in Zechariah 1–8	121
8. Freeing the Burden of Prophecy: משא and the Legitimacy of Prophecy in Zechariah 9–14	135
9. Zechariah 11:4–16 in Its Literary Contexts	153
10. Inner Biblical Allusions in the Shepherd Units of Zechariah 9–14	169
11. Reading Zechariah 9–14 with the Law and the Prophets: Sibling Rivalry and Prophetic Crisis	183
12. Afterword	197
Bibliography	199
Ancient Sources Index	225
Modern Authors Index	249

Preface

During the past three decades the book of Zechariah has received increasing attention within the Hebrew Bible guild. This was due no doubt to the appearance of the influential commentaries of Eric and Carol Meyers as well as David Petersen beginning in the 1980s, but also to the increasing focus on the Persian period in historical and biblical scholarship. Research during this period has been diverse, focusing on the composition, the structure, and the reception of this ancient text and all points in between. The guild has been witness to a shift from dominantly diachronic methodologies to a diversity of diachronic, synchronic and a-chronic approaches, reflecting a (con)fusion of modern, postmodern and even premodern sensibilities.

It was the book of Zechariah that provided me a fresh direction for research after spending my doctoral years focusing nearly all my attention on Ezra–Nehemiah. My dissertation on Neh 9 ended by giving attention to connections between that penitential prayer and Zech 7–8. Little did I realize that this conclusion was my invitation to two decades of focused attention on this "post-exilic" prophet. Shifting to Zechariah provided me a new challenge to engage deeply with a different genre and tradition (prophetic), but also the opportunity to build on my newfound knowledge of the Persian period. It was a perfect time to enter into the study of Zechariah since there was a growing community of scholars with whom I could converse, dialogue, and debate.

During these two decades of work I have written two commentaries and in the process have sought to test my ideas in the Hebrew Bible scholarly guild. As I look back I can discern two major streams in my research. On the one hand, I have pursued the question of the composition of the book of Zechariah and the limits of the literary activity related to this prophet and his tradition. On the other hand, I have continued the line of research that I began in my doctoral work, investigating the presence of inner biblical allusions within Zechariah and the impact of these allusions on the reading of the prophetic book. In the present two volumes I have brought together several articles that have been published in various literary contexts (journals, collected volumes) or presented at scholarly conferences in which I tested my ideas among learned colleagues. Drawing them together into one collection hopefully will help scholars identify the basis, trace the trajectory, and engage the conclusions to which I have arrived after two decades of working with the text of Zechariah.

This second volume focuses on the phenomenon of inner biblical allusion in the book of Zechariah,[1] a topic to which many had contributed long before I began my work and to which many continued to contribute as I have researched over the past two decades. My interest began with this phenomenon in my doctoral dissertation on Neh 9, but it was Zech 9–14 that seemed to have the most potential for the use of this method. This soon extended to Zech 1–8. The allusions to other biblical materials are plenteous in the book of Zechariah, and I have provided a fuller account of this phenomenon in my detailed exegesis in my latest commentary (NICOT). In this present volume I provide some key studies on different sections of Zechariah which bring particular focus onto the role that the Latter Prophets played in Zechariah, with possible connections to the broader Torah and Prophets as canonical divisions. As with the first volume, at times I lay a foundation in one chapter and then extend the argument in the next, providing more evidence and teasing out the implications in greater ways. There will be some repetition, but in general each piece is distinct. I have also slightly revised the articles to fit into their new literary context and where necessary to align them with the later development in my thought, but most of the material is drawn verbatim from my earlier works cited at the outset of each chapter.[2]

My personal agenda for gathering scholars together for the sessions and eventually the edited book *Bringing Out the Treasure* was related to having arrived at Zech 9 in researching and writing a commentary and having no idea what to do with this material. Michael Floyd was gracious enough to join me on this venture as we drew together key scholars in Europe and North America who had worked or were presently working on Zech 9–14. This reveals how important the academic guild has been to me throughout my career to this point. I have found among other scholars a place to test my ideas, but more importantly to learn and be stretched and to remain accountable for my continued progress. Within the footnotes of *Exploring Zechariah* you will find many names of those who have impacted my scholarship, whether I agree with their conclusions or not. These people include both the great cloud of witnesses who have researched and written in decades past, but also those who are presently engaged in research. What a privilege we have to enjoy relationships while pursuing the academic love of our lives. One particular individual within the guild has been a faithful colleague along the way, not only through his superb work in editing now three volumes on

---

[1] For a similar preface but providing an overview of the first volume, see the preface to *Exploring Zechariah: Volume 1—The Development of Zechariah and Its Role within the Twelve*.

[2] When a chapter appeared in an earlier Festschrift I have removed specific reference to the honoree in the body of the text (though noted in the first footnote) so as not to distract from the argument. Of course, I mean no disrespect by this and still do fully honor and appreciate the colleague to which it was dedicated.

the prophets with me, but also through his stellar academic work which has informed my own and spurred me on in my academic pursuits. I dedicate this second volume of *Exploring Zechariah* to Michael Floyd for his faithful service to the guild and in particular his insights into the inner biblical nature of Zechariah.

I want to express my thanks to the Society of Biblical Literature ANEM editorial board for accepting these two volumes into their innovative and important series. I have appreciated Alan Lenzi for his guidance through the publication process, Nicole Tilford for help with copyediting and layout, and Dustin Burlet with indexing. Thanks especially goes to Alexander C. Stewart, my graduate assistant, who spent considerable time in the initial and final stages adapting these disparate essays into a usable form for publication. Much of the research for the articles within this volume was supported by a generous grant from the Canadian Government's Social Sciences and Humanities Research Council. This grant allowed me to test my ideas at various guild events and support research assistance for these articles, and for this support I am deeply thankful. Also I want to express my thanks to the Senate and Board of McMaster Divinity College for providing the freedom during a research leave to bring this volume together. Finally, I deeply appreciate the many publishing houses and journals who have granted me permission to republish these many essays in slightly revised form in this volume. I have noted the original place of publication at the outset of each essay. There have been some revisions to these essays, partly to bring the text into line with the Society of Biblical Literature ANEM style, but also small corrections and revisions relevant to the new literary place of these articles in this volume. I have kept these to a minimum. My hope is that this volume will provide some insight into my approach to the impact of broader biblical traditions on Zechariah and the role that Zechariah played in the preservation, explication, and possibly even formation of these broader traditions.

Ego ex eorum numero me esse profiteor qui scribunt proficiendo, et scribendo proficient.
      (Augustine, Epistle 143,2, via Jean Calvin)

Abbreviations

AB	Anchor Bible Commentary
ABD	*Anchor Bible Dictionary*. Edited by David Noel Freedman. 6 vols. New York: Doubleday, 1992
ABR	*Australian Biblical Review*
AcBib	Academia Biblica
AJSL	*American Journal of Semitic Languages and Literatures*
ANEM	Ancient Near East Monographs
AOAT	Alter Orient und Altes Testament
ATANT	Abhandlungen zur Theologie des Alten und Neuen Testaments
ATD	Das Alte Testament Deutsch
AUSS	*Andrews University Seminary Studies*
BBB	Bonner biblische Beiträge
BETL	Bibliotheca Ephemeridum Theologicarum Lovaniensium
BHS	*Biblia Hebraica Stuttgartensia*. Edited by Karl Elliger and Wilhelm Rudolph. Stuttgart: Deutsche Bibelgesellschaft, 1983
Bib	*Biblica*
BibInt	*Biblical Interpretation*
BibS(N)	Biblische Studien (Neukirchen, 1951–)
BJRL	*Bulletin of the John Rylands University Library of Manchester*
BJSUCSD	Biblical and Judaic Studies from the University of California, San Diego
BR	*Biblical Research*
BT	*Bible Translator*
BZAW	Beihefte zur Zeitschrift für die alttestamentliche Wissenschaft
CBC	Cambridge Bible Commentary
CBET	Contributions to Biblical Exegesis and Theology
CBQ	*Catholic Biblical Quarterly*
CC	Continental Commentaries
CJ	*Classical Journal*
CMBC	Canadian Mennonite Bible College
Colloq	*Colloquium*
ConBOT	Coniectanea Biblica: Old Testament Series
CTM	*Concordia Theological Monthly*
CurBR	*Currents in Biblical Research* (formerly *Currents in Research: Biblical Studies*)
CurBS	*Currents in Research: Biblical Studies*
DB	Darius I's Bisitun inscription
Did	*Didaskalia*
Dtr	Deuteronomic

EBib	Etudes bibliques
EJL	Early Judaism and Its Literature
Enc	*Encounter*
ErIsr	*Eretz-Israel*
ETL	*Ephemerides Theologicae Lovanienses*
EvT	*Evangelische Theologie*
FAT	Forschungen zum Alten Testament
FOTL	Forms of the Old Testament Literature
FRLANT	Forschungen zur Religion und Literatur des Alten und Neuen Testaments
GKC	*Gesenius' Hebrew Grammar*. Edited by Emil Kautzsch. Translated by Arthur E. Cowley. 2nd ed. Oxford: Clarendon, 1910
HAT	Handbuch zum Alten Testament
HBAI	*Hebrew Bible and Ancient Israel*
HCOT	Historical Commentary on the Old Testament
HeyJ	*Heythrop Journal*
HSM	Harvard Semitic Monographs
HTR	*Harvard Theological Review*
HUCA	*Hebrew Union College Annual*
IBC	Interpretation: A Bible Commentary for Teaching and Preaching
IBHS	*An Introduction to Biblical Hebrew Syntax*. Bruce K. Waltke and Michael O'Connor. Winona Lake, IN: Eisenbrauns, 1990
IBS	*Irish Biblical Studies*
ICC	International Critical Commentary
IDBSup	*Interpreter's Dictionary of the Bible: Supplementary Volume*. Edited by Keith Crim. Nashville: Abingdon, 1976
IECOT	International Exegetical Commentary on the Old Testament
IEJ	*Israel Exploration Journal*
inf. constr.	infinitive construct
Int	*Interpretation*
ITC	International Theological Commentary
IVP	InterVarsity Press
JAOS	*Journal of the American Oriental Society*
JBL	*Journal of Biblical Literature*
JETS	*Journal of the Evangelical Theological Society*
JHS	*Journal of Hebrew Scriptures*
JJS	*Journal of Jewish Studies*
JNES	*Journal of Near Eastern Studies*
Joüon	Joüon, Paul, and Takamitsu Muraoka. *A Grammar of Biblical Hebrew* SubBi 14. Rome: Pontifical Biblical Institute, 2000.
JQR	*Jewish Quarterly Review*

JSJ	*Journal for the Study of Judaism in the Persian, Hellenistic, and Roman Periods*
JSNT	*Journal of the Study of the New Testament*
JSNTSup	Journal for the Study of the New Testament Supplement Series
JSOT	*Journal for the Study of the Old Testament*
JSOTSup	Journal for the Study of the Old Testament Supplement Series
KAT	Kommentar zum Alten Testament
KBW	Katholisches Bibelwerk
LD	Lectio Divina
LHBOTS	The Library of Hebrew Bible/Old Testament Studies
LSTS	The Library of Second Temple Studies
LXX	Septuagint/Old Greek
MT	Masoretic Text
NAC	New American Commentary
NCB	New Century Bible
Neot	*Neotestamentica*
NIBCOT	New International Biblical Commentary on the Old Testament
NICOT	New International Commentary on the Old Testament
NIVAC	The NIV Application Commentary
NRTh	*La nouvelle revue théologique*
NTTS	New Testament Tools and Studies
OBO	Oribis Biblicus et Orientalis
OTG	Old Testament Guides
OTL	Old Testament Library
OtSt	*Oudtestamentische Studiën*
PIBA	Proceedings of the Irish Biblical Association
PTL	*Poetics and Theory of Literature*
RB	*Revue biblique*
SBLDS	Society of Biblical Literature Dissertation Series
SBLMS	Society of Biblical Literature Monograph Series
SBLSP	Society of Biblical Literature Seminar Papers
SCM	Student Christian Movement Press
SHBC	Smyth & Helwys Bible Commentary
SHR	Studies in the History of Religions (supplements to *Numen*)
SJOT	*Scandinavian Journal of the Old Testament*
SSN	Studia Semitica Neerlandica
ST	*Studia Theologica*
STDJ	Studies on the Texts of the Desert of Judah
SubBi	Subsidia Biblica
SymS	Symposium Series

TLOT	*Theological Lexicon of the Old Testament*. Edited by Ernst Jenni, with assistance from Claus Westermann. Translated by Mark E. Biddle. 3 vols. Peabody, MA: Hendrickson, 1997
TOTC	Tyndale Old Testament Commentaries
Transeu	*Transeuphratène*
TUGAL	Texte und Untersuchungen zur Geschichte der altchristlichen Literatur
TynBul	*Tyndale Bulletin*
USFISFCJ	University of South Florida International Studies in Formative Christianity and Judaism
VT	*Vetus Testamentum*
VTSup	Supplements to Vetus Testamentum
WBC	Word Biblical Commentary
WMANT	Wissenschaftliche Monographien zum Alten und Neuen Testament
ZAW	*Zeitschrift für die altestamentliche Wissenschaft*
ZWT	*Zeitschrift für wissenschaftliche Theologie*

1
Reading between the Lines: Inner Biblical Allusion and Zechariah[1]

In this initial chapter I provide an overview of my approach and conclusions on the phenomenon of inner biblical allusion in Zechariah. After tracing the history of scholarship on this phenomenon in Zechariah, I provide a brief reflection on method before summarizing my general conclusions on key biblical influences on Zechariah. The chapter concludes with an orientation to the rest of the volume, a reference point to see how the more focused studies support key elements within my conclusions.

The opening pericope of the book of Zechariah (1:1–6) orients the reader to the role that earlier revelation will play in the book as a whole. The speech of Yahweh makes clear that while the prophets as revelatory conduits have died along with the rebellious generation they warned (1:5), Yahweh's revelation through those

---

[1] This chapter is drawn from earlier work in Mark J. Boda, *The Book of Zechariah*, NICOT (Grand Rapids: Eerdmans, 2016); Mark J. Boda, *Haggai and Zechariah Research: A Bibliographic Survey*, Tools for Biblical Study 5 (Leiden: Deo, 2003); Mark J. Boda, "Reading between the Lines: Zechariah 11:4–16 in Its Literary Contexts," in *Bringing out the Treasure: Inner Biblical Allusion and Zechariah 9–14*, ed. Mark J. Boda and Michael H. Floyd, JSOTSup 370 (Sheffield: Sheffield Academic, 2003), 277–91; Mark J. Boda and Stanley E. Porter, "Literature to the Third Degree: Prophecy in Zechariah 9–14 and the Passion of Christ," in *Traduire la Bible hébraïque: De la Septante à la Nouvelle Bible Segond = Translating the Hebrew Bible: From the Septuagint to the Nouvelle Bible Segond*, ed. Robert David and Manuel Jinbachian, Sciences Bibliques 15 (Montreal: Médiaspaul, 2005), 215–54. These sources are combined and revised for inclusion in this volume.

he called "my servants the prophets" endures (1:6a). That revelation is identified as "my words" and "my statutes," terms which point to both prophecy and law, those revelatory traditions which begin with Moses and endure throughout the history of Israel and Judah (see 2 Kgs 17:13). Zechariah 1:4 contains an example of the words which endure ("Turn from your evil ways and from your evil deeds"), drawn from the literary tradition of Jeremiah. In similar fashion Zech 7:1–14 also notes the words proclaimed through the "earlier prophets" (7:7), echoing again the words of Jeremiah (7:9–10).

In light of this emphasis on earlier revelation preserved in the message of Zechariah, it is not surprising that scholars have consistently highlighted connections between texts in the book of Zechariah and other biblical materials (whether through study of inner biblical allusions or traditio-historical connections). In the late 1960s and early 1970s four key scholars provided an important foundation for scholarship on this topic over the past half century. Beuken, Petitjean, and Jeremias focused on Zech 1–8,[2] while Lutz, Mason, and Willi-Plein attended to Zech 9–14.[3]

---

[2] Wim A. M. Beuken, *Haggai–Sacharja 1–8: Studien zur Überlieferungsgeschichte der frühnachexilischen Prophetie*, SSN 10 (Assen: Van Gorcum, 1967); Albert Petitjean, *Les oracles du proto-Zacharie: Un programme de restauration pour la communauté juive après l'exil* (Paris: Librairie Lecoffre, 1969); Christian Jeremias, *Die Nachtgesichte des Sacharja: Untersuchungen zu ihrer Stellung im Zusammenhang der Visionsberichte im Alten Testament und zu ihrem Bildmaterial*, FRLANT 117 (Göttingen: Vandehoeck & Ruprecht, 1977); cf. Christian Jeremias, "Sacharja und die prophetische Tradition, untersucht im Zusammenhang der Exodus-, Zion-, und Davidüberlieferung" (PhD diss., University of Göttingen, 1966).

[3] Hanns-Martin Lutz, *Jahwe, Jerusalem und die Völker: Zur Vorgeschichte von Sach. 12, 1–8, und 14, 1–5*, WMANT 27 (Neukirchen-Vluyn: Neukirchener, 1968); Rex A. Mason, "The Use of Earlier Biblical Material in Zechariah IX–XIV: A Study in Inner Biblical Exegesis" (PhD diss., University of London, 1973) = Rex A. Mason, "The Use of Earlier Biblical Material in Zechariah 9–14: A Study in Inner Biblical Exegesis," in *Bringing out the Treasure: Inner Biblical Allusion and Zechariah 9–14*, ed. Mark J. Boda and Michael H. Floyd, JSOTSup 370 (Sheffield: Sheffield Academic, 2003), 1–208; Rex A. Mason, "The Relation of Zech 9–14 to Proto-Zechariah," *ZAW* 88 (1976): 227–39; Rex A. Mason, "Some Examples of Inner Biblical Exegesis in Zech. IX–XIV," in *Studia Evangelica Vol. 7: Papers Presented to the 5th International Congress on Biblical Studies Held at Oxford, 1973*, ed. Elizabeth A. Livingstone, TUGAL 126 (Berlin: Akademie, 1982), 343–54; Rex A. Mason, "Inner Biblical Exegesis in Zech. 9–14," *Grace Theological Journal* 3 (1982): 51–65; Ina Willi-Plein, *Prophetie am Ende: Untersuchungen zu Sacharja 9–14*, BBB 42 (Köln: Hanstein, 1974). Of course the earlier shorter studies of Bernhard Stade, "Deuterosacharja: Eine kritische Studie I," *ZAW* 1 (1881): 1–96; Bernhard Stade, "Deuterosacharja: Eine kritische Studie II," *ZAW* 2 (1882): 151–72; Bernhard Stade, "Deuterosacharja: Eine kritische Studie III," *ZAW* 2 (1882): 275–309; Mathias Delcor, " Les sources du Deutero-Zacharie et ses procédés d'emprunt," *RB* 59 (1952): 385–411, created a key platform for Mason and Willi-Plein.

Many have followed in the footsteps of these foundational scholars,[4] beginning with a flurry of activity in the early 1990s.[5] Mason's student Tollington focused her attention on the first half of the book of Zechariah, noting connections between Haggai–Zech 1–8 and the pre-exilic prophets through a close examination of continuities and discontinuities in style and tradition.[6] In terms of style she concluded that these prophets employ similar forms to their classical predecessors (oracles, visions, symbolic action). In terms of tradition, however, she highlights varying levels of continuity and discontinuity. As the earlier prophets, Zechariah (and Haggai) drew prophetic authority from a divine calling and revealed similar struggles for credibility, even if he was more successful than the preexilic prophets in eliciting a response. In contrast to the earlier prophets who attacked the religious hierarchy of their day, Zechariah (and Haggai) rally the people around the temple and religious identity. Zechariah (and Haggai) approached the leadership tradition in similar ways to the earlier prophets by affirming the Davidic line represented by Zerubbabel. However, there are indications in Zech 1–8 (and the framework of Haggai, which is linked by Tollington to Zechariah) that the prophet came to the conclusion that a diarchic rule of religious and civil leaders would sustain the community until the arrival of a Davidic royal. Although there are

---

[4] Not included in this survey are the helpful contributions from the commentary tradition during this period, especially from David L. Petersen, *Haggai and Zechariah 1–8: A Commentary*, OTL (Philadelphia: Westminster, 1984); David L. Petersen, *Zechariah 9–14 and Malachi: A Commentary*, OTL (Louisville: Westminster John Knox, 1995); Carol L. Meyers and Eric M. Meyers, *Haggai, Zechariah 1–8: A New Translation with Introduction and Commentary*, AB 25B (Garden City, NY: Doubleday, 1987); Carol L. Meyers and Eric M. Meyers, *Zechariah 9–14: A New Translation with Introduction and Commentary*, AB 25C (New York: Doubleday, 1993).
[5] At two junctures during the past fifteen years I along with my colleague Michael Floyd have brought together scholars working on inner biblical allusion/intertextuality, showcasing the results in the following volumes: Mark J. Boda and Michael H. Floyd, eds., *Bringing out the Treasure: Inner Biblical Allusion and Zechariah 9–14*, JSOTSup 370 (Sheffield: Sheffield Academic, 2003), with articles by Petersen, Floyd, Nurmela, Tigchelaar, Person, Boda, Nogalski, Redditt, Schart, and response from Mason; Mark J. Boda and Michael H. Floyd, eds., *Tradition in Transition: Haggai and Zechariah 1–8 in the Trajectory of Hebrew Theology*, LHBOTS 475 (London: T&T Clark, 2008), with articles by Kessler, Patrick, Redditt, Phinney, Tiemeyer, Wolters, Stead, Boda, Rudman, Floyd, Delkurt, Schnocks, Sweeney, and Pola, and responses from Beuken, Mason, Petersen, and Tollington.
[6] Janet E. Tollington, *Tradition and Innovation in Haggai and Zechariah 1–8*, JSOTSup 150 (Sheffield: JSOT Press, 1993); Janet E. Tollington, "Readings in Haggai: From the Prophet to the Completed Book, a Changing Message in Changing Times," in *The Crisis of Israelite Religion: Transformation of Religious Tradition in Exilic and Post-Exilic Times*, ed. Bob Becking and Marjo C. A. Korpel, OtSt 42 (Leiden: Brill, 1999), 194–208.

many links to the earlier prophetic tradition regarding Yahweh's judgment of the people, the historical and theological perspective of Zechariah (and Haggai), that is, that he proclaimed in the Persian period and can declare that the punishment was deserved, results in significant differences. Zechariah also considers the future for non-Israelite nations, presenting new hope for these nations as they recognize Yahweh's sovereignty and join together as the people of God (Haggai focuses more on Israel's supremacy in the world). Tollington concludes that although Zechariah (and Haggai) was a prophet in the classical tradition, unlike Haggai, he functions somewhat as an innovator who challenged the people to remain open to a new experience of Yahweh and a different view of the future. According to Tollington in the end the people were unable to grasp his vision and hope.

Tollington's work on Zech 1–8, however, was followed by several key works which focused on Zech 9–14. Schaefer restricted his attention to Zech 14 and concluded that the author composer relied heavily upon earlier sections of Zechariah (chs. 1–13) as well as Jeremiah and Ezekiel.[7] Person highlighted many links between Deutero-Zechariah and Deuteronomic literature and concluded that Deutero-Zechariah represents the activity of a Deuteronomic school that continued until the time of Ezra.[8] These links were established through many lexical connections, but also through similarities in tradition, with special focus on shared eschatology and common approach to prophecy.[9] Larkin was sensitive to inner biblical connections, even if in the end her focus was on mantological features and techniques in Zech 9–14.[10] Larkin highlighted exegesis of earlier scriptures drawn from various parts of the Hebrew Bible (Isaiah, Ezekiel, Amos, Genesis, Psalms, Jeremiah, Hosea, and Deuteronomy), allusions to Proto-Zechariah and typological connections to Old Testament motifs. Tai analyzed both the tradition and redaction of Zech 9–14.[11] He concluded that these chapters were formed in four stages and that each stage reveals a distinct tradition orientation. The first stage (9:1–11:3) drew heavily on the text of Jeremiah not only in its use of the shepherd motif, but also in its announcement of judgment and salvation for Israel

---

[7] Konrad R. Schaefer, "Zechariah 14 and the Formation of the Book of Zechariah" (SSD diss., Ecole biblique et archéologique française, 1992); Konrad R. Schaefer, "Zechariah 14 and the Composition of the Book of Zechariah," *RB* 100 (1993): 368–98; Konrad R. Schaefer, "The Ending of the Book of Zechariah: A Commentary," *RB* 100 (1993): 165–238; Konrad R. Schaefer, "Zechariah 14: A Study in Allusion," *CBQ* 57 (1995): 66–91.
[8] Raymond F. Person, *Second Zechariah and the Deuteronomic School*, JSOTSup 167 (Sheffield: JSOT Press, 1993).
[9] Raymond F. Person, *The Deuteronomic School: History, Social Setting, and Literature*, SBLMS 2 (Atlanta: Society of Biblical Literature, 2002).
[10] Katrina J. Larkin, *The Eschatology of Second Zechariah: A Study of the Formation of a Mantological Wisdom Anthology*, CBET 6 (Kampen: Kok, 1994).
[11] Nicholas Ho Fai Tai, *Prophetie als Schriftauslegung in Sacharja 9–14: Traditions- und kompositionsgeschichtliche Studien*, Calwer Theologische Monographien 17 (Stuttgart: Calwer, 1996).

and warning against divination. In contrast, the second stage (11:4–16) drew upon the text of Ezekiel, a trend that was continued into the third stage (12:1–13:9), although there was some evidence of Deuteronomic influence, seen in connections to Hosea, especially in the final pericope (13:1–9). Zechariah 14:1–21 comprises the fourth and final stage and draws on the Day of Yahweh motif in prophetic literature. Tai concluded that Zech 9–14 reveals a new approach to prophecy which entails application of preexisting prophetic texts to new situations. Nurmela also undertook an investigation of similarities between Zechariah and other Old Testament books.[12] He concluded that Zech 9–14 depends mostly on Isaiah (although only chs. 1–11 and 29–31, not 40–55), Jeremiah, and Ezekiel and is internally dependent upon Zech 1–8.

With Delkurt, however, there was a shift back to the first half of Zechariah. Delkurt interpreted Zech 1–6 within the Hebrew prophetic tradition, highlighting relationships between the night visions and the earlier prophets.[13] He concluded that Zechariah draws on Deutero-Isaiah's salvation and Zion traditions in order to demonstrate that God is trustworthy. Zechariah also regularly alludes to the book of Ezekiel. On the one hand he echoes the message of Ezekiel by criticizing cultic outrages (esp. chs. 1–3, 8–11), while on the other, he diverges from his predecessor by taking a different approach to the temple and city (cf. Ezek 40–48).[14] Zechariah also draws on other prophetic writings with allusions to Proto-Isaiah (chs. 6, 30–31), Amos (4:11; 8:4–14), Hosea (1:9; 2:10; 8:6; 13:2; 14:7), Micah (7:18–20), Habakkuk (2:9–11), and Jeremiah (7:9; 15:19; 36). Delkurt's investigation showed that Zechariah knew the earlier prophets well, but that he often created ambiguities in his terms in order to allow several levels of interpretation. Stead's research continued this work on Zech 1–8 and in the process helped refine methodology.[15] His analysis highlighted the key influence of earlier prophetic materials and the book of Deuteronomy on Zech 1–8. He sees in Zech 1–2 allusions to Isa 40–55 (esp. ch. 54), Jer 30–33, 48–51, Ezek 38–39, 40–48, Joel 2, and Lam 2. Zechariah 3 draws on priestly (Exod 28–29; Lev 8; 16; Ezek 40; 44), but also prophetic (Amos 4; Isa 6) texts. Zechariah 4 draws on Exod 25–27 and Deut 18.

---

[12] Risto Nurmela, *Prophets in Dialogue: Inner-Biblical Allusions in Zechariah 1–8 and 9–14* (Åbo: Åbo Akademi University, 1996).
[13] Holger Delkurt, *Sacharjas Nachtgesichte: Zur Aufnahme und Abwandlung prophetischer Traditionen*, BZAW 302 (Berlin: de Gruyter, 2000).
[14] See also Holger Delkurt, "Sacharja und der Kult," in *Verbindungslinien: Festschrift für Werner H. Schmidt zum 65. Geburtstag*, ed. Axel Graupner, Holger Delkurt, and Alexander B. Ernst (Neukirchen-Vluyn: Neukirchener, 2000), 27–39.
[15] Michael R. Stead, *The Intertextuality of Zechariah 1–8*, LHBOTS 506 (London: T&T Clark, 2009); cf. Michael R. Stead, "Sustained Allusion in Zechariah 1–2," in *Tradition in Transition: Haggai and Zechariah 1–8 in the Trajectory of Hebrew Theology*, ed. Mark J. Boda and Michael H. Floyd, LHBOTS 475 (New York: T&T Clark, 2008), 144–70.

Zechariah 5:1–4 draws on Jer 7 and Deut 29 together with Exod 11–12, while Zech 5:5–11 looks to Ezek 1–11, 2 Sam 7, Exod 25, as well as Amos 8 and Ezek 8. In Zech 6:1–8 he finds the influence of Job 1–2, something recognized in the first night vision in Zech 1:7–17, but also a conflation of Isa 45:2 and Hab 3. Zechariah 6:9–15 is influenced by 2 Sam 7, Isa 44–45, Jer 22, 23, and 33. Finally, Zech 7 draws consistently on Jer 7, while Zech 8 on Deut 28–30, Haggai, and Jeremiah 30–31, ending with an allusion to Isa 2:3. His concern to situate Zech 1–8 within its two key contexts—a literary context of the earlier prophets and a historical context of the early post-exilic period—reflects a much needed shift identified below. His work observed new techniques in intertextuality beyond the typical focus on verbal repetition. While some may question the validity of thematic allusions, his focus on ungrammaticalities and especially sustained allusion, composite metaphors, and the interweaving of intratexts and intertexts will endure as key contributions to methodology.

The most recent work by Lee returned once again to Zech 9–14, although her limitation to Zech 9–10 allowed for a more focused analysis.[16] She identified the key role played by earlier prophetic texts in the shaping of the vision for restoration in these two chapters, in particular Isaiah, Jeremiah, and Ezekiel. She concluded that this reuse of earlier prophetic material is designed to shape the perspective of the Yehudite community associated with these texts in the early Persian period, a perspective which envisions "the return of Yahweh who inaugurates the new age, ushering in prosperity and blessings" and anticipates "the formation of an ideal remnant settling in an ideal homeland, with Yahweh as king and David as vice-regent, reigning in Zion" but also a society which is "a cosmic one, with Judah, Ephraim, and the nations living together in peace."[17]

This history of scholarship highlights the dominance of intertextual/inner biblical approaches for the study of book of Zechariah and the rich results arising from this sustained interest. Before presenting my own overview on the intertextual shape and character of the book of Zechariah, a brief consideration of methodology is in order.

A BRIEF REFLECTION ON METHOD

Most are aware that there is a long tradition of Jewish and Christian biblical interpretation that stressed the interconnectedness of Scripture, developed in Judaism through hermeneutical principles such as the sevenfold *middot* of Hillel[18] and

---

[16] Suk Yee Lee, *An Intertextual Analysis of Zechariah 9–10: The Earlier Restoration Expectations of Second Zechariah*, LHBOTS 599 (London: Bloomsbury, 2015).
[17] Lee, *An Intertextual Analysis*, 254.
[18] D. I. Brewer, *Techniques and Assumptions in Jewish Exegesis before 70 C.E.* (Tübingen: Mohr Siebeck, 1992), 226; cf. William Yarchin, ed., *History of Biblical Interpretation: A Reader* (Peabody, MA: Hendrickson, 2004) 114 n. 5; also see Gershon Hepner, "Verbal

in Christianity through the more general hermeneutical principle: *Scriptura Scripturae interpres* (Scripture interprets Scripture).[19] In the post-Enlightenment era this same sensibility may be discerned in the dominant traditio-historical technique of biblical scholarship as scholars sought to discover the pre-literary development of biblical traditions.[20] Similar principles were also identified in the post-literary development of biblical traditions leading to the recognition of "Inner Biblical Exegesis" by scholars such as Fishbane and Mason.[21] These two post-Enlightenment developments, however, focused on the diachronic character of the connections between biblical traditions and texts. Mason, in particular, noted in his introduction to his dissertation that the aim of his work was to identify "principles of exegesis" and "above all" to see if such principles afford "any clue to the place of this author, or authors, in the developing traditio-history of the community of post-exilic Judaism."[22] Mason's aims were natural for a scholar working within the parameters of the historical-critical paradigm, but even in his own day a hermeneutical shift was already underway. This shift would move the focus from authorial intention to reader impression and redefine (or at least supplement) the methodologies used for the study of the Hebrew Bible. This shift in approach is evidenced in the increasing description of such inner biblical connections as

---

Resonances in the Bible and Intertextuality," *JSOT* 96 (2001): 3–27 who speaks of the thirteen principles of Tanna Rabbi Ishmael and in particular the second rule: "lexical analogy."

[19] On the phenomenon of quotation, allusion, and intertextuality, see Mark J. Boda, "Quotation, Allusion," in *Dictionary of Biblical Criticism and Interpretation*, ed. Stanley E. Porter (New York: Routledge, 2006), 298–300.

[20] Walter E. Rast, *Tradition History and the Old Testament* (Philadelphia: Fortress, 1971); Douglas A. Knight, *Rediscovering the Traditions of Israel: The Development of the Traditio-Historical Research of the Old Testament, with Special Consideration of Scandinavian Contributions*, rev. ed., SBLDS 9 (Missoula, MT: Scholars Press, 1975); Douglas A. Knight, "Tradition History," in *ABD* 6:633–38.

[21] Michael A. Fishbane, *Biblical Interpretation in Ancient Israel* (Oxford: Clarendon, 1985); Michael A. Fishbane, "Inner-Biblical Exegesis," in *Hebrew Bible/Old Testament: The History of Its Interpretation—I: From the Beginnings to the Middle Ages (until 1300). Part I: Antiquity*, ed. Magne Sæbø (Göttingen: Vandenhoeck & Ruprecht, 1996), 33–48; Rex A. Mason, "Inner-Biblical Exegesis," in *A Dictionary of Biblical Interpretation*, ed. R. J. Coggins and J. L. Houlden (London: SCM, 1990), 312–14; Mason, "Use."

[22] Ibid., ii.

"intertextuality,"[23] a term that brings this interpretive tradition into conversation with broader trends in linguistics and hermeneutics.[24]

This shift to "intertextuality" was more than just a change in nomenclature, as demonstrated by Kirsten Nielsen in her application of this technique to biblical studies. Although Nielsen rejects post-structuralist assassinations of the author, whom she says lives on in the text, she also rejects the historical-critical definition of the relationship between author, text, and reader. Nielsen then is able to affirm an intertextuality rooted in the author alongside one rooted in the reader. As she writes:

> What is worth noting is that it is an ongoing dialogue which can be restricted neither to the author's deliberate choice of intertextuality nor to the reader's free choice of intertextuality. There may be other kinds of intertextuality than the author himself is aware of, new readers may add to this dialogue as well, but new intertextuality does not abolish the first one, the one intended by the author.[25]

Nielsen's identification of two kinds of intertextuality can also be discerned in Moyise's review of the subject where he distinguishes between intertextual echo (the classic diachronic approach), on the one side, and dialogical and postmodern intertextuality, on the other.[26]

---

[23] Some have trumpeted "intertextuality" as the way forward for writing Biblical Theology: Christopher R. Seitz, *Word without End: The Old Testament as Abiding Theological Witness* (Grand Rapids: Eerdmans, 1998), 12: "A fresh intellectual horizon for Old Testament studies is the rediscovery of the complex network of intertextuality that binds all texts together, not only in their canonical shape in the Old, but more especially as this intertextuality is taken up and filled to fullest capacity in the New. If I have said nothing else here, it is that special attention needs to be paid to reconnecting Old and New Testament studies." See also Elmer Martens, "Reaching for a Biblical Theology of the Whole Bible," in *Reclaiming the Old Testament: Essays in Honour of Waldemar Janzen*, ed. Gordon Zerbe (Winnipeg, MB: CMBC Publications, 2001), 83–101.

[24] The term itself (*intertextualité*) appears to have been first coined by Julia Kristeva in 1969. Building on the work of Bakhtin, Kristeva argued the interconnectedness of texts was essential to all reading. Other notable figures include Roland Barthes and Michel Foucault. See superb review in Robert P. Carroll, "The Book of J: Intertextuality and Ideological Criticism," in *Troubling Jeremiah*, ed. A. R. Pete Diamond, Kathleen M. O'Connor, and Louis Stulman, JSOTSup 260 (Sheffield: Sheffield Academic, 1999), 220–43 and Steve Moyise, "Intertextuality and the Study of the Old Testament in the New," in *The Old Testament in the New Testament: Essays in Honour of J. L. North*, ed. Steve Moyise, JSNTSup 189 (Sheffield: Sheffield Academic, 2000), 14–41; and the accessible works of Daniel Chandler, *Semiotics: The Basics* (London: Routledge, 2002); Basil Hatim and Ian Mason, *Discourse and the Translator* (London: Longman, 1990); Basil Hatim and Ian Mason, *The Translator as Communicator* (London: Routledge, 1997).

[25] Kirsten Nielsen, "Intertextuality and Biblical Scholarship," *SJOT* 2 (1990): 89–95 (92).

[26] Moyise, "Intertextuality."

The radically different character of these two types of intertextual analysis has led some to justifiably question the wisdom of using the same term for both exercises.²⁷ Moyise is well aware of this condition when he writes: "Frequent use of the term intertextuality is threatening to make it meaningless unless more attention is given to definitions."²⁸ However, because of the present ubiquity of the term Moyise affirms its enduring use "as an umbrella term for the complex interactions that exist between 'texts' (in the broadest sense)."²⁹

This terminological and methodological tension can be discerned in two key works from the late 1990s which focused on the book of Isaiah. Benjamin Sommer introduces his book on allusion in Isa 40–66 by orienting his readers to the academic discipline of intertextual studies. Sommer wisely identifies two main streams of scholarship, distinguishing between those focused on "influence/allusion" and those focused on what he calls "intertextuality."³⁰ According to Sommer, the approach of the former group is diachronic in character, "asking how a composition evokes its antecedents, how one author is affected by another, and what sources a text utilizes."³¹ In this way it is focused on the author-text relationship. The approach of the latter is synchronic in nature, focusing "not on the author of a text but either on the text itself (as part of a larger system) or on the reader."³² This synchronic method "interprets signs in the text by associating them with related signs in the reader's own mind."³³

---

²⁷ Cf. Stanley E. Porter, "The Use of the Old Testament in the New Testament: A Brief Comment on Method and Terminology," in *Early Christian Interpretation of the Scriptures of Israel: Investigations and Proposals*, ed. Craig A. Evans and James A. Sanders, JSNTSup 148 (Sheffield: Sheffield Academic, 1997), 79–96 (84–88).
²⁸ Moyise, "Intertextuality," 40–41.
²⁹ Ibid., 41.
³⁰ Benjamin D. Sommer, *A Prophet Reads Scripture: Allusion in Isaiah 40–66*, Contraversions Series (Stanford, CA: Stanford University Press, 1998), 6–14; cf. Benjamin D. Sommer, "Exegesis, Allusion and Intertextuality in the Hebrew Bible: A Response to Lyle Eslinger," *VT* 46 (1996): 479–89. See also the essays in Sipke Draisma, ed., *Intertextuality in Biblical Writings: Essays in Honour of Bas van Iersel* (Kampen: Kok, 1989), especially Vorster, Voelz, Delorme, and van Wolde; the essays in Danna Nolan Fewell, *Reading between Texts: Intertextuality and the Hebrew Bible*, Literary Currents in Biblical Interpretation (Louisville: Westminster John Knox, 1992), especially those by Fewell, Beal, and Miscall. Both Gerrie Snyman, "Who Is Speaking? Intertextuality and Textual Influence," *Neot* 30 (1996): 427–49 and Thomas R. Hatina, "Intertextuality and Historical Criticism in New Testament Studies: Is There a Relationship?" *BibInt* 7 (1999): 28–43 note the fundamental difference between intertextuality and historical studies.
³¹ Sommer, *A Prophet Reads*, 7.
³² Ibid.
³³ Ibid.

Although presenting the two approaches fairly, Sommer adopts the diachronic approach of influence/allusion to guide his study of Isa 40–66 because "[s]ome authors call attention to their own allusivity; they seem to insist on their relation to earlier texts." An exclusive intertextual approach "would lead a critic to overlook an important aspect of the text at hand."[34]

Similar to Sommer, Richard Schultz (1999), in his volume on "verbal parallels" in prophetic material, also identifies these same two aspects of intertextual analysis. For Schultz, the *diachronic* phase of analysis examines the "historical factors which may have produced or influenced the use of quotation."[35] This phase demands attention to the identification of the source and its context and also the determination of the historical context which prompted the quotation. His *synchronic* phase shifts attention to the function of the repeated language within texts to examine its literary impact on the reader.[36] In contrast to Sommer, however, Schultz encourages an intertextual approach which incorporates both diachronic and synchronic analyses.[37]

---

[34] Ibid., 9. See further the vigorous debate between Eslinger and Sommer. Lyle Eslinger, "Inner-Biblical Exegesis and Inner-Biblical Allusion: The Question of Category," *VT* 42 (1992): 47–58, advocates an abandonment of traditional inner biblical exegesis in favor of a synchronic ahistorical approach. Sommer, "Exegesis," 488 maintains a place for both diachronic and synchronic studies, although wary that at times the synchronic "masks an abdication of critical rigor." Similar debates are underway in New Testament studies; cf. Richard B. Hays and Joel B. Green, "The Use of the Old Testament by New Testament Writers," in *Hearing the New Testament: Strategies for Interpretation*, ed. Joel B. Green (Grand Rapids: Eerdmans, 1995), 224–38; Kenneth D. Litwak, "Echoes of Scripture? A Critical Survey of Recent Works on Paul's Use of the Old Testament," *CurBS* 6 (1998): 260–88. This is displayed vividly in the debate between G. K. Beale, "Questions of Authorial Intent, Epistemology, and Presuppositions and Their Bearing on the Study of the Old Testament in the New: A Rejoinder to Steve Moyise," *IBS* 21 (1999): 152–80; G. K. Beale, "A Response to Jon Paulien on the Use of the Old Testament in Revelation," *AUSS* 39 (2001): 23–34; Steve Moyise, "The Language of the Old Testament in the Apocalypse," *JSNT* 76 (1999): 97–113; Jon Paulien, "Dreading the Whirlwind: Intertextuality and the Use of the Old Testament in Revelation," *AUSS* 39 (2001): 5–22 over the book of Revelation. Two recent collections reveal enduring variation in intertextual approaches within the biblical guild: Daniel Marguerat and Adrian Curtis, eds., *Intertextualités: La Bible en échos*, Le Monde de la Bible 40 (Geneva: Labor et Fides, 2000); Steve Moyise, ed., *The Old Testament in the New Testament: Essays in Honour of J. L. North*, JSNTSup 189 (Sheffield: Sheffield Academic, 2000).

[35] Richard L. Schultz, *The Search for Quotation: Verbal Parallels in the Prophets*, JSOTSup 180 (Sheffield: Sheffield Academic, 1999), 229.

[36] Ibid., 232–33.

[37] One should not forget that Sommer does see a place for synchronic approaches as the previous note asserted. It should also be admitted that Schultz's "synchronic" analysis is not concerned with the discovery of further intertext, but rather how the intertext identified diachronically impacts the reading process.

It is this attention to both the diachronic and synchronic dimensions that underlies my own work.[38] Often inner biblical allusion/exegesis studies have been reduced to mere cataloguing exercises, identifying evidence of influence from earlier texts, without reflection on the impact of these influences from source texts on the reading of the host texts. The theoretical foundation for this moving beyond mere cataloging is showcased, for example, in the work of Hatim and Mason who describe intertextuality "in terms of semiotic systems of signification."[39] Their work reminds us that one should not treat intertexts merely as "'bits and pieces' culled from other texts," but rather as texts that have been transformed to adjust to their new environment."[40] Thus, similar to Schultz, by incorporating both approaches into the interpretive framework, we avoid the extreme of an intertextual analysis that merely catalogues connections to earlier texts (diachronic extreme) as well as the extreme of an intertextual analysis that only explores the musings of the postmodern mind (synchronic extreme). In my intertextual analysis I have striven not to limit the method to identifying pre-texts, but rather to also reflect on the accommodation and adaptation of these pre-texts into the new host text, what I call reading between the lines.

ANALYZING ZECHARIAH: AN OVERVIEW

As noted at the outset of this introduction the explicit claims of Zech 1:1–6 concerning the relationship between Zechariah's words and those of the prophets which preceded him establishes a hermeneutical grid which is essential for reading the remainder of the book of Zechariah, creating expectation in the reader that they will continue to hear the words of the earlier prophets proclaimed as fresh revelation for this new generation emerging from the devastating period of destruction and exile. The reader is not disappointed since as the book progresses earlier biblical traditions within the Torah, the Former Prophets, and especially the Latter Prophets can be discerned in the form and language of the various pericopae.

---

[38] In doing so I am risking the displeasure of Ellen van Wolde, "Trendy Intertextuality?" in *Intertextuality in Biblical Writings: Essays in Honour of Bas van Iersel*, ed. Sipke Draisma (Kampen: Kok, 1989), 43–49 (43), who has attacked recent studies for using "intertextuality as a modern literary theoretical coat of veneer over the old comparative approach." One should not overlook the work of Konrad R. Schaefer, "Zechariah 14: A Study in Allusion," *CBQ* 57 (1995): 66–91 who has considered the allusion technique of Zech 14. Although a superb effort, his work remains focused on the diachronic level, registering connections and techniques within Zech 14 with little consideration of the overall shape of Zech 9–14.
[39] Hatim and Mason, *Discourse*, 123.
[40] Ibid., 128–29.

First of all, the forms which appear throughout Zechariah have been drawn from earlier biblical materials. Zechariah 1:1–6 and 7:1–8:23 have been shaped according to the Jeremianic tradition with its "brief apologetic historical narratives" (Jer 26; 36; 37–41). Throughout Zech 1:7–6:15 one can discern the influence of two key prophetic visionary form traditions, one represented by Amos (chs. 7, 9) and Jeremiah (chs. 1, 24) and the other Ezekiel (chs. 1, 2, 8, 10, 37, 44). The report of a divine council scene form depicted in passages like 1 Kgs 22:19–21, Isa 6:1–13, and Job 1–2 has influenced Zech 3 as well as Zech 1:7–17, 4:1–14, and 6:1–8, while the Report of a Prophetic Sign-Act form of Jeremiah and Ezekiel (Jer 13; 16; 19; 27–28; 32; 35; 43; 51; Ezek 3; 4–5; 6; 12; 24; 33; 37) can also be discerned in Zech 3 and 6:9–15. The Summons to Joy (*Aufruf zur Freude*) form tradition found throughout the prophetic corpus is employed in Zech 2:14 [Eng. 10]. The influence of earlier prophetic form traditions continues into Zech 9–14 with the more generic tag of "oracle" (משא, 9:1; 12:1) structuring a collection which has been influenced by various prophetic form traditions, including: the Summons to Joy (9:9), the Entrance Liturgy (11:1; cf. Isa 26:2; Ps 24), the Call to Lament (11:2; cf. Isa 14:31; Jer 6:26; Joel 1:2–14), the Report of a Prophetic Sign-Act (11:4–16, see above), the Woe Oracle (11:17; cf. Isa 5), and the Sword Oracle (11:17; 13:7–9; cf. Jer 50:35–38).

Secondly, not only prophetic forms, but also prophetic language drawn from particular texts can be discerned throughout all the sections of the book of Zechariah. Of particular importance are the three major prophetic traditions of Isaiah, Jeremiah, and Ezekiel. Connections can also be discerned at times to other books within the Book of the Twelve, especially Joel, but also Hosea, Amos, Micah, and Habakkuk. Although not as popular as the prophets, the Torah's influence can also be discerned within the book of Zechariah, at times in more general ways through the priestly tabernacle traditions (Zech 3–4), but at other times in terms of language from the legal codes, as well as the narrative traditions in Genesis and Exodus, and the tradition of Deuteronomy. Of minor importance is the Deuteronomic historiographic tradition, although one does find allusions at various points to Joshua, Samuel, and Kings. The books found in the Writings play very little role in Zechariah, although four of the visions in Zech 1:7–6:15 rely on Job 1–2, and other texts throughout Zechariah are reliant on the liturgical traditions found in the books of Psalms and Lamentations.

While the influence of the earlier prophets (whether through the Law, Former or Latter Prophets) can be discerned in the book of Zechariah, the formation of a book related to Zechariah is testimony to the fact that he also took his place in this line of prophets. This reality, suggested by the very fact of the prophetic book named Zechariah, is demonstrated explicitly in Zech 8:1–8 in which the earlier words of Zechariah (from the oracles in the visionary material) are declared afresh in a new context (see commentary on 8:1–8). The same is true for the words of Haggai which are echoed in Zech 8:9–13 and reveal the continuing process of revelation, now based on earlier revelation.

The above overview is based on careful study of the various texts of the book of Zechariah, much of which is provided in my recent commentary on Zechariah.[41] What follows in this volume are key works which showcase intertextual analysis of key passages throughout the book of Zechariah. In many of these articles I have highlighted the key role of traditions, forms, and texts from the book of Jeremiah, but also more broadly the prophets, but in the end provide evidence of a canonical consciousness that was suggested by my more general observations above.

I begin with the inner core of Zech 1–8, the vision reports with oracles and sign-act section in 1:7–6:15. Chapter 2, "Terrifying the Horns" investigates the impact of the Babylon and foreign nation tradition from the rest of the Hebrew Bible on the vision reports. While some may find it odd for a prophetic tradition to speak of Babylon in connection with vision reports linked to the early reign of Darius, I show that it is precisely during Darius's early reign that the prophetic hopes related to Babylon (that is, divine punishment for the nation that judged Judah) and even Assyria were seen as fulfilled. Here we see Zecharian tradition grappling with the relevance of earlier prophetic traditions related to the nations. Chapter 3, "*Hoy, Hoy,*" continues the investigation of the Babylon tradition by focusing on Zech 2:10–17 (Eng. 6–13). This collection of oracles which brings closure to the first three vision reports belies reliance on a breadth of prophetic traditions focused on Babylon and its punishment, including Isaiah (chs. 12–14), Jeremiah (chs. 25, 50–51), Ezekiel (chs. 38–39), and Habakkuk (ch. 2). This shows the importance of the prophetic corpus for interpreting world events during the reign of Darius. The oracular material encourages a response from the community which entails flight from Babylon and a return to Zion for a covenantal encounter with Yahweh which will include the nations. In Chapter 4, "Oil, Crowns, and Thrones," the focus shifts the internal social context of Yehud as the Zecharian tradition grapples with the enduring relevance and present shape of the sociofunctionaries of prophet, priest and king. While some scholars see evidence of promotion of the priestly caste at the expense of the royal line, I show how the Zecharian tradition in Zechariah 3, 4:6b–10a, and 6:9–15 relies on key Jeremiah texts to show that the reemergence of priestly function at the temple is a sign of the soon reemergence of the royal line. Chapter 5, "Writing the Vision," shifts the focus from traditio-lexical connectivity between Zechariah and the prophets to links in terms of form. A comparison between the vision report forms used in Zechariah with those used in Jeremiah, Amos, and Ezekiel, reveals evidence of influence and points of innovation.

After these investigations into Zech 1:7–6:15, I then focus attention on the prose sermon inclusion in Zech 1:1–6 and 7:1–8:23. Chapter 6, "Zechariah: Mas-

---

[41] Boda, *The Book of Zechariah*.

ter Mason or Penitential Prophet?," highlights the impact of both the earlier penitential prayer tradition and the Deuteronomic-Jeremianic tradition on the prose sermon inclusion in Zech 1:1–6 and 7:1–8:23. Following this, Chapter 7, "When God's Voice Breaks Through," highlights rhetorical features of both Zech 1:1–6 and 7:1–8:23 which are designed to make the earlier prophetic words fresh for a Persian period audience.

Attention then shifts in the volume to Zech 9–14. I begin in Chapter 8, "Freeing the Burden of Prophecy," with an analysis of the oracular introductions which structure the overall collection in Zech 9–14, appearing at two key junctures in Zech 9:1 and 12:1 (as well as Mal 1:1). After criticizing the earlier influential work of Weis, Sweeney, and Floyd which identified the term משׂא as a genre tag indicating a text interpreting earlier revelation, I then argued that this term has been drawn from Jeremiah and signals the reemergence of authoritative prophecy in the Persian Period. Zechariah 9–14 (as well as Malachi) is to be taken seriously by the reading community as the word of Yahweh. In Chapter 9, "Zechariah 11:4–16 in Its Literary Contexts," I focus attention on the key sign act report which lies at the center of the literary complex of Zech 9–14. Clear connections are established between Zech 11:4–16 and two passages in Ezekiel (34:1–31 and 37:15–28). A close look at the two Ezekiel passages reveals that they share in common a focus on positive leadership from a Davidic figure. This evidence is used to bring clarity to the issue of shepherd leadership in Zech 11:4–16, identifying the crisis as one revolving around the rise and fall of Davidic leadership in the Persian period. Insights from this analysis provide an opportunity to read Zech 9–14 again and shows how Zech 11:4–16 explains key contrasts between the first (9:1–11:3) and the second (chs. 12–14) halves of Zech 9–14. Chapter 10, "Innerbiblical Allusions in the Shepherd Units of Zechariah 9–14," analyzes the remaining elements of the redactional skeleton of Zech 9–14, that is, the Shepherd Units which appear at regular intervals throughout the collection: 10:1–3; 11:1–3; 11:17; 13:7–9. The chapter traces evidence of influence from especially Jeremiah but also from Ezekiel. Again the impact of these allusions on the reading of Zech 9–14 is provided. My final chapter in the section on Zech 9–14, Chapter 11, "Reading Zechariah 9–14 with the Law and the Prophets," highlights evidence outside the redactional skeleton of Zech 9–14 that suggests that the material in Zech 9–10 and 12–14 has been influenced by sibling rivalry texts in Genesis combined with prophetic crisis texts in 1 Kings, Amos, and Jeremiah. The interlinking of these Torah traditions (sibling rivalry) with Prophets traditions (prophetic crisis) suggests a canon consciousness by those responsible for Zech 9–14, something that has been suggested for those responsible for the final verses of Malachi.

Analyzing Zechariah for evidence of influence from other biblical materials shows that Zechariah and his tradition have drawn from the breadth of biblical resources now found in the Tanak. The first volume of *Exploring Zechariah* concluded that those responsible for Haggai–Malachi also played a role in the final shaping of the Book of the Twelve. In one essay, however, evidence was provided that those responsible for the final form of Haggai–Malachi were cognizant of a corpus which included the Torah and the Prophets (Chapter 5). Our focus on inner biblical allusion in Zechariah has confirmed resonance with a breadth of biblical materials and in the final article evidence of material drawn simultaneously from Torah and Prophets (Former and Latter) strengthens the case that those responsible for Haggai–Malachi were working with canonical materials that we now recognize as the Torah and the Prophets. This suggests that those associated with the Zecharian tradition may have played a role in the development of or at least were conscious of a cohesive canonical tradition, not surprising in light of Zechariah's explicit appropriation of these earlier traditions he called "the earlier prophets" (Zech 1:4; 7:7, 12).

2
Terrifying the Horns:
Persia and Babylon in Zechariah 1:7–6:15[1]

In this chapter I investigate the impact of the Babylon tradition (especially as articulated in the Hebrew prophets) on the vision report-oracle-sign-act section of Zech 1:7–6:15.

The majority of books within the corpus known as the Latter Prophets employ superscriptions connecting prophetic literature with a particular era in the history of Israel and Judah.[2] Some of these superscriptions link the texts generally to the reign of one or more monarchs (Hos 1:1, Amos 1:1, Mic 1:1, Zeph 1:1), while others cite a specific year (Isa 6:1; 14:28). The book of Jeremiah shows the even more precise practice of citing not only the king's reign but at times even the month alongside the year, using both Judean and Babylonian kings as reference points (e.g., 25:1; 28:1). Ezekiel takes this further by including year, month, and day, referring also to the year of the exile of the monarch (e.g., 1:2; 8:1; 20:1).

---

[1] Based on my original publication, Mark J. Boda, "Terrifying the Horns: Persia and Babylon in Zechariah 1:7–6:15," *CBQ* 67 (2005): 22–41. Slightly revised for inclusion in this volume. Special thanks to Rainer Albertz, whose paper at sessions we co-chaired at the joint EABS/ISBL meeting (Rome, 2001) provided inspiration for this article; see now Rainer Albertz, "Darius in Place of Cyrus: The First Edition of Deutero-Isaiah (Isaiah 40.1–52.12) in 521 B.C.E.," *JSOT* 27 (2003): 371–88 (371–88). Thanks also to J. Kessler (Tyndale), L. Fried (Michigan), and D. Vanderhooft (Boston) for helpful comments on earlier drafts.

[2] All except Joel, Obadiah, Nahum, Habakkuk, and Malachi.

The final stage in the development of prophetic temporal superscriptions is demonstrated in the books of Haggai and Zechariah, in which the temporal reference point is exclusively the reign of a foreign king and the precise year, month, and day are provided. This level of precision suggests that those responsible for the final form of these books were deeply concerned that the readers grasp the connection between these prophecies and the historical circumstances of the prophet and community. This crucial literary signal should shape one's strategy of reading the particular book[3] and appears to be reflected in the fact that most research on Zech 1–8 over the past century has had a strong historical dimension. This trend has only been enhanced by the recent surge of research and reflection on the Persian period in relation to Yehud as well as to the entire ancient Near East.[4]

In this article I will highlight an important motif of the vision-oracle section in Zech 1:7–6:15,[5] that is, the depiction of the enemy of God's purposes and people. I will examine this literary motif in Zech 1:7–6:15 in particular and the Hebrew prophets in general, before considering the connection between this motif and the historical context suggested in the superscription which introduces this section of Zechariah.

IMAGERY OF ENEMIES

ZECHARIAH 1:7–17

In the initial vision-oracle (1:7–17) the prophet observes the report of a reconnaissance party, fresh from patrolling the earth.[6] Their observation of global rest and peace prompts the impassioned cry of the angel of Yahweh, asking how long God

---

[3] Contrast Edgar W. Conrad, *Zechariah*, Readings: A New Biblical Commentary (Sheffield: Sheffield Academic, 1999).

[4] See Mark J. Boda, "Majoring on the Minors: Recent Research on Haggai and Zechariah," *CurBR* 2 (2003): 33–68; Mark J. Boda, *Haggai and Zechariah Research: A Bibliographic Survey*, Tools for Biblical Study 5 (Leiden: Deo, 2003).

[5] For how Zech 1:7–6:15 relates to the larger literary corpus of Zech 1–14, see Mark J. Boda, "Zechariah: Master Mason or Penitential Prophet?," in *Yahwism after the Exile: Perspectives on Israelite Religion in the Persian Era*, ed. Bob Becking and Rainer Albertz, Studies in Theology and Religion 5 (Assen: Van Gorcum, 2003), 49–69 = chapter 6 in this present volume; Mark J. Boda, "From Fasts to Feasts: The Literary Function of Zechariah 7–8," *CBQ* 65 (2003): 390–407 = *Exploring Zechariah*, volume 1, chapter 2.

[6] Contrast, e.g., David L. Petersen, *Haggai and Zechariah 1–8: A Commentary*, OTL (Philadelphia: Westminster, 1984), 139–40), who sees here the cosmic deep, with e.g., Carol L. Meyers and Eric M. Meyers, *Haggai, Zechariah 1–8: A New Translation with Introduction and Commentary*, AB 25B (Garden City, NY: Doubleday, 1987), 107–34, who do not see the elements in this passage suggesting anything but a normal reconnaissance in the Levant.

will continue to withhold mercy from Jerusalem and the towns of Judah (1:12).⁷ This question is answered with a comforting oracle relayed to the prophet by the interpreting angel in which God expresses his passion for Jerusalem and his anger with הגוים השאננים, "the nations that feel secure." He declares: אני קצפתי מעט והמה עזרו לרעה, "I was angry a little, but they added to the disaster" (1:15). The oracle continues with the promise of God's return to Jerusalem to rebuild the temple and the city and restore prosperity (1:16–17).

Here the enemy is merely referred to as הגוים השאננים, "the nations that feel secure." However, evidence from the surrounding material strongly suggests that Babylon is meant.⁸ First of all, the motif of "seventy years" is clearly drawn from the Jeremianic tradition (25:11–12; 29:10), where it refers to the period of Jewish servitude to the king of Babylon.⁹ According to Jeremiah, this period begins with the exile of the people and desolation of the land (25:11; 29:1–7) and ends with the punishment of Babylon—the ruin of the land and the enslavement of its people (25:12)—and the return of the Jews to Jerusalem from exile (29:10).¹⁰ Second, because the present predicament is related to Jerusalem (Zion) and the towns of Judah (1:12, 14, 16, 17) and because the reversal of the present predicament is depicted as the rebuilding of the temple and the city, the angry divine

---

⁷ On the various characters in this vision, see David J. Clark, "The Case of the Vanishing Angel," *BT* 33 (1982): 213–18.
⁸ The plural הגוים ("nations") does not disqualify Babylon as referent, as demonstrated in the reference to both "many nations" as well as Babylonians in Ezekiel's prophecy on the siege of Tyre (26:1–14).
⁹ On this motif, see C. F. Whitley, "The Term Seventy Years Captivity," *VT* 4 (1954): 60–72; C. F. Whitley, "The Seventy Years Desolation—a Rejoinder," *VT* 7 (1957): 416–18; Avigdor Orr, "The Seventy Years of Babylon," *VT* 6 (1956): 304–06; Ross E. Winkle, "Jeremiah's Seventy Years for Babylon: A Re-Assessment (Part I: The Scriptural Data)," *AUSS* 25 (1987): 201–14; John Applegate, "Jeremiah and the Seventy Years in the Hebrew Bible," in *The Book of Jeremiah and Its Reception: Le Livre de Jérémie et sa réception*, ed. Adrian H. W. Curtis and Thomas C. Römer, BETL 128 (Leuven: Peeters, 1997), 91–110; and Michael A. Fishbane, *Biblical Interpretation in Ancient Israel* (Oxford: Clarendon, 1985), 479–85. Several commentators have proposed a precise seventy-year period (e.g., 609–539 or 587–517 BCE). The connection of this symbol with the length of human life (Ps 90:10) and through this to the length of punishment of a city (Isa 23:15–18) shows how it functions in a similar way to the motif of "forty years" in the narrative of the wilderness. The period of forty years ensures that the offending generation will have been eradicated from the community. In this way, the image does relate to a particular and limited period of time, even if the speaker/writer is not timing that period down to the second.
¹⁰ When the seventy-year motif is picked up in the book of Chronicles (2 Chr 36:21), it is used to refer to the period from the Babylonian destruction of Jerusalem until the Persian defeat of Babylon. In Dan 9:1, the reference is linked to the reign of a figure named Darius.

action against Israel most likely points to the destruction of the temple and the city by the Babylonian armies in 587 BCE.

ZECHARIAH 2:1–4 (ENG. 1:18–21)

Whereas the first vision-oracle describes the positive aspects of the promised restoration, that is, the restoration of infrastructure (temple, city) and prosperity to Jerusalem and Judah, the second vision-oracle (2:1–4 [Eng. 1:18–21]) traces the negative aspect, that is, the punishment of the offending nations. The prophet sees four horns, which are mentioned three times (2:1 [Eng. 1:18], 4a, 4b [1:21]). Some interprets take this as a reference to the horns of an animal. This image is used elsewhere in the Hebrew Bible to represent the power of a nation, usually with a view to its military prowess (see Deut 33:17; Jer 48:25; Mic 4:13).[11] The number four and the term חרשים, understood as craftsmen, together with allusions elsewhere in Zech 1–6 to building the temple, suggest to others that a four-horned altar is in view here (cf. Ezek 43:15; Amos 3:14).[12] Still other commentators take a *via media*, understanding this as a reference to a metal helmet to which horns have been attached. This approach allows for both craftsmen and horns.[13]

Of these interpretations it is difficult to accept the horned altar approach, since these horns were "lifted up against" (נשא אל) the land of Judah and "scattered" (זרה) Judah, Israel, and Jerusalem, activities difficult for an altar to perform.[14] Rather, these activities are appropriate for an animal with horns, an image suggested also by the collocation קרנות הגוים, "horns of the nations." The term חרשים may indeed refer to "craftsmen" if the horns are metal horns representative of the power of the nations (as in 1 Kgs 22:11; 2 Chr 18:10; Mic 4:13), but more likely this term is a plural participial or nominal form of the Hebrew gloss

---

[11] E.g., Meyers and Meyers, *Haggai, Zechariah 1–8*, 143. For various uses of image of the horn, see Margit L. Süring, *The Horn-Motif in the Hebrew Bible and Related Ancient Near Eastern Literature and Iconography*, Andrews University Seminary Dissertation Series 4 (Berrien Springs, MI: Andrews University Press, 1980), 323–28.

[12] E.g., Petersen, *Haggai and Zechariah 1–8*, 165; Baruch Halpern, "The Ritual Background of Zechariah's Temple Song," *CBQ* 40 (1978): 167–90; Marvin A. Sweeney, *The Twelve Prophets*, 2 vols., Berit Olam (Collegeville, MN: Liturgical Press, 2000), 2:582. Petersen also adopts the previous view (horns as military power).

[13] Commentators have been forced to do semantic gymnastics to make the two images fit (horns and craftsmen); see, e.g., Joyce G. Baldwin, *Haggai, Zechariah, Malachi: An Introduction and Commentary*, TOTC (Downers Grove, IL: InterVarsity Press, 1972), 104.

[14] Usually a horn (קרן) is raised (both positively as divine support and negatively as human arrogance) using the verb רום (1 Sam 2:1, 10; Pss 75:5–6, 11; 89:18, 25; 92:11; 112:9; 148:14; Lam 2:17). Elsewhere קרן is never used with the verb נשא, but רום and נשא regularly appear as a word pair, which suggests that they have a similar semantic range and function (Gen 7:17; Num 24:7; 2 Kgs 19:22; Prov 30:13; Isa 2:12–14; 6:1; 13:2; 49:22; 52:13; 57:15; Ezek 10:16).

"plough" and should be translated "ploughmen."[15] This view is supported by the use of the term להחריד ("to terrify"), which is used to describe the act of driving off a group of animals (see Isa 17:2; Deut 28:26; Jer 7:33). These "ploughmen" are also said "to throw" (לידות, *piel* inf. constr. of ידה). This stem occurs only two others times in the MT: in Lam 3:53 to refer to casting stones at an enemy, and in Jer 50:14 to refer to shooting arrows at an enemy (interestingly, Babylon is that enemy). The imagery here is that of horned animals, likely two horned animals, being driven away by a group of ploughmen. The number four appears in relation to both ploughmen and horns to show that the ploughmen are a match for (or, if two animals are indicated, have a clear advantage over) the horned animals.[16]

Is there any indication of how this image is used in Zech 2:1–4? Three times in the vision these horns are said to have "scattered" (זרה) the people of God, an action often associated with the exile of the Jewish people (e.g., Isa 41:15; Jer 15:7; 31:10; Lev 26:33). In the last two of these occurrences the horns have scattered "Judah," while in the first instance a longer list—"Judah, Israel, and Jerusalem"—is given.[17] It appears that the focus of attention in this vision is again Judah, and thus the referent is most likely Babylon, which scattered Judah, although Assyria, which exiled the northern kingdom Israel, may also be in view, which may explain the image of two animals. Even if this latter is the case, Assyria must be viewed together with Babylon as an imperial complex whose power is broken by later Persian forces. The emphasis is on the breaking of Babylonian power.[18]

---

[15] Robert M. Good, "Zechariah's Second Night Vision (Zech 2, 1–4)," *Bib* 63 (1982): 56–59.

[16] Janet E. Tollington, *Tradition and Innovation in Haggai and Zechariah 1–8*, JSOTSup 150 (Sheffield: JSOT Press, 1993), 225 claims that the number four suggests a "wider interpretation" beyond Babylon (and possibly Assyria), while Merrill F. Unger, *Zechariah: Prophet of Messiah's Glory* (Grand Rapids: Zondervan, 1970), 38), views it as an apocalyptic foreshadowing of four coming kingdoms. William Emery Barnes, *Haggai, Zechariah and Malachi: With Notes and Introduction*, 2nd ed., Cambridge Bible for Schools and Colleges 38 (Cambridge: Cambridge University Press, 1934), 32, thinks it refers to Samaria (north), Ammon (east), Edom (south), Tyre/Philistia (west); see also Süring, *Horn-Motif*, 323–28. Considering that animals have two horns, this terminology may be a reference to the Assyrian-Babylonian hegemony over Judah and Israel, which ended with the defeat of Babylon.

[17] Some LXX manuscripts omit "Israel," and others omit "Jerusalem." The Naḥal Ḥever Greek scroll agrees with the MT; see Meyers and Meyers, *Haggai, Zechariah 1–8*, 138.

[18] Assyria and Babylon are joined also in Jer 50:17–18 and Gen 10:8–12. David S. Vanderhooft, *The Neo-Babylonian Empire and Babylon in the Latter Prophets*, HSM 59 (Atlanta: Scholars Press, 2000), 207, cf. 122, notes this fusion of traditions in Mic 4:10; Isa 14:4b–21; and Jer 50:17. See also Peter Machinist, "Assyria and Its Image in the First Isaiah," *JAOS* 103 (1983): 719–37 (736–37). For evidence from the Sibylline Oracles, see

ZECHARIAH 2:10–17 (ENG. 2:6–13)

Following the third night vision, in which the prophet sees the rebuilding of the city, the prophetic cry הוֹי appears three times (2:10, 11; cf. Isa 55:1), calling attention to the imperatives נוּס ("flee") and מלט ("escape").[19] The prophet is inviting the exiled people to return and fill the restored city of Jerusalem. In verse 10 the point of origin of the exiles is "the land of the north," a location that is made explicit in verse 11 as the "daughter of Babylon."[20] Although there are enigmatic textual and grammatical features in what follows in verses 12–13,[21] there is little question that the prophet is announcing judgment on "the nations that have plundered" the people of God, envisioning a reversal in which the people of God (the slaves of the nations) would plunder the nations (v. 13). As with the earlier messages, great emphasis is placed on the punishment of an enemy that had abused the people of God, and this enemy is identified explicitly as "Babylon."

David J. Reimer, *The Oracles against Babylon in Jeremiah 50–51: A Horror among the Nations* (San Francisco: Mellen Research University Press, 1993), 282.

[19] The relationship between vv. 10–17 (Eng. vv. 6–13) and vv. 5–9 (Eng. vv. 1–4) is a matter of debate. Some commentators see the two sections as intricately linked, e.g., Adam S. van der Woude, "Zion as Primeval Stone in Zechariah 3 and 4," in *Text and Context: Old Testament and Semitic Studies for F. C. Fensham*, ed. W. Claassen, JSOTSup 48 (Sheffield: Sheffield Academic, 1988), 237–48. Others view them as distinct, e.g., Petersen, *Haggai and Zechariah 1–8*, 185. Although other visions in Zech 1:7–6:15 contain oracles (e.g., 1:7–17), 2:10–17 is distinguished from 2:5–9 by the absence of a narrative formula (cf. 1:14, 17; 2:4; 5:3) and the change of audience (from young man to exilic community); see Burke O. Long, "Reports of Visions among the Prophets," *JBL* 95 (1976): 353–65, for the use of oracles within visions. For the role 2:10–17 plays at the end of the first three night visions, see Mark J. Boda, *Haggai/Zechariah*, NIVAC (Grand Rapids: Zondervan, 2004).

[20] For the image of daughter as more than personification, see Elaine R. Follis, "The Holy City as Daughter," in *Directions in Biblical Hebrew Poetry*, ed. Elaine R. Follis, JSOTSup 40 (Sheffield: Sheffield Academic, 1987), 173–84; Elaine R. Follis, "Zion, Daughter of," in *ABD* 6:1103, and Mark Biddle, "The Figure of Lady Jerusalem: Identification, Deification, and Personification of Cities in the Ancient Near East," in *The Biblical Canon in Comparative Perspective*, ed. William W. Hallo (Lewiston, NY: Mellen, 1991), 173–94 (184–85). The reference to being scattered to the four winds of heaven does not disqualify the referent as Babylon. Jeremiah will often speak of a return from the land of the north and the ends of the earth (Jer 3:18; 16:15; 23:8; 31:8). The odd term "scattered" (פרשׂ, פרס) is probably a play on the word "Persia."

[21] See T. C. Vriezen, "Two Old Cruces," *OtSt* 5 (1948): 80–91; Carola J. L. Kloos, "Zech. II 12: Really a Crux Interpretum?" *VT* 25 (1975): 729–36.

Zechariah 5:5–11

After the two central visionary reports in chapters 3 and 4, which make no allusion to an enemy, one encounters the two related visions of Zech 5. Although distinct, these two visions address betrayal of the covenant within the Yehudite community: verses 1–4 confront infidelity in human relationships, and verses 5–11 confront unfaithfulness in the people's relationship with God.[22] It is in this latter vision that an additional allusion to Babylon occurs.

The vision proceeds through three phases of revelation and interpretation. In the first phase (5:5–6) the measuring basket is identified as the "guilt of the people in all the land"; this guilt is linked to idolatry in the second phase (5:7–8) through the portrayal of the image of a goddess inside the basket. In the final phase of the vision (5:9–11), two women wearing wings like that of the unclean stork appear and transport both guilt and idols away from the land. Their destination is identified as ארץ שנער, "the land of Shinar," the name in the biblical tradition for the Mesopotamian plain where lay the cities of Babel, Erech, Akkad, and Calneh (Gen 10:10).[23] This name appears in the infamous episode in Gen 11 in which rebellious humanity's attempt to build a tower to heaven is thwarted by the creation of languages, thus giving rise to the name Babel (Babylon) itself. In Zech 5:5–11 the

---

[22] There is a difference of opinion about vv. 5–11. Some commentators see these verses as continuing the theme of social injustice of vv. 1–4, e.g., Petersen, *Haggai and Zechariah 1–8*, 255–59; Margaret Barker, "The Evil in Zechariah," *HeyJ* 19 (1978): 12–27 (23); Carroll Stuhlmueller, *Rebuilding with Hope. A Commentary on the Books of Haggai and Zechariah*, ITC (Grand Rapids: Eerdmans, 1988), 92; Eugene H. Merrill, *Haggai, Zechariah, Malachi: An Exegetical Commentary* (Chicago: Moody Press, 1994), 174; Dominic Rudman, "Zechariah 5 and the Priestly Law," *SJOT* 14 (2000): 194–206. Others see here a reference to idolatry, Peter R. Ackroyd, *Exile and Restoration: A Study of Hebrew Thought of the Sixth Century B.C.*, OTL (Philadelphia: Westminster, 1968), 204; Christian Jeremias, *Die Nachtgesichte des Sacharja: Untersuchungen zu ihrer Stellung im Zusammenhang der Visionsberichte im Alten Testament und zu ihrem Bildmaterial*, FRLANT 117 (Göttingen: Vandenhoeck & Ruprecht, 1977), 195–96; Meyers and Meyers, *Haggai, Zechariah 1–8*, 296–316; Rex A. Mason, *The Books of Haggai, Zechariah and Malachi*, CBC (Cambridge: Cambridge University Press, 1977), 58; Paul L. Redditt, *Haggai, Zechariah and Malachi*, NCB (London: Marshall Pickering, 1995), 75; Michael H. Floyd, *Minor Prophets, Part 2*, FOTL 22 (Grand Rapids: Eerdmans, 2000), 391–96; Diana Edelman, "Proving Yahweh Killed His Wife (Zechariah 5:5–11)," *BibInt* 11 (2003): 335–44. However, even Rudman admits that there is a cultic flavor to this section.

[23] Shinar appears to be a Hebrew modification of the name Sumer, which is used more technically to refer to southern, in contrast to northern, Babylon, but can be used for the entire region. In biblical tradition the term Shinar is associated with cities in both north and south (Gen 10:10; Dan 1:2). Although Isa 11:11 has a reference to שנער in relation to the return of exiles, it does not contain the collocation ארץ שנער, "land of Shinar."

winged women are expected to take their idolatrous cargo to the land of Shinar and there build a house for it, where the basket will be "set there in its place." This final phrase is used elsewhere to speak of religious objects within a temple complex (1 Kgs 7:27, 29; 2 Kgs 25:13, 16 // Jer 52:17, 20; Jer 27:19; Ezra 3:3). Because it appears alongside the phrase לבנות־לה בית, "to build for it a house," a phrase used for building not only houses but also temples (1 Kgs 3:1; cf. 2 Sam 7:5, 7, 13, 27), it must be a reference to the creation of a shrine for the idol. Although the name "Babylon" does not appear in this vision, the allusion to land of Shinar is clearly drawing on the Hebraic Babylon tradition.

ZECHARIAH 6:1–8

The final vision (6:1–8) joins the first vision to form an *inclusio* around the collection, creating the expectation of a great action of God.[24] The scene is most likely the entrance to the divine council, where the four winds of heaven, God's agents of judgment depicted as chariots drawn by variously colored horses, are released to enact judgment.[25] Although there are textual and grammatical uncertainties over the number if horses and directions in which they go, there is little question that emphasis is again placed on ארץ צפון, "the land of the north" (v. 8). Probably two chariots (black and white) are sent to this ארץ צפון,[26] and, according to *BHS*, upon their arrival they "have given my Spirit rest" (הניחו את־

---

[24] N. L. A. Tidwell, "*Wā'ōmar* (Zech 3:5) and the Genre of Zechariah's Fourth Vision," *JBL* 94 (1975): 343–55, and Halpern, "Ritual Background," note connections in visions 1, 4, 5, and 8 to imagery of the divine council.
[25] See Meyers and Meyers, *Haggai, Zechariah 1–8*, 319–20.
[26] There are notorious textual difficulties related to the various colors and directions of the chariot teams, due to differences between 6:2 and 6:6–7. On the issue of color, some emend אמצים ("powerful") in 6:7 to אדמים ("red"), and others insert a reference to a chariot with red horses at the beginning of 6:6. However, there is no manuscript support for emending אמצים ("powerful"), which appears to be modifying all the chariots. The supposed awkward syntax of v. 6 can be understood as the "so-called 'independent relative' clause," as used in verbal or verbless clauses; see Gen 7:23; Num 22:6; and esp. 2 Kgs 6:16; *IBHS* §19.3c. The red team is not mentioned in 6:6–7 either because it is pulling the chariot of the commanding officer (see 1:8, 11) or because it is stationed in the east, where the scene takes place. On the issue of directions, as the MT stands (matching the LXX), the black horses head to the north, the dappled horses to the south, but the white horses follow the black ones (אל־אחריהם [lit., "to behind them"]; cf. 2 Sam 5:23; esp. 2 Kgs 9:18–19). It has often been assumed, however, that the reference to "four spirits/winds" (ארבע רוחות) suggests four directions, and yet in the two major textual witnesses only two directions are mentioned. This discrepancy has led some commentators to emend the phrase אל־אחריהם (lit., "to behind them") to אל־אחר הים, lit., "to the behind, the sea," that is, the west, resonating with הים האחרון (the Mediterranean Sea; Deut 11:24; 34:2; Joel 2:20; Zech 14:8); see Petersen, *Haggai and Zechariah 1–8*, 264, following A. B. Ehrlich. Although the four

רוחי). The construction of the *hiphil* of the verb נוח here, followed by the preposition ב- introducing the object of wrath is found regularly throughout Ezekiel, with the term חמתי ("my wrath") rather than רוחי ("my spirit/wind/breadth") (5:13; 16:42; 24:13). This difference, however, is inconsequential, since רוח and חמה are closely associated in the book of Ezekiel (3:14; 13:13).[27] This close connection between רוח and anger is demonstrated in Jer 49:36–37, where interestingly the four winds (ארבע רוחות) are employed as agents of God to express his "fierce anger," and in other passages where the term רוח is used on its own to signify anger (Judg 8:3; Prov 16:32; 29:11).[28] This evidence confirms that the purpose of these רוח-chariots is punishment, to satisfy the disciplinary wrath of God.

This punishment is directed towards "the land of the north" (ארץ צפון). The precise referent of this land is most likely Babylon for the following reasons. First, Zech 6:1–8 is closely associated with the first vision in Zech 1:7–17; the final vision appears to depict the fulfillment of the anger of God expressed in 1:15 against nations already identified above as Babylon.[29] Second, the reappearance of two phrases from 2:10, "four winds/spirits of heaven" (ארבע רוחות השמים) and "land of the north" (ארץ צפון), where the land is clearly identified as Babylon, suggests that Babylon is in view here as well. Finally, in the prophetic piece that follows this final vision (6:9–15), a contingent of people appears who have arrived from none other than "Babylon" (6:9), showing the response of the community to the earlier prophetic cry of 2:10–17 and to the divine action depicted in the prophetic vision of 6:1–8.

---

winds do originate in the four extremities (compass points) of the earth, their movement is not restricted to these four directions (cf. Jer 49:36 with Ezek 37:9). Therefore, the reading of the MT should be retained, denoting that the black and white teams head to the north and the dappled team to the south. Since the scene here depicts the entrance to the divine council in the mountains east of Mesopotamia (cf. Petersen, *Haggai and Zechariah 1–8*, 267–68), there may be no need to send a team to the east since the meeting takes place there, nor is there need to send a team to the west because it is a desert. The approach in W. D. McHardy, "The Horses in Zechariah," in *In Memoriam: Paul Kahle*, ed. Matthew Black and Georg Fohrer, BZAW 103 (Berlin: Töpelmann, 1968), 174–79, based on abbreviations that were confused by scribes, is too speculative.

[27] A violent wind (רוח) is used to express the anger (חמה) of God in Ezek 13:13, and Ezekiel's anger is expressed as "the anger of my spirit" (בחמת רוחי) in Ezek 3:14.

[28] See Petersen, *Haggai and Zechariah 1–8*, 271.

[29] Although the tradition of the "land of the north," which is restricted in the Hebrew Bible to Jeremiah and Zechariah, is more generically a reference to Mesopotamia (esp. Jer 46:10; 50:9), it is consistently related to the destruction/exile (Jer 6:22; 10:22) and return/restoration of Judah (Jer 3:18; 16:15; 23:8; 31:8), actions intimately related to the rise and fall of Babylon.

SUMMARY

A consistent feature of Zech 1:7–6:15 is reference to a foreign entity, descriptions of which appear to be linked to Babylon.[30] This enemy is cast in negative light, seen as an agent of God's discipline that exceeded the divine calling by abusing God's people and threatened God's covenant relationship with his people through idolatrous practices. God responds by promising and enacting punishment on Babylon, inviting his people to escape Babylon, and removing Babylonian religion from his people.

HISTORY AND IMAGE

These various allusions to Babylon arise within a literary complex of vision-oracles explicitly connected to a particular historical context. This historical connection is created through use of a superscription at 1:7 that joins two others in 1:1 and 7:1 to form a tripartite structure for Zech 1–8. Each of these superscriptions include the following two components: citation of date (1:1: 8th month, 2nd year of Darius; 1:7: 24th day, 11th month [Shebat], 2nd year of Darius; 7:1: 4th year of Darius the king ... 4th day, 9th month [Kislev]) and announcement of the prophetic word (1:1: the word of Yahweh came to the prophet Zechariah, son of Berekiah, the son of Iddo; 1:7: the word of Yahweh came to the prophet Zechariah, son of Berekiah, the son of Iddo; 7:1: the word of Yahweh came to Zechariah). Two key issues have arisen in the study of these superscriptions: (1) their historical referent and (2) their historical authenticity.

HISTORICAL REFERENT

The first issue, that of the precise historical referent, was a point of great debate in the middle of the twentieth century owing to connections that were drawn between revolts in the transition from Cambyses to Darius and the message of the books of Haggai and Zechariah.[31] This attention led to a careful analysis of the precise dating system used by the editor of Zech 1–8 and the relationship between

---

[30] On this Tollington, *Tradition*, 219–20, agrees: there is "clear evidence of a negative attitude towards Babylon" (Zech 2:19–11; 5:11; and probably 2:2–4), even if she finds this "surprising" (see below). In her work on these visions/oracles she consistently sees the reference to Babylon, but then generalizes this to include all nations who mistreat Israel (pp. 219–20, 225, 228).

[31] A. T. Olmstead, *History of the Persian Empire* (Chicago: University of Chicago Press, 1948), 135–41; Leroy Waterman, "The Camouflaged Purge of Three Messianic Conspirators," *JNES* 13 (1954): 73–78; see more recently E. J. Bickerman, "En marge de l'écriture II: La seconde année de Darius," *RB* 88 (1981): 23–28; Sidney G. Sowers, "Did Xerxes Wage War on Jerusalem?," *HUCA* 67 (1997): 43–53.

these dates and various events in this tumultuous period of Persian history. The careful work of Peter R. Ackroyd in an earlier period and more recently that of John Kessler reflect the strong consensus that the superscriptions in Haggai and Zech 1 point to the second regnal year of Darius using the accession year system; that is, they refer to the year April 520–April 519.[32]

HISTORICAL AUTHENTICITY

The second issue, that of the authenticity of these superscriptions and their relationship to their respective prophetic material, has also been controversial. Although the consensus is not as strong in this case, the majority of scholars have affirmed historical authenticity for at least most of the material in these sections. That these superscriptions were created by an editor to lend credibility to later prophetic material is unlikely. Close consideration of the form of the superscriptions shows diversity in formulas for both date and messenger.[33] One would not expect an editor to display such variety in composing introductory statements. It appears that the editor was constrained by sources that used different formulas.[34] However, even if one does not accept the historical authenticity of the material, it is clear that the vision-oracles have been linked to the second regnal year of Darius.

---

[32] Peter R. Ackroyd, "Two Old Testament Historical Problems of the Early Persian Period," *JNES* 17 (1958): 13–27; Peter R. Ackroyd, "Historical Problems of the Early Achaemenian Period," *Orient* 20 (1984): 1–15; Peter R. Ackroyd, "Some Historical Problems of the Early Achaemenian Period," in *Proceedings, Eastern Great Lakes and Midwest Biblical Societies*, ed. Philip Sigal, Proceedings, Eastern Great Lakes and Midwest Biblical Societies 4 (Grand Rapids: Eastern Great Lakes Biblical Society, 1984), 37–53; John Kessler, "The Second Year of Darius and the Prophet Haggai," *Transeu* 5 (1992): 63–84 (84); John Kessler, *The Book of Haggai: Prophecy and Society in Early Persian Yehud*, VTSup 91 (Leiden: Brill, 2002). Contrast, however, Diana Edelman, *The Origins of the Second Temple: Persian Imperial Policy and the Rebuilding of Jerusalem* (London: Equinox, 2005), in which she argues that the restoration of the temple has been displaced from the reign of Artaxerxes I (445–432 BCE) to that of Darius I (521–485 BCE). For my response to Edelman, see Mark J. Boda, "Review of Edelman: *The Origins of the 'Second' Temple: Persian Imperial Policy and the Rebuilding of Jerusalem* (2005)," *JHS* (2006).

[33] On this, see especially the articles by Kessler and Ackroyd in the preceding note and Boda, "Fasts to Feasts" = *Exploring Zechariah*, volume 1, chapter 2.

[34] Even if one rejects the authenticity of these formulas, the editor has linked these messages to the transitional period from Cambyses to Darius.

PROBLEM

To this point I have introduced two key issues. First, an examination of the imagery of enemy nations in Zech 1:7–6:15 has identified Babylon as the most likely referent. Second, past research on the superscriptions in the book has connected this material to the early phase of Darius's rule. It is the intersection of these two issues, however, that raises the key questions of this article. Why does one find focused attention on the punishment of Babylon in prophetic messages linked to the early period of Darius's reign? Do not Hebrew, Greek, and Mesopotamian sources agree that Cyrus II (the Great) was the one who overthrew the regime led by Nabonidus in 539 BCE, bringing an end to Babylonian hegemony over the ancient Near East?

Several solutions to this tension have been suggested.[35] For one group of scholars, Zech 1:8–6:15 originated late in the reign of the Babylonian Nabonidus and looks to the impending overthrow of Babylon by Cyrus. This older material has been taken up and either delivered to the people in the reign of Darius or at least linked to this reign in order to highlight/rehearse God's action on behalf of his people. Representative of this viewpoint is Rex A. Mason, who, although open to the fact that references to the enemy could reflect the upheavals at the beginning of Darius's reign ("the Darius upheavals had passed without sign of earth-shattering events foretold by Haggai"), favors the first view because references to the seventy years and the anger toward the nations suggest an origin in the time of the Babylonian exile.[36] Recently, this view has been taken up afresh by Paul L. Redditt, who suggests that Zechariah could have received his call before the fall of Babylon in 539 BCE ("the decisive defeat of the enemies lay yet in the future") and that this earlier vision was enlarged and reapplied to 520 BCE because "Cyrus' defeat of Babylon had had little real impact on the lives of the exiles who remained far from home."[37]

For a second group of commentators, Zech 1:8–6:15 originated early in the reign of Darius and looks to the future overthrow of Persia or any nation that subjugates and abuses God's people. This view is reflected in David L. Petersen's work on the vision in 1:8–17; while linking it to the indictment of Babylon in Isa 47:5–7,[38] he notes that for Zechariah (as opposed to Deutero-Isaiah), "Babylonian hegemony had ended two decades prior to the time of Zechariah's visions" and thus "anger at specific foreign nations is no longer appropriate in quite the same

---

[35] See further Boda, "Majoring"; Boda, *Research*.
[36] Mason, *Haggai*, 37–39, 43, 61.
[37] Redditt, *Haggai, Zechariah and Malachi*, 54–55.
[38] This is far from certain, however, since the vocabulary is different and seems (with many of the other passages, especially 2:10–17) to reflect the influence of the Jeremianic tradition, especially Jer 50–51 and other oracles against the foreign nations at the end of Jeremiah; see Jer 48 and indictment of Moab.

way as for Deutero-Isaiah."[39] In similar fashion, Janet E. Tollington, having placed this section securely in the reign of Darius, suggests that the remembrance of the destruction of Jerusalem was "etched so deeply on the consciousness of the Jewish people that 'Babylon' came to be used to symbolize any, or all enemy people."[40] Carol L. Meyers and Eric M. Meyers also note that Babylonian rule was "completed at the time of Cyrus nearly two decades before Zechariah's prophecy"; as a result, they suggest that this is "an unspecified and generalized reference to Persia in all its imperial extent."[41]

Meyers and Meyers, however, were also open to a third view, one espoused in an earlier era by Hinckley G. T. Mitchell and Joyce G. Baldwin, which combines elements of the first two views by arguing that Zech 1:8–6:15 originated early in the reign of Darius, but rehearses the past overthrow of the enemy Babylon by Cyrus II. As Mitchell put it: "it seems best to interpret this first vision as a picture of the past, that is, of the period of the Exile ... it is probably this period that Zechariah had in mind when he put into the mouths of the returned horsemen the report that, wherever they went, they found undisturbed quiet."[42] Finally, there is a suggestion by Tollington that Zech 1:8–6:15 originated early in the reign of Darius and that its Babylonian focus reflects an undocumented opposition to Jewish restoration by Babylon.[43]

Solution

This diversity of opinion reveals a serious dilemma in the interpretation of Zech 1:7–6:15. Resolving this dilemma, created by the intersection of image and history, demands revisiting the place of Zechariah within the broader literary development of the prophetic image of Babylon and the historical experience of it as political entity in the Persian period. First, I will revisit the image of Babylon within prophetic expectation, especially in the books of Isaiah, Jeremiah, Ezekiel, and Habakkuk; second, I will consider afresh evidence of the realization of the prophetic expectation in the early Persian period.

---

[39] Petersen, *Haggai and Zechariah 1–8*, 154–55.
[40] Tollington, *Tradition*, 219–20.
[41] Meyers and Meyers, *Haggai, Zechariah 1–8*, 121.
[42] Hinckley Gilbert Mitchell, John Merlin Powis Smith, and Julius August Brewer, *A Critical and Exegetical Commentary on Haggai, Zechariah, Malachi and Jonah*, ICC (Edinburgh: T&T Clark, 1912), 122–23, 28; cf. Meyers and Meyers, *Haggai, Zechariah 1–8*, 117.
[43] Tollington, *Tradition*, 219–20.

Hebrew Prophetic Expectation

Babylon is treated in various ways throughout the Hebrew Bible. As already mentioned, readers of the Torah are introduced to the universal need for redemption through the recitation of the story of the Tower of Babel, associating Babylon with the human drive to be divine (Gen 11:1–9). In the Former Prophets, Chronicles, and Ezra, Babylon is the threatening enemy who enacts God's judgment upon Judah (2 Kgs 20 // Isa 39; 2 Kgs 24–25; 2 Chr 32:31; 33:11; 36; Ezra 5:12). Tucked within the book of Psalms is the vengeful Ps 137, in which exiles remember the cruel demands for songs by their Babylonian captors and call for retribution.

In the prophetic tradition, however, Babylon receives extensive treatment.[44] Babylon is the agent of discipline upon rebellious nations and the destination of the exile of his people, especially in the central part of the books of Jeremiah (chs. 20–39) and Ezekiel (chs. 17–32). At two key points in Jer 25, however, a different nuance is offered. Jeremiah 25:11–12 promises that after the nations serve Babylon for seventy years, God would punish the king, land, and people of Babylon, making it desolate forever (see 29:10). Later in the chapter in the review of the nations's consumption of God's wrathful cup, Babylon is the final nation to partake of this devastating cup. This dark nuance for Babylon is developed more vividly in the collection of oracles against Babylon in Jer 50–51.[45] There the prophet states that Babylon will be captured, its king punished, its gods shamed, and its city and land laid waste. This will be accomplished by a foreign destroyer (51:1–2), a foe from the north (50:8–13), identified as "the kings of the Medes" (51:11, 28). The Jewish exiles are invited to flee from Babylon (50:8).

A similar treatment of Babylon can be discerned in the book of Isaiah, where, besides the narrative linkage in Isa 39, Babylon's future is depicted as disastrous. Babylon is compared to Sodom and Gomorrah, its inhabitants exiled and eradicated, its gods shattered (13:1–14:23; 21:1–10; 43:14; 47:1–15; 48:14–15). In Isaiah the discipline of Babylon is linked to two foreign powers. As in Jer 50–51,

---

[44] On the image of Babylon in the prophets, see further Christopher T. Begg, "Babylon in the Book of Isaiah," in *The Book of Isaiah—Le Livre d'Isaïe: Les oracles et leurs relectures. Unité et complexité de l'ouvrage*, ed. J. Vermeylen, BETL 81 (Leuven: Peeters, 1989), 121–25; Reimer, *Oracles*; Majella Franzmann, "The City as Woman: The Case of Babylon in Isaiah 47," *ABR* 43 (1995): 1–9 (1–9); Chris A. Franke, "Reversals of Fortune in the Ancient Near East: A Study of the Babylon Oracles in the Book of Isaiah," in *New Visions of Isaiah*, ed. Roy F. Melugin and Marvin A. Sweeney, JSOTSup 214 (Sheffield: Sheffield Academic, 1996), 104–23; and especially Vanderhooft, *Babylon*.

[45] Interestingly, the darker nuance of Jer 25:26 uses the *Athbash* name for Babylon (*Sheshach*), a name that appears elsewhere only in Jer 50–51. The reference to Babylon in Jer 25:26 may be a piece that was added when chs. 50–51 were inserted into Jeremiah. See the superb work by Reimer, *Oracles*, 268–73, which also notes connections and development in Zech 2:10–17.

the one force is the Medes (Isa 13:17–18; 21:2).[46] But in Isa 40–48 a more specific foe is identified, "Yahweh's chosen ally" (48:14–15), who appears to be the anointed shepherd, Cyrus, from 44:28; 45:1; and 45:13.[47] In this same section (Isa 40–48) one hears again the prophetic encouragement to flee from punished Babylon (48:20; cf. 48:14–15).

These two approaches to the portrait of Babylon, both as agent and recipient of wrath, are associated closely in the book of Habakkuk. The divine response to the prophet's first complaint announces the role of Babylon as abuser of the nations (Hab 1:5–11),[48] while the second complaint prompts a divine announcement of judgment upon Babylon itself (Hab 2:2–20).

This evidence from the prophetic corpus highlights a strong stream of anti-Babylonian rhetoric within the Hebrew prophetic tradition.[49] Although an agent of God's wrath, Babylon is not insulated from discipline and will ultimately be punished. This discipline would be accomplished by a foreign power that is consistently linked to the land of Media in Jeremiah and to the land of Media and probably also the figure of Cyrus in Isaiah.

CYRUS AND BABYLON

In light of this prophetic expectation for Babylon's demise, what does the evidence of history tell us about fulfillment in the early Persian period? Our answer to this question takes as its point of departure the famous dream of Nabonidus that assembles a fascinating trio of ancient near Eastern rulers in the mid-sixth century BCE: Nabonidus, emperor of Babylon; Astyages, king of Media; and Cyrus, king of Anshan. In the dream Nabonidus identifies Cyrus's defeat of Astyages as the work of Marduk on his behalf to enable him to rebuild the temple of his mother's cult of Sin in Harran. Nabonidus's joy at Cyrus's success, however, would soon turn to terror as he watched the young Iranian conquering territory along the

---

[46] In Isa 21:2 they are linked to Elam, as in Jer 25:25.
[47] See recently on Cyrus in Second Isaiah, Lisbeth S. Fried, "Cyrus the Messiah? The Historical Background of Isaiah 45:1," *HTR* 95 (2002): 373–93.
[48] It is never explicitly stated in Habakkuk that Babylon functioned as God's disciplinary tool; cf. Sweeney, *Twelve*.
[49] I have left out Ezekiel because no reference is made to the punishment of Babylon in this book, although there is a possibility that Magog in Ezek 38–39 is a coded reference to Babylon, similar to Sheshach in Jer 25:26; 51:41 and Leb-qamai in Jer 51:1, both of which use the encoding system called *Athbash*. Cf. J. Boehmer, "Wer ist Gog von Magog? Ein Beitrag zur Auslegung des Buches Ezechiel," *ZWT* 40 (1897): 321–55; but see critique in Daniel I. Block, *The Book of Ezekiel: Chapters 25–48*, NICOT (Grand Rapids: Eerdmans, 1998), 434 n. 36.

fringes of the Babylonian empire, territory that would ultimately dwarf Nabonidus's holdings. By 539 BCE Cyrus would move across the Zagros Mountains, ford the Tigris at Opis, and march toward Babylon.[50] One of Cyrus's key supporters, Ugbaru, the Persian governor of Gutium, would actually defeat the Babylonian forces and enter the city first, so that when Cyrus entered it was secure and under the control of Gutian troops.[51] Although Cyrus's self-presentation assuredly has a propagandistic tone, it does reveal that Cyrus positioned himself wisely both politically and religiously.

It appears that Cyrus secured his Babylonian holdings through employing two key strategies.[52] First, he favored the priests and their temples, especially the

---

[50] On this, see Max Mallowan, "Cyrus the Great," in *The Cambridge History of Iran: Volume 2—The Median and Achaemenian Periods*, ed. Ilya Gershevitch (Cambridge: Cambridge University Press, 1985), 392–419; A. L. Oppenheim, "The Babylonian Evidence of Achaemenian Rule in Mesopotamia," in *The Cambridge History of Iran: Volume 2—The Median and Achaemenian Periods*, ed. Ilya Gershevitch (Cambridge: Cambridge University Press, 1985), 529–87; Pierre Briant, *From Cyrus to Alexander: A History of the Persian Empire*, trans. Peter T. Daniels (Winona Lake, IN: Eisenbrauns, 2002).

[51] Amélie Kuhrt, "Babylonia from Cyrus to Xerxes," in *The Cambridge Ancient History—Volume IV: Persia, Greece and the Western Mediterranean c. 525 to 479 B.C.*, ed. John Boardman et al. (Cambridge: Cambridge University Press, 1988), 112–38 (122). This may explain why Persian sources are more positive about the transition to Cyrus's rule than the Greek sources, the Greek relating more of the struggle between Ugbaru and Nabonidus and the Persian concentrating on the arrival of Cyrus (compare, e.g., the Cyrus Cylinder and *Nabonidus Chronicle* with Herodotus's *Hist.* 1.188–91 and Xenophon's *Cyr.* 7.5.7–32, 58). See also Vanderhooft, *Babylon*, 194–202, who weighs the evidence of Mesopotamian and Greek sources but then draws on Jer 51:30–32, which he suggests affirms the Greek version. For this period and the movements of Ugbaru and Cyrus, see J. M. Cook, *The Persian Empire* (New York: Barnes & Noble, 1983), 30–31; Mallowan, "Cyrus"; Oppenheim, "Babylonian Evidence," 542–44; T. Cuyler Young, "The Early History of the Medes and the Persians and the Achaemenid Empire to the Death of Cambyses," in *The Cambridge Ancient History—Volume IV: Persia, Greece and the Western Mediterranean c. 525 to 479 B.C.*, ed. John Boardman et al. (Cambridge: Cambridge University Press, 1988), 1–52 (38–41); E. Haerinck, "Babylonia under Achaemenid Rule," in *Mesopotamia and Iran in the Persian Period: Conquest and Imperialism 539–331 B.C. (Proceedings of a Seminar in Memory of Vladimir G. Lukonin)*, ed. John Curtis (London: British Museum, 1997), 26–34 (26–27).

[52] See Muhammad A. Dandamaev, *Iranians in Achaemenid Babylonia*, Columbia Lectures on Iranian Studies 6 (Costa Mesa, CA: Mazda/Bibliotheca Persica, 1992); Muhammad A. Dandamaev and Vladimir G. Lukonin, *The Culture and Social Institutions of Ancient Iran*, trans. Philip L. Kohl and D. J. Dadson (Cambridge: Cambridge University Press, 1989), 90, and Briant, *Cyrus*, 71. Besides these two key strategies, Dandamaev also mentions the lack of interruption of law and economy, the designation of Babylon as a winter royal residence, and the assumption by Cyrus of the title King of Babylon, King of the Lands.

priests at the temple of Esagila in Babylon.[53] Second, he retained high-ranking bureaucrats who had served under Nabonidus. So Amélie Kuhrt notes that "the very high office of *šākin māti* (the highest in the Neo-Babylonian period, superior to that of *šākin ṭēmi*) was held by Nabû-ahhē-bullit from Nabonidus' eighth regnal year to the end of Cyrus' third regnal year."[54] Furthermore, Dandamaev emphasizes this continuity when he writes:

> After the Persian conquest Cyrus II permitted the Babylonian kingdom to continue as a nominal entity, with its traditional methods of administration and social institution.... Even the most highly placed Babylonian officials retained their positions in the administrative apparatus.... Priests were encouraged to revive their ancient cults, which had been somewhat neglected during the rule of the last Chaldean king, Nabonidus.[55]

Such evidence has led Pierre Briant to conclude that "Cyrus himself, beginning with the conquest of Babylon, wished to put the accent more on the continuities than on the discontinuities, at least in his propagandistic assertions."[56]

Thus, Cyrus does match the hoped-for shattering of Babylonian power over the ancient Near East and appears to have provided conditions conducive to freedom for Jewish exiles and restoration of their temple,[57] but the city of Babylon appears to have escaped any serious disaster. For some within the Jewish tradition, namely, those responsible for Chronicles and Ezra, this event was celebrated as a key moment in the story of Jewish redemption; however, one must admit that it does fall short of many of the prophetic expectations.

Briant notes also that temple administrators continued to refer to regulations issued during Babylonian hegemony (from Nebuchadnezzar II, Neriglissar, and Nabonidus).

[53] The famous Cyrus Cylinder was a foundation document at Esagila; see Kuhrt, "Babylonia," 124; cf. Haerinck, "Babylonia," 26–27; Peter R. Bedford, "Early Achaemenid Monarchs and Indigenous Cults: Towards the Definition of Imperial Policy," in *Religion in the Ancient World: New Themes and Approaches*, ed. Matthew Dillon (Amsterdam: Hakkert, 1996), 17–39; Briant, *Cyrus*, 43.

[54] Kuhrt, "Babylonia," 125–26.

[55] Dandamaev, *Iranians*, 3; cf. Dandamaev and Lukonin, *Culture*, 100; Haerinck, "Babylonia," 26–28.

[56] Briant, *Cyrus*, 71.

[57] For recent work on Cyrus's connection to Jewish tradition, see Fried, "Cyrus the Messiah?"; and for reflection on political realities in Yehud, see Lisbeth S. Fried, *The Priest and the Great King: Temple-Palace Relations in the Persian Empire*, BJSUCSD 10 (Winona Lake, IN: Eisenbrauns, 2004).

DARIUS AND BABYLON

Any sign of the fulfillment of these expectations would have to wait until the reign of Darius, who, in the wake of the death of Cambyses wrested control of the empire and established a new Persian dynasty.[58] Darius's Bisitun Inscription sketches a tale of Babylonian rebellion. In early 522 BCE Babylon was among the first provinces of the empire to join the revolt against Cambyses's rule.[59] By the end of September 522 Darius ascended the throne and then moved within the week to retake Babylon. But when Darius left the city later in the year, the northern part of Babylon again revolted under Nidintu-Bel (October 522), who claimed to be Nebuchadnezzar, son of Nabonidus. This prompted Darius to march against Nidintu-Bel, finally defeating his forces after two battles near the end of 522. In August of the following year (521), however, Babylon revolted a third time under the Armenian Arkha, who began the revolt in Ur by claiming, as Nidintu-Bel, to be Nebuchadnezzar, son of Nabonidus. He would prove a more formidable opponent and was not be defeated until Darius's general outmaneuvered him on November 27, 521. This was the final revolt for Babylon under Darius's rule.

Piecing together the extent of Darius's punishment of Babylon is a great challenge. Darius impaled Nidintu-Bel and forty-nine of his followers.[60] However, because of the serious character of the third rebellion under Arkha, the inscription notes that Arkha and 2,497 of his supporters were impaled in Babylon.[61] This event seems to be reflected in Herodotus's claim (3.150–59) that Darius punished the Babylonians by impaling three thousand citizens. Herodotus's account, however, includes a reference to the destruction of walls and gates (3.159), something that has been seriously questioned by scholars because it is not mentioned in Persian sources.[62] Moreover, when Herodotus visited the city within a century, he

---

[58] For a fascinating viewpoint on the veracity of Darius's blood relationship to Cyrus and of Cyrus's "Achaemenid" heritage, see M. M. Waters, "Darius and the Achaemenid Line," *Ancient History Bulletin* 10 (1996): 11–18 (11–18); cf. Briant, *Cyrus*, 110–11, 138. Briant concludes: "he manipulated dynastic circumstances with a great deal of skill" (p. 138).

[59] On the history of the revolts, see Cook, *The Persian Empire*, 55–57; J. M. Cook, "The Rise of the Achaemenids and Establishment of Their Empire," in *The Cambridge History of Iran: Volume 2—The Median and Achaemenian Periods*, ed. Ilya Gershevitch (Cambridge: Cambridge University Press, 1985), 200–91 (218–19); Jon L. Berquist, *Judaism in Persia's Shadow: A Social and Cultural Approach* (Philadelphia: Fortress, 1995), 52–53; Edwin M. Yamauchi, *Persia and the Bible* (Grand Rapids: Baker, 1990), 147; Young, "Consolidation"; Kuhrt, "Babylonia," 129; Dandamaev and Lukonin, *Culture*, 91–94; Briant, *Cyrus*, 114–22, 899.

[60] Briant, *Cyrus*, 123; *DB Bab.* 19 (Darius's Bisitun Inscription, Akkadian column).

[61] Kuhrt, "Babylonia," 129.

[62] Ibid. The evidence of archaeology is also negative; see Robert Koldewey, *The Excavations at Babylon* (London: MacMillan, 1914).

described it as intact (1.178–200).⁶³ These rebellions not only resulted in severe punishment on Babylonians but also set in motion the impetus for political reorganization. As Dandamaev has noted:

> The uprisings of 522–521 revealed the weaknesses of the Achaemenid empire. Striving to avert separatist tendencies, Darius I carried out important administrative-financial reforms, which facilitated the creation of a stable system of state administration and control over the conquered countries, created order in the collection of taxes, and increased the contingent of troops. The implementation of these reforms took several years, and apparently began with the reorganization and unification of the system of administration of the provinces undertaken around 519 B.C.⁶⁴

Interestingly, in March 520 the Persian Ushtani became the governor of Mesopotamia and Across the River, the former governor, Gubaru, having died in the revolts of 522–521 BCE. By 516 BCE, however, the first signs of a rift in this large satrapy can be discerned in the political reorganization that placed Ushtani over Mesopotamia and Tattenai over Across the River.⁶⁵ Although Tattenai was still accountable to Ushtani, this division of the two was the first evidence of a breakup of the territory that had comprised the former Babylonian imperial lands.⁶⁶

Although it is difficult to attain certainty on all details, the various historical sources for the early Persian period on the one side stress continuity for Babylon

---

⁶³ Yamauchi, *Persia*, 159, 72. Kuhrt, "Babylonia," 129, does not accept Herodotus's view of the ruse of Zopyrus and destruction of gates and defenses. However, Kenneth G. Hoglund, *Achaemenid Imperial Administration in Syria-Palestine and the Mission of Ezra and Nehemiah*, SBLDS 125 (Atlanta: Scholars, 1992), 210, claims that Darius I destroyed the inner citadel walls in 521 BCE and Xerxes the entire city wall system in 484 BCE. See also Maurice Meuleau, "Mesopotamia under Persian Rule," in *The Greeks and the Persians from the Sixth to the Fourth Centuries*, ed. H. Bengston, Delacorte World History 5 (New York: Delacorte, 1968), 354–85 (357–61).

⁶⁴ Dandamaev and Lukonin, *Culture*, 97.

⁶⁵ Ibid., 100.

⁶⁶ It appears that the final and clear division between Babylon and Abar-Nahara would occur under Xerxes (sometime after 486 BCE, most likely 482 BCE); see Dandamaev, *Iranians*, 3–4; also Ephraim Stern, "The Persian Empire and the Political and Social History of Palestine in the Persian Period," in *The Cambridge History of Judaism, Volume One—Introduction: The Persian Period*, ed. W. D. Davies and Louis Finkelstein (Cambridge: Cambridge University Press, 1984), 70–87 (73, 78); Matthew W. Stolper, "The Governor of Babylon and Across-the-River in 486 B.C.," *JNES* 48 (1989): 283–305; Michael Heltzer, "A Recently Published Babylonian Tablet and the Province of Judah after 516 B.C.E.," *Transeu* 5 (1992): 57–61; Israel Eph'al, "Changes in Palestine During the Persian Period in Light of Epigraphic Sources," *IEJ* 48 (1998): 106–19 (109).

in the transition from Nabonidus to Cyrus, both in terms of treatment of the population and political structure, while stressing discontinuity for Babylon in terms of both treatment of the population and political structure in the transition from Cambyses to Darius.[67]

ZECHARIAH 1:7–6:15 IN HISTORY

This historical evidence suggests that the treatment of Babylon in Zech 1:7–6:15 is appropriate within the historical context noted in the superscription in 1:7.[68] It is unnecessary to posit an original historical or narrative setting for these visions and oracles in the transition from Nabonidus to Cyrus. Zechariah 1:7–6:15 finds in the recent upheaval of the Persian empire significant progress towards the Persian fulfillment of prophetic expectations. This means not just the breaking of Babylonian hegemony over Yehud, but punishment of Babylonian excesses, structural transformation of the former empire, and reversal of the devastating actions of the Babylonians through releasing significant numbers of people and rebuilding the temple structure.[69] Although Cyrus had begun the process in 539

---

[67] Reimer, *Oracles*, 284, notes the three "falls" of Babylon as 689, 539, and 482 BCE, skipping over the period of Darius.

[68] Another key period of Babylonian revolt and Persian punishment that remains a possibility is that of Xerxes's rule. It is often noted that the Babylonians were severely punished in 482 BCE for their revolt against Xerxes, who dismantled the fortifications of the city and its temple, killed priests, and removed the statue of Marduk from Esagila, bringing an end to the Akitu festival; see Olmstead, *History*, 237; Cook, *The Persian Empire*, 100; Young, "Consolidation," 73–75; Dandamaev and Lukonin, *Culture*, 4–5, 95, 366; Muhammad A. Dandamayev, "Xerxes and the Esagila Temple in Babylon," in *Encyclopaedia Iranica*, ed. Ehsan Yarshater (New York: Encyclopaedia Iranica Foundation/Columbia University, 1993), 3:326–34; Haerinck, "Babylonia," 28. The historicity of this event, which is limited to Greek sources, has been seriously contested by Amélie Kuhrt and S. Sherwin-White, "Xerxes' Destruction of Babylonian Temples," in *The Greek Sources: Proceedings of the Groningen 1984 Achaemenid History Workshop*. Edited by H. Sancisi-Weerdenburg and Amélie Kuhrt. Achaemenid History 2 (Leiden: Nederlands Instituut Voor Het Nabije Oosten, 1987), 69–78; Kuhrt, "Babylonia," 133–34; and Pierre Briant, "La date des révoltes babyloniennes contre Xerxès," *Studia Iranica* 21.1 (1992): 7–20; Briant, *Cyrus*, 525, 35, 43–44, 963. All agree, however, that there were serious revolts in Babylon near the beginning of Xerxes's rule. What is contested is the character of Xerxes's punishment of the city. Although this is a possible historical referent for the anti-Babylonian rhetoric in the night visions and may even offer the impetus for its publication, the evidence tips in favor of the period of Darius in light of the superscription, at least for the origination of the rhetoric.

[69] Ackroyd, "Historical Problems," 21, rightly attacks the work of Waterman and Olmstead, who saw in the message of Haggai and Zechariah a call to rebel against Persia alongside the Babylonians. By this, however, Ackroyd is not denying any connection between the Babylonian rebellions and the text of Zechariah, for he notes that hostility toward

BCE, in the Zecharian tradition it was Darius who displayed greater progress in the fulfillment of the prophetic hope.[70]

IMPLICATIONS

This examination of the period of Darius in Zech 1:7–6:15 provides perspective on the development not only of the Babylonian tradition in the period after the reign of Nabonidus but also of the Persian tradition. In biblical studies Cyrus has often taken center stage in rehearsals of the early Persian period, owing to his defeat of Nabonidus and establishment of the Persian empire, reflected in the traditions of 2 Chr 36 and Ezra. However, one should not miss the importance of Darius in biblical tradition and how significant the Cyrus-Darius tradition complex is for later rehearsals of this period. This importance is demonstrated in Ezra 1–6, in which Cyrus and Darius participate together to bring completion to the temple, the later Darius affirming the proclamation of the earlier Cyrus, lending renewed authority and resources to the frustrated project (Ezra 5:1–6:15; esp. 6:14).[71] A close association between the traditions about Cyrus and Darius in Jewish literature may also explain the oddities in the Danielic tradition that appear to

---

Babylon in Zechariah "may with greater probability reflect the situation in the time of Darius I, when there is a possibility that the Jews had less sympathy with the Babylonian rebels than with the Persians in whom they had hope of restoration" (Ackroyd, *Exile*, 37–38, 180). Furthermore, Ackroyd, "Historical Problems," 20 n. 51, notes with Kurt Galling, "Die Exilswende in der Sicht des Propheten Sacharja," *VT* 2 (1952): 18–36, that some oracles in Zechariah seem to presuppose a Babylonian geographical background, although during the period of Cambyses–Darius.

[70] Since completing this piece, I have discovered a similar argument (based on the general prophetic tradition) in Konrad Schmid and Odil Hannes Steck, "Restoration Expectations in the Prophetic Tradition of the Old Testament," in *Restoration: Old Testament, Jewish and Christian Conceptions*, ed. James M. Scott, Supplements to JSJ 72 (Leiden: Brill, 2001), 41–82 (73–74). Floyd, *Minor Prophets*, 357, recently came to the same conclusion, although for different reasons. He finds it difficult to see here anti-Persian sentiment, in light "of the fact that the new world order so favorable to Judah has been created precisely by the Persians." Thus, although Floyd says that 1:8–17 could be dated as early as the time of Cyrus (ca. 535 BCE), he concludes that since 1:16 envisions a return of Yahweh, a later date is to be preferred: after the upheavals following the death of Cambyses.

[71] Peter R. Bedford, *Temple Restoration in Early Achaemenid Judah*, Supplements to the JSJ 65 (Leiden: Brill, 2001), 181, writes: "From the perspective of Haggai and Zechariah 1–8, there was no delay since the fall of the Babylonian empire and the edict of Cyrus did not mark the end of Yahweh's ire against his people and his land. For these prophets the abatement of the anger of Yahweh and his return to Jerusalem had come only in their day."

forge together two figures named Cyrus and Darius.⁷² This close association between Cyrus and Darius, however, is most likely not merely a Jewish innovation, as M. M. Waters argues so cogently in his recent work, but appears to be reflected in Darius's own historical monuments.⁷³

---

⁷² It is interesting that Darius is called the Mede in Daniel, since the prophetic tradition consistently named the Medians as the force that would defeat the Babylonians (see above). Commenting on Cyrus's defeat of Astyages, Cook, "Rise," 211, notes that "to the Eastern Mediterranean world it may have appeared nothing more than a change of dynasty; for in the eyes of Jews, Greeks, Egyptians and Arabs the ruling power long after continued to be the 'Mede'"; however notice how Ugbaru was the governor of Gutium, which Cook, *The Persian Empire*, 30, identifies as an "anachronistic name in keeping with the conservatism of priests who were trying to keep their old language and cuneiform script alive.... It is not really possible to say more than that Gutium at this time meant a region east of the Tigris." For other approaches to the "Darius" tradition in Daniel, especially in relationship to the prophetic tradition of Israel, see Lester L. Grabbe, "Another Look at the Gestalt of 'Darius the Mede'," *CBQ* 50 (1988): 198–213 (esp. 212); Brian E. Colless, "Cyrus the Persian as Darius the Mede in the Book of Daniel," *JSOT* 56 (1992): 113–26.

⁷³ Waters, "Darius"; so also Briant, *Cyrus*, 138, who concludes about Darius: "he intended to promote skillful propaganda at Pasargadae that would allow him to establish a fictitious link with Cyrus, just as he did with his matrimonial policy."

3
Hoy, Hoy: The Prophetic Origins of the Babylonian Tradition in Zechariah 2:10–17[1]

Having analyzed the use of the Babylon tradition in Zech 1:7–6:15 in the previous chapter, I now focus attention on a particular text, Zech 2:10–17, culling it for further evidence of influence from the Hebrew prophets. This pericope belies reliance on a breadth of prophetic traditions focused on Babylon and its punishment, including Isaiah (chs. 12–14), Jeremiah (chs. 25, 50–51), Ezekiel (chs. 38–39) and Habakkuk (ch. 2).

In his commentary on the books of Haggai and Zech 1–8, David Petersen singles out two prophetic tradition streams, Isaiah and Ezekiel, as key to the development of Zech 1–8. On the one side, Petersen argues that the Zecharian tradents present "an alternative to or a revision of the notions of restoration present in Ezek. 40–

---

[1] Based on my original publication, Mark J. Boda, "*Hoy, Hoy*: The Prophetic Origins of the Babylonian Tradition in Zechariah 2:10–17," in *Tradition in Transition: Haggai and Zechariah 1–8 in the Trajectory of Hebrew Theology*, ed. Mark J. Boda and Michael H. Floyd, LHBOTS 475 (London: T&T Clark, 2008), 171–90. Slightly revised for inclusion in this volume. The numbering system of the MT will be used in the present study. Most English translations number these verses as Zech 2:6–13.

48."[2] On the other side, however, he argues that there is "shared discourse between the prophetic traditionists of the Isaianic circle, the prophet Zechariah, and those preserving Zechariah's visions and oracles."[3]

Marvin Sweeney's recent commentary takes this claim for Isaianic impact to a new level.[4] While it is true that Sweeney admits that Zechariah cites other prophetic books (Jeremiah, Ezekiel, Hosea, Amos, Haggai), he gives pride of place to the book of Isaiah. This inter-prophetic connection can be discerned from the outset of the book of Zechariah where Sweeney finds the genealogy of a prophet Zechariah who is called "son of Berechiah." According to Sweeney, this serves as a play on the character "Zechariah son of Jeberechiah" who served as a witness to the birth of Isaiah's son in Isa 8:1–4, an identification which "is apparently intended to point to Zechariah's book as a representation of the fulfillment of Isaiah's prophecies at the time of the building of the second temple and beyond."[5] This evidence, however, does not stand alone, for Sweeney concludes that the "book of Zechariah alludes extensively to passages from the book of Isaiah to make the point that Isaiah's prophecies are about to achieve their fulfillment."[6] He notes that while the book of Isaiah prophesied the fall of Assyria and Babylon, the book of Zechariah looks to the fall of Persia. Thus Sweeney calls the authors of Zechariah "early readers of Isaiah" who "sought to cast Zechariah as the witness to the fulfillment of Isaiah's message."[7] He does note, however, that these readers "appear to have been heavily influenced by Micah as well as by other prophetic writings, particularly Jeremiah."[8]

A passage that has often been used to bolster this claim for Isaianic influence is the prophetic oracle found in Zech 2:10–17. For Petersen, the evidence for this claim is exemplified by the similarity of the reference to the escape of Zion in

---

[2] David L. Petersen, *Haggai and Zechariah 1–8: A Commentary*, OTL (Philadelphia: Westminster, 1984), 119.

[3] Petersen, *Haggai and Zechariah 1–8*, 122. Also note Petitjean's conclusion on the oracles in Zech 1–6: "Fortement marques par l'influence des prophètes antérieurs, principalement de Jérémie, d'Ézéchiel et du Second Isaïe, les oracles de Zacharie experiment cependant une pensée dense et originale," Albert Petitjean, *Les oracles du proto-Zacharie: Un programme de restauration pour la communauté juive après l'exil* (Paris: Librairie Lecoffre, 1969), 441.

[4] Marvin A. Sweeney, *The Twelve Prophets*, 2 vols., Berit Olam (Collegeville, MN: Liturgical Press, 2000); note also Marvin A. Sweeney, "Zechariah's Debate with Isaiah," in *The Changing Face of Form Criticism for the Twenty-first Century*, ed. Marvin A. Sweeney and Ehud Ben Zvi (Grand Rapids: Eerdmans, 2003), 335–50, where Sweeney focuses exclusively on the influence of Isaiah on the entire book of Zechariah. His lack of attention to Jeremiah and Ezekiel is surprising.

[5] Sweeney, *Twelve*, 2:563–64.

[6] Ibid., 2:563.

[7] Ibid.

[8] Ibid., 2:564.

Zech 2:11 to Isa 51:16, the reference to the singing upon the return of Yahweh in Zech 2:14 as typical of Isaiah (with the language similar to Isa 12:6) and the reference to gentiles joining the covenant people in Zech 2:15 echoing the language of Isa 56:6–7. Petersen admits that in the final case there is some discontinuity: "The distinctions that will be maintained according to Isa. 56:7 (and for that matter Isa. 2:1–4) will, according to Zech. 2:15 [11 E.], be abrogated."[9]

Sweeney adds more details to Petersen's evidence. According to Sweeney, the reference to Daughter Babylon "draws heavily upon that of the book of Isaiah which frequently portrays Jerusalem and Babylon as women who suffer various misfortunes and restorations ... and calls upon the exiles to leave Babylon for Jerusalem" (citing Isa 3:25–4:1; 47; 49:18; 52:1–2; 54 for "Daughter Babylon/Zion" and Isa 48:20; 49:8–13; 51:9–11; 52:11–12 for leaving Babylon).[10] The submission of the nations to Yahweh at Jerusalem throughout 2:10–17 "corresponds well to Isaiah" (Isa 2:2–4, 6–21; 42:1–9; 45:9–14, 49:1–26; 51:1–11; 60–62), the imagery of God raising his hand against enemies of Israel found in Zech 2:13 is also used in Isa 11:15 and 19:16, the exhortations to Daughter Zion in Zech 2:14 are "reminiscent of Second Isaiah" (citing 42:11; 44:23; 49:13; 52:8, 9; 54:1; 61:7; cf. Isa 9:2; 12:1; 24:14; 26:19; 35:2, 6; 66:10).[11] As with Petersen, finally, the revelation that "many nations" will be "joined to YHWH" is akin to Isaiah, as Sweeney puts it: "Such a scenario corresponds to the overall outlook of Isaiah which envisions the nations coming to Zion together with Israel/Jacob to acknowledge YHWH's world-wide sovereignty" (citing Isa 2:2–4; 25:6–10; 56:1–8; 60–62; 66:18–24).[12]

The purpose of the present study is twofold. First, it is to test these claims for Isaianic influence on Zech 2:10–17 by searching for the key traditions that lie behind this passage. We will discover that the influential tradition is clearly prophetic, but extends well beyond Isaiah. Secondly, the purpose is also to describe the intertextual techniques evident in the use of these prophetic traditions. We will discover that the Zecharian tradent(s) incorporate earlier prophetic language from passages whose larger context is significant to the ideological program of Zech 2:10–17 in particular and Zech 1:7–6:15 in general.

---

[9] Petersen, *Haggai and Zechariah 1–8*, 182.
[10] Sweeney, *Twelve*, 2:588.
[11] Ibid., 2:589–90.
[12] Ibid., 2:590.

READING ZECHARIAH 2:10–17 WITH THE "EARLIER PROPHETS"

ZECHARIAH 2:10–11

| הוי הוי ונסו מארץ צפון נאם־יהוה כי
כארבע רוחות השמים פרשתי אתכם
נאם־יהוה: | Attention, attention, Flee from the land of the north, declares Yahweh, for as the four winds of the heavens I have scattered you, declares Yahweh. |

| הוי ציון המלטי יושבת בת־בבל: | Attention, Zion, escape you who dwell in Daughter Babylon.[13] |

The oracle opens with the words הוי הוי (2:10), calling the audience to attention with a word that is repeated again at the beginning of 2:11. This doublet style is typical in the Hebrew Bible, where the imperative is the most common word type for such constructions (Judg 5:12; 2 Sam 16:7; 20:16; Pss 47:7; 137:7; Prov 30:15; Song 7:1; Isa 40:1; 51:9, 17; 52:1, 11; 62:10; Lam 4:15; Ezek 3:1; 33:11; Nah 2:9; Hab 1:5). The use of double interjections is found elsewhere only in Ezek 16:23 where the closely related word אוי is used to gain the attention of the audience. The doublet style is very common in Isa 40–66 and thus this may betray influence from this corpus, but it must be admitted that "interjections" per se are never doubled in Isaiah. The verbs "flee" (נוס) and "escape" (מלט) are found together at several places in the Hebrew Bible (Gen 19:20; 1 Sam 19:10; 30:17; 1 Kgs 20:20; Isa 20:6; Jer 46:6; 48:6, 19; 51:6; Amos 9:1). However, as is evident in this list it is most common as a collocation in the Oracles Against the Nations in Jer 46–51, and Jer 51:6 is the only place that uses both verbs to call for flight from Babylon (cf. נוס in 50:16 and מלט in 51:45, 50 all in reference to flight from Babylon).[14]

The location from which this flight will take place is clearly identified as the ארץ צפון and בת־בבל. The phrase ארץ צפון is a regular component of the Jeremianic tradition, where it is identified with Babylon, the enemy of Israel and the one used of Yahweh to discipline the people (Jer 3:18; 6:22; 10:22; 16:15; 23:8; 31:8; 46:10; 50:9; cf. Zech 2:10; 6:6, 8). The בת־בבל only occurs four other times in the Hebrew Bible (Ps 137:8; Isa 47:1; Jer 50:42; 51:33).[15] Zechariah 2:10 and 2:11 place these two phrases in parallel, betraying influence from the Jeremianic tradition. Both phrases are found in Jer 50–51 (ארץ צפון: 50:9; cf. 50:3, 41; 51:48; בת־בבל: 50:42; 51:33), but interestingly it is linked to another people who are now identified as the enemies of Babylon. The term "Zion" for the disciplined people of Israel is a regular component in both Isaiah and Jeremiah traditions (Isa

---

[13] On the translation of "Daughter Zion," see n. 23 below.
[14] For this see David J. Reimer, *The Oracles against Babylon in Jeremiah 50–51: A Horror among the Nations* (San Francisco: Mellen Research University Press, 1993), 271.
[15] See also Reimer, *Oracles*, 270–71, for both ארץ צפון and בת־בבל.

40:9; 41:27; 46:13; 49:14; 51:3, 11, 16; 52:1, 2, 7, 8; 59:20; 60:14; 61:3; 62:1, 11; 64:9; 66:8; Jer 3:14; 4:6, 31; 6:2, 23; 8:19; 9:18; 14:19; 26:18; 30:17; 31:6, 12). However, it is only in Jer 50–51 that Zion is described in relationship to an escape from a place specifically identified as Babylon (Jer 50:5, 28; 51:10, 24, 35).[16] Finally the collocation יושבת בת־בבל at the end of Zech 2:11, which consists of the collective feminine singular participle יושבת followed by the term בת in construct with the name of a city/land, is found elsewhere only in the Jer 46–50 corpus (Jer 46:19; 48:18).[17]

The motif of the ארבע רוחות השמים is found in 1 Chr 9:24; Jer 49:36; Ezek 37:9; Dan 8:8; 11:4; and Zech 6:5. In Jer 49:36, this motif is used in a similar way to Zech 2:10, that is, the four winds of heaven are associated with the exile of a people and are the destination of a scattering of the people. It should be noted that Jer 49:36 uses the synonym זרה instead of פרש; however, the use of פרש here may be a purposeful allusion to Persia, a homonym.

The vocabulary of Zech 2:10–11, then, bears striking similarity to that of Jer 50–51 and the larger complex of the Oracles against the Nations in Jer 46–51 and the Jeremianic tradition in general.[18] The Isaianic tradition does not figure prominently in these two opening verses.[19]

ZECHARIAH 2:12–13

| כי כה אמר יהוה צבאות אחר כבוד שלחני אל־הגוים השללים אתכם כי הנגע בכם נגע בבבת עינו: | For thus says Yahweh Almighty, after glory he sent me to the nations which plundered you, for the one who touches you touches the pupil of his eye. |

---

[16] Petersen, *Haggai and Zechariah 1–8*, 176–77, makes reference to Isa 51:16 as typical of Deutero-Isaiah's use of Zion, but does not pursue the details of the vocabulary.
[17] See Carol L. Meyers and Eric M. Meyers, *Haggai, Zechariah 1–8: A New Translation with Introduction and Commentary*, AB 25B (Garden City, NY: Doubleday, 1987), 164.
[18] Reimer, *Oracles*, 270–71, noted several of these links between Jer 50–51 (46–51) and Zech 2:10–17 and others that will be noted throughout the present study.
[19] Meyers and Meyers, *Haggai, Zechariah 1–8*, 163, argue that 2:10 "can very well have been influenced by" both Jer 50–51 and Deutero-Isaiah (e.g., Jer 50:8, 28; 51:6, 45; Isa 48:20). Bernard Gosse, *Isaïe 13,1–14,23: Dans la tradition littéraire du livre d'Isaïe et dans la tradition des oracles contre les nations—Étude de la transformation du genre littéraire*, OBO 78 (Freiburg, Schweiz: Universitätsverlag; Göttingen: Vandenhoeck & Ruprecht, 1988), 208, highlights links between Jer 51:7 and Zech 2:10, 11; 50:42; 51:33 and Zech 2:11. Risto Nurmela, *Prophets in Dialogue: Inner-Biblical Allusions in Zechariah 1–8 and 9–14* (Åbo: Åbo Akademi University, 1996), 54–56, claimed that Jer 50–51 was reliant on Zech 2:10–17, but the evidence for the dating of Jer 50–51 presented below (n. 32) makes this unlikely.

כִּי הִנְנִי מֵנִיף אֶת־יָדִי עֲלֵיהֶם וְהָיוּ שָׁלָל   For behold I am raising my hand against
לְעַבְדֵיהֶם וִידַעְתֶּם כִּי־יהוה צְבָאוֹת   them and they will be plunder to their
שְׁלָחָנִי: slaves and you will know that Yahweh Almighty has sent me.

The root שלל is used on many occasions in the Hebrew Bible, where it is usually employed to refer to the simple act of despoiling a defeated enemy. The nuance found in Zech 2:12–13, that is, that those who once despoiled will now be despoiled by their former subjects, is restricted elsewhere to Ezek 39:10 and Hab 2:8.[20] Ezekiel 39:10 is the best candidate of these two because in it the Israelites are specified as the ones who enjoy the reversal, while in Hab 2:8 it is more generally the nations who remain.

The collocation נוף hiphil + יד occurs only elsewhere in Isa 11:15; 13:2, and 19:16, the first in reference to Yahweh's return of the exiles from Mesopotamia, the second in reference to God's judgment on Babylon, and the third in reference to God's judgment on Egypt.[21] Isaiah 13:2 is the closest conceptually to the use in Zech 2:13, for in both the action is one of judgment against a nation, and that nation has just been identified in 2:10–11 as Babylon.

The prophetic confirmation formula וִידַעְתֶּם כִּי־יהוה צְבָאוֹת שְׁלָחָנִי is unique to Zech 1–6, appearing at 2:12, 15; 4:9, and 6:15. The first part, וִידַעְתֶּם ("then you will know"), appears regularly in prophetic material, especially in the book of Ezekiel in the phrase וִידַעְתֶּם כִּי־אֲנִי יהוה (Ezek 6:7, 13; 7:4, 9; 11:10, 12; 12:20; 13:9, 14, 21, 23; 14:8; 15:7; 16:62; 17:21; 20:38, 42, 44; 22:16, 22; 23:49; 24:24; 25:5, 7; 35:4, 9, 12; 36:11; 37:6, 13, 14; 38:23; 39:6, 7, 22, 28; cf. Ezek 38:16; Is 43:10; 45:3; 49:23; 60:16). The second part, כִּי־יהוה צְבָאוֹת שְׁלָחָנִי, is reflected in the phrase יהוה שְׁלָחַנִי אֵלֶיךָ ("Yahweh has sent me to you"), which appears elsewhere in Exod 3:13, 14, 15; 7:16; Jer 42:21; Zech 4:9; 6:15; cf. 2 Kgs 8:9 (where a king sends a messenger). This phrase draws on the foundational narrative for prophecy, the calling of Moses. The shift in Zech 1–6 of the wording of the phrase from Ezekiel, however, moves the focus from the people knowing something about Yahweh (Ezekiel) to them knowing something about Yahweh's prophet. The influence of Ezekiel, however, is evident.

The Ezekielian tradition very likely lies behind the difficult phrase אַחַר כָּבוֹד ("after glory") as well. Ezekiel 39:21–29 uses the word כָּבוֹד ("glory") to refer to God's punishment of Judah, a punishment that the nations will see.[22] The

---

[20] Reimer, *Oracles*, 271, cites Jer 50:10 which uses שלל. Janet E. Tollington, *Tradition and Innovation in Haggai and Zechariah 1–8*, JSOTSup 150 (Sheffield: JSOT, 1993), 229, makes the helpful observation that this concept is found elsewhere in Ezek 39:10 and Isa 14:2 (leaving out Hab 2:8). Isa 14:2, however, uses the verb שבה.
[21] Ibid., 229 n. 1.
[22] Meyers and Meyers, *Haggai, Zechariah 1–8*, 165, note that כָּבוֹד ("glory") is a term "characteristic of priestly writing and also of Ezekiel."

prophet declares, however, that he will restore "Jacob," having compassion upon them. Thus the meaning here is that אחר כבוד ("after glory"), that is, after God's punishment of Judah, he then sent the prophet against the nations who have plundered them.

Common to most of these key words/phrases in Zech 2:12–13 is Ezek 38–39, a passage that, although shrouded in mystery, is linked to the punishment of Judah in exile and the reversal of this punishment on their enemies and the rescue of Judah from exile. It is possible that Isa 13:2 is the influence behind מניף את־ידי.

ZECHARIAH 2:14–16

רני ושמחי בת־ציון כי הנני־בא ושכנתי בתוכך נאם־יהוה:	Shout and rejoice, O Daughter Zion[23] for behold I am coming and I will dwell in your midst, declares Yahweh.
ונלוו גוים רבים אל־יהוה ביום ההוא והיו לי לעם ושכנתי בתוכך וידעת כי־יהוה צבאות שלחני אליך:	And many nations will be joined to Yahweh in that day and they will be my people and I will dwell in your midst and you will know that Yahweh Almighty has sent me to you.
ונחל יהוה את־יהודה חלקו על אדמת הקדש ובחר עוד בירושלם:	And Yahweh will inherit Judah as his portion in the holy land and will again choose Jerusalem.

Zechariah 2:14 represents a form identified by Crüsemann as *Aufruf zur Freude*, a form that can be traced through the following passages: Isa 12:4–6; 54:1; Joel 2:21–24; Lam 4:21; Zeph 3:14; Zech 2:14; 9:9 (cf. Hos 9:1).[24] This form consists

---

[23] For the translation "Daughter Zion" as an appositional genitive or genitive of association (and earlier "Daughter Babylon" in v. 11), see GKC §128k; Joüon §129f; as well as W. F. Stinespring, "No Daughter of Zion: A Study of the Appositional Genitive in Hebrew Grammar," *Enc* 26 (1965): 133–41; Adele Berlin, *Lamentations: A Commentary*, OTL (Louisville: Westminster John Knox, 2002), 11–12; contra F. W. Dobbs-Allsopp, "The Syntagma of *bat* Followed by a Geographical Name in the Hebrew Bible. A Reconsideration of Its Meaning and Grammar," *CBQ* 57 (1995): 45–70; see the excellent review in Hyukki Kim, "The Interpretation of בַּת־צִיּוֹן (Daughter Zion): An Approach of Cognitive Theories of Metaphor" (MA thesis, McMaster Divinity College, 2006). See now Mark J. Boda, *The Book of Zechariah*, NICOT (Grand Rapids: Eerdmans, 2016), 189, for my present view which is to translate as "Daughter of X."

[24] Frank Crüsemann, *Studien zur Formgeschichte von Hymnus und Danklied in Israel*, WMANT 32 (Neukirchen-Vluyn: Neukirchener, 1969), 55–65; cf. Katrina J. Larkin, *The Eschatology of Second Zechariah: A Study of the Formation of a Mantological Wisdom Anthology*, CBET 6 (Kampen: Kok, 1994), 73. Hosea 9:1 is clearly influenced by this form, but addresses a male figure: "Israel."

of three basic elements. First, it begins with an imperative drawn from a limited pool of verbal roots, the most common being: רנן, גיל, שמח, שיש, רוע, צהל, each inciting joyful shouts. Second, this imperative is addressed usually to a city/land personified as a woman and less frequently to male figures (Israel, sons of Zion) or animals. Thirdly, the imperative and vocative is followed by the particle כי ("for/because") which introduces a clause providing the reason for the exhortation. Of the occurrences of the form cited above, there is no question that Zeph 3:14 and Zech 9:9 are the closest to Zech 2:14. However, it appears that these two passages show signs of reliance on Zech 2:14.[25] It is Isa 12:6 that stands out from the others, the only other one addressed to a female inhabitant related to Zion (יושבת ציון, "inhabitant Zion"). It uses one of the two imperatives found in Zech 2:14 (רני, "shout for joy"), uses the particle כי to introduce the reason clause (contra Zeph 3:14 and Zech 9:9), and, similar to Zech 2:14, identifies the presence of God in their midst (בקרבך) as the motivation for the joy.

The verb לוה ("be joined," v. 15) appears only twelve times in the Hebrew Bible (Gen 29:34; Num 18:2, 4; Esth 9:27; Ps 83:9; Qoh 8:15; Isa 14:1; 56:3, 6; Jer 50:5; Dan 11:34; Zech 2:15). In light of previous connections in Zech 2:10–11, at first one may be drawn to Jer 50:5, which describes people seeking to join themselves to Yahweh in an everlasting covenant. The people in Jer 50:5, however, are not "many nations," as in Zech 2:15, but rather the "sons of Israel" and the "sons of Judah." Instead, the references in Isaiah (14:1; 56:3, 6) link gentiles with this verb.[26] The greater likelihood of this connection to Isaiah is increased when one observes further connections to Isa 14 in the use of the phrase בחר עוד ב (Zech 2:16; Isa 14:1; elsewhere only Zech 1:17), the verb נחל (Zech 2:16; Isa 14:2), the noun אדמה (Zech 2:16; Isa 14: 1, 2) and the common motifs of the reversal of captive/captors (Isa 14:2), and judgment upon Babylon (chs. 13–14). In light of this, Isa 12–14 appears to be the dominant source for verses 15–16,[27]

---

[25] I have argued this in Mark J. Boda, "Babylon in the Book of the Twelve," *HBAI* 3 (2014): 225–48 = *Exploring Zechariah*, volume 1, chapter 8. See also Nurmela, *Prophets in Dialogue*, 214–16; Risto Nurmela, "The Growth of the Book of Isaiah Illustrated by Allusions in Zechariah," in *Bringing out the Treasure: Inner Biblical Allusion and Zechariah 9–14*, ed. Mark J. Boda and Michael H. Floyd, JSOTSup 370 (Sheffield: Sheffield Academic, 2003), 245–59 (248–49).

[26] Petersen, *Haggai and Zechariah 1–8*, 181–82, chooses Isa 56:6–7 as "the strongest parallel expression to this text, apart from inner-Zechariah resonances," even though Zech 2:15 goes beyond Isa 56 in abrogating the distinctions between Israel and the nations.

[27] Cf. Reimer, *Oracles*, and see especially H. G. M. Williamson, *The Book Called Isaiah: Deutero-Isaiah's Role in Composition and Redaction* (Oxford: Oxford University Press; New York: Clarendon, 1994), 174–75, who argues for the reliance of Zechariah on Isa 14:1–2: "In my opinion, however, these similarities are to be explained in terms of Zechariah grappling with the apparent non-fulfillment of some aspects of earlier prophecies concerning the end of the exile." Although this may be true for the "seventy years" of 1:12 (in relationship to Jer 25:11; 29:10), this does not appear to be the case here in Zech 2:10–

even if again Jer 50 (esp. v. 5) may have influenced some of the vocabulary (לוה).²⁸

ZECHARIAH 2:17

| הס כל־בשׂר מפני יהוה | Hush all flesh before Yahweh for he has |
| כי נעור ממעון קדשו: | roused himself from his holy dwelling. |

The interjection הס ("be still/silent") is used seven times in the Hebrew Bible (Judg 3:19; Neh 8:11; Amos 6:10; 8:3; Hab 2:20; Zeph 1:7; Zech 2:17). Of these, Hab 2:20 resonates with the use in Zech 2:17, with its address to "all people" (Zech 2:17: כל־בשׂר; Hab 2:20: כל־הארץ) and reference to a holy dwelling (Zech 2:17: מעון קדשו; Hab 2:20: היכל קדשו).²⁹ Furthermore, both Hab 2:20 and Zech 2:17 function as conclusions to their respective prophetic messages.³⁰ However, Nurmela has observed that both כל־בשׂר and מעון קדשו appear in Jer 25:30–31, a passage that looks to the punishment of the nations, and, as we have seen already above, to the judgment of Babylon.³¹ In light of this, it is very likely that Zech 2:17 has been influenced by both Hab 2:20 and Jer 25:30–31.

OVERVIEW

The evidence above suggests that Zech 2:10–17, rather than relying predominantly on Isaiah, is actually drawing upon several key passages in the earlier prophetic tradition: Jer 25; 50–51; Ezek 38–39; Isa 12–14, and Hab 2. Of these, only Isa 12–14 is consistently linked by scholarship to "Deutero-Isaiah."³² Conspicuous by its absence is any firm allusion to the core of Deutero-Isaiah (Isa 40–55).

---

17. Rather, the present punishment of Babylon is seen as the evidence of the fulfillment of prophecy.
²⁸ For Jer 50 see Reimer, *Oracles*, 270–71. Notice also the use of חלק + נחלה for the language of inheritance and lot in Jer 51:19.
²⁹ See also Tollington, *Tradition*, 39, although she makes clear: "It is possible that the words of Zechariah have been influenced by these earlier prophetic uses but there is no indication of direct dependency on either of them."
³⁰ Ibid.
³¹ Nurmela, "Growth," 63. The phrase מעון קדשו also appears in Deut 26:15; 2 Chr 30:27; and Ps 68:6 [Eng. 68:5].
³² Williamson, *The Book Called Isaiah*, 118–25, 156–83; cf. Knud Jeppesen, "The *maśśā'* Babel in Isaiah 13–14," *PIBA* 9 (1985): 63–80, who writes: "if there are Deutero-Isaianic interpolations in Isa. 1–39, this text is one of the most obvious examples" (cited, affirmed, and bolstered in Williamson, *The Book Called Isaiah*, 165).

Reading the "Earlier Prophets" with Zechariah 2:10–17

The first half of this paper has highlighted evidence of intertextual links between Zech 2:10–17 and the "earlier prophets." The second section now mines these "earlier prophets" to discern why the one(s) responsible for Zech 2:10–17 chose their lexical stock from these particular passages.

Jeremiah 50–51

This investigation has highlighted the influential role played by Jer 50–51 in the development of Zech 2:10–17. Bellis has demonstrated that Jer 50–51 consists of six poems which existed originally in two collections (ch. 50 and ch. 51) drawn together by a third editor, or six poems assembled by one editor.[33] This collection of poems looks to the destruction of Babylon for its abuse of Jerusalem and Judah. The enemy who will carry out this divine judgment is identified as the king(s) of the Medes (51:11, 28), as well as Ararat, Minni, and Ashkenaz (51:27), the latter three being kingdoms conquered by the Median king Cyaxares II. The poems express an expectation that Babylon will soon be overthrown. Notwithstanding the subscription of Jer 51:59–64, this evidence has suggested to many scholars that these prophetic pieces originated in the period between the fall of Jerusalem and the fall of Media to the Persians (587–550 BCE) and most likely in the unsettled period between the death of Nebuchadnezzar and the Persian conquest of Media by Cyrus (562–550).[34]

---

[33] Alice Ogden Bellis, "The Structure and Composition of Jeremiah 50:2–51:58" (PhD diss., Catholic University of America, 1986), 216.

[34] Ibid., 15–17; similarly Martin Kessler, *Battle of the Gods: The God of Israel Versus Marduk of Babylon. A Literary/Theological Interpretation of Jeremiah 50–51*, SSN 42 (Assen: Van Gorcum, 2003), 206; and Klaas A. D. Smelik, "The Function of Jeremiah 50 and 51 in the Book of Jeremiah," in *Reading the Book of Jeremiah: A Search for Coherence*, ed. Martin Kessler (Winona Lake, IN: Eisenbrauns, 2004), 87–98 (96). For an excellent review of modern scholarship, see Kessler, *Battle*, 13–35. Wilhelm Rudolph, *Jeremia*, 3rd ed., HAT 12 (Tübingen: Mohr Siebeck, 1968), 299, dates this corpus to 559–538 BCE; John Bright, *Jeremiah: Introduction, Translation, and Notes*, AB 21 (Garden City, NY: Doubleday, 1965), 60, dates it to the period prior to 539; Robert P. Carroll, *Jeremiah: A Commentary*, OTL (Philadelphia: Westminster, 1986), 853–54, said it could be prior to 539, but that the language allows for later dates; William L. Holladay, *Jeremiah 2: A Commentary on the Book of the Prophet Jeremiah, Chapters 26–52*, Hermeneia (Minneapolis: Fortress, 1989), 414, dates it to 594 BCE as per the subscript in 51:59–64; Douglas R. Jones, *Jeremiah*, NCB (London: Marshall Pickering, 1992), 521, 23, dates it to the earlier part of the decade before until after the fall of Babylon; Terence E. Fretheim, *Jeremiah*, SHBC (Macon, GA: Smith & Helwys, 2002), 621, entertains the idea that there could have been a shift in Jeremiah's stance toward Babylon after 597 BCE, but that references to the temple in 50:28 and 51:11 indicate that 587 had taken place and thus, "it

A *Leitmotif* that binds these poems together is the emphasis upon "vengeance" (50:15, 28; 51:6, 11, 36),[35] a *leitmotif* that is related to the destruction of the temple. Noteworthy is the taunt of Jer 51:25–26, which not only addresses Babylon as a "mountain" which will be destroyed (cf. Zech 4:6b–10a) but also warns that it will never be rebuilt, using vocabulary familiar from ancient Near Eastern restoration inscriptions.[36] This intersection of rebuilding language alongside that of vengeance for the destruction of the temple may help us to understand why Jer 50–51 was so important to the one(s) responsible for Zech 2:10–17.[37] The rebuilding of Jerusalem and especially its temple was needed because of the destructive actions of Babylon. The signal that the vengeance of the temple had been fully satisfied was not merely the rebuilding of the temple under Persian patronage, but also the exacting of promised punishment on the ones who had destroyed it.

JEREMIAH 25

In the LXX tradition (which some see as original), Jer 50–51 is much more closely associated with Jer 25 than can be seen in the MT tradition since LXX Jer 25:1–32:38 has the order: MT Jer 25:1–13; 49:34–39; 46:2–25, 27–28; 50:1–46; 51:1–64; 47:1–7; 49:1–5, 23, 27, 33–38; 48:1–45; 25:15–38. As can be seen quite readily if the LXX precedes the MT, the MT has taken what was originally a bracket (25:1–13, 15–38) around the entire oracular complex against the nations and has fused it together, separated it from the oracles, and reordered the oracles. If the MT precedes the LXX, then the LXX has reordered the oracular material and

---

is possible that such texts represent a later editing of earlier oracles." David S. Vanderhooft, *The Neo-Babylonian Empire and Babylon in the Latter Prophets*, HSM 59 (Atlanta: Scholars Press, 2000), 189–90, 202, dates this to the late exilic era, being written by an author who knew something of Babylon's specific architecture. There are "some intriguing indications, most notably Jer 51:32, which suggest that the writer had already witnessed the fall of Babylon to the Persians" (p. 202). Bellis, "Jeremiah 50:2–51:58," 15, however, would appear to disagree, arguing in words first addressed to Carroll that "a provisional *terminus ad quem* is clearly 539, when Cyrus peacefully took over Babylon and all predictions of a violent overthrow of Babylon such as are found in Jeremiah 50–51, become pointless."

[35] The reference in 50:28 is not found in the Septuagint and may be a later addition under the influence of 51:11; see ibid., 215.

[36] Mark J. Boda, "From Dystopia to Myopia: Utopian (Re)Visions in Haggai and Zechariah 1–8," in *Utopia and Dystopia in Prophetic Literature*, ed. Ehud Ben Zvi, Publications of the Finnish Exegetical Society 92 (Helsinki: Finnish Exegetical Society; Göttingen: Vandenhoeck & Ruprecht, 2006), 211–49; Mark J. Boda and Jamie R. Novotny, *From the Foundations to the Crenellations: Essays on Temple Building in the Ancient Near East and Hebrew Bible*, AOAT 366 (Münster: Ugarit-Verlag, 2010).

[37] See the links cited in Reimer, *Oracles*, 270–71, between Jer 50–51 and Zech 2:10–17.

drawn it into the middle of chapter 25. In either case, what is interesting is to see the importance placed on Babylon in the material in Jer 25 which either was designed originally as a unified piece or as a bracket around the nations section.[38]

The first half of the chapter (MT 25:1–13) is clearly looking beyond the exile of Judah to the future of Israel. It emphasizes that Yahweh will use Babylon's Nebuchadnezzar to gather together "all the armies of the north" in order to exact punishment on Israel. However, it states that in seventy years Yahweh will in turn punish the king of Babylon. The focus in MT 25:1–13 is clearly on Babylon first as Divine Punisher and then as Divinely Punished.

The focus in MT 25:15–38 (LXX 32:15–38) expands to all the nations on earth. As in verses 1–13, so in verses 15–38 the focus on the nations is placed at first in the context of God's punishment on Jerusalem (25:28). However, then the punishment is expanded with the question to "all the nations of the earth": "should I let you go unpunished?" (25:29). This international flavor is showcased from the outset of the section as the prophet takes the cup of God's wrath to Judah before proceeding to Egypt, Uz, Philistia, Edom, Moab, Ammon, Tyre, Sidon, Dedan, Tema, Buz, Arabia, Zimri, Elam, Media, and Babylon. The naming of Babylon, however, is clearly climactic in the list because MT 25:26a offers a summarizing statement about the prophet's journey to all the kings before finally stating in 25:26b that the king of Babylon drank from the cup. Thus, in both sections of MT Jer 25 Babylon is the key player, and in both, after the punishment of Judah and Jerusalem, Babylon will receive punishment. The Zecharian tradents's use of tradition from Jer 25:30–31 is then not surprising, as it lays the prophetic foundation for the belief that the present punishment of Babylon by Persia was a fulfillment of God's promises of old. It also reveals that the command for "all flesh" to pay attention to Yahweh who has roused himself from the "holy habitation" should

---

[38] J. Gerald Janzen, *Studies in the Text of Jeremiah*, HSM 6 (Cambridge: Harvard University Press, 1973); Emanuel Tov, "Some Aspects of the Textual and Literary History of the Book of Jeremiah," in *Le Livre de Jérémie: Le prophète et son milieu, les oracles et leur transmission*, ed. P.-M. Bogaert, BETL 54 (Louvain: University of Louvain Press, 1981), 145–67; James W. Watts, "Text and Redaction in Jeremiah's Oracles against the Nations.," *CBQ* 54 (1992): 432–47; Robert P. Carroll, "Halfway through a Dark Wood: Reflections on Jeremiah 25," in *Troubling Jeremiah*, ed. A. R. Pete Diamond, Kathleen M. O'Connor, and Louis Stulman, JSOTSup 260 (Sheffield: Sheffield Academic, 1999), 73–86; Anneli Aejmelaeus, "Jeremiah at the Turning-Point of History: The Function of Jer. xxv 1–14 in the Book of Jeremiah," *VT* 52 (2002): 459–82; Martin Kessler, "The Function of Chapters 25 and 50–51 in the Book of Jeremiah," in *Troubling Jeremiah*, ed. A. R. Pete Diamond, Kathleen M. O'Connor, and Louis Stulman, JSOTSup 260 (Sheffield: Sheffield Academic, 1999), 64–72; Menahem Haran, "The Place of the Prophecies against the Nations in the Book of Jeremiah," in *Emanuel: Studies in Hebrew Bible, Septuagint, and Dead Sea Scrolls in Honor of Emanuel Tov*, ed. Shalom M. Paul et al., VTSup 94 (Leiden: Brill, 2003), 699–706; cf. Bernard Gosse, "The Masoretic Redaction of Jeremiah: An Explanation," *JSOT* 77 (1998): 75–80.

strike fear in the nations as the punishment that began "against his own land" (Jer 25:30) will now "reach the ends of the earth" (25:31).

This passage in Jeremiah not only emphasizes Babylon in its vision for future punishment of the nations, but appears to be doing so in order to answer a searching question for those in exile, one which is cited in 25:28: "should I let you [all the nations of the earth] go unpunished?" This Jeremianic tradition reveals that although Judah and Jerusalem were worthy of their punishment (25:1–11, 18, 29a), the unrighteous instruments used to bring this punishment will also be punished (25:12–14, 19–26, 29b–38). Furthermore, the importance of MT Jer 25 is that it offers insights into the timing of the divine plan for restoration, with the time identified as "seventy years" and the key turning point of events as the punishment of Babylon.

Ezekiel 38–39

The analysis of Zech 2:12–13 revealed possible links to the Ezekielian tradition and in particular to Ezek 38–39. This passage speaks of a day when a future prince of Magog will rise up and invade a land called the "the mountains of Israel" which has recovered from war and is inhabited by people gathered from the nations (38:8).[39] The evil scheme of this prince includes invading and plundering (לשלל שלל) a "land of unwalled villages" (פרזות; 38:11–12). This prince Gog along with his hordes, however, will meet defeat on those mountains of Israel (38:17–39:20) and the Israelites will instead "plunder those who plundered them" (ושללו את־שלליהם; 39:10]). The defeat of this enemy Gog of Magog is intricately linked to the revelation of God's glory (כבד; 39:13, 21), also expressed as God showing himself holy (קדש; 38:16, 23, cf. 39:7–8). The passage is honest about the exile of Israel as punishment (39:21–24), but also about the restoration of Israel as an expression of the zeal of God (קנא, 39:25). God will gather them from the nations and pour out his spirit on them. The final section of 39:23–29 reminds the reader that these events will occur after the restoration of Israel from an exile brought on by their sin. Thus, the defeat of Gog is a sign of God's favor on restored Israel.

The precise identity of Gog of Magog has been a point of great debate. Gog is identified as one who will come from what is called "the far north" (ירכתי צפון; 38:6, 15; 39:2). The enemy from the "north" is a consistent *Leitmotif* in Hebrew literature, referring to powerful Mesopotamian powers. The collocation "recesses of the north" (ירכתי צפון), however, is found elsewhere only on two occasions and in both cases refers to the place of the divine assembly on the "heights of Zaphon," once in the famous Zion psalm, Ps 48 (v. 3), and again,

---

[39] This is clearly Israel, see 38:14; 39:2, 4.

interestingly, in the taunt against the king of Babylon in Isa 14:13. Is this then the geographic origin of Gog? Are he and his cohorts sent from the divine assembly? Probably not. Rather, what we have in this collocation is a combining of usually differentiated phrases which identify the location of a powerful Mesopotamian enemy. For instance, the geographic origins of the enemy in Jer 6:22 as well as of the returning remnant of Israel in Jer 31:8 are traced in parallel lines to the "land of the north" (ארץ צפון) and to "the recesses of the earth (ירכתי־ארץ). Furthermore, the force used to bring judgment on Babylon in Jer 50:41 is identified as a people from "the north" (צפון), an area identified in the next line as "the recesses of the earth" (ירכתי־ארץ). This evidence suggests that words usually employed in parallel lines to refer to Mesopotamian lands have been fused together in a nominal construction. This evidence, combined with the fact that the book of Ezekiel, which places the prophet at the time of the Babylonian empire, contains no prophetic oracle against Babylon, suggests that Gog of Magog is a figurative or coded reference to Babylon.[40] If this can be accepted, Ezek 38–39 looks to the destruction of the enemy which had once brought legitimate divine punishment on Judah.[41]

A closer look at the structure of this section of the book of Ezekiel reveals the important role that Ezek 38–39 plays in its literary context. After a series of oracles against the nations in Ezek 25–32, Ezek 33 finally describes the fall of the city of Jerusalem. The chapters that follow, however, look to a promised restoration from exile to the land (cf. 36:24) and this restoration will involve a new heart/spirit (36:26–27) and repopulation of the devastated land (36:37–38). Ezekiel 37 looks to the resurrection of a valley of dry bones, an image which symbolizes the return of Israel to the land (37:12–14). This return is linked to the restoration of the Davidic line (37:22–25). The passage ends with the promise of the eternal covenant in 37:26–28 to which is intricately attached the promise of a new temple: "I will put my sanctuary among them forever" (37:26); "my dwelling place will be with them" (37:27); and "when my sanctuary is among them forever" (37:28). This passage appears to be preparing the way for the vision of the new temple in chapters 40–48, but before that vision complex is presented chapters 38–39 with their focus on God's victory over the nations are inserted.

---

[40] It is possible that this is a coded reference to Babylon (Magog), similar to Sheshach in Jer 25:26; 51:41 and Leb-qamai in Jer 51:1, both of which use an encoding system called *Athbash*. Cf. J. Boehmer, "Wer ist Gog von Magog? Ein Beitrag zur Auslegung des Buches Ezechiel," *ZWT* 40 (1897): 321–55; and now Margaret S. Odell, *Ezekiel*, SHBC (Macon, GA: Smyth & Helwys, 2006), 472–77; but see the critique in Daniel I. Block, *The Book of Ezekiel: Chapters 25–48*, NICOT (Grand Rapids: Eerdmans, 1998), 434, n. 36.

[41] The comments in Odell, *Ezekiel*, 9, are important: "Thus unlike his contemporary Jeremiah, Ezekiel does not promote Babylon as a source of peace, at least not in the way that Jeremiah does ... If Jeremiah counseled accommodation to a new life in exile, Ezekiel saw life among the Babylonians as a life of endurable shame."

The one(s) responsible for Zech 2:10–17 appear(s) to be sensitive to the literary flow of the book of Ezekiel. The hoped renewal of the community after the exile will be typified by the restoration of the sanctuary,[42] but in order for this to happen there must first be a great victory of God over the nations. Zechariah 2:10–17 identifies the punishment of Babylon as evidence of the key victory that must precede the construction of the Second Temple.

Furthermore, it is interesting that the first phase of the vision of the restored Temple in chapters 40–48 (chs. 40–42, that which precedes the key appearance of God's glory in ch. 43) is dominated by the vision of a man with a measuring line who measures a wall. This is fascinating in light of the fact that the oracle under discussion follows Zech 2:1–5, which has a visionary journey that involves a man with a measuring line in his hand measuring the city wall of Jerusalem. The fact that the wall in Ezek 40–48 is only constructed around the temple area may indicate that there is an expansion in expectations connected with this wall in the Zechariah vision, so that it would ultimately include the whole city. This expansion, however, does not make illegitimate the link to the Ezekielian tradition. The reference to the attack of Gog against the Israelite land of "unwalled villages" (38:11) may also be reflected in the preceding vision of Zech 2:5–9 in which Jerusalem is to be an "unwalled village" because of God's protection. They are to have no fear of Babylon, for Babylon will be defeated by God in their time.

Ezekiel 38–39, with its depiction of the punishment of Babylon, is key to the restoration of the temple and city and the return of God's presence in Ezek 25–48. It is not surprising that it was attractive to those Zecharian tradents seeking to interpret the events of their own times.

HABAKKUK 2

The analysis of Zech 2:17 above identified striking similarities with Hab 2:20, a passage that calls for the silencing of the nations in connection with God's renewed presence in the temple. The book begins with the lament of the prophet over God's lack of judgment on injustice within the prophet's community (Hab 1:2–4). The divine assurance to the prophet is that he plans to raise up a foreign nation (Babylon) to exact punishment (1:5–11). This answer, however, only raises a further complication and so the prophet questions why God would use such an

---

[42] See now Odell, *Ezekiel*, 9, who interprets the book of Ezekiel in line with ancient Near Eastern building restoration forms. There is thus great importance attached to the temple and city reconstruction in the shape of the book. See further Margaret S. Odell, "'The Wall Is No More': Architectural and Ritual Reform in Ezekiel 43:8," in *From the Foundations to the Crenellations: Essays on Temple Building in the Ancient Near East and Hebrew Bible*, ed. Mark J. Boda and Jamie R. Novotny, AOAT 366 (Münster: Ugarit-Verlag, 2010), 339–56.

evil agent to bring justice only to have that agent inflict further injustice among the people (1:12–2:1). Yahweh replies that he will in turn exact punishment on this foreign agent (2:2–20). The grand finale of the book is a prayer of Habakkuk which begins by rehearsing God's past theophany which brought deliverance for Israel (3:2–15) and ends by declaring trusting patience as he awaits God's future theophany (3:16–19), echoing the declaration of 2:4b that "the righteous will live by his faith."[43]

The particular verse that is alluded to in Zech 2:17, namely, Hab 2:20, is the final verse in the lament-debate between God and his prophet and serves as a transition to the final prayer which celebrates God's saving appearance. It presages, thus, the appearance of God to bring judgment on the unjust foreign agent (Babylon).[44] Again the one(s) responsible for Zech 2:10–17 has/have drawn language from a larger literary construct that looks to the punishment of Babylon after Babylon has in turn meted out God's judgment on Israel.

The themes found in Habakkuk as a whole are also evident throughout the night visions, in particular, disillusionment over God's use of an unrighteous foreign servant to carry out his punishment (cf. Hab 1:12–2:1 with Zech 1:15) and hope for a great reversal in which those who were plundered will now plunder their overlord (cf. Hab 2:8 with Zech 2:12). The use of Hab 2:20, with its focus on God's presence "in his holy temple," is significant in that it precedes the theophany of Hab 3 in which God threshes the nations in anger, rescues his people and anointed one, and crushes the leader of the land of wickedness (Hab 3:12–

---

[43] This final prayer (or at least 3:2–15) is often seen as predating the rest of the book due to its archaic style and themes. However, it plays a significant role in the final form of the book and for some contains intertextual links to chs. 1–2; cf. Theodore Hiebert, *God of My Victory: The Ancient Hymn in Habakkuk 3*, HSM 38 (Atlanta: Scholars, 1986); see Richard D. Patterson, *Nahum, Habakkuk, Zephaniah*, Wycliffe Exegetical Commentary (Chicago: Moody Press, 1991); Rex A. Mason, *Zephaniah, Habakkuk, Joel*, OTG (Sheffield: Sheffield Academic, 1994); and Adele Berlin, *Zephaniah: A New Translation with Introduction and Commentary*, AB 25A (New York: Doubleday, 1994), 14, 259–68; J. J. M. Roberts, *Nahum, Habakkuk, and Zephaniah: A Commentary*, OTL (Louisville: Westminster John Knox, 1991).

[44] That the Neo-Babylonian empire is in view is argued well by ibid., 84, even if the oracles in 2:6–20 were originally directed at others; cf. Francis I. Andersen, *Habakkuk*, AB 25 (New York: Doubleday, 2001), 18–19: "There is much in the prophecy that does not fit into this neat scheme." Ibid., 24–27, provides a superb review of the debate over the date of this material (ranging from the Assyrian to Seleucid periods), and settles on a date between 605 and 575 BCE.

14).⁴⁵ For the one(s) responsible for Zech 2:10–17, the temple-city project is inseparably linked with God's judgment on Babylon.⁴⁶ Zechariah 2:10–17 is thus claiming that the "appointed time" had now arrived for the fulfillment of Habakkuk's revelation which was written down on tablets (Hab 2:2).

ISAIAH 12–14

The analysis of Zech 2:15–16 highlighted several connections to Isa 14:1–4, a text which functions, in the words of Vanderhooft, as "an editorial link between the foregoing chapter and the poem preserved in 14:4b–21; vv. 1–2 provide a coda for Isa 13 and vv. 3–4a introduce the subsequent poem."⁴⁷ Isaiah 13–14 functions as the introduction to the nations complex of Isa 13–23. Interestingly, another oracle against Babylon appears in Isa 21 in this complex, there referred to as "the Desert by the Sea," with the words at 21:9 reading: "Babylon has fallen, has fallen! All the images of its gods lie shattered on the ground!"

The section in Isa 13:1–22, immediately preceding 14:1–2, describes the overthrow of Babylon by "the Medes" (13:17), focusing on the city of Babylon "the jewel" within the Babylonian empire (13:19).⁴⁸ The expectation is for total

---

⁴⁵ As Roberts, *Nahum, Habakkuk, and Zephaniah*, 128, has noted: "The verse [Hab 2:20] serves as a transition to the vision in chapter 3, a vision that may be understood as arising in the context of continued communal worship in the temple."

⁴⁶ See Vanderhooft, *Babylon*, 163, who notes the close relationship between the themes of Hab 1–2 and Neo-Babylonian imperial ideas and practices, especially these: "the idea that the king rules by divine fiat; that the one-way flow of material wealth and captives into Babylonia results from the recognition of Babylon's greatness by subject peoples; and that the king honors his deities through building programs."

⁴⁷ Ibid., 128. For redactional theories on Isa 13–14, see variously, Ronald E. Clements, *Isaiah 1–39*, NCB (Grand Rapids: Eerdmans, 1980), 129–37, John D. W. Watts, *Isaiah 1–33*, WBC 24 (Waco, TX: Word, 1985), 184–86, 95–96; John Goldingay, *Isaiah*, NIBC (Peabody, MA: Hendrickson, 2001), 97–98, and especially Marvin A. Sweeney, *Isaiah 1–39, with an Introduction to Prophetic Literature*, FOTL 16 (Grand Rapids: Eerdmans, 1996), 214–34; Hans Wildberger, *Isaiah 13–27*, trans. Thomas H. Trapp, CC (Minneapolis: Fortress, 1997), 12–18, 33–36; and Vanderhooft, *Babylon*, 124.

⁴⁸ Views on the origins of chs. 13–14 range from the Assyrian period to the Babylonian period—some arguing that it was directed at Babylon of Merodach-Baladan (Erlandsson) or originally at Assyria and then redirected against Babylon; cf. Seth Erlandsson, *The Burden of Babylon: A Study of Isaiah 13:2–14:23*, ConBOT 4 (Lund: Gleerup, 1970)—to the Persian period. Brevard S. Childs, *Isaiah*, OTL (Louisville: Westminster John Knox, 2001), 123, cf. 16, writes: "The theology expressed in 14:1–2—the election of Israel, the return to the land, the reversal of the oppressor—are all elements that are similar to those of Second Isaiah." Sweeney, *Isaiah 1–39*, 231–33, holds that 14:1–2 reflects the late sixth century when the return begins so that 13:1–14:23 was "edited into their present form in

destruction (like Sodom and Gomorrah) and annihilation of the population (13:19–22). Isaiah 13 thus functions as the foundation for the restoration described in 14:1–2. Isaiah 14:1–2 looks to Yahweh's compassionate choosing of Israel demonstrated through resettling them in their own land. Foreigners will join Israel and then nations will return the people to their own land. Isaiah 14:2 looks to a great reversal in which captors become captives. The Isaianic oracle against Babylon ends with a taunt to be taken up by the returned remnant of Israel (14:3–23). The one(s) responsible for Zech 2:10–17 has/have incorporated a limited amount of lexical stock from Isa 14:1–2, focusing on the restoration of God's people Judah after exile, but have chosen these words because they are part of a larger complex related to the punishment and destruction of Babylon.

This connection to Isa 13–14 helps us understand why Zech 2:14 draws from Isa 12:6 for the exhortation to Daughter Zion to rejoice at the return of God's presence. Isaiah 12:6 is the verse that immediately precedes the prophecy concerning Babylon in Isa 13–14, concluding a section focused on praise in 12:1–6.[49] This praise in turn ("in that day," 12:1a) follows a section of Isaiah that looks to the restoration of the remnant from exile (10:20–11:16). It is interesting that in this section two figures are key to the return of the remnant: Yahweh of hosts, the Holy One of Israel, as well as the "shoot" (11:1) or "root" (11:10) of Jesse. It is interesting that in Zech 2:10–3:10, the first figure to "come" (הנה בא) is Yahweh (2:14) who then promises to cause another figure to come (הנה בא), a figure who is identified as "Zemah," a Davidic royal (3:8). Both are essential to the return of the people to the land as well as the prosperity for which they long.

---

the mid- to late 6th century, in that they anticipate the fall of Babylon to the Medes and the end of the Babylonian ruling house" (234); see also Gosse, *Isaïe 13,1–14,23*, 201, who places this in the Persian period, and Christopher T. Begg, "Babylon in the Book of Isaiah," in *The Book of Isaiah—Le Livre d'Isaïe: Les oracles et leurs relectures. Unité et complexité de l'ouvrage*, ed. J. Vermeylen, BETL 81 (Leuven: Peeters, 1989), 121–25, and Wildberger, *Isaiah 13–27*, 34, who place it just before or after the fall of Babylon to Persia. However, see the superb critique of such late date theories (especially that of Gosse) in Williamson, *The Book Called Isaiah*, 156–83; cf. Vanderhooft, *Babylon*, 124. The reference to the Medes in ch. 13 especially discourages such a late date. It must predate the fall of Media to Cyrus.

[49] J. Vermeylen, *Du prophète Isaïe à l'apocalyptique: Isaïe, I–XXXV, miroir d'un demi-millénaire d'expérience religieuse en Israël*, EBib 1 (Paris: Gabalda, 1977), 280–82, highlights the redactional role of Isa 12 in relation to chs. 13–23, while Childs, *Isaiah*, 114, notes the literary role, observing how Isa 11–12 "provide a transition to chapters 13–23," especially with the allusions to various nations: Assyria, Egypt, Ethiopia, Philistia, Edom, Moab, and Ammon. Williamson, *The Book Called Isaiah*, 118–25, identifies Second Isaiah as the one responsible for Isa 12.

OVERVIEW

Reading the "earlier prophets" in light of Zech 2:10–17 has highlighted the significance of the broader context of the lexical stock incorporated by the Zecharian tradent(s). The evidence suggests that the one(s) responsible for Zech 2:10–17 was/were doing more than just incorporating random earlier prophetic lexical stock. In each case we have seen how the broader context of the passages from which this lexical stock has been drawn contains links to the overall message of Zech 2:10–17 within Zech 1:7–6:15. All of these passages (Jer 25; 50–51; Ezek 38–39; Isa 12–14; and Hab 2) are part of an enduring anti-Babylonian tradition in the Hebrew Bible. Jeremiah 25 and Ezek 38–39 are also concerned with the expected restoration of Israel to the land after the exile, and Jer 50–51; Ezek 38–39, and Hab 2 also highlight issues related to the temple and the return of God's presence. All the passages allude to the necessary punishment of the enemies of Israel and, in particular, Babylon, in order for this to be accomplished. Thus, Zech 2:10–17 is applying earlier prophetic tradition to present events, showing that the punishment of Babylon in the events surrounding Darius's rise to the throne is expected by the earlier prophets and demands a response by the people of God in exile.

IMPLICATIONS

In a recent article I have contended that the majority of pericopae within Zech 1:7–6:15 make some reference to the judgment of Babylon.[50] In that work I traced the history of the Babylonian revolts that arose in the wake of the overthrow of Pseudo-Smerdis (Gaumata) by Darius and the firm and brutal Persian responses. I also referred in general to the development of the prophetic tradition *contra* Babylon, highlighting that a key signal of restoration would have been the judgment of Babylon for their abuse of Israel during exile. The evidence of the present article reveals that this Zecharian reflection on Babylon's fate is drawn explicitly from a substantial body of earlier prophetic literature. In this we see the emphasis on the "words of the earlier prophets" (1:4–6; 7:7, 12) in the Prose Sermon inclusio of Zech 1:1–6 and 7:1–8:23, now reflected in the oracular material within the Night Visions.

Furthermore, the kinds of inner biblical allusion techniques and sources reflected in the oracle in Zech 2:10–17 are also strikingly similar to those long recognized in Zech 9–14. Here one finds, as in Zech 9–14, a pastiche of lexical stock drawn in from the "earlier prophets." Furthermore, there is sensitivity in both to

---

[50] Mark J. Boda, "Terrifying the Horns: Persia and Babylon in Zechariah 1:7–6:15," *CBQ* 67 (2005): 22–41 = chapter 2 in this present volume.

the broader context of the source text.⁵¹ This is further evidence that the one(s) responsible for the second phase of the Zecharian tradition (Zech 9–14) was/were not as innovative and distinct from the one(s) responsible for Zech 1–8 as was once thought.⁵²

Finally, Zech 2:10–17 shows evidence not only of mining the books of Isaiah, Jeremiah, Ezekiel, and Habakkuk, but also of drawing on passages that are considered among the latest redactional forms of these books. This suggests that those responsible for the book of Zechariah may have been instrumental in the assembling of the prophetic canon, or at the least may represent the first generation that was relying on a combined prophetic corpus.

---

⁵¹ As I have argued elsewhere for the redactional shepherd units of Zech 9–14: Mark J. Boda, "Reading between the Lines: Zechariah 11:4–16 in Its Literary Contexts," in *Bringing out the Treasure: Inner Biblical Allusion and Zechariah 9–14*, ed. Mark J. Boda and Michael H. Floyd, JSOTSup 370 (Sheffield: Sheffield Academic, 2003), 277–91 = chapter 9 in this present volume; Mark J. Boda and Stanley E. Porter, "Literature to the Third Degree: Prophecy in Zechariah 9–14 and the Passion of Christ," in *Traduire la Bible hébraïque: De la Septante à la Nouvelle Bible Segond = Translating the Hebrew Bible: From the Septuagint to the Nouvelle Bible Segond*, ed. Robert David and Manuel Jinbachian, Sciences Bibliques 15 (Montreal: Médiaspaul, 2005), 215–54 = chapter 10 in this present volume.

⁵² See Mark J. Boda, "From Fasts to Feasts: The Literary Function of Zechariah 7–8," *CBQ* 65 (2003): 390–407 = *Exploring Zechariah*, volume 1, chapter 2.

4
Oil, Crowns, and Thrones: Prophet, Priest, and King in Zechariah 1:7–6:15[1]

This chapter narrows our attention from the imperial stage to the internal social context of Yehud and Zechariah's articulation of the enduring relevance and present shape of the functionaries of prophet, priest, and king in Zech 3, 4, and 6. By drawing on Jeremianic tradition, Zechariah reveals that the reemergence of priestly functionaries at the temple is a sign of the soon reemergence of the royal line.

Throughout the monarchial history of Israel and Judah, three functionaries come to the fore consistently in the sociological structure of the society: king, priest, and prophet.[2] The scope of and relationship between these three types, however, is not constant, but fluctuates between personalities and generations throughout

---

[1] Based on my original publication, Mark J. Boda, "Oil, Crowns and Thrones: Prophet, Priest and King in Zechariah 1:7–6:15," *JHS* 3 (2001): Article 10. Slightly revised for inclusion in this volume. Versions of this paper were presented at Pacific Northwest Society of Biblical Literature Regional Meeting (Edmonton, AB), European Association of Biblical Studies (Rome, Italy), and Currents in Biblical and Theological Dialogue (St. John's College, University of Manitoba). Thanks to various participants in those conferences and especially to my colleague A. Reimer.

[2] Cf. Roland de Vaux, *Ancient Israel: Its Life and Institutions*, trans. John McHugh (New York: McGraw-Hill, 1961); Lester L. Grabbe, *Priests, Prophets, Diviners, Sages: A Socio-Historical Study of Religious Specialists in Ancient Israel* (Valley Forge, PA: Trinity Press International, 1995).

the history of Israel.[3] In some circumstances prophets and priests are closely tied to the royal court (2 Sam 6–7) and prophets join priests in the temple courts (Lam 2:20).[4] At other times the relationships are strained as prophets function removed from the palace and temple criticizing the royal and priestly offices (Hos 5:1) and priests act in defiance of royal authority (2 Kgs 11).

In the closing moments of the state of Judah, biblical texts reveal the endurance of these three types in the Judean community. Lists throughout Jeremiah regularly place kings, priests, and prophets together.[5] The narrative in Jer 37 reports that the king Zedekiah sent the priest Zephaniah to enquire of the prophet Jeremiah (37:3). This narrative reveals the strained character of the relationship between these three functionaries in the closing moments of the state of Judah.[6]

There is little evidence of the status of the various types during the post-587 exilic crisis. The attempt by the Babylonians to foster some form of Judean leadership under Gedaliah centered at Mizpah met with disaster (Jer 40–41). The Mesopotamian context was no more favorable for the expression of political royal leadership (without a kingdom) and temple priestly leadership (without a temple), although it appears that the prophetic function could be exercised in a limited way, as evidenced in the book of Ezekiel.[7]

The Persian Cyrus, however, introduced new conditions for identity for the various peoples. The opportunity to return to the land and restore the religious infrastructure was for many Jews an occasion for renewing communal identity and intertwined with such renewal was the restoration of a leadership core. The book of Haggai bears witness to this renewal by emphasizing the triumvirate of

---

[3] Grabbe emphasizes ideal types but notes that "such types seldom existed as such in society" as he proceeds to note relationships between and within type groups; ibid., 193.

[4] For cult prophecy, see G. W. Ahlström, *Joel and the Temple Cult of Jerusalem*, VTSup 21 (Leiden: Brill, 1971); W. H. Bellinger Jr., *Psalmody and Prophecy*, JSOTSup 27 (Sheffield: JSOT Press, 1984); Aubrey R. Johnson, *The Cultic Prophet in Ancient Israel*, 2nd ed. (Cardiff: University of Wales Press, 1962); Aubrey R. Johnson, *The Cultic Prophet and Israel's Psalmody* (Cardiff: University of Wales Press, 1979); Raymond Jacques Tournay, *Seeing and Hearing God with the Psalms: The Prophetic Liturgy of the Second Temple in Jerusalem*, trans. J. Edward Crowley, JSOTSup 118 (Sheffield: JSOT Press, 1991); Robert R. Wilson, *Prophecy and Society in Ancient Israel* (Philadelphia: Fortress, 1980).

[5] See Mark J. Boda, *Praying the Tradition: The Origin and Use of Tradition in Nehemiah 9*, BZAW 277 (Berlin: de Gruyter, 1999), 205–8; cf. Neh 9:32.

[6] Such tension is not only evident between the various offices, but also within the various offices; see Grabbe, *Priests, Prophets*.

[7] Although Niehr stresses continuity in leadership throughout the sixth century the evidence is not compelling; Herbert Niehr, "Religio-Historical Aspects of the 'Early Post-Exilic' Period," in *The Crisis of Israelite Religion: Transformation of Religious Tradition in Exilic and Post-Exilic Times*, ed. Bob Becking and Marjo C. A. Korpel, OtSt 42 (Leiden: Brill, 1999), 228–44.

prophet, governor, and priest: Haggai, Zerubbabel, and Joshua (Hag 1:1, 12–14; 2:1–2, 4, 21, 23),[8] which appears to be an echo of the preexilic prophet, king, and priest.[9]

Such renewal of leadership in the era of Darius, however, would not have been without its challenges. The return of successive waves of Jews to the land to join many who had remained or already returned would have been an occasion for defining the various leadership roles. Even if the roles corresponded to preexilic archetypes, the particular definition of these roles certainly would have been under negotiation on a sociological level.

Zechariah 1:7–6:15 is testimony to sociological upheaval and reconfiguration in early Persian period Yehud. While Haggai focuses particular attention on various leaders in the Jewish community, such focus is not immediately apparent in the night visions and oracles of Zechariah.[10] In contrast, the majority of visions treat the broader concerns of the community without reference to leadership figures (1:7–17; 2:1–4; 2:5–17; 5:1–4; 5:5–11; 6:1–8).

On three occasions, however, such reference can be discerned. Zechariah 3:1–10; 4:1–14 and 6:9–15 mention individuals connected to the leadership class as the prophet offers direction for the definition of the various functionaries in the Persian period. Not surprisingly, these three texts have attracted the attention of many seeking to delineate the sociological structure of the early Persian period community and to explain the development of that structure in the following centuries. Hanson's review of Israelite religion in the early Persian period represents a consistent trend in the interpretation of these texts. After commenting on Zech 3 and 4 and before considering 6:9–15, Hanson states:

---

[8] Rooke notes that the coupling of Zerubbabel and Joshua in Haggai "need not imply that their actual authority in practical terms was equivalent," Deborah W. Rooke, *Zadok's Heirs: The Role and Development of the High Priesthood in Ancient Israel*, Oxford Theological Monographs (Oxford: Oxford University Press, 2000), 129–30.

[9] Zerubbabel's connection to the Davidic line and hope is clear in Hag 2:20–23 because of the combination of terms found there; cf. Mark J. Boda, *Haggai/Zechariah*, NIVAC (Grand Rapids: Zondervan, 2004); Janet E. Tollington, *Tradition and Innovation in Haggai and Zechariah 1–8*, JSOTSup 150 (Sheffield: JSOT Press, 1993), 135–44; contra Wolter H. Rose, *Zemah and Zerubbabel: Messianic Expectations in the Early Postexilic Period*, JSOTSup 304 (Sheffield: Sheffield Academic, 2000), 208–43.

[10] For other differences between Haggai and Zechariah see Mark J. Boda, "Zechariah: Master Mason or Penitential Prophet?," in *Yahwism after the Exile: Perspectives on Israelite Religion in the Persian Era*, ed. Bob Becking and Rainer Albertz, Studies in Theology and Religion 5 (Assen: Van Gorcum, 2003), 49–69 = chapter 6 in this present volume.

Zechariah thus bears witness to a stream of tradition in the early postexilic period that synthesized royal and priestly elements in a well-defined program of restoration and, for reasons no longer transparent to us, expanded the authority of the Zadokite priests so as to encompass areas earlier controlled by prophets and kings. The history of the growth and transmission of the book of Zechariah thus gives us a glimpse of the development of the Jewish community from a diarchy under a Davidic prince and a Zadokite priest to a hierocracy under a Zadokite functioning as high priest.[11]

Although differing on many details, this viewpoint is a consistent feature in other works on Zech 1:7–6:15. Carol and Eric Meyers note: "The sixth century saw developments that anticipated the fifth-century events. Prophets and Davidides were still visible and vocal, but they were already moving toward the sidelines—especially the latter, since there was no longer a kingdom."[12] So also Antti Laato concludes that the "High Priest during the Persian period was regarded as representative of the Davidic dynasty,"[13] while Rex Mason suggests that "there are priestly, royal and prophetic overtones about Joshua and presumably, the postexilic line of which he is (re)founder, forerunner and representative."[14]

These various scholars are representative of a major strain of research on Zech 1:7–6:15 which uses Zech 3, 4, and 6 to argue for an expansion of priestly control into arenas of royal and prophetic influence.[15] But is this justifiable in light

---

[11] Paul D. Hanson, "Israelite Religion in the Early Postexilic Period," in *Ancient Israelite Religion: Essays in Honor of Frank Moore Cross*, ed. Patrick D. Miller, Paul D. Hanson, and S. Dean McBride (Philadelphia: Fortress, 1987), 485–508 (498).

[12] Carol L. Meyers and Eric M. Meyers, *Haggai, Zechariah 1–8: A New Translation with Introduction and Commentary*, AB 25B (Garden City, NY: Doubleday, 1987), 201.

[13] Antti Laato, *A Star Is Rising: The Historical Development of the Old Testament Royal Ideology and the Rise of the Jewish Messianic Expectations*, USFISFCJ 5 (Atlanta: Scholars Press, 1997), 203.

[14] Rex A. Mason, "The Messiah in the Postexilic Old Testament Literature," in *King and Messiah in Israel and the Ancient Near East: Proceedings of the Oxford Old Testament Seminar*, ed. John Day, JSOTSup 270 (Sheffield: Sheffield University Press, 1998), 338–64 (345, cf. 349).

[15] Cf. Miloš Bič, *Die Nachtgesichte des Sacharja: Eine Auslegung von Sacharja 1–6*, BibS(N) 42 (Neukirchen-Vluyn: Neukirchener, 1964), 70; David L. Petersen, "Zechariah's Visions: A Theological Perspective," *VT* 34 (1984): 195–206 (204–5); Niehr, "Aspects," 233; R. J. Coggins, *Haggai, Zechariah, Malachi*, OTG (Sheffield: JSOT, 1987), 45–46. For a very different approach to the two figures in view in Zechariah see Barker who identifies here two priests, not a priest and king; Margaret Barker, "The Two Figures in Zechariah," *HeyJ* 18 (1977): 33–46. Floyd retains distinctions between the various offices but consistently gives the upper hand to the priestly caste by arguing that Zechariah is using the Davidide (Zerubbabel/Zemah) to bolster priestly status; Michael H. Floyd, *Minor Prophets, Part 2*, FOTL 22 (Grand Rapids: Eerdmans, 2000), 375, 406–7. Similarly Tollington sees enhancing of Joshua with little support for restoration of monarchy under Zerubbabel; Tollington, *Tradition*, 178–79. Rooke has recently challenged the consensus

of these texts? The focus of this paper is to examine afresh these three primary texts from the early Persian period in order to understand the perspective of the Zecharian tradent community on the socio-political structure of the nascent Persian province of Yehud.

PROPHET, PRIEST, AND KING IN ZECHARIAH 3

ORIENTATION

Many throughout the history of interpretation of Zech 1:7–6:15 have noted the unique character of the vision found in Zech 3.[16] Although it contains some of the characteristics of the other visions, the introductory verse contrasts with those found in the other visions. In addition, the scene involves a historical figure contemporary with Zechariah (Joshua), rather than enigmatic objects or characters and the interpreting angel, המלאך הדבר בי = "the angel who talked with me,"[17] a faithful and helpful guide in other scenes, is absent. Furthermore, the prophet enters the visionary action, demanding that Joshua be clothed with a turban.

Zechariah 3 represents an amalgamation of several socio-ritual types evident elsewhere in Hebrew literature, plucked from the royal, priestly, and prophetic worlds. First, the scene itself reflects the proceedings of a legal court scene in the heavenly royal council. Secondly, the consistent use of vocabulary from priestly rituals strongly suggests that the scene reflects the investiture and atonement rituals of the high priest. Thirdly, our consideration below will show that the entire scene functions as a prophetic sign act. Thus in terms of socio-ritual types alone,

---

of a priestly takeover of monarchical powers both through a fresh look at Zechariah (p. 151, and other ancient corpora) as well as a revaluation of the fourth century coinage data (pp. 219–37). The only evidence she can find for encroachment on an office is the royal infringement on priestly duties in the preexilic and Maccabean periods; Rooke, *Zadok's Heirs*; cf. Deborah W. Rooke, "Kingship as Priesthood: The Relationship between the High Priesthood and the Monarchy," in *King and Messiah in Israel and the Ancient Near East: Proceedings of the Oxford Old Testament Seminar*, ed. John Day, JSOTSup 270 (Sheffield: Sheffield Academic, 1998), 187–208. Also Cook calls the claim of priestly ascendancy to "governmental hegemony" "overstated"; cf. Stephen L. Cook, "The Metamorphosis of a Shepherd: The Tradition History of Zechariah 11:17 + 13:7–9," *CBQ* 55 (1993): 453–66. Rose's recent consideration of the passages dealt with in this paper lends positive support to my conclusions. On most issues we agree and so I will not provide detailed noting of his work. There are some differences in opinion on details and on the relationship between Zemah and Zerubbabel as will become evident in this paper; Rose, *Zemah*.
[16] See list in Christian Jeremias, *Die Nachtgesichte des Sacharja: Untersuchungen zu ihrer Stellung im Zusammenhang der Visionsberichte im Alten Testament und zu ihrem Bildmaterial*, FRLANT 117 (Göttingen: Vandehoeck & Ruprecht, 1977), 201–3.
[17] English translations follow the NRSV, unless explicitly stated otherwise.

Zech 3 reflects a convergence of three key functionaries evident throughout the history of Israel: prophetic, priestly, and royal.

PAST INTERPRETATION

This observation of a convergence of types on the socio-ritual level raises the question of the relationship between these various functionaries in restoration Yehud. Several elements in Zech 3 have been used by those who argue for an expansion of the priestly role into prophetic and royal areas. First, the focus in the chapter is on the instatement of the Zadokite high priest affording great exposure to this office. Secondly, the prophet instructs the divine council to place a צניף ("turban," 3:5) on Joshua's head, a term which some have suggested has royal overtones.[18] Thirdly, the angel speaks of the figure Zemah in a speech directed to the priests, intimating that for Zechariah this figure is priestly (3:8).[19] Fourthly, the angel of Yahweh promises Joshua מהלכים בין העמדים האלה a phrase often translated as "a way/right of access among those standing here," that is, access to the heavenly council (3:7). For some this is seen as evidence of Joshua receiving "prophet-like authority."[20]

---

[18] So also Petersen: "The use of *ṣanîp* gives royal overtones to this scene. Clearly, the prerogatives of Joshua were noteworthy, especially now that there was no invested king on the throne," David L. Petersen, *Haggai and Zechariah 1–8: A Commentary*, OTL (Philadelphia: Westminster, 1984), 198; Meyers: "an official headpiece with monarchic associations ... a conscious departure from priestly terminology ... Joshua as 'high priest' both continues the traditional role of 'chief priest' ... and also incorporates into the scope of his office some responsibilities previously assumed by the Judean kings," Meyers and Meyers, *Haggai, Zechariah 1–8*, 192; Mason (on Zech 3): "Now no dyarchy is envisaged. All the attention is on the priesthood which, by divine appointment, has taken over all the old pre-exilic royal privileges and prerogatives. A 'messianic hope' is indeed expressed, but attached in no way to Zerubbabel," Rex A. Mason, *Preaching the Tradition: Homily and Hermeneutics after the Exile* (Cambridge: Cambridge University Press, 1990), 208; cf. Laato, *A Star is Rising*, 203; James C. VanderKam, "Joshua the High Priest and the Interpretation of Zechariah 3," *CBQ* 53 (1991): 553–70.

[19] So Bič, *Nachtgesichte*; Coggins, *Haggai*, 46; cf. Rooke, *Zadok's Heirs*, 142 n. 50.

[20] So Petersen, who adds that the priest "might even be entrusted with a definitive word for a particular situation, as were the prophets," Petersen, *Haggai and Zechariah 1–8*, 208. Cf. Meyers and Meyers, who claim: "it appears as if Joshua himself were to have the same privileges as prophets," Meyers and Meyers, *Haggai, Zechariah 1–8*, 196–97; also see Conrad, who translates this as "goings [or walkings]" and concludes: "That the high priest will have access to those who, like the messenger of the Lord, the standing ones, suggests that Joshua will also gain the status of messenger by walking among the messengers"; Edgar W. Conrad, *Zechariah*, Readings: A New Biblical Commentary (Sheffield: Sheffield Academic, 1999), 94–95; Edgar W. Conrad, "Messengers in Isaiah and the Twelve: Implications for Reading Prophetic Books," *JSOT* 91 (2000): 83–97 (96). Tollington follows the "access" approach, but does not see prophetic authority but rather an invitation

Oil, Crowns, and Thrones

But does this evidence in Zech 3 sustain the weight of the argument? Is Zechariah a priestly promoter, advocating hierocratic intrusion into prophetic and royal arenas?

EVALUATION

1. Prophet and Priest: מהלכים—*"A Right of Access"? (3:7)*

Zechariah 3:6 marks an important transition in this vision as the angel launches into a speech directed to Joshua. The initial section presents a series of four conditions, the first two of which are more general in nature and the second two specific to priestly duties.[21] There is nothing surprising in this charge. Such a commission is expected in an investiture context. What is surprising is the promised consequence that appears at the end of 3:7. If such conditions are met the angel promises the high priest מהלכים בין העמדים האלה ("a right of access among those standing here").

The identity of העמדים האלה ("those standing here") is certain since the participle עמד ("standing") has been used six times in the vision in reference to members of the heavenly council (3:1, 3, 4, 5). Jeremiah asserts that "to stand" (עמד) in the divine council is "to see and to hear his word" (23:18), that is, to participate in the deliberations of the heavenly court.

---

to intercede for the people; cf. Tollington, *Tradition*, 160–61. Mason links the granting of "access" to a royal function; Mason, *Preaching*, 207; but see contra Tollington, *Tradition*, 160 n. 3, 161 n. 2. Jeremias notes links to prophetic call genre here which would grant him access to the divine council; Jeremias, *Die Nachgesichte des Sacharja*, 203–5.

[21] There has been considerable debate over how many of the clauses in v. 7 are part of the protasis of this condition. There is no question that the first two clauses are part of the protasis (condition) because they both begin with the Hebrew particle אם ("if") and quite clearly the final clause ("I will give you a place among these standing here") is part of the apodosis (consequence). The controversy circles around the middle two clauses ("you will govern my house ... have charge of my courts"), both of which begin with the particle וגם (often translated "and also"). While a conditional relationship can be created by juxtaposing אם + protasis (condition) with וגם + apodosis (consequence) as in Gen 13:16; Jer 31:36, 37, there are no cases where the apodosis is introduced by וגם. Rather when וגם appears after the conditional particle אם ("if") it denotes an additional member of the protasis (1 Sam 12:14) or the apodosis (Exod 8:17; 18:23; Mal 2:2). This evidence means that the third and fourth clauses in 3:7 belong to the protasis (condition), a position bolstered by the fact that in the final clause the subject changes from Joshua ("you") to the Lord ("I"). Some have seen in these conditions an expansion of priestly powers into royal areas; cf. Rose, *Zemah*, 79–83; but based on Deut 17:8–11, Tollington argues that such responsibilities were priestly in former times; Tollington, *Tradition*, 158–60.

Challenging, however, is the meaning of the first word in the Hebrew text, מהלכים ("right of access"). Most have traced this plural word to the singular form מהלך ("passage/walk/journey") that is used in three other texts to refer to a passageway or journey (Ezek 42:4; Jonah 3:3–4; Neh 2:6), by positing the gloss: "access." However, not only is this gloss unattested, but the vowels in the Hebrew text are not the ones expected for the plural of this word, and even if they were, it is difficult to explain why this would be rendered in the plural. Taking the lead from the ancient versions which attest participial forms, it appears that this Hebrew form is the plural participle of the *piel* of הלך and with the verbal clause נתן + ל ("give you," Zech 3:7) refers to the angel providing "those who move between those who stand."[22]

Rather than giving Joshua "access," the angel is providing for Joshua individuals who already enjoy such access. Considering the only individuals who have access to the heavenly council in the Hebrew Bible are the prophets, this would suggest that God will restore temple prophecy, a conclusion which would explain the presence of "prophets" with "the priests of the house of the LORD of hosts" in Zech 7:3.[23] Therefore, Zechariah is not granting the Zadokites prophetic authority or function, but rather securing an enduring role for the prophet in the future operation of the temple cult.

2. Priest and King

a. צניף—*Royal turban? (3:5).* In 3:5, Zechariah surprises the reader by participating in the scene, commanding the attendants to set a clean turban on

---

[22] See the excellent discussion of this in Rose, *Zemah*, 73–83. Rose notes that for the *piel* participle one would expect מְהַלְּכִים (p. 77). The Septuagint translates this word as a masculine plural participle of the verb ἀναστρέφω and results in the translation: "those who dwell among these standing here" (ἀναστρεφομένους ἐν μέσῳ τῶν ἑστηκότων τούτων; similarly Syriac and Vulgate). In Ezek 3:15; 22:30, two other cases where this same word and form are used in the Septuagint, one finds references to a person who stands with or for another. On the other hand, in those passages where the MT has מהלך, LXX has περίπατος (Ezek 42:4, passageway), πορεία (Jonah 3:3, 4; Neh 2:6, journey). VanderKam suggests it may be an Aramaic loanword "in which the causative participial form has an intransitive meaning"; VanderKam, "Joshua"; cf. also Wim A. M. Beuken, *Haggai–Sacharja 1–8: Studien zur Überlieferungsgeschichte der frühnachexilischen Prophetie*, SSN 10 (Assen: Van Gorcum, 1967), 293–96, who translates "Männer, die gehen." See also the Aramaic participial forms in Dan 3:25; 4:34 and the Hebrew participle in Eccl 4:15. Cf. Floyd, *Minor Prophets*, 375.

[23] Thus, as VanderKam has suggested, it removes Joshua one step from the divine council for he is "given individuals who have direct access to the divine presence" and intimates: "In fact, the promise may refer to the ongoing presence of people such as Zechariah," VanderKam, "Joshua," 560. Rose identifies these as angelic beings; cf. Rose, *Zemah*.

Joshua's head.²⁴ The term used (צָנִיף, "turban") is not the normal term in the Torah for the headgear of the high priest (מִצְנֶפֶת, "turban"; cf. Exod 29:6; Lev 8:9; Num 20:26–28) but is one used only three other times in the Hebrew Bible, none of them in reference to a priest (Job 29:14; Isa 3:23; 62:3).²⁵ However, although the word צָנִיף does appear with the terms מְלוּכָה ("royal") and עֲטָרָה ("crown") in Isa 62:3, words often used in connection with royalty, the occurrences in Job 29:14 and Isa 3:23 lack such royal vocabulary.²⁶ On the other hand, מִצְנֶפֶת ("turban" of the high priest in the Torah), is not limited to the High Priest, for in Ezek 21:31 it is used with a prince. One cannot confine either of these words to royal or priestly contexts. צָנִיף ("turban," Zech 3:7) has no more royal overtones than the term מִצְנֶפֶת ("turban," Exod 29:6).

b. *אַנְשֵׁי מוֹפֵת*—*Men of signs (3:8)*. With the clothing ceremony completed in 3:5, the angel delivers two speeches. The reference to אַנְשֵׁי מוֹפֵת ("an omen of things to come") in the second of these speeches links this entire scene to the prophetic sign act form (Ezek 12:6, 11; 24:24, 27; cf. Isa 20:3), with the investiture ceremony serving as the prophetic action and the angelic speeches as the interpretive components.²⁷

---

²⁴ Some see this interjection as an addition; cf. Thomas Pola, "Form and Meaning in Zechariah 3," in *Yahwism after the Exile: Perspectives on Israelite Religion in the Persian Era*, ed. Bob Becking and Rainer Albertz, Studies in Theology and Religion 5 (Assen: Van Gorcum, 2003), 156–67. Some have opted to emend this text with the ancient translations (LXX, Syriac, Vulgate, Targums), e.g., Petersen, *Haggai and Zechariah 1–8*, 197, to "he said," but Tidwell has demonstrated the appropriateness of a first person interjection of this sort in similar divine council texts; N. L. A. Tidwell, "*Wā'ōmar* (Zech 3:5) and the Genre of Zechariah's Fourth Vision," *JBL* 94 (1975): 343–55.

²⁵ VanderKam, "Joshua," 557, refutes those who see in Zechariah's choice of the word צָנִיף a more royalist nuance, but rather argues that both this term and the technical high priestly term (מִצְנֶפֶת) have royal connotations (cf. Ezek 21:31 [Eng. 21:26]).

²⁶ See also Tollington, *Tradition*, 157.

²⁷ The term מוֹפֵת is used often in the Hebrew Bible to refer to God's visible signs before humanity, and regularly in a word pair with אוֹת. It is employed for the great acts Yahweh performed through Moses before Pharaoh (Exod 7:3, "signs and wonders"), but also for signs promised by a prophet (Deut 13:1, "omens or portents"). The word does not necessarily refer to miraculous demonstrations of divine power, for it is used in connection with the sign acts or object lessons of the prophets. See Kelvin G. Friebel, *Jeremiah's and Ezekiel's Sign-Acts*, JSOTSup 283 (Sheffield: Sheffield Academic, 1999); Kelvin G. Friebel, "A Hermeneutical Paradigm for Interpreting Prophetic Sign-Actions," *Did* 12.2 (2001): 25–45; cf. Georg Fohrer, "Die Gattung der Berichte über symbolische Handlungen der Propheten," *ZAW* 64 (1952): 101–20; Georg Fohrer, *Die symbolische Handlungen der Propheten*, 2nd ed., ATANT 54 (Zurich: Zwingli, 1968); W. D. Stacey, *Prophetic Drama in the Old Testament* (London: Epworth, 1990). Thus Isa 20:3 reveals that Isaiah's act of going naked and barefoot was an אוֹת וּמוֹפֵת ("a sign and a portent") against Egypt and

Such sign acts are intended to teach a lesson or symbolise a coming event and both intentions can be discerned in the interpretive comments of the angel. First, he commissions Joshua for his role as high priest in 3:6–7. Secondly, he expands his address to the entire Zadokite priesthood in 3:8–10 with his reference to רעיך הישבים לפניך ("your associates sitting before you"), a phrase which most likely does not refer to additional priests in the visionary scene but rather to priests who assist Joshua in his duties.[28] This is most likely an allusion to the instatement of the Zadokite priesthood in the priestly service as promised by Ezek 44. Zechariah 3:8–10 moves the discussion beyond teaching a lesson to symbolizing a coming event.

This future event, to which the instatement of the Zadokite priesthood points, is the arrival of someone whose is called עבדי צמח ("my servant, the Branch," hereafter "my servant, Zemah").[29] Zechariah 3:8, by preceding it with עבדי ("my servant"), clearly identifies צמח (Zemah) as a person. Jeremiah 23:5–6 and 33:15–16 are the only passages outside of Zech 1–8 which use this image to refer to a person and in these cases he is clearly a descendant from David, one who was

---

Cush. Similarly, Ezekiel's acts of packing his belongings and digging through the wall (Ezek 12:6, 11, "sign") and his silence at the death of his wife (Ezek 24:24, 27, "sign") are called מופת (so also Isa 8:18 for Isaiah and his children, "signs and portents"; cf. Peter R. Ackroyd, *Exile and Restoration: A Study of Hebrew Thought of the Sixth Century B.C.*, OTL (Philadelphia: Westminster, 1968), 188–89. In these examples from the prophets we have a precedence for human beings being מופת as in Zech 3, and of the two Ezekiel is the closest to Zech 3 because it consistently uses the word מופת ("wonders") without אות ("signs"). This evidence confirms that Zech 3 has been influenced by the prophetic sign act form.

[28] The term רע ("colleague") is common in the Hebrew Bible and can be used for anyone from a close friend or mere acquaintance to a fellow-citizen or other person. Thus, based on this word alone, the angel could be referring to fellow priests, members of the Jewish community, or even other human beings within the divine council, that is, the prophets. However, these associates are modified by the phrase "seated before you," a surprising development because there has been no mention to this point in the vision of any other humans besides Joshua and Zechariah. This phrase does not necessarily mean that there were other humans in the divine council, for it appears in 2 Kgs 4:38; 6:1 to describe the relationship between a religious figure and his disciples. The technical nature of this phrase in such contexts becomes clear in 2 Kgs 6:1 where Elisha's disciples refer to their meeting place as "the place where we live under your charge" (המקום אשר אנחנו ישבים שם לפניך). So also in Ezek 33:31; cf. 8:1; 14:1; 20:1 it is used to speak of the prophet declaring the word of Yahweh to the elders of Israel in exile. Thus "your colleagues who sit before you" are Joshua's priestly associates who assist him with the temple justice and rituals and who need not be present in the visionary scene. Tollington, *Tradition*, 161 n. 3, cites Gen 43:33 to argue that this idiom points to the supremacy of Joshua over the other priests.

[29] The traditional translation of צמח as "branch" is inappropriate and an imposition of the royal expectation of Isa 11:1 (where נצר appears). See Rose for a superb argument on the translation of this word; Rose, *Zemah*, 91–120.

regularly called by God, עבדי ("my servant"; Jer 33:21; cf. 2 Sam 3:18; 7:5; 1 Kgs 11:13, 32, 34, 36, 38; 14:8; 2 Kgs 19:34; 20:6).[30] A closer look at one of these two Jeremianic prophecies about צמח (Zemah), Jer 33:15–16, will help clarify the relationship between these priests and צמח (Zemah).

Jeremiah 33:15–16 is a piece of prophetic poetry set within a larger prose piece focused on the restoration of Judah and Israel from captivity (33:7).[31] The larger prophecy promises not only a return to and resettlement of the land, but a cleansing of the people's sin (עון "sin/sins"; 33:8 twice) and a restoration of the fame of Jerusalem (33:9). These points of connection can also be traced in the vision of Zech 3:1–5 where עון (3:4, 9; "guilt") connected with the exile is removed and Jerusalem is chosen once again. After describing the resettlement of the land, the prose prophecy cites the poetic piece about the Davidic descendant. At the close of this piece in Jeremiah, however, we find a fascinating development: the promise to David is intimately linked with the promise to "the levitical priests" (33:17–18). Jeremiah 33 does not collapse the Davidic house into the priestly, but rather links their fate together: both enjoy perpetual covenants. By

---

[30] See also Laato, *A Star Is Rising*, 201. In these passages Zemah is identified as a Davidic descendant who is called "The LORD is our righteousness" (יהוה צדקנו), a play on the name of the final king over Judah, Zedekiah; cf. Robert P. Carroll, *Jeremiah: A Commentary*, OTL (Philadelphia: Westminster, 1986), 445–47; contra Barker, "Two Figures." Barker seeks to eliminate the Davidic connection by drawing in other passages which do not use Zemah to refer to a Davidic descendant (e.g., Isa 4:2). However, the connections to the Jeremianic tradition, especially in Zech 6:12–13, are far stronger.

[31] According to Grothe, Jer 33:14–26 represents "the longest continuous passage which is present in the MT but lacking in the LXX." Grothe argued for the originality of Jer 33:14–26 based on trends in Alexandrian treatment of priestly texts; Jonathan F. Grothe, "An Argument for the Textual Genuineness of Jeremiah 33:14–26 (Massoretic Text)," *CJ* 7 (1981): 188–91. In contrast, Tollington sees Jer 33 as late and postdating Zech 1–8; Tollington, *Tradition*, 170 n. 2. This pericope appears to be playing off of the earlier Zemah oracle in Jer 23:5–6 and expanding it to consider the durability of the priestly line; cf. Michael A. Fishbane, *Biblical Interpretation in Ancient Israel* (Oxford: Clarendon, 1985), 471–74. Jeremiah 33:14–26 speaks of הכהנים הלוים (Jer 33:18, 21; notice reversal in v. 21), which is found regularly in Dtr literature (Deut 17:9, 18; 18:1; 24:8; 27:9; Josh 3:3; 8:33) and then appears in Persian period literature (1 Chr 9:2; 2 Chr 5:5; 23:18; 30:27; Ezra 10:6; Neh 10:29, 35; 11:20). It is used in Ezekiel (43:19; 44:15), but in both cases a phrase referring to the descendants of Zadok is appended. Zechariah thus appears to be the later text and represents a reading of Jer 33 through the lens of the Ezekielian tradition; see also Douglas K. Stuart, "The Prophetic Ideal of Government in the Restoration Era," in *Israel's Apostasy and Restoration: Essays in Honor of Roland K. Harrison*, ed. Abraham Gileadi (Grand Rapids: Baker, 1988), 283–92. In the end, however, no matter how one treats Jer 33:14–26 and its relationship to Zechariah it remains as early evidence of the linkage without amalgamation of royal and priestly lines.

playing off this earlier prophetic message, the vision in Zech 3 reveals that the instatement of the Zadokite priesthood foreshadows the ultimate arrival of a Davidic king and the era he will inaugurate.[32]

SUMMARY

Although the greater focus of the vision in Zech 3 is on the renewal of the priestly house in restoration Yehud, through it the prophet clarifies the relationship between royal, priestly, and prophetic personnel in this new era. Rather than promoting priestly extension or usurpation of prophetic and royal prerogatives, this vision-sign act advocates a balance of influence, sustaining preexilic patterns.

PROPHET, PRIEST, AND KING IN ZECHARIAH 4

ORIENTATION

Zechariah 4 consistently appears in discussions of the role of governor and priest in the early Persian period. In this passage the prophet is granted a vision of a lampstand fueled by oil flowing directly from two olive trees. Although there are many enigmatic features to this vision, greatest attention has been focused on the meaning of 4:14, the explanation of the two olive trees. The angel reveals: אלה שני בני־היצהר העמדים על־אדון כל־הארץ ("these are the two anointed ones who stand by the Lord of the whole earth"). Clearly this shows that the olive tree imagery symbolizes two individuals (שני בני־היצהר; "the two anointed ones") intimately linked to the "Lord of all the earth" (אדון כל־הארץ).

PAST INTERPRETATION

Past interpretations consistently have identified these two individuals as Zerubbabel, the governor, and Joshua, the high priest.[33] This has been based on the imagery of anointing with olive oil, a ritual practice setting apart royal and priestly

---

[32] Baldwin notices the important role that Jer 33 plays in Zechariah's interpretation of Zemah, but misinterprets the Jeremiah passage: "Already in Jeremiah's usage the term combines priestly and kingly functions. The priestly aspect is to the fore in Zechariah's first use of the term (3:8)"; Joyce G. Baldwin, *Haggai, Zechariah, Malachi: An Introduction and Commentary*, TOTC (Downers Grove, IL: InterVarsity Press, 1972), 135. In this I agree with Laato who concludes: "the High Priest and his colleagues serve as a good omen of the coming messianic era"; Laato, *A Star Is Rising*, 207.

[33] See most commentators; cf. Robert T. Siebeneck, "Messianism of Aggeus and Proto-Zacharias," *CBQ* 19 (1957): 312–28 (321), and Laato, *A Star Is Rising*, 201. See Barker for the view that two priestly lines are in view; Barker, "Two Figures"; Morgenstern for the view that high priest and assistant are in view; J. Morgenstern, "A Chapter in the

figures in Hebrew tradition (e.g., 1 Sam 16:13; Exod 29:7), and on the strong tradition of Zerubbabel and Joshua as inheritors of the royal and priestly lines in the Persian period (Ezra 2–6; Hag 1–2). However, a closer look at this Hebrew text casts doubt over this interpretive strain.

EVALUATION

1. בני־היצהר: Anointed Ones? (4:14)

First of all, one needs to revisit the phrase שני בני־היצהר ("the two anointed ones"). The term for oil here (יצהר, "anointed") is never used elsewhere for anointing, a role reserved for the Hebrew word שמן.[34] The term here is one reserved for unmanufactured oil from the olive tree, appropriate because it flows directly from tree to lampstand. Thus even if the oil here was used for "anointing," it is not received by the two figures, but rather flowing from the two figures.

History of the High-Priesthood," *AJSL* 55 (1938): 1–24, 183–97, 366–77 (5). Halpern (see also Tollington) suggests a pun here on the Levitical clan יצהר (cf. Exod 6:18, 21; Num 3:19; 16:1; 1 Chr 5:28; 6:3, 23; 23:12, 18); Baruch Halpern, "The Ritual Background of Zechariah's Temple Song," *CBQ* 40 (1978): 167–90 (177); Tollington, *Tradition*, 177 n. 4.

[34] It is used for anointing kings (1 Sam 16:13; 1 Kgs 1:39), priests (Lev 8:12; Exod 30:23–33), and the tabernacle (Lev 8:10). שמן is the more general term encompassing all forms and uses of oil while יצהר is reserved for the unmanufactured state. Cf. Kenneth A. Strand, "The Two Olive Trees of Zechariah 4 and Revelation 11," *AUSS* 20 (1982): 257–61; Petersen, *Haggai and Zechariah 1–8*, 230; Tollington, *Tradition*, 177; contra Wilhelm Rudolph, *Haggai, Sacharja 1–8, Sacharja 9–14, Maleachi*, KAT 13 (Gütersloh: Mohn, 1976), 107–8; Jeremias, *Die Nachgesichte des Sacharja*, 184; Rex A. Mason, *The Books of Haggai, Zechariah and Malachi*, CBC (Cambridge: Cambridge University Press, 1977), 48; Baldwin, *Haggai*, 124; Susan Niditch, *The Symbolic Vision in Biblical Tradition* (Chico, CA: Scholars Press, 1983), 108–18; Eugene H. Merrill, *Haggai, Zechariah, Malachi: An Exegetical Commentary* (Chicago: Moody Press, 1994), 155. Redditt has noted that the word שמן ("oil") is used in a similar phrase (son of שמן, as here son of יצהר) in Isa 5:1 and there designates something very fertile. He proposes that here the image is of olive trees sated with oil; cf. Paul L. Redditt, "Zerubbabel, Joshua, and the Night Visions of Zechariah," *CBQ* 54 (1992): 249–59 (251); Van der Woude suggests fertility figures; Adam S. van der Woude, "Die beiden Söhne des Öls (Sach 4:14): Messianische Gestalten?" in *Travels in the World of the Old Testament: Studies Presented to M. A. Beek*, ed. M. S. H. G. Heerma van Vos, Ph. H. Houwink ten Cate, and N. A. van Uchelen (Assen: Van Gorcum, 1974), 262–68. Rooke directs similar criticism to mine against the traditional interpretation, but retains Zerubbabel and Joshua as referents, seeing them as the source of blessing on Yehud. Even then, however, she is careful to note that there is no proof in Zech 4 of the High Priest taking on royal power nor of diarchy; Rooke, *Zadok's Heirs*, 136–37, 45; cf. Ackroyd, *Exile*, 193; contra Tollington, *Tradition*, 178.

Secondly, the position of these two individuals in the vision needs to be noted carefully. They "stand by the Lord of all the earth." This combination of the verb עָמַד ("stand") with the preposition עַל ("by") followed by a reference to deity is found elsewhere only in 1 Kgs 22:19 (// 2 Chr 18:18).[35] In this instance the prophet Micaiah observes God deliberating with the host of heaven, the divine council of angelic spirits who are "standing" (עָמַד) "by" (עַל) God.[36] It is instructive that Micaiah has access to this scene, and the calls of other prophets reveal that the prophet was the one human allowed into this privileged position (Isa 6; Ezek 1–3; Jer 23:16–22; Amos 3:7; cf. Ps 89:6–7; Job 15:8).[37]

This evidence brings into question the traditional connection between Zech 4:14 and Zerubbabel and Joshua. If these two individuals are human beings in this passage they are most likely prophetic figures.[38] The prominence of Haggai and Zechariah in the traditions of the early Persian period community and their crucial role in the rebuilding of the temple may explain the presence of two prophetic figures in this vision (Hag 1–2; Zech 8:9–13; Ezra 5:1–2; 6:14).

The vision of the lampstand and olive trees, thus, emphasizes the role of the prophet in the restoration of the early Persian period. The lampstand, signifying the position of the temple as the location from which God's presence and sovereignty emanates throughout the earth, is fueled by oil supplied by the prophets. Therefore, at the center of the vision complex lies a strong reminder of the importance of the prophetic office and word within the restoration community.[39]

---

[35] Genesis 18:8 also pictures Abraham "standing" (עָמַד) "by" (עַל) divine beings, but this is an appearance of God in human form and Abraham is pictured as serving these beings food.

[36] This combination also occurs in Zech 3:1, but there it is difficult to determine if the adversary is standing beside the angel of Yahweh or beside Joshua. Notice also the similar construction in the prophetic call experience in Isa 6:1–2, עַל + עָמַד for the position of the seraphim.

[37] See Rose, *Zemah*, for detailed evidence on these combinations. Niditch sees the connection to the divine council and 1 Kgs 22:19, but not the prophetic nuance; Niditch, *Symbolic Vision*, 113.

[38] Interestingly when elements within this vision are taken up in Rev 11, these two individuals are clearly seen as prophetic, not royal or priestly figures; cf. Strand, "Olive Trees"; Meredith G. Kline, "By My Spirit," *Kerux* 9.1 (1994): 3–15; Craig A. Evans, "'The Two Sons of Oil': Early Evidence of Messianic Interpretation of Zechariah 4:14 in 4Q254 4 2," in *The Provo International Conference on the Dead Sea Scrolls: Technological Innovations, New Texts, and Reformulated Issues*, ed. Donald W. Parry and Eugene Ulrich, STDJ 30 (Leiden: Brill, 1999), 566–75 (567); although see ibid. for Rabbinic and Qumran interpretations of Zech 4:14 (priest/king). Rose identifies them as angelic beings; Rose, *Zemah*, 202–6.

[39] Baldwin struggles with any interpretation that would suggest that olive trees signifying humans (for her Joshua and Zerubbabel) could be the source of the lamps signifying divine presence. However, the prophet is well aware that any resources of the prophetic office are

2. בְּרוּחִי—*By My Spirit (4:6)*

This approach sheds new light on the reason for the insertion into the center of this vision of two oracles addressed to Zerubbabel (4:6b–10a). The power of the Spirit, well associated with the prophetic office in the Hebrew Bible and linked to the empowerment of the royal office, is promised to Zerubbabel who undertakes the temple building project in the first oracle. The promise of the prophet confronts the skepticism against Zerubbabel in the second oracle. Surely the empowering "oil" of prophecy fueled the building project, bringing the presence of God on earth.

Summary

Therefore, rather than affirming a diarchy in the political structure of early Persian Yehud, Zech 4 highlights the key role that prophecy will play within the Jewish community both in the royal task of rebuilding the temple structure (Zerubbabel, 4:6b–10a) as well as in the priestly responsibility for the enduring temple cult (lampstand, 4:1–6a, 10b–14).

Prophet, Priest, and King in Zechariah 6:9–15

Orientation

The third pericope in Zech 1:7–6:15 that alludes to the leadership of Persian period Yehud is 6:9–15. This passage appears to be linked to the night visions/oracles by the final editors of Zech 1–8 because of its position prior to the superscription of 7:1. In addition, Zech 6:9–15 shares several points of similarity with 3:1–10 and 4:1–14.[40] The same cast of characters from chapter 3 appears: prophet, Joshua, צֶמַח ("the Branch," Zemah), and priestly associates while Zerubbabel is noticeably absent. Furthermore, one can discern here allusions to socio-ritual types drawn from royal, priestly, and prophetic contexts: a royal investiture ceremony, a priestly temple memorial rite, and a prophetic sign act. So also it will be demonstrated that the prophetic empowerment of the royal building program highlighted in chapter 4 is accentuated in 6:9–15. This array of characters, rituals, and themes provides another opportunity to consider the relationship between the various functionaries in restoration Yehud.

---

derived from God; Joyce G. Baldwin, "Tsemach as a Technical Term in the Prophets," *VT* 14 (1964): 93–97.

[40] Ackroyd notes similarity between 3:8–10 and 6:9–15; Ackroyd, *Exile*, 199.

Past interpretation

Past approaches have exploited 6:9–15 for evidence of tension between royal and priestly groups in the Persian period. In this pericope the prophet describes a sign act involving three recent priestly exilic returnees (Heldai, Tobijah, Jedaiah)[41] whose precious cargo is to be made into crowns. At least one crown is to be placed on the head of Joshua.[42] The speech to Joshua which follows this sign act speaks of the figure צמח (Zemah) who will build the temple and to whom is attributed words often associated with royalty: "bear majesty ... sit and rule on his throne" (והוא־ישׂא הוד וישׁב ומשׁל על־כסאו). Then in the fourth poetic couplet of this speech the prophet declares "he will be a priest on his throne" (והיה כהן על־כסאו).[43]

These features have led some to conclude that this sign act is extending priestly control over royal prerogatives. It is argued that an oracle which originally affirmed either a diarchy between priest and prince or possibly the ascendancy of the prince over priest has been transformed into one which heightens the profile of the high priest either to undermine the royalist cause or to explain the absence of the royal line.[44] Is such a negative view of the present Hebrew text (MT) de-

---

[41] Although it is difficult to ascertain the precise identities of these men in 6:10, the few connections that can be discerned reveal links to priestly families; cf. Mark J. Boda, *Haggai/Zechariah*, NIVAC (Grand Rapids: Zondervan, 2004). Their priestly background is suggested by the later practice of Ezra. In Ezra's return, the priests were given care of the silver and gold collected from the Persian authorities and Jewish exilic community for safe travel to Palestine (8:24–32), and upon their arrival the materials were deposited at the temple into the care of other priests (8:33–34).

[42] There is no question that the second phrase ("set on the head of Joshua") refers to the placement of a crown on the head of Joshua. The Hebrew text does not have an object here, but it is quite certain that it is the crown which is placed on the head because of the phrase "on the head." Van der Woude suggested that the normal expression for putting something on someone is שׂים ב rather than שׂים על, which provides an opportunity for him to suggest an Akkadian expression which means "put at the disposal of somebody," thus, "you shall hand (it) over to Joshua"; van der Woude, "Söhne des Öls," 247 n. 31. However, the same construction as here ("set on the head of") is used for Xerxes's crowning of Esther in Esth 2:18, another Persian period text. See also the use of the synonym נתן with בראשׁ in Ezek 16:12 following two phrases which use the combination נתן with על; cf. Rose, *Zemah*, 48–50.

[43] This is a better translation than the NRSV which has here "there shall be a priest by his throne." A review of other instances where this phrase appears על־כסאו, the preposition speaks of "on" not "by." One would expect either "right" or "left" if "by" was intended (cf. 1 Kgs 2:19).

[44] Cf. Siebeneck, "Messianism," 323; Laato, *A Star Is Rising*, 206–7. Rooke's concern about the traditional emendation is that it would produce a text addressed to Zerubbabel that is about Zerubbabel and encourages interpretation of the "text as it stands"; Rooke,

fensible? Does this pericope really betray the deep rifts in the Persian period community that have been suggested? Another look at this pericope will chart a new course.

EVALUATION

1. Two Figures or One?

Two lexical features of the prophetic speech, one at the beginning and the other at the end, help clarify the number of individuals referred to in the speech. At the end of the prophetic speech directed to Joshua Zechariah tells the priest: ועצת שלום תהיה בין שניהם ("with peaceful understanding between the two of them"), a clear reference to two distinct people.[45] At the beginning of the speech in 6:12, Zechariah is instructed to speak אליו ("to him"), referring to Joshua the high priest who has just been introduced in the preceding phrase (6:11b). The speech which is then directed to Joshua begins with the words: הנה־איש ("Here is a man"). When this phrase appears in direct speech elsewhere in the Hebrew Bible, it does not refer to the one addressed, but rather to a third party who may be approaching from a distance (2 Sam 18:26), may be present in the scene (1 Sam 9:17), may be absent but accessible (1 Sam 9:6), or may have been encountered at an earlier point (1 Kgs 20:39).[46] Thus, צמח (Zemah) cannot be Joshua to whom the speech is addressed. It is possible that צמח (Zemah) could be someone in the scene (one of the four men mentioned or Zerubbabel who is not mentioned), but it is more likely that צמח (Zemah) is not present at all because in the one instance where

---

Zadok's Heirs, 146–47. Although her encouragement is appropriate, her concern is misguided because it is not sensitive to the fact that this is a prophetic interpretation of a sign act and could be using subtle rhetoric.

[45] In the vast majority of cases, the Hebrew construction "two of them" is used to refer to two people (Gen 2:25; 3:7; 9:23; etc.). However, in a few instances it speaks of two inanimate items (Num 7:13; Ezek 21:24; Prov 27:3), activities (Prov 17:15; 20:10); or body parts (Prov 20:12) and in a couple of places is used abstractly (Eccl 4:3: the dead and the living; Isa 1:31: a man and his work). These two instances may allow for an interpretation that would identify the "counsel of peace between two of them" as an allusion to the combining of two offices (see NASB). However, when the preposition "between" (Hebrew בין) is used with "two of them" (as in Zech 6:13) elsewhere it refers to two people (2 Kgs 2:11; Exod 22:10). The second instance (Exod 22:10) has nearly the same construction as here: noun construct chain (an oath of Yahweh) with היה (imperfect, "will be") with "between the two of them."

[46] This phrase is used as a narrative technique to introduce or progress a scene (1 Kgs 13:1, etc.) or as an apocalyptic device to introduce or progress a visionary description (Zech 1:8; 2:5; Ezek 40:3; Dan 10:5). In these cases it is accompanied by verbs for sight: "looked," "saw." Cf. the plural form in Josh 2:2.

the individual is in the scene the article accompanies the noun (הנה האיש, "Here is the man," 1 Sam 9:17), unlike Zech 6:12.[47]

2. Relationship between These Two Figures

These two initial pieces of evidence reveal that 6:9–15 refers to two distinct individuals, one of which is צמח (Zemah) who is not equated with Joshua.[48] The speech itself, modeling the cadence of poetic verse, appears to refer to two individuals in its four parallel lines.[49] The first line plays off of the root צמח ("to branch out," better "to grow") identifying the name.[50] The second line identifies the initial role of the צמח (Zemah) in the rebuilding project. The third line identifies the enduring role of the צמח (Zemah) in royal rule. With the fourth line, however, we are introduced to a priestly figure who sits on a throne in the first colon,[51] before the second colon defines the relationship between this priest and צמח (Zemah).

This relationship is defined as עצת שלום ("with peaceful understanding"), a phrase unique to Zech 6:13. Petersen has argued that the term עצה ("understanding") is not used elsewhere to indicate a "joint situation" or a "relationship" but rather "counsel received by a king" (2 Sam 15:31, 34).[52] The term "peaceful" describes this counsel which will be characterized by peace (positive counsel) or possibly result in peace/prosperity (counsel which produces peace). It appears, then, that the speech speaks of two individuals, צמח (Zemah) and priest, the latter functioning in the role of counselor for the former.

---

[47] Baldwin notes the lack of article as key, but mistakenly excludes Zerubbabel as a candidate; Baldwin, "Tsemach," 95. That the referent is not in the scene accords well with the only other allusion to Zemah in the book of Zechariah (3:8), in a speech also addressed to Joshua which refers to Zemah as someone whom Yahweh Almighty "is going to bring."
[48] Contra Baldwin who sees צמח as a future figure who combines both priestly and royal offices into one person; Baldwin, "Tsemach," 96–97.
[49] *BHS* structures this differently.
[50] Some have seen in the phrase "from his place" a reference to Joshua's displacement of the royal line or to the lowly stature of the royal line. The construction without "from" is used to describe one's dwelling or position when displacing someone either physically, as in the conquest (Deut 2:12, 21–23), or officially, as in the succession of a king (Gen 36:33–39) or priest (Exod 29:30; Lev 6:15). However, when used with the verb "grow" (צמח), it refers to the place from which something grows (Gen 2:9; Exod 10:5; Ps 85:12 [Eng. 85:11]; Job 5:6; 8:19).
[51] Laato says this priest cannot be Joshua for the speech is addressed to Joshua, but this conclusion is not sensitive to the fact that the prophet is interpreting the sign act; Laato, *A Star Is Rising*, 202.
[52] Petersen, *Haggai and Zechariah 1–8*, 278.

The appearance of a priest in close proximity to the royal צמח (Zemah) figure is not surprising if one remembers again the צמח (Zemah) passages in Jeremiah (Jer 23; 33) where the revelation of the צמח (Zemah) figure is connected with God's return of a remnant from captivity to a rebuilt and prosperous city filled with inhabitants (23:3, 8; 33:7–13). There is little question that 6:12–13 is alluding to the Jeremianic צמח (Zemah) tradition. Both Zechariah and Jeremiah employ identical vocabulary: combining the verbal form (צמח, "to branch out") with the nominal form צמח (Zemah, Jer 33:15–16; Zech 6:12),[53] focusing on renewal using the verbal root בנה ("to build")[54] and employing vocabulary often associated with the royal office (והוא־ישׂא הוד וישב ומשל על־כסאו; "royal honor ... sit upon his throne ... rule"; Jer 22:18, 30; Zech 6:13).[55]

As already noted the section which follows and elaborates the צמח (Zemah) prophecy in Jer 33:15–16 (33:17–26) intertwines the fortunes of the Davidic house and the "levitical priests."[56] This section never combines the two lines (royal and priestly) but rather argues that both covenants are as secure and eternal as the coming of day and night. The oracle in Zech 6:9–15, therefore, plays off of this Jeremianic tradition proclaiming that as the prophecy of priestly reinstatement is being realized, so also the prophecy of royal reestablishment will be fulfilled.[57] It also assures the priestly house that they will have a place of privilege and counsel within the Davidic court, while reminding them of the supremacy of the royal line in authority in the community and responsibility in the building project.

---

[53] One difference is that Jeremiah uses the *hiphil* while Zechariah uses the *qal*. Thus in Zech 6 the emphasis lies on the Zemah who is growing rather than Yahweh who will cause the growth as in Jer 33.

[54] The building in Zech 6, however, is slightly different. The one who builds in Jer 33:7–9 is Yahweh, while in Zech 6 it is Zemah. Additionally, the activity in Zech 6 is focused on the building of the temple of Yahweh, rather than the city and province in general.

[55] Note the correspondences: to be clothed with majesty (Pss 21 5; 45:4; Jer 22:18); to sit and rule on his throne (Jer 22:30; 1 Kgs 1:46; 16:11). Jeremiah 22 is a passage that prepares the way for the first of the two prophecies of Zemah in Jeremiah (Jer 23:5–6). Jeremiah 22:18 speaks of the loss of "majesty" (הוד) for Jehoiakim and 22:30 of the condemnation of Jehoiachin (Jehoiakim's son) whose sons would not "sit on the throne ... or rule" (ישׁב על־כסא דוד ומשל עוד ביהודה). This is the only other place in the Hebrew Bible where the combination: ישׁב; משׁל; כסא appears. The revelation of the Zemah who would come from David in the following chapter of Jeremiah is the answer to the disaster of the Davidic line proclaimed in the previous chapter. This confirms the Davidic lineage of the Zemah and the royal character of this couplet in Zech 6; contra Tollington who plays down the royal significance by missing the Jeremianic connections; Tollington, *Tradition*, 173–74.

[56] See discussion of this phrase and passage above under Zech 3.

[57] This may explain why the oracle refers to "priest" rather than "high priest," because Jer 33 says nothing about a "high priest."

3. Crowns and Thrones: Royal Allusions?

The Jeremianic tradition gives us a precedence for the reference to two individuals in 6:9–15. But this does not fully explain two other aspects of this text which appear to grant the priest royal status: the fact that a crown[58] is placed on Joshua's head in the sign act of 6:11 and that the priestly figure is seated on a throne in the prophetic speech of 6:13.

The word for crown in 6:11, 14, עטרה ("crown") often refers to the literal crown on a king's head (2 Sam 12:30 // 1Chr 20:2; Ps 21:3; Jer 13:18; Ezek 21:26; Song 3:11). In the majority of cases the word is employed metaphorically, as an extension of the literal meaning drawn from the royal court, usually with the sense of honor or beauty: Isa 28:1, 3, 5; 62:3; Ezek 16:12; 23:42; Job 19:9; 31:36; Prov

---

[58] There have been some challenges in discerning the number of crowns mentioned in this passage. The present Hebrew text (MT) reads the plural "crowns" at both 6:11, 14, while the versions reproduce several different combinations (e.g., Syriac Peshitta has the singular in both cases, the Greek Septuagint has the plural [11] and the singular [14], the Latin Vulgate the singular [11] and the plural [14]). In the Hebrew text the only verb associated with the word is written in the singular (14, תהיה). This diversity in textual witness and disagreement in syntax have led to a cacophony of interpretations. By retaining the Hebrew vocalic text (MT), some have argued that both references to crowns are plural. This would mean that multiple crowns were made and placed either on the heads of Joshua and Zemah/Zerubbabel or on the heads of the four individuals named in 6:10, 14. The first view is the traditional reading, while the second is argued by Redditt; Paul L. Redditt, *Haggai, Zechariah and Malachi*, NCB (London: Marhsall Pickering, 1995), 72–73. The use of a singular verb with the plural subject ("crowns") in v. 14 is not a problem since this is possible in Hebrew (cf. GKC §464k). Accepting the witness of the ancient versions, some have suggested reading the words here as singular, either as "plurals of excellence," referring to the excellence of a single crown (see NASB, "ornate crown"), or as descriptions of a composite headpiece, similar to the expression "many crowns" (διαδήματα πολλά, Rev 19:12), or as an archaic singular form which looks like the plural and is attested in other Semitic languages as well as in Hebrew. The common feminine plural ending, ות-, is found on the singular noun, חכמות (Prov 1:20; 9:1; 14:1; "wisdom"), which also has another form in the singular, חכמה. This parallels the suggestion here: a feminine noun with the usual ending (ה-, עטרה) also has a less common form (ות-, עטרת). Cf. Albert Petitjean, *Les oracles du proto-Zacharie: Un programme de restauration pour la communauté juive après l'exil* (Paris: Librairie Lecoffre, 1969), 281; Rose, *Zemah*, 47–48. A further option is that the first one is a plural referring to two crowns (v. 11a), one of which is placed on Joshua's head (v. 11b) and the other in the temple awaiting the coming of Zemah (v. 14). This may explain why the first use of crown has the plene spelling of ות- while the second has the defective form. Cf. Meyers and Meyers, *Haggai, Zechariah 1–8*, 363. The rules of text criticism would favor the Hebrew text (MT) as the preferred reading (the more difficult text) and the ancient versions as attempts to clarify this original text. Thus it most likely that the text should read "crowns" in both 6:11, 14, a conclusion that will be bolstered by further observations below.

4:9; 12:4; 14:24; 16:31; 17:6; Lam 5:16. In two places, however, the crown is placed on figures associated with the royal court: the queen mother (Jer 23:18) and an honored high official (Esth 8:15). This review reveals that עטרה has strong royal connotations, but is not limited to the king in his court. Even in literal court contexts, it can be used for a lesser member of the royal court.[59] Thus, to set a crown on the head of the high priest appears to have royal connotations, but does not necessarily signify that he is becoming a king.[60]

The presence of a priest on a throne in 6:13 also needs to be explained. Many have struggled with the appearance of a priestly figure on a כסא ("throne"), a term used in the previous phrase to refer to the seat of the royal Zemah figure and used regularly to refer to a royal throne throughout the Hebrew Bible, either in literal (e.g., Jer 1:15; 1 Kgs 22:10) or figurative ways (e.g., 1 Kgs 16:11).[61] The presence of two people on thrones is attested elsewhere in the Hebrew Bible in contexts where royal figures are taking counsel either from another king (1 Kgs 22:10) or from another figure in the court (1 Kgs 2:19, Queen Mother). In these cases one figure is clearly dominant over the other. Thus, as with the crown so also with the throne, it is possible for someone other than a king to be associated with this royal symbol, even in the presence of a king.[62]

---

[59] Notice how the Late Biblical Hebrew word for crown (כתר) is placed on queens (Esth 1:11; 2:17) and honored officials (6:8).
[60] Cf. Rose, *Zemah*, 51–56. A headdress word which would have bridged the high priestly and royal offices in Israel is נזר ("diadem") a term used of the golden crown plate attached to the high priest's turban (identified with ציץ, "plate," Exod 29:6; 39:30; Lev 8:9) and for the "crown" on a monarch's head (2 Sam 1:10; 2 Kgs 11:12 // 2 Chr 23:11; Pss 89:40; 132:18; cf. Zech 9:16; Prov 27:24). The most common term for the ceremonial headdress of the high priest is מצנפת ("turban") which was made of fine linen (Exod 28:24, 37, 39; 29:6; 39:28, 31; Lev 8:9; 16:4). However, Ezek 21:31 (Eng. 21:26) connects this word with a royal figure (wicked prince), parallel to עטרה. The term מצנפת is to be distinguished from the מגבעה which was worn by Aaron's sons ("headdress"; Exod 28:40; 29:9; 39:28; Lev 8:13). Two other general words could signify common or priestly headdresses: פאר ("headdress"; common: Isa 3:20; Ezek 24:17, 23; Isa 61:3; priestly: Exod 39:28; Ezek 44:18; Isa 61:3); צניף ("turban"; common: Isa 3:23; 62:3; Job 29:14; priestly: Zech 3:5). Rooke's view on the crown as symbolic of the rebuilt temple is odd, especially considering it is mentioned in a passage with so much royal language connected to צמח (Zemah); Rooke, *Zadok's Heirs*, 147–48.
[61] There is another priest, however, who sits on a throne: Eli in 1 Sam 1:9; 4:13, 18 and thus there is a precedence for someone other than a king, and particularly a priest, to sit on a throne.
[62] Quite clearly the Septuagint did not see Joshua as king, for rather than translating "he will be a priest on his throne," it produces "there will be a priest on his right hand" (ἔσται ὁ ἱερεὺς ἐκ δεξιῶν αὐτοῦ). See Brian A. Mastin, "A Note on Zechariah VI 13," *VT* 26 (1976): 113–16. Beuken follows LXX; Beuken, *Haggai–Sacharja 1–8*, 281. It is interesting that

This analysis has shown that the two figures assumed by the phrases at the beginning and end of this speech are royal and priestly.[63] The priestly figure, cast in the role of counselor, is subordinated to the royal figure who will be responsible for the building of the temple. The identity of the priestly figure is never revealed, although the fact that Joshua the high priest is the addressee suggests he is either the figure or a symbol of a future figure.[64] The identity of the royal figure is never offered, but there is reason to believe that his arrival is not far off. Looking at instances which employ the phrase הנה־איש ("here is a man") reveals that this person is within close spatial and temporal range and will soon be encountered (see above). Most likely, then, this is a reference to Zerubbabel who had not yet arrived from Babylon and whose efforts in the rebuilding project are highlighted elsewhere in Zechariah (Zech 4:6b–10a) and in other Persian period books: Haggai and Ezra 1–6.[65]

---

both royal terms associated with the priest in this passage, "crown" (6:11) and "throne" (6:13), are used of the queen mother in the preexilic royal court (Jer 13:18; 1 Kgs 2:19). Several texts indicate that the queen mother held a specific rank in the court. This is true of Solomon (2 Sam 11:3; 12:24) and the kings of Israel (1 Kgs 11:26; 16:31; 22:52; 2 Kgs 3:2; 9:22), but especially of the kings of Judah (1 Kgs 14:21; 15:2, 10; 22:42; 2 Kgs 8:26; 12:1; 14:2; 15:2, 33; 18:2; 21:1, 19; 22:1; 23:31, 36; 24:8; 24:18). Asa's need to remove his queen mother from her position (1 Kgs 15:11–13) and Athaliah's ability to order the murder of the Davidic family members (2 Kgs 11:1) reveals not only rank but also considerable power and influence in the court. The precise role is difficult to discern, but it appears to have had at least two aspects: political and religious. Politically the queen mother is depicted as involved in domestic affairs, as a key figure at the beginning of her son's rule to ensure transfer of power from her husband to her son (1 Kgs 1–2), but also wielding influence throughout his reign. However, there also appears to be a religious role for the queen mother for there are several examples of these figures introducing and supporting rival cults (1 Kgs 15:13; 1 Kgs 18–19). This second aspect may explain why the oracle associates the high priest with a "crown" and "throne." In place of the queen mother, who led preexilic Davidic kings away from pure religion, the high priest would sit with the king to offer advice and keep him faithful to Yahweh. See further the great reviews of Linda S. Schearing, "Queen," in *ABD* 5:583–86; Niels-Erik A. Andreasen, "The Role of the Queen Mother in Israelite Society," *CBQ* 45 (1983): 179–94.

[63] This speaks against those who have argued for an amalgamation of the priestly and royal offices in Zemah; cf. Baldwin, "Tsemach"; Baldwin, *Haggai*, 136–37. Merrill argues for two separate figures here, but then contradicts this with reference to the amalgamation of priest and king in Davidic (Pss 2:2, 6–8; 110:2, 4) and Christian tradition (Heb 5:1–10; 7:1–25); Merrill, *Haggai*, 199–201.

[64] Contra Rose, *Zemah*, 60.

[65] See Ackroyd for similar redactional dating; Ackroyd, *Exile*, 189, 197; contra Tollington and Rose who see a future figure; Tollington, *Tradition*, 172–73; Rose, *Zemah*.

In the closing verse of this pericope, 6:15, the prophet drives home his key point.[66] Those who are far away will come and build the temple. The priests, eager to begin the temple project, are encouraged to await the arrival of צמח (Zemah) and his entourage from exile. Rather than expanding priestly powers, the prophet is carefully delimiting them and subtly using his prophetic authority (you shall know that the LORD of hosts has sent me to you) to accomplish this.

SUMMARY

While Zech 6:9–15 has often been paraded as evidence of the expansion of priestly authority in restoration Yehud, this paper has argued that the passage does not sustain the weight of this conclusion. While Zechariah does provide a positive vision of the contribution of the priestly caste to the restoration community, he carefully distinguishes between priestly and royal roles. The fortunes of priest are intimately linked to those of the future king.

CONCLUSION

In the past scholars have detected within Zech 1:7–6:15 a prophetic justification for hierocratic aspirations.[67] This justification has been located either in the original prophetic declarations of the prophet Zechariah or in an elaborate scheme of

---

[66] In the sign act genre there is often an interpretation that accompanies the action (see note above). This is not to be disregarded as a later addition, but rather is intimately linked to the coming of Zemah.

[67] For discussion of the impact of Zech 1:7–6:15 on later messianic views (Qumran, Rabbinic, Christian), see: F. F. Bruce, "The Book of Zechariah and the Passion Narrative," *BJRL* 43 (1960–61): 167–90; Strand, "Olive Trees"; Seyoon Kim, "Jesus—the Son of God, the Stone, Son of Man, and the Servant: The Role of Zechariah in the Self-Identification of Jesus," in *Tradition and Interpretation in the New Testament*, ed. Gerald F. Hawthorne and Otto Betz (Grand Rapids: Eerdmans, 1987), 134–48; Walter Harrelson, "Messianic Expectations at the Time of Jesus," *Saint Luke's Journal of Theology* 32 (1988): 28–42; Hermann Lichtenberger, "Messianic Expectations and Messianic Figures in the Second Temple Period," in *Qumran-Messianism: Studies on the Messianic Expectations in the Dead Sea Scrolls*, ed. James H. Charlesworth, Hermann Lichtenberger, and Gerbern S. Oegema (Tübingen: Mohr Siebeck, 1998), 9–20; Craig A. Evans, "Jesus and Zechariah's Messianic Hope," in *Authenticating the Activities of Jesus*, ed. Bruce Chilton and Craig A. Evans, NTTS 28.2 (Leiden: Brill, 1998), 373–88; Evans, "Sons of Oil"; Craig A. Evans, "Did Jesus Predict His Death and Resurrection?" in *Resurrection*, ed. Stanley E. Porter, Michael A. Hayes, and David Tombs, JSNTSup 186 (Sheffield: Sheffield Academic, 1999), 82–97; Daniel Stökl, "Yom Kippur in the Apocalyptic Imaginaire and the Roots of Jesus' High Priesthood: Yom Kippur in Zechariah 3, 1 Enoch 10, 11QMelkizedeq, Hebrews and the Apocalypse of Abraham 13," in *Transformations of the Inner Self in*

redactional revisions to that prophet's visions and oracles. This paper has disputed this approach and argued that the Zecharian prophetic tradition retains clear distinctions between prophetic, royal, and priestly offices by relying on the Jeremianic tradition of the future of the royal and priestly lines.[68]

If there is an agenda in the Zecharian tradition in relation to leadership, it appears to be to curb priestly aspirations through emphasizing the key role that prophetic and royal streams must continue to play in Yehud. In this we may be observing the beginning phase of a trajectory, placing the prophetic stream on a collision course with the priestly. This growing tension may be reflected in Zechariah's strong indictment of the priests along with the people of the land in Zech 7:5 and possibly also help explain the addition of Zech 9–14 to Zech 1–8.

Ancient Religions, ed. Jan Assmann and Guy G. Stroumsa, SHR 83 (Leiden: Brill, 1999), 349–66.

[68] For the influence of the Jeremianic tradition on the prose inclusio of Zech 1:1–6; 7:1–8:23, see Boda, "Master Mason" = chapter 6 in this present volume.

5
Writing the Vision: Zechariah within the Visionary Traditions of the Hebrew Bible[1]

In this chapter I investigate the formal influence of earlier vision reports from Jeremiah, Amos, and Ezekiel on Zech 1:7–6:15. This analysis highlights innovations in the use of this form and the rhetorical impact of these innovations.

One of the most fascinating features of the book of Zechariah is the series of visionary experiences which dominate Zech 1:7–6:15. For readers of prophetic literature the form used immediately brings to mind other visionary traditions in the Hebrew Bible, especially those recorded in the books of Amos, Jeremiah, and Ezekiel.

Over the past century several scholars have offered a variety of analyses of these various visionary traditions in the Hebrew Bible.[2] Sister differentiated between three types of visions based on content, ranging from theophany, to self-

---

[1] Based on my original publication, Mark J. Boda, "Writing the Vision: Zechariah within the Visionary Traditions of the Hebrew Bible," in *'I Lifted My Eyes and Saw': Reading Dream and Vision Reports in the Hebrew Bible*, ed. Elizabeth R. Hayes and Lena-Sofia Tiemeyer, T&T Clark Library of Biblical Studies; LHBOTS 584 (London: Bloomsbury, 2014), 101–18. Slightly revised for inclusion in this volume.

[2] I am grateful to Michael Stead for his superb review of the prophetic visionary traditions: Michael R. Stead, "Visions, Prophetic," in *Dictionary of the Old Testament: Prophets*, ed. Mark J. Boda and J. Gordon McConville (Downers Grove, IL: IVP Academic, 2012), 818–26. Note also Michael A. Fishbane, *Biblical Interpretation in Ancient Israel* (Oxford: Clarendon, 1985), 447–57, who links these visionary texts to mantic wisdom which

explanatory images, to symbols needing interpretation.³ Lindblom focused on the religious experience of the prophet, distinguishing between ecstatic visions (with pictorial visions focused on objects or figures, e.g., Amos 7:1–3; and dramatic visions focused on dynamic scenes, e.g., Ezek 8–11), symbolic perceptions (e.g., Amos 8:1–2), and literary visions (e.g., Zech 1–2; 6:1–8).⁴ Horst distinguished between *die Anwesenheitsvisionen* (presence visions) in which the prophet experiences the divine presence, *die Wortsymbolvisionen* (word-symbol visions) which use visions as a foundation for proclamation (e.g., Amos 8:1–2), and *die Geschehnisvisionen* (event-visions) like Isa 21:1–10.⁵ Long lists three forms of vision reports with the first the oracle vision with its short report and dialogue used as platform for an oracle (e.g., Amos 7:7–8; Zech 5:1–4), the second the dramatic word vision with its depiction of a heavenly and/or dramatic scene (e.g., 1 Kgs 22:17–22; Zech 1:8–17), and the third the revelatory mysteries vision which deciphers veiled secrets of divine activity (e.g., Zech 4:1–14; Dan 8).⁶ Amsler focused on the literary use of visions within prophetic material, distinguishing between cases where a prophet reports what he has seen but which are not considered "visions" (e.g., Isa 21:2, 7) and twenty-two passages which share in common a depiction of what the prophet saw, followed by a dialogue with a heavenly figure, and the proclamation of a divine word (e.g., the visions in Amos, Jeremiah, Ezekiel, and Isa 6).⁷ With Niditch the focus becomes more diachronic in nature as she differentiates three stages in the development of symbolic visions in the Hebrew Bible, beginning with an economic-rhetorical style in Amos and Jeremiah, and developing into a more ornate and prosaic form in most of the Zecharian visionary materials, before reaching a baroque and narrative phase in Daniel, 2

---

explicates visual forms of prophecy. For those who have focused more particularly on the Zecharian visionary tradition, see especially Christian Jeremias, *Die Nachtgesichte des Sacharja: Untersuchungen zu ihrer Stellung im Zusammenhang der Visionsberichte im Alten Testament und zu ihrem Bildmaterial*, FRLANT 117 (Göttingen: Vandehoeck & Ruprecht, 1977); David L. Petersen, *Haggai and Zechariah 1–8: A Commentary*, OTL (Philadelphia: Westminster, 1984), 113–15; Janet E. Tollington, *Tradition and Innovation in Haggai and Zechariah 1–8*, JSOTSup 150 (Sheffield: JSOT Press, 1993), 78–124; cf. Antonios Finitsis, *Visions and Eschatology: A Socio-historical Analysis of Zechariah 1–6*, LSTS 79 (London: T&T Clark, 2011).

³ Moses Sister, "Die Typen der prophetischen Visionen in der Bibel," *Monatsschrift für Geschichte und Wissenschaft des Judentums* 78 (1934): 399–430.

⁴ Johannes Lindblom, *Prophecy in Ancient Israel* (Philadelphia: Fortress, 1962).

⁵ Friedrich Horst, "Die Visionsschilderungen der alttestamentlichen Propheten," *EvT* 20 (1960): 193–205.

⁶ Burke O. Long, "Reports of Visions among the Prophets," *JBL* 95 (1976): 353–65.

⁷ S. Amsler, "La parole visionnaire des prophètes," *VT* 31 (1981): 359–63.

Baruch, and 4 Ezra.⁸ Behrens highlights two elements which are core to the prophetic vision report, that is, first a vision element employing the verb ראה usually in the *hiphil* with Yahweh as subject, followed by והנה introducing an *Überraschungssatz* (surprise clause) depicting the visionary scene, and second a dialogue element employing the *waw*-relative prefix conjugation of אמר and then either a question from the prophet or an imperative from the heavenly figure, and finally a concluding word from the heavenly figure.⁹ For Behrens there are two streams of visionary materials, first the basic prophetic vision report identified above (Amos 7–8; Jer 1:11–14; 24:1) and second a throne vision stream (Isa 6; 1 Kgs 22:17, 19; Amos 9:1–4). These two streams flow together in Ezek 1–3 (basic form in 2:9–3:9; throne vision in 1:4–2:8a), and are influenced by priestly conceptions in Ezek 8–11. This Ezekielian priestly form can be discerned in Zechariah and Daniel.

This review of scholarship highlights the key Hebrew Bible passages which are often associated with the visionary report tradition. Various approaches have been taken in the past, most emphasizing a different aspect of the traditional form critical agenda, that is, attention to formal structure, lexical content, and life setting, with some attention to literary setting typical of more recent form critical approaches.¹⁰ Often form critical research emphasizes the similarities between the various texts under review and planes out the unique qualities of each composition. The present article will seek to heed the call to shift from form to rhetorical criticism as we consider the visionary traditions in the Hebrew Bible.¹¹

The article will begin with the reports of a symbolic vision in Zech 1:7–6:15, seeking to identify the building blocks of these vision reports within Zechariah.¹² Then it will show the way that earlier vision reports in prophetic books relate to these building blocks. This comparison reveals two major streams of earlier vision reports which relate to Zechariah: one found in Jeremiah and Amos and the other

---

⁸ Susan Niditch, *The Symbolic Vision in Biblical Tradition* (Chico, CA: Scholars Press, 1983).
⁹ Achim Behrens, *Prophetische Visionsschilderungen im Alten Testament: Sprachliche Eigenarten, Funktion und Geschichte einer Gattung*, AOAT 292 (Münster: Ugarit-Verlag, 2002).
¹⁰ For this recent trend, see Colin M. Toffelmire, "Form Criticism," in *Dictionary of the Old Testament: Prophets*, ed. Mark J. Boda and J. Gordon McConville (Downers Grove, IL: IVP Academic, 2012), 257–71; see now Mark J. Boda, Michael H. Floyd, and Colin M. Toffelmire, eds., *The Book of the Twelve and the New Form Criticism*, ANEM 10 (Atlanta: SBL Press, 2015).
¹¹ James Muilenburg, "Form Criticism and Beyond," *JBL* 88 (1969): 1–18, and Rolf P. Knierim, "Old Testament Form Criticism Reconsidered," *Int* 27 (1973): 435–68.
¹² For the tables and discussion in this article, see further Mark J. Boda, *The Book of Zechariah*, NICOT (Grand Rapids: Eerdmans, 2016), 87–100.

in Ezekiel.[13] This analysis will lay the foundation for a closer look at the unique expression of the vision reports in Zechariah and the rhetorical effect of these later vision reports.

ZECHARIAH'S VISION REPORTS

One can discern a basic structure and lexical stock common to the various vision reports in Zech 1:7–6:15 (see Table 1).[14] Each of the reports begins with an Introductory Observation Note (A.) which within Zechariah is rendered usually as a depiction of the personal cognition of the prophetic observer, most commonly employing the phrase ואשא את־עיני וארא (2:1a, 5a; 5:1a, 9a; 6:1a) but in two places ראיתי (1:8a; 4:2a).[15] In a few cases the Introductory Observation Note is initiated by someone other than the prophetic observer, with Yahweh showing the scene (ויראני) to the observer in 2:3 and 3:1, some heavenly figure asking the prophetic observer a question about the scene (ויאמר אלי מה אתה ראה ויאמר ראיתי/אני ראה) in 4:2 and 5:2, and finally the interpreting messenger commanding the prophetic observer to view the scene (שא נא עיניך וראה) in 5:5. Every type employs the verb ראה, but utilizes different verbal forms. Closely linked with the Introductory Observation Note is the Observation Report (B.) which immediately follows. In most cases this element is introduced by the phrase והנה (1:8; 2:1, 5; 4:2; 5:1, 7, 9; 6:1), although it is missing in 2:3, 3:1, and 5:2.

---

[13] The absence of Daniel in this analysis is due to the later genesis of the forms in this book.
[14] In a recent study, Martin Hallaschka, "Zechariah's Angels: Their Role in the Night Visions and in the Redaction History of Zech 1,7–6,8," *SJOT* 24 (2010): 13–27 (16) observes that all other visions in Zech 1:7–6:15 contain the pattern "seeing—asking—interpreting," except for Zech 3. This evidence, along with the fact that the interpreting angel is not mentioned and the fact that for him ch. 3 disturbs the original symmetry of the cycle (which he sees as concentric in shape), leads him to the conclusion that ch. 3 is a later addition to the vision-oracle section of Zech 1:7–6:15. There are some initial rebuttals to Hallaschka's observations. First, there is an assumption that a single "center" is key to concentricity in biblical texts. One could say that the removal of ch. 3 would disrupt the concentricity created by similarities between Zech 3 and 4 which together may constitute the "center" of the literary complex. Second, in terms of the pattern "seeing—asking—interpreting," one must admit that the "asking" element is different in 5:1–4 where it some other figure who asks the prophet rather than the prophet asking a question. Furthermore, this kind of general formal structure does not appear to be sensitive enough to capture the intricacies and diversities of form used within the broader visionary report tradition.
[15] ראיתי appears at two key points in the vision sequence: at the beginning (1:8) and at what seems to be (since the interpreting messenger returns to the prophetic observer and rouses him) the start of a second phase of the revelatory experience.

The second phase in Zechariah's vision reports comprises a question and response exchange between the prophetic observer and the heavenly being. Usually the query is related to the identification of elements in the scene using the phrase מה־אלה/היא (1:9; 2:2; 4:4, 11; 5:6; 6:4). In 2:6 and 5:10 the question is related to the identification of a destination of an element in the scene (אנה) while in 2:4 the question is related to a purpose of an element in the scene (מה אלה באים לעשות). No question appears in three cases (3:1–10; 5:1–4; 5:7–8). The syntax of the response which follows the question is determined by the type of query. Those questions seeking the identity of elements in the scene employ the demonstrative which ended the question (ויאמר [אלי] אלה/זאת; 1:10; 2:2, 4; 4:6a/10b, 14; 5:6; 6:5–6), while those questions seeking after a destination or purpose employ an infinitive (2:4, 6; 5:11). Interestingly the vocabulary associated with the heavenly response appears in 5:3 and 5:8, even though a question is not provided. In a couple of the visions extra material appears in the transition between the question and the response. In 1:9b the heavenly being declares his intention to show the prophetic observer the identity of the element queried (אני אראך מה־המה אלה), while in 4:5, 13 the heavenly being responds first by declaring ידעת מה(־המה) אלה(4:5a, 13a) to which the prophetic observer must respond לא אדני (4:5b, 13b).

Following this second phase, four (possibly five) of the vision reports provide a second phase of description of the scene (E.) without repeating the Introductory Observation Note/Observation Report, Question/Response elements (1:11–13; 2:7–8; 5:8b; 6:7; possibly 3:1–10).[16] Usually these further descriptions are related to additional dialogue and/or action that occurs.

In nearly every case the vision report is concluded (1:14–17; 2:9, 10–17; 3:7–10; 5:4; 6:8, 9–15) and in one case it is interrupted (4:6b–10a) by a Prophetic Oracle (F.) which is related to the visionary elements.

Although all elements are not always present, these basic elements are arranged in consistent sequence throughout the vision reports. The sequence may only occur once in a visionary report unit, such as in 1:8–17; 2:5–9 (+10–17) [Eng. 2:1–5 (+6–13)]; 3:1–10; and 6:1–8 (+9–15) or may be repeated either two (2:1–4 [Eng. 1:18–21]; 5:1–4) or even three times (5:5–11). It is informative that of the five cases where one finds "Further Description of Scene" (see above), four of them are classified as single linear sequences, suggesting that the single linear sequences are merely multiple linear sequences without the initial elements (Introductory Observation Note/ Observation Report, Question/ Response).

---

[16] It is possible that this element is what is found in Zech 3:2–6 after the Introductory Observation Note in 3:1a and the Observation Report in 3:1b.

Table 1. Visions in Zechariah 1:8–6:15

			1:8–17	2:1–4	2:5–17	3:1–10	4:1–14	5:1–4	5:5–11	6:1–15
A. Introductory Observation Note	1. Command prompting observation	שׂא נא עיניך וראה							5a	
	2. Question/answer prompting observation	ויאמר אלי מה אתה ראה / ואמר					1–2a	2a	5b	
	3. Autobiographical Depiction	ואראה ואנה / ואשׂא את־עיני	8a	1a	5a		2	1a		9a	1a
	4. Yahweh showed me	ויראני		3a		1a				
B. Observation Report	1. Introduced by behold	והנה	8b	1b	5b	1b	2b–3	1b		7	9b	1b–3
	2. No behold							2b			
C. Question From Observer concerning scene	1. To identify elements in scene ("what are these/is this?")	מה־אלה/מה (אתה)	9a	2a			4		6a	11	4
	2. To identify destination of action in scene ("where?")	אנה			6a					10	
	3. To identify purpose of elements in scene ("why?" or what are X coming to do?")	מה־אלה		4a							

		Hebrew										
X. Extra piece	1. Heavenly being response: intention to show observer	אן אראה מה / הנה אלה	9b									
	2. Heavenly being question: "do you not know?"	הן אליה / הנה(הדבר) / ידע					5a		13a			
	3. Observer response: "no"	לא ידע					5b		13b			
D. Response from heavenly being (answering C.)	1. Introduced by demonstrative (if C is "what?")	ויאמר (אלי) / זאת/אלה	10	2b	4bα			3	6b	8a	14	5–6
	2. Introduced by infinitive (if "where?" or "why?" question)				4bβ	6b	6a, 10b					11
E. Further description of scene			11–13		7–8					8b		7
F. Prophetic Oracle		כה אמר יהוה (צבאות) / הנה ימי באים / אלה/אלהם דבר־יהוה	14–17			9	6b–10a	4				8
						10–17	7–10					9–15

Table 2. Visions in Zechariah and Amos/Jeremiah			Zech 1:8–6:15	Amos 7			Amos 8	Jer 1			Jer 24	
A. Introductory Observation Note	1. Command prompting observation	ראה נא עיניך וראה	5:5									
	2. Question/answer prompting observation	מה אתה ראה / ואמר את מה אתה ראה				8a	ויאמר … מה אתה ראה (Amos 7:8; 8:2; Jer 24:3) מה אתה ראה … ויאמר מה אתה ראה אל ירמיהו (Jer 1:11, 13)		2a			3a
	3. Autobiographical Depiction	ראה	1:8a; 4:2b									
		ראה אתה עיני עד ראות	2:1a, 5a; 5:1a, 9a; 6:1a									
	4. Yahweh showed me	הראני	2:3a; 3:1a	1a		7a	1a	הראני יהוה (כה) (Amos 7:1, 4, 7; 8:1; Jer 24:1)				1b
B. Observation Report	1. Introduced by behold	הנה	1:8b; 2:1b, 5b; 4:2b; 5:1b; 5:7, 9b; 6:1b–3	1b 1c	4b	7b	1b		11a	13a	1c–2	
	2. No behold		2:3b; 3:1b; 5:2b				8b	2b	11b	13b		3b
C. Question from Observer concerning scene	1. To identify elements in scene ("what are these?")	מה אלה/הראה (אדני)	1:9a; 2:2a; 4:4, 11; 5:6a; 6:4									
	2. To identify destination of action in scene ("where?")	אנה	2:6a; 5:10									
	3. To identify purpose of elements in scene ("why?" or what are X coming to do?")	הראה	2:4a									

D. Response from heavenly being (answering C.)	1. Introduced by demonstrative (if C is "what?")	וַיֹּאמֶר (אֵל) זֹאת/אֵלֶּה	1:10; 2:2b, 4bα; 4:6a/10b, 14; 5:3, 6b, 8a; 6:5–6				
	2. Introduced by infinitive (if "where?" or "why?" question)		2:4bβ, 6b; 5:11				
E. Further description of scene			1:11–13; 2:7–8; 3:2–6; 5:8b; 6:7				
F. Prophetic Oracle		כה אמר יהוה (צבאות)	1:14–17; 2:9, 10–17; 3:7–10; 4:6b–10a; 5:4; 6:8, 9–15				
		נאם יהוה (צבאות)		8c–9	2c–3	12	14–19
		אל תיראו/אלכם הדברים					4–10
				נאם (אדני) יהוה (Amos 8:2; Jer 1:15, 19)			
				כה אמר (אדני) יהוה (Jer 24:5, 8)			
G. Prophetic Intercession					2b–3	5–6	

Table 3. Visions in Zechariah and Ezekiel

			Zech 1:8–6:15	Ezekiel					
				1	2	8	10	37	44
A. Introductory Observation Note	1. Command prompting observation	שָׂא נָא עֵינֶיךָ וּרְאֵה	5:5						
	2. Question/answer prompting observation	וַיֹּאמֶר אֵלַי מָה אַתָּה רֹאֶה / וַיֹּאמֶר אֶל ... הֲרֹאֶה אַתָּה	4:2a; 5:2a	וַיֹּאמֶר אֶל ... הֲרֹאֶה אַתָּה (8:6: "then he said to me ... do you see?") / וַיֹּאמֶר אֵלַי הֲרָאִיתָ (8:12, 15, 17: "then he said to me, did you see?")		5a			
	3. Autobiographical Depiction	וָאֶרְאֶה / וָאֶרְאֶה אֶת	1:8a; 4:2b; 2:1a, 5a; 5:1a, 9a; 6:1a			5b		8a	
	4. Yahweh showed me	וַיַּרְאֵנִי	2:3a; 3:1a	4a	9a	2	1a		4b
B. Observation Report	1. Introduced by behold	וְהִנֵּה	1:8b; 2:1b, 5b; 4:2b; 5:1b, 5:7, 9b; 6:1b–3	4b–14	15b–28	2–4	7b	9a	
	2. No behold		2:3b; 3:1b; 5:2b			5c	7c	10a	4c
C. Question from Observer concerning scene	1. To identify elements in scene ("what are these?")	מָה־אֵלֶּה/הָאֵלֶּה (אֲדֹנִי)	1:9a; 2:2a; 4:4, 11; 5:6a; 6:4				10b–11	8b	
	2. To identify destination of action in scene ("where?")	אָנָה	2:6a; 5:10				1b	9b–22	
	3. To identify purpose of elements in scene ("why? or what are X coming to do?")	מָה־אֵלֶּה	2:4a						

	1. Introduced by demonstrative (if C is "what?")	וָאֹמַר (אֶל) אֵלָה/זֹאת	1:10; 2:2b, 4bα; 4:6a/10b, 14; 5:3, 6b, 8a; 6:5–6			
D. Response from heavenly being (answering C.)	2. Introduced by infinitive (if "where?" or "why?" question)		2:4bβ, 6b; 5:11			
E. Further description of scene		כֹה אָמַר יְהוָה (צְבָאוֹת)	1:11–13; 2:7–8; 3:2–6; 5:8b; 6:7			
F. Prophetic Oracle		נְאֻם יְהוָה (צְבָאוֹת) הִנְנִי עֹשֶׂה/מֵבִיא בְּיַד יְהוָה צְבָאוֹת דִּבֶּר־יְהוָה אֶל	1:14–17; 2:9, 10–17; 3:7–10; 4:6b–10a; 5:4; 6:8, 9–15	Imperative Instructions/fulfillment (2:1–2; 3:1-11; 8:8–9; 37:9–10; 44:5–31)		
G. Prophetic Intercession						

This evidence highlights a tension between form and rhetoric. On the one side one can discern a general sequence that is followed throughout the vision reports, but on the other there is clear evidence of flexibility and creativity. Before analyzing the rhetorical significance of the use of this form in Zech 1:7–6:15 we need to look at the broader vision report tradition within the Hebrew Bible to see if some of the flexibility and creativity can be attributed to the form tradition itself or if this is a rhetorical strategy for those responsible for the Zecharian tradition.

ZECHARIAH'S VISION REPORTS AMONG VISIONARY LITERATURE IN THE HEBREW BIBLE

Prophetic Visionary Reports are not unique to the book of Zechariah, and in the review of scholarship on visionary materials in the Hebrew Bible passages from the books of Amos, Jeremiah, and Ezekiel were regularly cited.[17] Even with only a cursory glance at these various corpora one can discern two distinct streams, one found in Amos and Jeremiah and the other in Ezekiel.

AMOS AND JEREMIAH

Prophetic Visionary Reports occur six times in the books of Amos and Jeremiah (see Table 2).[18] Each of them employs an Introductory Observation Note (A.), all of them initiated by the heavenly figure Yahweh. Amos 7:1, 4, 7; 8:1; and Jer 24:1 use the *hiphil* of ראה (cf. Zech 2:3; 3:1) while Amos 7:8; 8:2; Jer 1:11, 13; and 24:3 have the heavenly figure Yahweh prompt observation by asking the question מה־אתה ראה, the answer to which is introduced always by ואמר, in two cases followed by אני ראה in Jer 1:11 and 13 (cf. 4:2a; 5:2a). As expected the Introductory Observation Note is always followed by an Observation Report (B.), with only Amos 7:1, 4, 7; 8:1; and Jer 24:1–2 introducing the report with והנה (contrast Amos 7:8; 8:2; Jer 1:11, 13; 24:3). A Prophetic Oracle (F.) ends the sequence in Amos 7:8–9; 8:2–3; Jer 1:12, 14–19; 24:4–10, while Amos 7:2–3 and 7:5–6 end with an intercessory dialogue between the prophet and Yahweh (G.).

---

[17] One other vision type appears in Isa 6 and 1 Kgs 22, which are Reports of a Vision in the Divine Court. These do employ a form of the verb ראה at the outset, as found in the visionary traditions traced in the present work, but contain few other connections.

[18] See also Jer 4:23–28 and 38:21–23 where utilization of the introductory elements of the Visionary Report can be discerned. Thus Jer 4:23–28 employs ראיתי ... והנה four times in a row and then provides a prophetic oracle introduced by כי־כה אמר יהוה. Jeremiah 38:20–23 employs הראני יהוה ... והנה, but no prophetic oracle follows. The second example is simply using elements of the Visionary Report form without any visionary elements. The first example is closer to the visionary tradition in our focus, but instead of focuses on a symbolic object, it focuses on future cosmic conditions which reverse creation.

EZEKIEL

Prophetic Visionary Reports can also be found in Ezekiel (see Table 3), but the style and form is distinct from that found in Amos and Jeremiah. The Introductory Observation Note (A.) is without except a depiction of the personal cognition of the prophetic observer, nearly always employing the form וארא (1:4a, 15a; 2:9a; 8:2, 7b, 10a; 10:1a, 9a; 44:4b), but in one case the phrase ואשא את־עיני (8:5b) and in another ראיתי (37:8a). Alongside the personal cognition of the prophetic observer in chapter 8, one finds the form of Introductory Observation Note which employs a question (ויאמר אלי הראית, 8:6, 12, 15, 17), but unlike Amos, Jeremiah, and Zechariah, this is merely a rhetorical question to which there is no reply from the prophetic observer.[19] Also without exception, the Introductory Observation Note is followed by an Observation Report containing והנה (B.).[20] In Amos and Jeremiah the Visionary Report climaxes with the provision of a prophetic oracle, but in Ezekiel with imperative instructions to the prophet by the heavenly figure (F.) followed by a depiction of the fulfillment of the instruction (2:1–2; 3:1–11; 8:8–9; 37:9–10; 44:5–31). As with Amos and Jeremiah, Yahweh is normally the heavenly figure leading and interacting with the prophetic observer, but other figures also emerge at certain points, in particular in chapters 8–10 (cf. Ezek 9:2–4, 11; 10:2, 6, 7)[21] and chapters 40–48 (cf. 40:4, 17; 42:13, 15).

---

[19] Notice also Ezek 37:3 where the question "can these bones live?" is answered by the prophet with "O Yahweh God, you know." There appears to be little room for dialogue between heavenly and earthly figures in Ezekiel.

[20] In contrast to Amos and Jeremiah as well as Zechariah, in Ezekiel והנה may be preceded by verbs describing the movement of the prophet either initiated by himself (3:23; 47:7) or God (8:14, 16; 37:1–2; 40:3, 17, 24; 43:5; 46:19, 21; 47:1, 2). In addition, while Amos, Jeremiah, and Zechariah focus on "seeing," Ezekiel speaks also of "hearing" (שמע, 1:24, 28; 2:2; 3:12) and "knowing" (ידע, 10:20) in relation to visionary experiences; cf. D. Nathan Phinney, "Life Writing in Ezekiel and First Zechariah," in *Tradition in Transition: Haggai and Zechariah 1–8 in the Trajectory of Hebrew Theology*, ed. Mark J. Boda and Michael H. Floyd, LHBOTS 475 (London: T&T Clark, 2008), 83–103, and D. Nathan Phinney, "Portraying Prophetic Experience and Tradition in Ezekiel," in *Thus Says the Lord: Essays on the Former and Latter Prophets in Honor of Robert R. Wilson*, ed. John J. Ahn and Stephen L. Cook, LHBOTS 502 (New York: T&T Clark, 2009), 234–43.

[21] There has been some debate over the identity of the "man" in 8:2, whether a secondary heavenly being or Yahweh. For the first opinion, see Walther Zimmerli, *Ezekiel: A Commentary on the Book of the Prophet Ezekiel*, Hermeneia (Philadelphia: Fortress, 1979), 1:236. For the second opinion, see Daniel I. Block, *The Book of Ezekiel: Chapters 1–24*, NICOT (Grand Rapids: Eerdmans, 1997), 279–80, and David L. Thompson, "Ezekiel," in *Ezekiel, Daniel*, ed. David L. Thompson and Eugene E. Carpenter, Cornerstone Biblical Commentary (Carol Stream, IL: Tyndale House, 2010), 1–284 (79). For priestly aspects of the figure in chs. 9–10, see Margaret S. Odell, *Ezekiel*, SHBC (Macon, GA: Smyth &

Comparing Earlier Visionary Traditions with Zechariah

Taking the structure of the vision reports in Zechariah as our guide, one can discern points of contact and contrast between these earlier prophetic visionary traditions and Zech 1:7–6:15. It is in the contrast that one can discern some of the key rhetorical power of Zechariah's visionary reports.

1. Introductory Observation Note (A.) and Observation Report (B.)

Common to all these visionary traditions are elements A. and B., the Introductory Observation Note and the Observation Report. Amos and Jeremiah use a simple construction for element A., employing only the verb ראה, whether in the *hiphil* or *qal*. Ezekiel follows this trend in its use of ראה. While employing the phrase "I lifted up my eyes" on one occasion (Ezek 8:5b), Ezekiel never combines it with ראה as in Zechariah.

This simpler construction is common throughout accounts of revelatory experiences throughout the Hebrew Bible. In many cases the *hiphil* of ראה is employed (Exod 25:9; 27:8; 33:18; Num 8:4; Num 23:3; 2 Kgs 8:13; Jer 24:1; 38:21; Ezek 11:25; 40:4; Hab 1:3; cf. Exod 25:40; 26:30). Notable are the deity visions of 1 Kgs 22:19 // 2 Chr 18:18; Amos 9:1; and Isa 6:1.

Various forms of the simpler construction do occur in Zechariah, but more common is the complex phrase which combines the collocation נשא with עין (lift up the eye) with the verb ראה. This more complicated style can be discerned throughout the Hebrew Bible in scenes describing a person who is either observing or inviting a person to observe a non-revelatory scene. In these passages these verbs may be followed by the particle הנה (e.g., Gen 24:63; 33:1, 5; 37:25; 2 Sam 13:34; 18:24), or not (Gen 13:14; 22:4; 24:64; 43:29; Num 24:2; Deut 3:27; 4:19; Judg 19:17; 1 Sam 6:13; Isa 40:26; 49:18; 60:4; Jer 3:2; 13:20). In a few cases this more complicated style does occur in revelatory scenes or in scenes where a human encounters a heavenly being, whether that is Jacob's dream encounter in Gen 31:11–13,[22] David's encounter with the threatening messenger of Yahweh in 1 Chr 21:16, Abraham's encounter with Yahweh and his two messengers in Gen 18:2, or Joshua's encounter with the captain of Yahweh's host in Josh 5:13.[23]

Helwys, 2006), 117. Zimmerli, *Ezekiel*, 1:246, and Steven Shawn Tuell, *Ezekiel*, NIBCOT 15 (Peabody, MA: Hendrickson; Milton Keynes, UK: Paternoster, 2009), 53, note his heavenly origins. Block, *The Book of Ezekiel: Chapters 1–24*, 304, notes both, but favors the latter.

[22] Tollington, *Tradition*, 97–99; Michael R. Stead, *The Intertextuality of Zechariah 1–8*, LHBOTS 506 (London: T&T Clark, 2009), 89, see Gen 31:11–13 as the source of this collocation in Zechariah.

[23] Notice also Gen 22:11–13 where Abraham sees the ram announced by Yahweh's messenger. The more complex style may be discerned in 2 Kgs 6:17 where Elisha prays

What is the rhetorical effect of Zechariah's use of the complex autobiographical Introductory Observation Note? It shifts rhetorical focus onto the experience of the prophetic observer.[24] The form of Introductory Observation Note used in Jeremiah and Amos focuses the attention at the outset on the heavenly figure who prompts the revelatory experience.[25] In Ezekiel and Zechariah it is the prophetic observer who initiates the sequence, highlighting the importance of the one receiving revelation. The use of the complex form of the Introductory Observation Note in Zechariah expands this rhetorical focus even further.

2. Question from Observer Concerning the Scene (C.) and Response from Heavenly Being (D.)

The key differences between the vision reports in Zechariah and those found in Amos, Jeremiah, and Ezekiel appear in the rhetorical space between the Introductory Observation Note and Observation Note (A. and B.) and the concluding Prophetic Oracle/Intercession (F. and G.).[26]

The addition of the two elements, Question from Observer Concerning Scene (C.) and Response from Heavenly Being (D.), is a unique feature in the Zechariah visionary tradition. This can possibly be linked to the near absence in Zechariah of the Introductory Observation Note type which employed a question/answer exchange (מה אתה ראה ... אני ראה) that only appears in Zech 4:2a; 5:2a. In Zechariah the questions arise from the prophetic figure, again rhetorically shifting the focus from the heavenly figure towards the prophetic observer.[27]

---

for his servant's eyes to be opened (פתח עין) and he saw (*waw*/relative prefix conjugation of ראה). The content of the servant's revelatory experience is introduced with the particle והנה.

[24] On connections between Zechariah and Ezekiel in terms of their autobiographical style, see Phinney, "Life Writing."

[25] Notice how the heavenly figure in Jeremiah and Amos is always Yahweh, but in Zechariah (and Ezekiel) there is a distinct shift away from Yahweh (who only functions in 2:3 and possibly 3:1) to other heavenly beings.

[26] See Niditch, *Symbolic Vision*, 173, for the expansionary trends in what she calls Zechariah visions stage II.

[27] Possibly another indication of this shift in focus to the prophetic observer is in the greater role played by the prophetic observer in Zech 3:5 where the observer initiates an action in the scene. A greater role can be seen for the observer in Ezekiel (e.g., Ezek 1:28; 2:1–8; 3:1–2), as opposed to Amos and Jeremiah, although the intercessory pieces which conclude the reports in Amos 7:1–3, 4–6 may be akin to this. On the shift in the role of messengers in such visions, see Tollington, *Tradition*, 97–99, Finitsis, *Visions and Eschatology*, 102–3 n. 3, and Karin Schöpflin, "God's Interpreter: The Interpreting Angel in Post-Exilic Prophetic Visions of the Old Testament," in *Angels: The Concept of Celestial Beings— Origins, Development and Reception*, ed. Friedrich V. Reiterer, Tobias Nicklas, and Karin

Interestingly it is within the Question/Response elements that one finds what I have identified as expansionistic elements (X. Extra Piece).²⁸ All three of the examples (1:9b; 4:5, 13) employ the phrase אלה (מה־)(המה), identical to those words which comprise the question from the prophetic observer. In each case, however, these words appear on the lips of the heavenly being. In the first case in 1:9b by using the unnecessary personal pronoun (אני אראך מה־המה אלה) the emphasis is placed on the role of the heavenly being in interpreting the vision. In the second cases in chapter 4, the heavenly being appears to be depicted as challenging the revelatory capacity of the prophetic observer (הלוא ידעת מה־המה אלה), a question which demands and receives a simple negative reply followed by an acknowledgement of superiority (לא אדני). The fact that in chapter 4 this sequence occurs twice increases this rhetorical effect even further. While 1:9b appears to draw attention to the necessity of the heavenly messenger to provide insight into the revelation, 4:5, 13 seem to accentuate the incompetence of the prophetic observer to gain insight into the revelation.²⁹

On the one hand, then, it appears that the Zecharian visionary tradition brings greater emphasis on the ability of the prophetic observer, as one who takes a greater role in initiating the revelatory experience and also in initiating the revelatory interpretation. However, on the other hand, there appears to be even greater emphasis on the exclusive right of heavenly beings to interpret the visionary scene.

3. Further Description of Scene (E.)

The Zecharian vision reports also stand apart from the earlier visionary traditions by elongating the observation report through the provision of further description at a later point after the initial question/response exchange (1:11–13; 2:7–8; 3:2–6; 5:8b; 6:7). This feature makes the visionary scene more complex and gives even further voice to the prophetic observer at least as he depicts the scene. In the earlier visionary traditions, the Observation Report is followed immediately by the Divine Oracular material, placing all the rhetorical focus on the word from God. The purpose of the visionary scene is thus the divine proclamation. The Zecharian tradition, however, by providing further description of the scene after

---

Schöpflin, *Deuterocanonical and Cognate Literature Yearbook 2007* (Berlin: de Gruyter, 2007), 189–203 (197). See now David P. Melvin, *The Interpreting Angel Motif in Prophetic and Apocalyptic Literature*, Emerging Scholars (Minneapolis: Fortress, 2013).

²⁸ This is not a diachronic description, but a statement based on the most common rhetorical structure of the vision reports in Zechariah.

²⁹ My approach contrasts with that of Lena-Sofia Tiemeyer, "Through a Glass Darkly: Zechariah's Unprocessed Visionary Experience," *VT* 58 (2008): 573–94 (581), who treats these features as indicating that the vision reports were "unprocessed" and thus somehow deficient or at least lacking in sophistication.

the initial identification of elements and further description that is often important for the climactic divine oracle, shifts greater rhetorical emphasis onto the visionary scene itself rather than focusing exclusively on the divine oracle. This is an important shift as it highlights that the visionary scene is not just a symbolic introduction to a divine oracle, but appears actually to be essential to the enactment and realization of what is contained in the divine oracle. Thus, the interchange between the messenger of Yahweh and the horse teams in 1:11 followed by the interchange between the messenger of Yahweh, the interpreting messenger, and Yahweh in 1:12–13 is key to setting up the divine oracles in 1:14–17. The interchange between the messengers in 2:7–8 lays the foundation for the concluding oracle in 2:9. The description in 5:8b sets up the action that follows through which this wicked idol will be removed from the land. The further description in 6:7 highlights the action of the chariot teams whose patrol actually made the venting of Yahweh's wrath a reality (6:8). Whereas in the earlier visionary traditions the basic scene at the outset is what sets up the oracular piece, in Zechariah's visionary material the initial scene is often only introductory and the prophetic observer must linger and watch for further elements which actually are key to the accomplishment of the concluding oracle.

Thus, God's promises in the concluding heavenly speeches are made possible by the work of the heavenly messengers described in these pieces of further description, whether it is the intercession of the messenger of Yahweh in 1:11–13, the engineering guidance of the messenger in 2:3–4, the violent action of the interpreting messenger in 5:8b, or the military maneuvers of the chariot teams in 6:7. This suggests that the visionary materials are now not as much treated as symbolic as they are enacting something within the realm between heaven and earth which facilitates the divine word that follows. This brings greater rhetorical focus onto the visionary scene and its actions and dialogues than in earlier traditions.

Conclusion

The Vision Reports throughout Zech 1:7–6:15 show clear indebtedness to a form tradition well attested in the prophetic corpus of the Hebrew Bible. The one(s) responsible for Zech 1:7–6:15, however, have not been constrained by this earlier tradition, but have introduced innovative elements which relay visionary experiences to a written audience in unique ways. Even among the vision reports of Zechariah one can discern significant variation, revealing the rhetorical creativity of prophetic literature. Such innovation is motivated by rhetorical intention as the one(s) responsible for Zech 1:7–6:15 communicate to a new audience. Through Zech 1:7–6:15 one can discern a greater focus on the prophetic observer as recipient of revelation and on the heavenly figure as an interpreter of revelation and a greater focus on the visionary scene as an enactment of the divine agenda revealed through the prophetic message.

6
Zechariah: Master Mason or Penitential Prophet?[1]

While the chapters to this point have focused on the internal core of Zech 1–8, with this chapter I shift my attention to the prose sermon bracket around this inner core: Zech 1:1–6; 7:1–8:23. In this chapter I highlight the impact of both the earlier penitential prayer and Deuteronomic-Jeremianic traditions on this inclusio.

There is little doubt that the community that emerged in the early Persian Period in the province of Yehud was faced with the task of the reformulation of their world amidst questions of identity. One key component in the various responses to these new circumstances was the rebuilding of the temple structure with its attendant cultic ceremonies, a component well attested in two significant narrative rehearsals from the Persian Period, Ezra 1–6 and the books of Chronicles. There the building of the temple forms a strong link to the past while signaling the beginning of the new age of renewal.[2]

---

[1] Based on my original publication, Mark J. Boda, "Zechariah: Master Mason or Penitential Prophet?" in *Yahwism after the Exile: Perspectives on Israelite Religion in the Persian Era*, ed. Bob Becking and Rainer Albertz, Studies in Theology and Religion 5 (Assen: Van Gorcum, 2003), 49–69. Revised for inclusion in this volume. While I do now embrace a Haggai–Zech 1–8 early collection, enduring is my concern that the theme of temple rebuilding in Haggai should not overshadow the broader themes in Zech 1–8, but rather the reverse.

[2] For the importance of the temple for the Chronicler(s) see R. J. Coggins, *The First and Second Books of the Chronicles*, CBC (Cambridge: Cambridge University Press, 1976), 6–7; H. G. M. Williamson, *1 and 2 Chronicles*, NCB (Grand Rapids: Eerdmans, 1982), 28–

To many, the prophets Haggai and Zechariah echo the priority of temple restoration established in Ezra 1–6 and Chronicles.[3] Ezra 5–6 clearly presents these two figures as a prophetic tag team championing the temple restoration cause (Ezra 5:1–3; 6:14). Taken on its own terms, the book of Haggai resonates with this presentation, revealing the fixation of the prophet and his narrator with the rebuilding project. At several points Zechariah exhibits a similar interest in the restoration of the temple structure (Zech 1:16; 4:6b–10a; 6:9–15; 8:9–13), evidence that has led to the assumption that the prophet Zechariah shares with Ezra, Chronicles and Haggai the central concern of temple rebuilding.

This link to the temple restoration agenda has been bolstered by arguments for the redactional unity of the books of Haggai and Zech 1–8.[4] This unity has been based not only on the similar historical setting (Persian Period Yehud) with related characters (Joshua, Zerubbabel, remnant), but more importantly on the utilization of similar superscriptions (both date and messenger formulae). For some,

---

31; Roddy L. Braun, *1 Chronicles*, WBC 14 (Waco, TX: Word, 1986), xxix–xxxi; and especially Roddy L. Braun, "Message of Chronicles: Rally 'Round the Temple," *CTM* 42 (1971): 502–14; Sara Japhet, *I and II Chronicles: A Commentary*, OTL (Louisville: Westminster John Knox, 1993), 45; J. A. Thompson, *1, 2 Chronicles*, NAC 9 (Nashville: Broadman & Holman, 1994), 35–36; for Ezra 1–6 see Coggins, *Chronicles*, 6; H. G. M. Williamson, *Ezra, Nehemiah*, WBC (Waco, TX: Word, 1985), xlix; Joseph Blenkinsopp, *Ezra–Nehemiah: A Commentary*, OTL (Philadelphia: Westminster, 1988), 53–54; Tamara Cohn Eskenazi, *In an Age of Prose: A Literary Approach to Ezra–Nehemiah*, SBLMS 36 (Atlanta: Scholars Press, 1988).

[3] On the intimate connection between the Chronicler(s) and Haggai–Zech 1–8 see Wim A. M. Beuken, *Haggai–Sacharja 1–8: Studien zur Überlieferungsgeschichte der frühnachexilischen Prophetie*, SSN 10 (Assen: Van Gorcum, 1967); Peter R. Ackroyd, "Studies in the Book of Haggai (Part One)," *JJS* 2 (1951): 163–76; Peter R. Ackroyd, "Studies in the Book of Haggai (Part Two)," *JJS* 3 (1952): 1–13. Although Mason opposes Beuken, he still places those responsible for Haggai–Zech 1–8 in the same circles which ultimately produced the books of Chronicles. Cf. Rex A. Mason, *The Books of Haggai, Zechariah and Malachi*, CBC (Cambridge: Cambridge University Press, 1977), 9–10; Rex A. Mason, *Preaching the Tradition: Homily and Hermeneutics after the Exile* (Cambridge: Cambridge University Press, 1990), 195.

[4] There is little need today to highlight discontinuity between Zech 1–8 and 9–14. The initial eight chapters use a date formula followed by the messenger formula, "the word of the Lord came to Zechariah" (היה דבר־יהוה אל־זכריה), to create a tripartite structure (see 1:1, 7; 7:1), whereas the final six chapters utilize the simple editorial marker: "An oracle. The word of the Lord..." (משא דבר־יהוה) to create a bipartite structure (see 9:1; 12:1). Additionally, the character of Zechariah, so essential to both the narrative sections and the prophetic messages in the first part, is absent in the second part. Finally, although the genres in the first part are quite diverse (prose sermons, visions, oracles, narrative), the second section utilizes a mixture of prose sermon and prophetic poetry. See now, however, my view on cohesion in *Exploring Zechariah*, volume 1, chapter 1.

Zechariah: Master Mason or Penitential Prophet? 103

this demonstrates only that the same hand was at work on two distinct works (Haggai, Zech 1–8), while for an increasing number Haggai–Zech 1–8 was a unified piece of literature at an early stage.[5]

The purpose of this chapter is to challenge this reigning consensus in the study of Zech 1–8 and to propose that this corpus in its final form transcends the agenda of temple rebuilding by accentuating the ethical agenda of two key exilic traditions: the literary tradition of the prophet Jeremiah and the oral tradition of penitential prayer both of which developed in response to the fall of Jerusalem. In this way Zech 1–8 reformulates the world of the Jewish community and addresses the question of identity in a way which supplements and transcends the message of Haggai.

---

[5] See especially, Beuken, *Haggai–Sacharja 1–8*, 10–20, 331–36; Ackroyd, "Studies 2," 152; Peter R. Ackroyd, *Exile and Restoration: A Study of Hebrew Thought of the Sixth Century B.C.*, OTL (Philadelphia: Westminster, 1968), 154; Paul D. Hanson, "Zechariah, Book of," in *IDBSup* 982–83; Paul L. Redditt, "Zerubbabel, Joshua, and the Night Visions of Zechariah," *CBQ* 54 (1992): 249–59; Paul L. Redditt, *Haggai, Zechariah and Malachi*, NCB (London: Marshall Pickering, 1995), 42–43; Rex A. Mason, "The Purpose of the 'Editorial Framework' of the Book of Haggai," *VT* 27 (1977): 413–21; Mason, *Haggai*, 10–11, 29; Carol L. Meyers and Eric M. Meyers, *Haggai, Zechariah 1–8: A New Translation with Introduction and Commentary*, AB 25B (Garden City, NY: Doubleday, 1987), xliv–lxiii; Janet E. Tollington, *Tradition and Innovation in Haggai and Zechariah 1–8*, JSOTSup 150 (Sheffield: JSOT Press, 1993), 47, 247. In recent years there has been a veritable explosion of studies on the redaction of the Book of the Twelve in which a Haggai–Zech 1–8 or Haggai–Zechariah–Malachi collection is assumed to have existed prior to its incorporation into the Book of the Twelve. See especially James D. Nogalski, *Literary Precursors to the Book of the Twelve*, BZAW 217 (Berlin: de Gruyter, 1993); James D. Nogalski, *Redactional Processes in the Book of the Twelve*, BZAW 218 (Berlin: de Gruyter, 1993); James W. Watts and Paul R. House, eds., *Forming Prophetic Literature: Essays on Isaiah and the Twelve in Honor of John D.W. Watts*, JSOTSup 235 (Sheffield: Sheffield Academic, 1996); Erich Bosshard-Nepustil, *Rezeptionen von Jesaja 1–39 im Zwölfprophetenbuch: Untersuchungen zur literarischen Verbindung von Prophetenbüchern in babylonischer und persischer Zeit*, OBO 154 (Göttingen: Vandenhoeck & Ruprecht, 1997); Burkard M. Zapff, *Redaktionsgeschichtliche Studien zum Michabuch im Kontext des Dodekapropheton*, BZAW 256 (Berlin: de Gruyter, 1997); Aaron Schart, "Redactional Models: Comparisons, Contrasts, Agreements, Disagreements," in *Society of Biblical Literature 1998 Seminar Papers Part Two*, SBLSP 37 (Atlanta: Scholars Press, 1998), 893–908; Aaron Schart, *Die Entstehung des Zwölfprophetenbuchs*, BZAW 260 (Berlin: de Gruyter, 1998) and the earlier arguments of Ronald W. Pierce, "Literary Connectors and a Haggai–Zechariah–Malachi Corpus," *JETS* 27 (1984): 277–89; Ronald W. Pierce, "A Thematic Development of the Haggai–Zechariah–Malachi Corpus," *JETS* 27 (1984): 401–11.

CONTINUITY AND DISCONTINUITY BETWEEN HAGGAI 1–2 AND ZECHARIAH 1–8

Zechariah 1–8 indeed shares several emphases in common with Haggai.[6] Both speak of the physical restoration of Judah, emphasize the important role that leadership will play in this restoration, and trace the cosmic impact of restoration. However, there are also clear differences.[7] Haggai speaks of the nations in connection with the rebuilding of the temple, but presents them in largely negative light as those who will be defeated by a great work of God (Hag 2:6–9; 2:21–22). Likewise, Zechariah proclaims a message of doom for the nations who oppressed the Jews (1:15; 2:4; 2:10–17). However, he contrasts this punishment with an inclusive view of the nations who will be incorporated into the covenant people of God (2:15; 8:20–23).

The most striking difference between the two corpora is revealed when considering the issue of the rebuilding the temple.[8] Each of the pericopae in Haggai is connected to the rebuilding project in some fashion and every other topic is introduced in service of this larger theme.[9] In Zechariah, however, we find a radically different situation. Although the rebuilding project can be discerned at several junctures in the book, it is not the main focus of the prophet's message.[10] Zechariah expands restoration beyond a rebuilt temple (1:16; 2:5; 4:6–10a; 6:15)

---

[6] They also appear to have shared the prophetic stage at the refoundation of the temple. Compare Hag 2:10–23 and Zech 8:9–13.

[7] Mason notes some differences, but then stresses: "the parallels between the two are more striking than the differences," Rex A. Mason, "Prophets of the Restoration," in *Israel's Prophetic Tradition: Essays in Honour of Peter Ackroyd*, ed. Richard Coggins, Anthony Phillips, and Michael Knibb (Cambridge: Cambridge University Press, 1982), 137–54 (146).

[8] In this I differ from Tollington for whom Haggai–Zech 1–8 is concerned with reconstruction and leadership but not ethical issues: "Unlike the major pre-exilic prophets, neither Haggai nor Zechariah focused attention on the ethical standards of their society" (Tollington, *Tradition*, 77). This does not do justice to the message of Zech 5:1–4; 7:8–10; 8:16–17.

[9] See Mark J. Boda, *Haggai/Zechariah*, NIVAC (Grand Rapids: Zondervan, 2004); Mark J. Boda, "From Dystopia to Myopia: Utopian (Re)Visions in Haggai and Zechariah 1–8," in *Utopia and Dystopia in Prophetic Literature*, ed. Ehud Ben Zvi, Publications of the Finnish Exegetical Society 92 (Helsinki: Finnish Exegetical Society; Göttingen: Vandenhoeck & Ruprecht, 2006), 211–49.

[10] Halpern's attempt to place each of the night visions into a temple rebuilding mold, although helpful at points, appears forced especially in Zech 5. He wisely does not extend his work to Zech 1:1–6 or 7:1–8:23; cf. Baruch Halpern, "The Ritual Background of Zechariah's Temple Song," *CBQ* 40 (1978): 167–90; Mason, "Prophets," 146; and Klaus Seybold, *Bilder zum Tempelbau: Die Visionen des Propheten Sacharja* (Stuttgart: KBW, 1974).

to include a renewed city and province (1:14, 16, 17, 2:2–5; 8:1–7) and moves beyond physical issues to consider the socio-religious rhythms necessary for life with a new temple and city.[11] This explains the greater emphasis on leadership at the center of the night vision series (Zech 4) as well as in the secondary redaction levels (Zech 3:1–10; 6:9–15). This explains the encouragement for the exilic community to return and participate in the life of Yehud (2:10–17; 6:9–15). It also explains how sin is distanced from the rebuilding project and expressed in religio-ethical terms.

Most of the evidence so far has been drawn from the central series of night visions with accompanying oracles (1:7–6:15). However, the greatest obstacles to the theory of a unified Haggai–Zech 1–8 corpus defined only in terms of the temple rebuilding project are the two prose sections which begin and end Zech 1–8 (1:1–6; 7:1–8:23). These two sections, so influential in the reading of the final form of Zech 1–8, are nearly silent on the rebuilding project.

A quick review of the Meyers's interpretation of these two prose sections reveals the inadequacy of the argument for a Haggai–Zech 1–8 corpus unified around the theme of the temple rebuilding project. When considering Zech 1:1–6 they admit that the reference to "evil ways" and "evil deeds" in 1:4 refers to Jeremiah's indictments of injustice, oppression, theft, murder, adultery and idolatry.[12] However, because of their belief that the entire night vision series concerns the rebuilding project and that Zechariah is attested in the book of Ezra as a prophet concerned with temple rebuilding, they conclude that Zechariah is attacking the failure of the people to restore the temple structure,[13] even though there is no mention in the prose section of the temple project. When they interpret Zech 7:1–8:23 they cannot ignore the shift away from the rebuilding project in the message, a shift which is explained by appeal to the changed historical circumstances.[14]

The preceding discussion argues that the focus assumed by the Meyers and others for the redaction of a combined Haggai–Zech 1–8 (that is, temple rebuilding) does not do justice to the entire night vision section (1:7–6:15), let alone the prose sections (1:1–6; 7:1–8:23). This raises serious questions about the validity of this approach. The content of Zech 1–8 cannot be explained solely by reference

---

[11] See the Meyers who attack Rignell and Rudolph for interpreting Zechariah "on a much broader level" by arguing that this "does not do justice to the object that has inspired them, namely the temple," but then admit that 1:1–6 and 7:1–8:23 broaden the message "elaborating and interpreting themes of the visions in a more universalistic language," Meyers and Meyers, *Haggai, Zechariah 1–8*, lxxi.

[12] Ibid., 95.

[13] Ibid., 96.

[14] Ibid., 390. In their minds the focus of Zech 7–8 is on "an authoritative legal system."

to the rebuilding of the Second Temple and thus this theme should not be used as the main thrust for Zechariah or the unified collection of Haggai and Zech 1–8.

If Zech 1–8 does not rely entirely on the rebuilding project to provide the new identity needed by this community, on what then does it depend? A closer look at the prose inclusio of Zech 1:1–6 and 7:1–8:23 will intimate connections to two key exilic traditions: the Jeremianic prophetic tradition and the Penitential prayer tradition. These connections emphasize that Zechariah was viewed not merely as a prophetic voice encouraging the rebuilding of the physical temple, but more importantly as a penitential prophet calling for ethical renewal among the people.

ZECHARIAH'S PROSE SERMONS, THE MESSAGE OF THE PROPHETS, THE RESPONSE OF THE FATHERS, AND THE DISCIPLINE OF GOD

In nearly every redactional theory, the final shaping of the prose sections in Zech 1:1–6 and 7:1–8:23 is attributed to the same source (either Zechariah himself or his disciples) and plays an influential role in the final audience's understanding of the night visions.[15] These two sections share a similar rhetorical pattern. After a short message of challenge to the present generation (1:3; 7:5–6), they both launch into a review of the message of the "earlier prophets" (1:4a; 7:7–10) before describing the response of the "fathers" (1:4b; 7:11–12b) and finally the resultant discipline from God (1:5–6a; 7:12c–14; 8:14). Not only are these two sections similar in vocabulary and style,[16] but, as we shall soon see, they appear to be drawing from the same sources.

THE MESSAGE OF THE PROPHETS

Both prose sermons in Zechariah accentuate what is identified as the message of the הנביאים הראשנים (1:4; 7:7, 12). Zechariah 7:7, 12 speak of the agency of these prophets by employing the phrase: ביד הנביאים (7:7, 12). The use of this construction when speaking of the prophet as an instrument of warning to earlier

---

[15] Zechariah 1:1–6 does not have a complicated redactional history as it takes up a prophetic sermon of Zechariah and casts it into a narrative context. However, Zech 7:1–8:23 is more complex. David J. Clark, "Discourse Structure in Zechariah 7:1–8:23," *BT* 36 (1985): 328–35 argues for a literary unity, but glosses over clear differences between the various prophetic introductory formulae (7:1, 4, 8; 8:1, 18). It appears that 8:1–13 consists of at least two prophetic oracles which have been inserted into a prophetic narrative account which consisted of 7:1–14 + 8:14–22 (or –23). See Mark J. Boda, *The Book of Zechariah*, NICOT (Grand Rapids: Eerdmans, 2016), 469–74, and *Exploring Zechariah*, volume 1, chapter 3.

[16] For lexical and thematic connections see Tollington, *Tradition*, 208–9 and Meyers and Meyers, *Haggai, Zechariah 1–8*, l–lv.

generations is well-attested in Deuteronomic literature (1 Kgs 14:18; 16:7, 12; 2 Kgs 14:25; 17:13a, 13b, 23; 21:10; 24:2; Jer 37:2; 50:1; cf. Hos 12:11; Ezek 38:17; 2 Chr 10:15; 29:25). In addition, the reference to the prophets as עבדי הנביאים (Zech 1:6a) is a Dtr expression found throughout Jeremiah (Jer 7:25; 25:4; 26:5; 29:19; 35:15; 44:4; cf. 2 Kgs 9:7; 17:13, 23; 21:10; 25:2).[17]

The message itself comprises a short anthology of imperatives reflecting the message of Jeremiah, introduced by the messenger formula: כה אמר יהוה צבאות (Zech 1:4; 7:9). In Zech 1:4 the prophet draws on the idiom found in the Dtr prose of Jeremiah (Jer 18:11; 23:22; 25:5; 35:15).[18] In doing this Zechariah

---

[17] See Lawrence A. Sinclair, "Redaction of Zechariah 1–8," *BR* 20 (1975): 36–47 (43); Moshe Weinfeld, *Deuteronomy and the Deuteronomic School* (Oxford: Clarendon, 1972), 351; Tollington, *Tradition*, 206–7; Mark J. Boda, *Praying the Tradition: The Origin and Use of Tradition in Nehemiah 9*, BZAW 277 (Berlin: de Gruyter, 1999), 140. Joyce G. Baldwin, *Haggai, Zechariah, Malachi: An Introduction and Commentary*, TOTC (Downers Grove, IL: InterVarsity Press, 1972), 90, claims Zechariah has Jer 35:15 in mind. Connections to the Dtr prose and redaction of the book of Jeremiah will be regularly noted. The passages usually tagged to this "C" level in Jeremiah are: 7:1–8:3; 11:1–5, 9–14; 18:1–12; 21:1–10; 25:1–11a; 32:1–2, 6–16, 24–44; 34:1–7, 8–22; 35:1–19; 44:1–14 (with Carroll, see below). The passages usually tagged as "B" level consist of prophetic narratives: 19:1–2, 10–11a; 19:14–20:6; 26–44. There has been great debate over whether one can distinguish between the "B" and "C" levels, whether the Dtr sections could have originated with Jeremiah, and whether the Dtr sections match the style of DtrH. However, this present work will follow the view that the oracles of Jeremiah were taken up in the exilic period and presented by those responsible for the DtrH. The limits and history of this redactional level has been well-documented and debated in the following scholarly contributions. Cf. Ernest Wilson Nicholson, *Preaching to the Exiles: A Study of the Prose Tradition in the Book of Jeremiah* (New York: Schocken, 1971), 20–37; J. A. Thompson, *The Book of Jeremiah*, NICOT (Grand Rapids: Eerdmans, 1980), 33–50; William McKane, *A Critical and Exegetical Commentary on Jeremiah*, ICC (Edinburgh: T&T Clark, 1986), xli–xcix; Robert P. Carroll, *From Chaos to Covenant: Prophecy in the Book of Jeremiah* (New York: Crossroad, 1981), 5–30; Robert P. Carroll, *Jeremiah*, OTG (Sheffield: JSOT Press, 1989), 31–40; Leo G. Perdue and Brian W. Kovacs, eds., *A Prophet to the Nations: Essays in Jeremiah Studies* (Winona Lake, IN: Eisenbrauns, 1984); Louis Stulman, *The Prose Sermons of the Book of Jeremiah: A Redescription of the Correspondences with Deuteronomistic Literature in the Light of Recent Text-Critical Research*, SBLDS 83 (Atlanta: Scholars Press, 1987); Douglas R. Jones, *Jeremiah*, NCB (London: Marshall Pickering, 1992), 17–37; Walter Brueggemann, *A Commentary on Jeremiah: Exile and Homecoming* (Grand Rapids: Eerdmans, 1998), viii–11.

[18] This is claimed by nearly all commentators: e.g., Elizabeth Achtemeier, *Nahum–Malachi*, IBC (Atlanta: Westminster John Knox, 1986), 112; Mason, *Preaching*, 201; David L. Petersen, *Haggai and Zechariah 1–8: A Commentary*, OTL (Philadelphia: Westminster, 1984), 132. See Tollington, *Tradition*, 205–6. Sinclair, "Redaction," 43, has noted that the use of the particle נא confirms the Jeremianic connection, for this is typical

joins hands with the Dtr tradents of Jeremiah to clarify and expand the initial exhortation to return in 1:3. In 7:9–10 the audience is provided with another collection of the message of the earlier prophets. Again there are links to idioms found in the Dtr prose of Jeremiah (Jer 5:28; 7:5–6; 9:23; 22:3; 32:18). In neither of these cases, however, do we have a direct quotation from these sections of Jeremiah, rather an echo of the message in which the composer incorporates unique constructions (see further below).

THE RESPONSE OF THE FATHERS

The prose sermons in Zechariah emphasise not only the message of the earlier prophets, but also the response of an earlier generation identified as "your fathers" to whom the earlier prophets proclaimed (1:4, 5, 6; 8:14). The practice of alluding to "your fathers" (אבתיכם) in a prophetic message is attested more often in Jeremiah and particularly in the Dtr prose of Jeremiah than in any other prophetic corpus.[19]

However, not only is this generation identified in the sermon, but their response to the prophetic message is described in detail. These descriptions in 1:4b and 7:11–12 reveal affinity with the Dtr prose in Jeremiah. As Zech 1:4, Jer 7:24–26 links the Hebrew construction ולא שמעו with the message of the prophets.[20] So also Jer 11:1–13 shares the same vocabulary (11:8) while employing a second term used in Zech 7:11: מאן (Jer 11:10). The verb מאן appears many times throughout the Hebrew Bible, but usually in the sense of refusing to do some action (e.g., Num 22:13, 14). In connection with listening to the word of God, however, it is restricted to Dtr literature, especially the Dtr prose level of Jeremiah (Jer 11:10; 13:10; cf. 1 Sam 8:19).[21]

---

of Jeremiah. He also highlights the repeated use of the phrase "return to me" (1:3) in Jeremiah (3:1, 7, 10; 4:1; 24:7; cf. Isa 44:22; Joel 2:12).

[19] Jer 7:14, 22, 25; 11:4, 5, 7; 16:11, 12, 13; 17:22; 34:13, 14; 44:3, 9, 10, 21 (cf. Jer 2:15; 3:18; Ezek 20:18, 27, 30, 36, 42; 47:14; Hos 9:10; Joel 1:2; Mal. 3:7; Isa 65:7).

[20] Cf. Tollington, *Tradition*, 209 n. 2. Notice also the allusion to the stubborn animal imagery which is picked up and transformed in the second prose section in 7:11–12 (see below).

[21] Cf. Mason, *Preaching*, 219; Boda, *Praying the Tradition*, 148–49. Interestingly in the poetic sections of Jeremiah another combination predominates: מאנו לשוב (Jer 5:3; 8:5; cf. Hos 11:5).

THE DISCIPLINE OF GOD

The rhetorical pattern in both prose sermons ends with a description of the discipline of God. Here again there are connections to the tradition of Jeremiah and his Dtr tradents.

The description of God's discipline consistently roots this discipline in the anger of God (Zech 1:2; 7:12; 8:14; קצף + קצף). This vocabulary is used regularly of God's anger in prophetic literature (Isa 34:2; 47:6; 54:8, 9; 57:16, 17; 60:10; Jer 10:10; 21:5; 32:37; 50:13). However, the expression in Zech 7:12 (קצף גדול) betrays Dtr influence, for this phrase is only found elsewhere in connection with God's anger in Deut 29:27; Jer 21:5; 32:37 (cf. 2 Kgs 3:27).[22]

The description of the expression of this anger in disciplinary actions shows further connections to Jeremiah and Dtr contexts. The rhetorical play: "when he called, they did not listen, so when they called, I would not listen" (כאשר־קרא ולא שמעו כן יקראו ולא אשמע) in Zech 7:13a draws on the rhetoric of Dtr prose in Jeremiah (7:2, 13, 27; 11:6, 11, 14; 29:12; 35:17).[23] The use of storm imagery (here the verb סער; cf. nouns סער and סערה) in Zech 7:14 to describe the discipline of exile is a regular feature of Jeremiah (23:19; 25:32; 30:23; cf. Isa 29:6).[24] The description of the destination of the exile as nations אשר לא־ידעום in 7:14 is "particularly prominent" in the Dtr corpus and when speaking of exile it occurs regularly in Jeremiah.[25] The depiction of the state of the land after judgment in 7:14 (וישימו ... לשמה) can be traced to Jeremianic literature (4:7; 18:16; 19:8; 25:9; 51:29)[26] as well as the former state of the land (ארץ־חמדה) which is used elsewhere with land only in Jer 3:19 and Ps 106:24.[27]

---

[22] Notice also the use of קצף + קצף in Lam 5:22; Ps 102:11; Isa 64:4, 8 in laments longing for restoration of Zion.
[23] See Tollington, *Tradition*, 209. Cf. similar rhetoric in Isa 65:12, 24; 66:4; and Ezek 8:18 where Ezekiel adds: באזני קול גדול.
[24] Cf. ibid. Zechariah is unique in using the verbal form in connection with the judgment of God (cf. Amos 1:14). Habakkuk 3:14 speaks of Pharaoh sending his troops.
[25] Cf. Beuken, *Haggai–Sacharja 1–8*, 132; Sinclair, "Redaction," 43; Weinfeld, *Deuteronomy*, 357; Tollington, *Tradition*, 209; Petersen, *Haggai and Zechariah 1–8*, 294–95. This idiom is used in reference to gods (Jer 7:9; Deut 13:3); people (Deut 28:33); and land (Jer 15:14; 16:13; 17:4; 22:28).
[26] Cf. Petersen, *Haggai and Zechariah 1–8*, 296 who also cites Beuken's agreement. Contrast Ezek 25:3; 36:33–36.
[27] Cf. Tollington, *Tradition*, 209; Mason, *Preaching*, 219. Mason has noted a connection between the description of the land as "secure' (שלוה) in 7:7 and Jer 22:20–23 where the people do not listen (although he also cites Ezek 16:49). Psalm 106 as we will see below is a member of the penitential prayer *Gattung*.

When the prose sermon picks up again in 8:14 there are again links to Jeremianic literature. The verb זמם (1:6b; 8:14–15) is used for God's action of discipline against Judah elsewhere only in Jer 4:28 (cf. 4:13–28) and Lam 2:17.[28] Additionally, God's judgment in not showing mercy (לא נחמתי; 8:14) is used in this sense also in Jer 4:28; 20:16 (cf. Ezek 24:14).[29] Finally, in the announcement of salvation in Zech 8:19 we find a play on a Jeremianic expression. There the change to feasting is described by the word pair לששון ולשמחה. The Dtr prose level in Jeremiah uses this word pair from bridal feasts regularly when speaking of what will be lost in the coming judgment and in the context of the land's desolation: Jer 7:34; 16:9; 25:10; 33:10–11.[30]

As the presentation of the message of the earlier prophets and the response of the earlier generation, so also the depiction of the discipline of God in the prose sermons exhibits affinity with the Jeremianic tradition and in particular the Dtr prose sermon material in Jeremiah.[31]

NARRATIVE CONTEXTS

All three key components in the prose sermons of Zechariah have been linked to the Jeremianic tradition and in particular to the Dtr prose material in Jeremiah. The influence of either this corpus or the tradition group responsible for it is demonstrated also in the style of the prose sermons themselves. Both corpora place the prophetic word in a narrative context in which we catch glimpses of the audience and at times their reaction to the prophecies.[32]

Even beyond this stylistic similarity, an examination of the narratives surrounding the prose sermons in Zechariah reveals some fascinating parallels with the Dtr prose of Jeremiah. Jeremiah 36 relates an instruction received by Jeremiah

---

[28] Cf. Sinclair, "Redaction," 43. See Jer 51:12 where it is used of God's judgment of Babylon.
[29] So also Tollington, *Tradition*, 212.
[30] Although also found in other prophets speaking about restoration period: Isa 35:10; 51:3, 11; 61:3.
[31] Further Dtr influence can be seen in the use of נשג to describe the fulfillment of God's curse warnings in 1:6a (cf. Deut 28:2, 15, 45). The footnotes above reveal that Tollington noted many of these connections to Jeremiah in her work. However, in the end she denied this influence in the presentation of the discipline of God because of connections in Ezekiel. Although a few elements in Ezekiel are similar, several others can be discounted. The cumulative weight is in favor of Jeremiah.
[32] This may reflect what Lohfink called the "historische Kurzgeschichte" and Petersen called the "brief apologetic historical narrative." They saw this style in Jer 26, 36, and 37–41. Cf. N. Lohfink, "Die Gattung der 'historischen Kurzgeschichte' in den letzten Jahren von Juda und in der Zeit des babylonischen Exils," *ZAW* 90 (1978): 319–47; Petersen, *Haggai and Zechariah 1–8*, 35.

from God in the fourth year of King Jehoiakim (36:1). This instruction commands Jeremiah to record all his prophecies on a scroll in order to call the people to repentance (36:2–3, 7). This scroll was destined to be read on a day of fasting by Jeremiah's scribe Baruch when all the people came in from their towns (36:6).[33] The fasting day on which this scroll was finally read to the people took place in the ninth month of the following year of Jehoiakim's reign (36:9, 22). In the following narrative, the scroll finds its way to King Jehoiakim who, in a brazen act of rebellion against God, destroys the scroll piece by piece. The story concludes with the assurance that another scroll was produced to replace the destroyed one (36:32).

There are several connections to the prose sermon in Zech 7–8.[34] First of all, both accounts are similar in dating, connecting the prophetic message to the fourth year and the ninth month.[35] Secondly, both accounts refer to fasting practices connected to the destruction of Judah by the Babylonians (Jeremiah's anticipates the destruction, Zechariah's remembers it). Thirdly, both accounts involve hearing the prophecies of Jeremiah without him being present. Once again we see the intimate link between the sermon in Zech 7–8 and the Dtr presentation of Jeremiah.[36]

Another possible connection to the Dtr prose of Jeremiah is Jer 26. We have already noted connections to this chapter, but have yet to mention the appearance of the phrase חלה + פני יהוה in verse 19. It refers to an obedient generation which heeded the prophetic warning of Micah, all in the context of Jeremiah's prophecy of disaster against Jerusalem and the temple by comparing the temple to Shiloh. In a similar way Zech 7:2 depicts a community from Bethel, ten miles south of Shiloh, coming and being confronted by another prophetic message.[37]

A third possible connection can be discerned in Zech 7:5 where the prophet clarifies the more ambiguous phrase of the delegation (זה כמה שנים) by defining

---

[33] Jeremiah's involvement on days of fasting and penitence can be seen elsewhere in the book of Jeremiah. See further on this: Mark J. Boda, "From Complaint to Contrition: Peering through the Liturgical Window of Jer 14,1–15,4," *ZAW* 113 (2001): 186–97.

[34] Meyers and Meyers, *Haggai, Zechariah 1–8*, 381.

[35] This may explain why the editor has awkwardly split the date in Zech 7:1 into two pieces with the insertion of the messenger formula. In Jer 36:1 a similar, but not identical, messenger formula comes immediately after the citation of the year of the king's reign.

[36] The Meyers and Meyers, *Haggai, Zechariah 1–8*, 381, also note a historical similarity between the two accounts in that in both an eastern king is giving attention to his western territories (Nebuchadnezzar, Darius).

[37] Jeremiah compares Jerusalem to Shiloh also in Jer 7, another Dtr prose passage and already cited above.

it as זה שבעים שנה. This is an allusion to the predictions of Jeremiah presented in the Dtr prose of Jer 25:11, 12; 29:10.[38]

CONCLUSION

The composer of the prose sections in Zech 1:1–6 and 7:1–8:23 is deeply rooted in the tradition of Jeremiah.[39] Although there are some signs of reliance on non-Dtr sections of Jeremiah, there is strong allegiance to the Dtr prose sections.[40] Because of this we can expand Petersen's conclusion on Zech 8:14–15 to encompass the entire prose sermon sections: "One senses that Jeremiah's rhetoric has been carried into and interpreted for a new generation by one of Zechariah's tradents."[41]

It is not surprising that the Dtr prose sections of Jeremiah appear to be most influential on the prose sermons in Zechariah. These sections confront behavioral patterns within the community that led to the destruction of Judah and these confrontations are closely related to religious activity and rituals surrounding the temple in Jerusalem. This corpus would have provided superb preaching material for the one responsible for the prose sermons as the temple edifice was arising in the early Persian period.[42]

---

[38] See further below how important this is to penitential liturgy in Dan 9:2, 24 and how it is closely associated in the Persian period with Jeremiah; cf. Dan 9:2; 2 Chr 36:21.

[39] Some of the connections in the preceding discussion cannot be isolated to a Jeremianic or even Dtr source. However, the cumulative evidence points to the Jeremianic tradition as the common denominator.

[40] A point made by Sinclair, "Redaction," 42–43.

[41] Cf. ibid.; Petersen, *Haggai and Zechariah 1–8*, 309; Tollington, *Tradition*, 206. Tollington writes: "it was the prophecies of Jeremiah threatening the disaster of the exile which were in the mind of the originator of Zech 1.2–6."

[42] Tollington may be correct that the appeal to the earlier prophets served also to bolster Zechariah's authority in the Persian period community; cf. ibid., 76–77. The regular use of the phrase וידעתם כי־יהוה צבאות שלחני (2:13, 15; 4:9; 6:15) may indicate that there were questions about his authority; cf. Mark J. Boda, "Haggai: Master Rhetorician," *TynBul* 51 (2000): 295–304; Mark J. Boda, "Oil, Crowns and Thrones: Prophet, Priest and King in Zechariah 1:7–6:15," *JHS* 3 (2001): Article 10 = chapter 4 in this present volume.

ZECHARIAH 1–8 AND PENITENTIAL PRAYER LITURGY

ZECHARIAH PROSE AND NEHEMIAH 9

Comparison of the prose sermons in Zechariah with the Dtr prose of Jeremiah has revealed connections in terms of idiom, expression, and style.[43] The one responsible for the prose sermons, however, has not woodenly quoted from the Dtr prose of Jeremiah, but rather offered summaries of the message of the prophet, depictions of the response of the people and the discipline of God in Dtr prose style. This results in a presentation which sounds like the Dtr prose of Jeremiah, and yet has some unique twists.[44]

Some of this unique coloring can be linked to the creativity of the one responsible for these sermons, but at several junctures throughout the prose sermons another influence can be discerned.

The call to repentance in Zech 1:4 is reminiscent of Dtr prose, but the second part of the expression is restricted elsewhere in the Hebrew Bible to the penitential prayer of Neh 9:[45]

Zech 1:4   שׁובו ... ומעליליכם הרעים
Neh 9:35   ולא־שׁבו ממעלליהם הרעים

---

[43] Although Petersen recognized the strong influence of the Dtr prose of Jeremiah on the prose sermons of Zechariah, he refused to accept its significance: "It is interesting that so many parallels to this rhetoric appear in the book of Jeremiah, and more particularly in the so-called Jeremianic prose. Nevertheless, it remains difficult to argue that Jeremiah was uniquely significant for the writer of Zechariah" (Petersen, *Haggai and Zechariah 1–8*, 290). Part of this has to do with his view of the dating of the Dtr prose level in Jeremiah. In his work on 1:4 he accepts that the author "had access to some form of the nascent prophetic collections, one that in the case of Jeremiah included the recently written deuteronomistic prose" (133). However, in his comments on 7:9–10 he denies this connection: "Since this text [Jer 7:5–6] is almost certainly a late element in the composition of the book of Jeremiah, it is difficult to argue for literary dependence of Zechariah on Jeremiah" (ibid.).

[44] Petersen follows Beuken and Petitjean in highlighting the creativity of the sermons's presentation of the earlier prophets's message: "Rather than providing a pale copy of prophetic speech, he has provided a vigorous prophetic discourse" (ibid., 291); Beuken, *Haggai–Sacharja 1–8*, 125; Albert Petitjean, *Les oracles du proto-Zacharie: Un programme de restauration pour la communauté juive après l'exil* (Paris: Librairie Lecoffre, 1969), 335.

[45] Boda, *Praying the Tradition*, 183–84.

While the Dtr/JerC expression for the lack of attention of the earlier generation to the message of the Hebrew prophets is typically שמע (see above),[46] in the Zech sermons we find also the verb קשב (*hiphil*), "to pay attention" (Zech 1:4; 7:11). The only other place where this verb is used in connection with the people's rejection of the earlier prophets is in Neh 9:34.[47]

Although the image of the stubborn animal is common in Dtr literature (Deut 9:6, 13, 27; 2 Kgs 17:14; Jer 7:26; cf. Exod 32:9), the expression used in Zech 7:11 only occurs elsewhere in Neh 9:29:[48]

ויקשו את־ערפם	Jer 7:26
ויתנו כתף סררת	Zech 7:11
ויתנו כתף סוררת וערפם הקשו	Neh 9:29

As already noted above, the phrase ביד to describe the prophets as instruments of warning to earlier generations occurs regularly in Dtr literature. However, the particular combination in Zech 7:12, linking God's Spirit with the prophets, occurs elsewhere only in Neh 9:30.[49]

ברוחו ביד הנביאים	Zech 7:12
ברוחך ביד־נביאיך	Neh 9:30

In each of the preceding examples Dtr/JerC vocabulary or imagery has been transformed into new forms reflected elsewhere only in the penitential prayer in Neh 9. Two further features in the Zech prose sermons already linked to Dtr/JerC also appear in Neh 9: the use of the verbs שמע and מאן to depict the unresponsiveness of the earlier generation (9:17, 29).

NEHEMIAH 9 AND PENITENTIAL PRAYER

These points of contact with the prayer in Neh 9 prompt the question of its origins and function within the Jewish community. In its present literary position it is recited by a group of Levites on a day of fasting, confession, and prayer followed by a renewal of covenant (Neh 10). This is not the appropriate place to tackle the redaction history of the book of Nehemiah, but no matter what theory is used to explain this history the prayer in Neh 9 must have existed prior to its incorporation

---

[46] See ibid., 147–49, esp. 49 n. 303.
[47] Ibid., 182.
[48] Ibid., 177–78 nn. 433–34.
[49] Ibid., 138–39, 178.

Zechariah: Master Mason or Penitential Prophet? 115

into either the literary context of Neh 8–10 or the historical context described in Neh 9.[50]

This literary context, however, is a helpful guide to the function of this prayer within the Jewish community. The narrative introduction (Neh 9:1–4) informs us that it was recited in connection with the following activities: communal assembly, confession, Scripture reading, fasting, wearing sackcloth, and putting dust on heads. Several of these activities are those typical of communal lament days on which the people would cry out to God for help.[51] The prayer itself (Neh 9:5–37) reveals the cry of a people who have lost control of their land. These same characteristics are also found in a series of biblical prayers which find their genesis in the centuries following the fall of Jerusalem and which can be tagged "Penitential Prayer" (Ezra 9; Neh 1; 9; Dan 9; Ps 106).[52] Because all four of the prayers in biblical narrative are recited in the context of the fasting rituals (Ezra 10:6; Neh 1:4; 9:1; Dan 9:3) and because the prayers share the common purpose "to bring an end to the devastating effects of the fall of the state—either to captivity, oppression, or the sorry condition of Palestine," the supposed *Sitz im Leben* has been the fasts established in the exilic period in response to the fall of Jerusalem and Judah (Jer 41:4–5; Zech 7:3, 5; 8:19).[53]

The prayers themselves share these features in common: praise, supplication (depiction of need, muted lament, implicit request), confession of sin (admission

---

[50] See ibid., 6–16.

[51] Cf. Hermann Gunkel and Joachim Begrich, *Einleitung in die Psalmen: Die Gattungen der religiösen Lyrik Israels*, 2nd ed. (Göttingen: Vandenhoeck & Ruprecht, 1933), 117–21; E. Lipinski, *La liturgie pénitentielle dans la Bible*, LD 52 (Paris: Cerf, 1969), 27–35.

[52] See Boda, *Praying the Tradition*; Volker Pröbstl, *Nehemia 9, Psalm 106 und Psalms 136 und die Rezeption des Pentateuchs* (Göttingen: Cuvillier, 1997), 47; Rodney A. Werline, *Penitential Prayer in Second Temple Judaism: The Development of a Religious Institution*, EJL 13 (Atlanta: Scholars Press, 1998). Further examples can be seen in non-biblical literature: Bar 1:15–3:8; Dan 3:26–45 LXX; 1QS 1:18–3:12; 4QDibHam [= 4Q504–506]; 4Q393. The biblical prayers in Isa 63:7–64:11; Jer 32:17–25 and possibly Isa 59:9–15; Lamentations; and Pss 74, 79, and 89 represent proto-penitential prayers; see Boda, *Praying the Tradition*, 27 n. 28 and literature cited there.

[53] These fasts commemorated various events surrounding the fall of the state: fourth month (the breach of Jerusalem's walls and flight of leadership; 2 Kgs 25:3–7; Jer 39:1–10; 52:6–11); fifth month (Jerusalem destroyed; 2 Kgs 25:8–12 // Jer 52:12–16); seventh month (assassination of Gedaliah; 2 Kgs 25:25–26; Jer 41:1–3); tenth month (beginning of the siege of Jerusalem; 2 Kgs 25:1; Jer 39:1). Cf. commentaries on Zechariah and Ackroyd, *Exile*, 270 n. 122. The fact that the delegation from Bethel in Zech 7:3 only refers to the fast of the fifth month, while Zechariah expands the message to encompass the entire Jewish community along with four different fasts, suggests that different communities followed different practices. This may explain the number of these prayers in the Persian period books.

of culpability, declaration of solidarity with former generations, consistent use of התודה ("to confess"), history (anthological use of historical sources, use of contrast motif: God's grace/Israel's disobedience), and themes (covenant, land, law). These prayers represent the response of the "exilic" community to the guidance of Lev 26:39–45 and 1 Kgs 8:46–53. They signify a substantial leap from the pre-exilic lament with its questioning of God to this exilic response with the silencing of lament and clear justification of God.[54]

ZECHARIAH PROSE SERMONS AND PENITENTIAL PRAYER

As many of the Dtr connections from Jeremiah have been mediated to the composer of the prose sermons of Zechariah through the prayer in Neh 9, so also several features of the penitential prayer tradition have been mediated to the composer through this prayer. In both we see the key role of the prophets in warning the earlier generation (Zech 1:4, 5, 6; 7:7, 12; cf. Neh 9:26, 30; Ezra 9:10–11; Dan 9:6, 10) and the use of the construction of ביד to speak of the agency of these prophets (Zech 7:12; cf. Neh 9:30; Ezra 9:11; Dan 9:10). In both we see the function of the law as the standard rejected by the earlier generation (Zech 7:12; cf. Neh 9:16, 29, 34; Ezra 9:10, 14; Neh 1:7; Dan 9:5, 10–11) and the near identity of the words of the prophets and the law (Zech 7:12; 1:6a; cf. Neh 9:29, 34; Dan 9:10–11).[55] In both the earlier generation is identified as אבות (Zech 1:2, 4, 5, 6; 8:14; cf. Neh 9:2, 9, 34, 36; Ezra 9:7; Neh 1:6; Dan 9:16; Ps 106:6, 7) and the sin of that generation is linked with the present generation (Zech 1:6b, 8:14; cf. Neh 9:32–37; Ezra 9:6–7; Neh 1:6–7; Dan 9; Ps 106:6). Finally, in both there is an admission of the justice of God (Zech 1:6b; cf. Neh 9:33; Ezra 9:15; Dan 9:6, 14).[56]

In addition to this evidence, one cannot ignore the setting presupposed by the second prose sermon in Zech 7–8. This sermon was delivered in response to a query about the ongoing relevance of the "exilic" fasting liturgy. As already noted, the penitential prayer tradition fits comfortably into this *Sitz im Leben*.

---

[54] See Richard J. Bautch, *Developments in Genre between Post-Exilic Penitential Prayers and the Psalms of Communal Lament*, AcBib 7 (Atlanta: Society of Biblical Literature, 2003).

[55] Cf. Mason, *Preaching*, 203.

[56] Although absent from Neh 9, other penitential prayers stress the righteous anger of God towards the earlier generation (Zech 1:2; 7:12 [cf. 8:2]; cf. Ps 106:23, 29, 32, 40; Ezra 9:14; Dan 9:16); as well as the reference to "my servants the prophets" (cf. Zech 1:6a; Ezra 9:11; Dan 9:6, 10), examples of Dtr expression, cf. Weinfeld, *Deuteronomy*, 351; Boda, *Praying the Tradition*, 140.

Conclusion

The number of links identified in our preceding discussion between the prose inclusio of Zechariah and the penitential prayer tradition strongly suggests that the composer is playing off this prayer tradition.[57] Our research may have also unearthed the very prayer that the prose sections presupposed.[58] This connection to the penitential prayer tradition and the attendant fasting liturgy is not surprising, considering the link we have already noted between Zech 7–8 and the Dtr presentation of Jeremiah's involvement in a preexilic fasting day.

The penitential prayer tradition, however, is not the exclusive influence on the prose sermons in Zechariah. The sermons betray close affinity with Dtr/JerC prose as well, and although in some cases this prose has been relayed through the penitential prayer tradition, this cannot explain every example.

Reading Zechariah 1–8 Again for the Very First Time

With these new insights into the background to the prose sermon inclusio surrounding Zech 1–8, let us now return to the redactional discussion of Zech 1–8 and identify the way these insights shape our reading of the corpus.

Zechariah 7–8

This identification of the key influence of fasting and penitential liturgies is extremely helpful for understanding the original impact of the sermon in Zech 7–8. To confront their fasting practices the composer alludes to the content of their liturgy which highlights the prophetic word while rehearsing the prophetic example and message of Jeremiah. Through this Zechariah is depicted as calling his

---

[57] Connections between portions of the prose sermons in Zechariah and exilic fasting liturgies or penitential prayers have been noted in the past by various scholars: Petitjean, *Oracles*, 333–41, 48–49; Mason, *Haggai*, 67; Baldwin, *Haggai*, 147. Petitjean sees in Neh 9:30 and Zech 7:12, "les marques d'un emprunt à une pièce liturgique plus ancienne" (349), while Baldwin asserts: "a well known psalm may underlie both Neh 9:30 and Zech 7:12" (147). There is no reason to follow several commentators when they assert that Zechariah is attacking the fasting liturgy as an institution (Baldwin, *Haggai*, 140; Petersen, *Haggai and Zechariah 1–8*, 283; Redditt, *Haggai, Zechariah and Malachi*, 81). Rather Zechariah is arguing that appropriate fasting will lead to feasting.

[58] See Williamson who noted a connection between Zech 1:2–6 and Neh 9; H. G. M. Williamson, "Structure and Historiography in Nehemiah 9," in *Proceedings of the Ninth World Congress of Jewish Studies (Panel Sessions: Bible Studies and Ancient Near East, Jerusalem 1988)*, ed. M. Goshen-Gottstein (Jerusalem: Magnes, 1988), 117–32 (130 n. 40).

present generation to transcend the example of their ancestors by obeying the enduring message of the earlier prophets.[59]

ZECHARIAH 1:1–6

This connection to Jeremiah and the penitential prayer tradition is helpful for understanding the strategy of the composer in Zech 7–8, but it also sheds some light on the function of Zech 1:1–6. Zechariah 1:1–6 depicts Zechariah as a second Jeremiah, declaring the old message afresh to a new generation.[60] It also depicts the appropriate penitential response of the community to the prophetic word. As opposed to Jeremiah's community which rejected the prophet's message and did not repent and avert God's wrath (Jer 36:3, 7), the prose envisions a community which returns to God. The narrative in 1:6b depicts the success of the sermon by alluding to an important component of the penitential prayer tradition (justification of God's discipline) and the foundational purpose of the prayer (expression of repentance). The message of the earlier prophets has finally been accepted, setting a new trajectory for the community.[61] Is it possible that this sermon has been placed at the outset of the book of Zechariah to show that God's promises in the following night visions were precipitated by a penitent community?

ZECHARIAH 1:7–6:15

Although distinct in genre and style, there is some justification for seeing a close connection between the initial sermon and the first night vision. First of all, there are a few points of contact in terms of vocabulary: קרא (1:4; 1:14), קצף and קצף (1:2, 15) and שוב (1:3, 4, 6; 16).[62] Secondly, a couple of features in this night vision point to the influence of the penitential prayer tradition. Petersen suggests that the appearance of the phrase "seventy years" in Zech 1:12 (cp. 7:4) in the mouth of a distraught Angel of the Lord who employs language familiar from the laments of the Psalter (עד־מתי) may echo the exilic fasting liturgy.[63] Similarly,

---

[59] These sermons remind the reader that Zechariah has assumed the mantle of the earlier prophets. This is seen in the reference to the death of the prophets in 1:5 and the echo of the prophetic message in 8:16–17 (cf. 7:8–10).

[60] For signs of Jeremiah's involvement as prophet in fasting liturgies in the last days of the kingdom of Judah, see Boda, "Complaint."

[61] Note the importance of repentance and confession to restoration in Lev 26:39–40 and 1 Kgs 8:46–53. See Boda, *Praying the Tradition*, 47–54. It is possible that the first sermon is used to show the normative penitence of the Jerusalem community that is contrasted in the second sermon by the inappropriate penitence of those outside of Jerusalem.

[62] Cf. Meyers and Meyers, *Haggai*, li–liv.

[63] Petersen, *Haggai and Zechariah 1–8*, 146–47.

Tollington compares Zech 1:12 with Ps 79 and "the occasions of national fasting such as those mentioned in Zech 7.5; 8.18–19."[64]

If both the initial prose sermon and the first night vision can be linked to the fasting liturgy, we may be able to discern the design behind the positioning of the prose sermon and the night visions. This design may be informed by the preexilic fasting liturgy which was an avenue for the community to express their need to God and receive a prophetic answer from God (cf. Jer 14).[65] In this prophetic fasting liturgy the people would depict their dire situation and express their penitence before God. The prophet was then to enquire of God for his answer to their dilemma.

Echoes of this pattern can be discerned in Zech 1. Promising the "return" of God, the prophet calls the people to "return" (1:3). In response to the prophet's review of the past disobedience and discipline, the people respond with humble repentance (1:6b). At the point when the prophet in the liturgical pattern is to enquire of God for his answer (positive or negative) to their prayer, the prophet relates the first new vision in which he hears the Angel of Yahweh pleading with God for an end to the exilic experience. The answer to be proclaimed is a positive answer from God in which he promises a "return" to his people (1:16).

Recognition of this connection between the initial sermon and the first night vision forces us to read the entire night vision section in a new way. The focus is not on the call to rebuild, as in Haggai, but rather on the call to ethical purity and covenantal loyalty in line with the message of Jeremiah. The night visions in Zech 5 are thus not tangents off topic, but rather in keeping with the fundamental conviction of Zech 1–8. The vision of the cleansing of Joshua in Zech 3 with its additional prophecy of the cleansing of the land also takes up the strong concern with the sin of the people and land.

Conclusion

This chapter has used the prose sections of Zech 1–8 as a window through which we can gaze into the life of the Persian period community. Through this literature we have viewed a community living under a burden created by an earlier generation. Into this community has stepped Zechariah and his tradents who, rather than denying the past, have embraced it in order to transcend it. For them the way forward is back, not distancing themselves from it nor denying its reality, but rather facing it.

Filled with allusions and patterns drawn from the exilic liturgy of penitential fasting, the sermons blend present and past generations. This penitential prayer

---

[64] Tollington, *Tradition*, 184–85.
[65] For this, see Boda, "Complaint."

traces and faces past patterns of disobedience, admitting imperfections, expressing repentance, and pleading for relief from the present predicament.

However, this is not all. The sermons transport the community back to the streets of Jerusalem in the waning days of the kingdom of Judah. There they have the opportunity to hear afresh the message of Jeremiah in order that they may respond with the repentance demanded by that prophet.

In this, we also discover two forms which help create and sustain identity in the Persian period community. The first is oral: the liturgy of penitential prayer, while the second is written: the text of prophetic witness. Liturgical expression and Scriptural recitation will form a close partnership in the coming years as the Jewish community continues to struggle with identity. This association is attested in other contexts in which the liturgy of penitential prayer appears. In Dan 9 a pious individual reads the prophet Jeremiah and responds with penitential prayer. In Neh 9 a pious community reads extensively from the book of the Law and responds with penitential prayer.[66] These two forms, liturgy and canon, through which the community goes back to their future, will endure alongside the temple, and in the end will outlast that physical structure, sustaining the identity of the community to the present day.

---

[66] Although the narrative contexts surrounding the penitential prayers in Ezra 9 and Neh 1 do not mention reading authoritative books, the prayers themselves reveal strong affinity with elements within such books (cf. Ezra 9:11–12; Neh 1:8–9). Cf. Boda, *Praying the Tradition*, 30–32. See especially Werline and Newman for evidence of the integration of interpretation and prayer throughout the Second Temple period; Werline, *Penitential Prayer*; Judith H. Newman, *Praying by the Book: The Scripturalization of Prayer in Second Temple Judaism*, EJL 14 (Atlanta: Scholars Press, 1999). Werline expresses his conclusion in reference to Dan 9 and Bar 1–3: "prayer and the interpretation of authoritative texts have become the method for understanding and responding to Israel's sins and the people's recurring political crises" (p. 108).

7
When God's Voice Breaks Through: Shifts in Revelatory Rhetoric in Zechariah 1–8[1]

In this chapter I continue my reflection on the impact of the earlier prophetic tradition on the prose-sermon bracket of Zech 1:1–6 and 7:1–8:23. Here the focus is on the rhetorical features which are designed to make the earlier prophets's words fresh for a Persian period audience.

Interpreters of the book of Zechariah have often noted the close relationship between the opening pericope of the book in 1:1–6 and the later pericope in 7:1–8:23.[2] The two sections are dominated by prose material, refer to the "earlier prophets" whose message is cited, draw particularly from the Jeremianic Dtr tradition, and are structured in similar ways. They share a similar rhetorical structure, especially 1:1–6 and 7:1–14:

---

[1] Based on my original publication, Mark J. Boda, "When God's Voice Breaks Through: Shifts in Revelatory Rhetoric in Zechariah 1–8," in *History, Memory, Hebrew Scriptures: A Festschrift for Ehud Ben Zvi*, ed. Diana Edelman and Ian Wilson (Winona Lake, IN: Eisenbrauns, 2015), 169–86, in honor of Ehud Ben Zvi. Slightly revised for inclusion in this volume.
[2] See Mark J. Boda, "Zechariah: Master Mason or Penitential Prophet?," in *Yahwism after the Exile: Perspectives on Israelite Religion in the Persian Era*, ed. Bob Becking and Rainer Albertz, Studies in Theology and Religion 5 (Assen: Van Gorcum, 2003), 49–69 = chapter 6 in this present volume.

1. Short message of challenge to the present generation (1:3; 7:5–6)
2. Review of the message of the "earlier prophets" (1:4a; 7:7–10)
3. Depiction of the response of the "ancestors" (1:4b; 7:11–12b)
4. Depiction of divine discipline (1:5–6a; 7:12c–14)

These two pericopes bracket the material that has received the most attention in studies of the book of Zechariah, that is, the vision reports with accompanying oracular and sign-act report material in 1:7–6:15. What is often missed is the key role played by the bracketing pericopes in the reading experience of the book of Zechariah in its final form. Zechariah 1:1–6 initially sets up the vision-oracle-sign-act material in 1:7–6:15, a role made clear by intratextual links between 1:1–6 and the first vision report in 1:7–17.[3] Through this technique those responsible for the book of Zechariah identify 1:7–6:15 as a depiction of Yahweh's covenantal "return" to the people due to their "return" to Yahweh.[4] The final phrase of 1:7–6:15, the conditional clause אִם־שָׁמוֹעַ תִּשְׁמְעוּן בְּקוֹל יהוה אֱלֹהֵיכֶם ("if you entirely obey Yahweh your God"), however, introduces ambiguity into the fulfillment of the hopes expressed in 1:7–6:15 and the reason for this ambiguity is then articulated in 7:1–8:23. Thus for those encountering the first half of the book of Zechariah, 1:1–6 and 7:1–8:23 have a dominating role over the reading of the material in 1:7–6:15. While the material in 1:7–6:15 is presented in a way that suggests sure fulfillment, placing the accent on heavenly action, the bracketing material in 1:1–6 and 7:1–8:23 reminds the reader that such fulfillment is not assured but is conditional on human response.

The present article looks more closely at a particular rhetorical strategy that can be discerned in these two influential pericopes (1:1–6; 7:1–8:23). Many scholars have noted an awkward flow in the rhetoric of Zech 1:1–6 and 7:1–14, highlighting confusing levels of quoted material in Zech 1:1–6 as well as diverse prophetic formulae and confusing shifts in speaker in Zech 7:1–14 (see Tables 1, 2, and 3 at end of chapter). These challenges to reading these prophetic passages

---

[3] For instance: compare קרא ("call") in 1:4 // 1:14; קצף/קצף ("anger"/"be angry") in 1:2 // 1:15; שוב ("turn") in 1:3, 4, 6 // 1:16. See Carol L. Meyers and Eric M. Meyers, *Haggai, Zechariah 1–8: A New Translation with Introduction and Commentary*, AB 25B (Garden City, NY: Doubleday, 1987), li–liv; Mike Butterworth, *Structure and the Book of Zechariah*, JSOTSup 130 (Sheffield: Sheffield Academic, 1992), 80–81, 241; Jakob Wöhrle, *Die frühen Sammlungen des Zwölfprophetenbuches: Entstehung und Komposition*, BZAW 360 (Berlin: de Gruyter, 2006), 328.

[4] A distinction appears to be made between returning and taking up dwelling at the temple; Mark J. Boda, *The Book of Zechariah*, NICOT (Grand Rapids: Eerdmans, 2016); see also Jakob Wöhrle, "The Formation and Intention of the Haggai–Zechariah Corpus," *JHS* 6 (2006): Article 10; Michael R. Stead, *The Intertextuality of Zechariah 1–8*, LHBOTS 506 (London: T&T Clark, 2009), 234–35.

appear to me to be precisely what Ehud Ben Zvi has identified as key to the kind of texts that we find within the Hebrew Bible and particularly within the prophetic corpus. As he noted in his work on Micah:

> the way people reread texts differs significantly from their first reading of the same texts. For instance, rereaders, and particularly those who meditate on the text, are aware of the entire text even as they reread its first line ... texts that are suitable for continuous rereading show at least some degree of double meaning, ambiguity, and literary sophistication. Furthermore, the continuous rereading of YHWH's word—within a community that accepts the text as such—involves a particular mode of reading: careful reading, studious and meditative (cf. Josh 1:8; Hos 14:10 [Eng. 14:9]; Sir 38:34–39:3) as opposed to rushed reading.[5]

Past modes of biblical scholarship have been tempted to deal with confusing rhetoric through developmental approaches, looking to underlying sources or redactional activities to explain these features in the text. Ben Zvi has encouraged the guild to embrace the text as its stands to see within its ambiguity a literary sophistication that is discovered only through continuous rereading, one that involves "careful reading, studious and meditative." I hope the interpretation below will reflect the results of such rereading. The conclusion is that no matter what the sources were for these texts, the resulting rhetoric appears to be designed to impact the reader to hear the message of past generations as fresh revelation for the present generation. This subtle rhetoric resonates with the explicit reference to "the earlier prophets" in these texts, and lays a foundation for what follows in Zech 9–14.

ZECHARIAH 1:1–6

The first sentence of the "word of Yahweh" which came to Zechariah, קָצַף יהוה עַל־אֲבוֹתֵיכֶם קָצֶף ("Yahweh was extremely angry with your ancestors") (1:2), is clearly addressed to a plural audience, the referent of the second masculine plural pronominal suffix on the word "ancestors." This audience contrasts that of the phrase which follows immediately after: וְאָמַרְתָּ אֲלֵהֶם ("You [ms] must say to them [mp]") (1:3a), which is addressed to a masculine singular audience, who must be the prophet since the verb is אָמַר. The referent of the third masculine plural pronominal suffix ("them") on the preposition אֶל in this same phrase, however, is not as clear. Floyd has suggested that the referent of this third masculine plural pronominal suffix is the "ancestors" of verse 2 and thus the וְאָמַרְתָּ at the beginning of verse 3 initiates a description of Zechariah's past declaration to the ancestors ("and you [repeatedly] said to them [ancestors]") which consists of the

---

[5] Ehud Ben Zvi, *Micah*, FOTL 21B (Grand Rapids: Eerdmans, 2000), 5–6.

remainder of verse 3.⁶ In this scenario verse 4 is the continuation of the speech which began in verse 2. The more common approach to verse 3 is that the referent of the third masculine plural pronominal suffix is the present audience of the prophet Zechariah and ואמרת is an injunction for the prophet to declare the message to this present audience which then follows.⁷ In both cases a portion or all of verse 3 represents an aside comment from the deity to the prophet in the revelation given to Zechariah for the present generation. The disadvantage of Floyd's approach is that it does not fit as well with the speech which follows in verses 4–6a which links אבותיכם ("your ancestors") with words from הנביאים הראשנים ("earlier prophets"), both of whom appear to have passed from the scene. It must be noted, however, that this clarity only emerges as the pericope progresses. At the outset there is ambiguity in the speech, an ambiguity that blurs the line between generations.

Similar ambiguity can be discerned in the second half of 1:6. The speech of 1:2–6a ends precisely where it began, with a reference to אבתיכם ("your [mp] ancestors") noting now the final step in a process which included the anger of Yahweh (1:2) and the prophetic warning of Yahweh (1:4b) and now ends with the fulfillment of the warnings through judgment (1:6a). Zechariah 1:6b then reports about an ambiguous masculine plural group returning and declaring a speech that justifies God's actions as in line with his intentions and warnings. The speech suggests that it is a group which has received the punishment of Yahweh (זמם יהוה צבאות לעשות לנו ... כן עשה אתנו; "Yahweh planned to do us ... so he has dealt with us") due to their culpability (כדרכינו וכמעלילינו; "according to our ways and according to our deeds"). The immediately preceding verses identify this culpable and punished group as the ancestors's generation. Furthermore, the terms used for culpability (דרך "way" and מעלל "deed") are the same terms used by the earlier prophets in the penitential speech addressed to the ancestors's generation in 1:4 (שובו נא מדרכיכם הרעים ומעליליכם הרעים; "turn from your evil ways and from your evil deeds").⁸ Not surprisingly some have suggested that the group whose actions and words are depicted in 1:6b is the ancestors's generation, so that 1:6b is a continuation of the depiction of the earlier generation from

---

⁶ Michael H. Floyd, *Minor Prophets, Part 2*, FOTL 22 (Grand Rapids: Eerdmans, 2000), 318–19.

⁷ Some have suggested that ואמרת is a truncated form which was preceded originally by an imperative form or forms expressing preliminary action (e.g., Isa 6:9) or speaking (e.g., Jer 3:12); see Hinckley Gilbert Mitchell, John Merlin Powis Smith, and Julius August Brewer, *A Critical and Exegetical Commentary on Haggai, Zechariah, Malachi and Jonah*, ICC (Edinburgh: T&T Clark, 1912), 110; Friedrich Horst, *Die zwölf kleinen Propheten*, 2nd ed., HAT 14 (Tübingen: Mohr Siebeck, 1964), 216.

⁸ Following the *qere* in v. 4, but even if following the *ketiv* the connectivity remains.

1:4b ("but they did not listen nor pay attention to me").[9] However, undermining this interpretation is the depiction of the ancestors in 1:5–6 in which Zechariah notes that the fulfillment of the prophetic warnings in judgment resulted in the demise of these ancestors (אבותיכם איה־הם; "your ancestors, where are they?") and even the prophets who delivered the message (והנבאים הלעולם יחיו; "and the prophets, did they go on living forever?"). The judgment did not then provide an opportunity for repentance for this earlier generation, but led to their elimination. This suggests then that the masculine plural subjects of the verbs וישובו ("returned") and ויאמרו ("said") in 1:6b are the same masculine plural subjects which were identified in 1:3a and the referents behind the second masculine plural pronominal suffixes on אבותיכם ("your ancestors") throughout 1:2–6a, that is, Zechariah's present generation.

The ambiguity in the rhetoric which has given rise to debates over the referents of the subjects of verbs and pronominal suffixes need not be considered evidence of sloppy writing by the one(s) responsible for Zech 1:1–6. This ambiguity matches the message of the pericope. First, the connection between generations is established from the outset of the message as God's anger towards the ancestors (1:2) is immediately linked to the call to the present generation to repent (1:3). Second, two prophetic penitential messages are cited, one addressed through Zechariah to the present generation (1:3) and the other through the earlier prophets to the ancestors's generation (1:4). Both calls to repentance employ the root שוב. Third, a potential parallel between generations is explicitly stated at the outset of 1:4 as the prophet exhorts the present generation: אל־תהיו כאבתיכם ("do not be like your ancestors"). Fourth, the words cited in 1:6b make clear that the present generation assumes solidarity with the former generation both in terms of their culpability and their experience of judgment.

This discussion of Zech 1:1–6 has sought to resolve some of the challenges and debates related to the flow of thought and the confusion over which words and actions are related to various generations of prophets and audiences in the Babylonian and Persian periods. One key challenge alone for those of us commissioned to provide fresh translations of Zech 1:1–6 is discerning how to punctuate the material within quotation marks throughout this passage. Prophetic material is often a challenge to punctuate, as often (as here in Zechariah) the narrator depicts the prophet receiving a message from Yahweh, and then the prophet depicts the reception of that message ("Thus has said Yahweh of hosts" or "declaration of Yahweh of hosts"), and then cites the actual message which was given (e.g.,

---

[9] See Mitchell, Smith, and Brewer, *Haggai*, 113; David L. Petersen, *Haggai and Zechariah 1–8: A Commentary*, OTL (Philadelphia: Westminster, 1984), 110; Marvin A. Sweeney, *The Twelve Prophets*, 2 vols., Berit Olam (Collegeville, MN: Liturgical Press, 2000), 2:573.

"return to me"), but in Zech 1:1–6 we hear Yahweh speaking to the prophet directly ("You must say to them"), and then within the cited speech of Yahweh, Yahweh cites an earlier message which he had delivered to other prophets ("turn from your evil ways and from your evil deeds") and we even hear those prophets's depiction of their revelatory experience ("Thus has said Yahweh of hosts"). The levels of embedded quotation, already a bit confusing within prophetic material, now moves to a whole new level as messages to multiple generations are rehearsed.

It is the challenge of such translation, and the presence of the debate over addressees throughout these short six verses, which I believe lays bare a key feature of this pericope. One of its driving purposes appears to be to connect generations, whether prophetic speakers or audiences, and thus the confusing rhetoric and especially the layers of embedded quotation (see Tables 1, 2, and 3 at end of chapter), serve to fuse the generations, even to confuse the generations, as the message of the earlier prophets is taken up afresh and rehearsed while the response to the earlier prophets is rehearsed and overcome by a present generation standing in solidarity with its ancestors.

ZECHARIAH 7–8

One can discern similar tensions in chapters 7–8. After an initial narrative introduction in 7:1 which is very similar to 1:1, the passage depicts the approach of a contingent (most likely linked to Bethel) to seek the favor of Yahweh from the religious leaders at the house of Yahweh (most likely in Jerusalem), in order to receive discernment on whether they should continue their fasting practices (7:2–3).[10] While the initial prose sermon report in Zech 1:1–6 began with a prophetic revelation which prompted the response of the people, this second prose sermon report in Zech 7–8 begins with the people approaching the prophet which prompts a prophetic revelation. Rhetorically this suggests from the outset a reversal of the situation which appeared to be resolved in the opening pericope of the book.[11]

The initial speech of Zechariah in 7:5b–6 is the first indication that multiple generations are again key to this speech, as the prophet refers to a fasting and lamenting tradition which had endured for seventy years.[12] This becomes clearer in the verses which follow. First comes the rhetorical question of 7:7 which, as in 1:1–6, refers to the revelation through the earlier prophets:

---

[10] See further: Boda, *The Book of Zechariah*, 415–39.

[11] Bolstering this is the final verse of 1:7–6:15, which reminds the audience of the conditionality of human response to ensure the fulfillment of the promises articulated throughout 1:7–6:15 (see above).

[12] For connections to the early penitential prayer tradition, see Boda, "Master Mason" = chapter 6 in this present volume.

הלוא את־הדברים אשר קרא יהוה	Are not these the words which Yahweh an-
ביד הנביאים הראשנים בהיות	nounced through the earlier prophets, when Je-
ירושלם ישבת ושלוה ועריה	rusalem was inhabited and at ease and its cities
סביבתיה והנגב והשפלה ישב	were surrounding it, and the Negev and Sheph-
	elah were inhabited?

Later 7:11–14 depicts, as 1:1–6, the response of the earlier generation confronted by the earlier prophets. This earlier generation is identified in 8:14 as אבתיכם ("your ancestors") who אתי ... בהקציף ("aroused me to anger").[13]

There are, however, key debates over the flow and meaning of 7:5b–14. First of all, it is unclear what words are in view at the outset of 7:7 (הלוא את־ הדברים; "are not these the words"). For some they are those already declared in 7:5b–6 (e.g., Petersen)[14]:

כי־צמתם וספוד בחמישי ובשביעי	When you fasted, lamenting in the fifth and in
וזה שבעים שנה הצום צמתני אני:	the seventh month, these seventy years, did you
וכי תאכלו וכי תשתו הלוא אתם	really fast for me? And when you are eating
האכלים ואתם השתים	and when you are drinking, are not only you
	the ones eating and only you the ones drinking?

For others they are the words cited following in 7:9–10 (e.g., Meyers and Meyers, Redditt, and Stead)[15]:

משפט אמת שפטו וחסד ורחמים	Render true judgment and practice covenant
עשו איש את־אחיו: ואלמנה ויתום	loyalty and mercy, each of you to one another.
גר ועני אל־תעשקו ורעת איש	And do not exploit widow or orphan, sojourner
אחיו אל־תחשבו בלבבכם:	or poor. Do not devise in your minds evil
	against one another.

In either case, there is no question that what follows in 7:8–14 presents prophetic words and describes prophetic critique, as well as descriptions of the lack of response of the community from late monarchic Judah, that is, from the ancestors's generation.

While it is difficult to establish a link between the words declared in 7:5b–6 and any extant prophetic material in the Hebrew Bible, many have noted links between 7:9–10 and the Jeremianic tradition.[16] Jeremiah 7:5–6 contains much of

---

[13] See ibid. = chapter 6 in this present volume, for evidence that 8:14 is the original continuation of 7:14.
[14] Petersen, *Haggai and Zechariah 1–8*, 287.
[15] Meyers and Meyers, *Haggai, Zechariah 1–8*, 396; Paul L. Redditt, *Haggai, Zechariah and Malachi*, NCB (London: Marshall Pickering, 1995), 82; Stead, *Intertextuality*, 223.
[16] See Petersen, *Haggai and Zechariah 1–8*, 289–90; Risto Nurmela, *Prophets in Dialogue: Inner-Biblical Allusions in Zechariah 1–8 and 9–14* (Åbo: Åbo Akademi

the vocabulary used in Zech 7:9–10 (משפט, עשה, איש, עשק, אלמנה, יתום, גר), but Jer 5:27–28 may also be influential with its reference to rendering justice (משפט ... שפט) and to the orphan (יתום). While one can discern Jeremianic influence here (as in other ways throughout Zech 7:1–14) one does not find here direct citation, as Petersen so aptly noted: "rather than providing a pale copy of prophetic speech, he has provided vigorous prophetic discourse."[17] Strengthening this view of earlier prophetic speech employed in fresh rhetoric is the highly debated phrase which now constitutes Zech 7:8: "Then the word of Yahweh came to Zechariah saying"). Just prior to the prophetic message relying heavily upon the tradition of the earlier prophets (Jeremiah) the one(s) responsible for Zech 7–8 remind the reader that these words are considered contemporary revelation from Yahweh through Zechariah. This fuses the two generations of prophets, earlier (Jeremiah) and contemporary (Zechariah) and at the same time the two generations of audiences, that of Zechariah and the ancestors.

A similar strategy can be discerned in another anomaly in this passage that has confused commentators in the past, one that comes to light in Zech 7:13. The opening verb of 7:13 identifies the activities described in 7:13–14 as part of Zechariah's rehearsal of the experience of the ancestors's generation, a rehearsal which began in 7:7, included the echoing of the words of the earlier prophets in 7:9–10, and included the depiction of the inappropriate response of the ancestors's generation in 7:11–12a. This disobedience prompted the anger of God described in 7:12b using the same term (קצף) employed in 1:2 to describe God's response to the disobedience of the ancestors. The disciplinary phases already highlighted in Zech 1:1–6 (anger, warning, judgment) can also be discerned in Zech 7:7–14 (anger in 7:12b, warning in 7:9–12a, judgment in 7:14). But in Zech 7 another phase is included, one that lies between anger/warning and judgment in which the deity's patience runs out, refusing to respond to the cries of the people due to their enduring refusal to respond to the deity's warnings. This added phase is appropriate for the response of the prophet to the Bethel contingent in Zech 7–8, because this group had requested clarification over whether they should continue their practice of fasting and mourning over the destroyed temple, penitential practices which entailed calling out for the deity's response. While 7:13–14 represents a

---

University, 1996), 69–72; Stead, *Intertextuality*, 232–33. Contra claims by John D. W. Watts, "Zechariah," in *The Broadman Bible Commentary, Volume 7: Hosea–Malachi*, ed. C. J. Allen (London: Marshall, Morgan & Scott, 1972), 7:308–65 (333), and Sweeney, *Twelve*, 2:644, for connections to Isaianic material such as Isa 1:10–17.

[17] Petersen, *Haggai and Zechariah 1–8*, 291. See also Wim A. M. Beuken, *Haggai–Sacharja 1–8: Studien zur Überlieferungsgeschichte der frühnachexilischen Prophetie*, SSN 10 (Assen: Van Gorcum, 1967), 125; Albert Petitjean, *Les oracles du proto-Zacharie: Un programme de restauration pour la communauté juive après l'exil* (Paris: Librairie Lecoffre, 1969), 335.

description of the experience of the earlier generation (ancestors), the verbal forms used reveal a rhetorical strategy to make this historical presentation vivid and relevant to Zechariah's contemporary audience.

ויהי כאשר־קרא ולא שמעו כן יקראו ולא אשמע אמר יהוה צבאות:	¹³Then it came about (waw/r prefix) that just as he called (suffix) and they did not respond (suffix), so they are calling (prefix) and I am not responding (prefix), has said Yahweh of hosts.
ואסערם על כל־הגוים אשר לא־ידעום	¹⁴But I am blowing them away in a storm (simple waw prefix) onto all the nations which they did not know.
והארץ נשמה אחריהם מעבר ומשב וישׂימו ארץ־חמדה לשמה:	And the land was desolated (suffix) behind them in order to prevent passing over and returning. So they made (waw/r prefix) a precious land uninhabited.

The prophet begins in 7:13a by describing the experience of the earlier generation (ancestors) with Yahweh: he called and they did not respond (קרא ולא שמעו), utilizing suffix conjugation verbs, a conjugation usually employed for activities in the past. In 7:13b, however, the speaker shifts from the prophet to Yahweh describing the activity of deity and people. In addition, the verbal forms used are no longer suffix conjugations but prefix conjugations (יקראו ולא אשמע, "they are calling and I am not responding"), a conjugation usually employed for activities in the present or future. Through this shift in conjugations the audience is transported back into the ancestors's generation, the audience of the earlier prophets, to hear the final verbal judgment of Yahweh against that earlier generation cast in Yahweh's personal voice and employing verbal forms typical of present and progressive action. This would have been poignant for the audience typified by the Bethel contingent of chapter 7, as they ask whether to continue their practice of crying out to Yahweh (7:3).

The use of the prefix conjugation does not end with the depiction of the deity's disciplinary unresponsiveness to the people's cries in 7:13. The depiction of the deity's judgment in 7:14a continues the use of the prefix conjugation (ואסערם; "I am blowing them away in a storm") before shifting back into the suffix conjugation (נשמה; "was desolated") and preterite (וישׂימו; "they made") expected for depictions of the past in 7:14b. In this way not only is the lack of divine response to the people's cries made contemporary in this depiction, but so also the act of judgment is made vividly present for Zechariah's contemporary audience.

Conclusion

Thus, in Zech 7:1–14 one can discern a similar pattern to what was observed in 1:1–6. Through ambiguity and subtle shifts in rhetoric generations of both prophets and people are fused and the word of Yahweh endures to motivate a new generation to respond to the prophetic cries. One key difference between 1:1–6 and chapters 7–8, however, is that while in 1:1–6 the response of the people is recorded, chapters 7–8 do not provide any such depiction as completed, looking only to the future, and leaving such response in the hands of its readers. The message of the earlier prophets will continue to exert its influence in the chapters which follow in Zech 9–14,[18] as the solution for the realization of restoration becomes increasingly epic. While 1:1–6 provides a picture of the appropriate response to this intergenerational prophetic strategy, chapters 7–8 justify why restoration remains unrealized even though the temple is completed.

---

[18] See Ina Willi-Plein, *Prophetie am Ende: Untersuchungen zu Sacharja 9–14*, BBB 42 (Köln: Hanstein, 1974); Raymond F. Person, *Second Zechariah and the Deuteronomic School*, JSOTSup 167 (Sheffield: JSOT Press, 1993); Katrina J. Larkin, *The Eschatology of Second Zechariah: A Study of the Formation of a Mantological Wisdom Anthology*, CBET 6 (Kampen: Kok, 1994); Nicholas Ho Fai Tai, *Prophetie als Schriftauslegung in Sacharja 9–14: Traditions- und kompositionsgeschichtliche Studien*, Calwer Theologische Monographien 17 (Stuttgart: Calwer, 1996); Nurmela, *Prophets in Dialogue*; Mark J. Boda and Michael H. Floyd, eds., *Bringing out the Treasure: Inner Biblical Allusion and Zechariah 9–14*, JSOTSup 370 (Sheffield: Sheffield Academic, 2003); Suk Yee Lee, *An Intertextual Analysis of Zechariah 9–10: The Earlier Restoration Expectations of Second Zechariah*, LHBOTS 599 (London: Bloomsbury, 2015).

Table 1: Rhetorical Levels in Zechariah 1:1–6

Narrator (or Zechariah) describing actions of Zechariah and present generation
    Direct address of present generation
        Direct address from Yahweh to Zechariah
            Zechariah's address to present generation
                Yahweh's address to present generation (through Zechariah)
                    Earlier prophets's address to ancestor generation
                        Yahweh's address to ancestor generation
                        (through earlier prophets)

$^{1:1}$In the eighth month, in year two of Darius, the word of Yahweh came to Zechariah son of Berechiah son of Iddo, the prophet, saying:
        ^{2}" *'Yahweh was extremely angry with your (mp) ancestors.'*
      ^{3} You (ms) must say to them (mp):
            Thus has said Yahweh of hosts,
                "return (mp) to me,"
            declaration of Yahweh of Hosts,
                "that I may return to you (mp),"
            has said Yahweh of Hosts.
            ^{4}"Do not be (mp) like your (mp) ancestors to whom the earlier prophets proclaimed saying:
                'thus has said Yahweh of Hosts:
                      "Turn (mp) from your (mp) evil ways and from your (mp) evil deeds."'
            But they (mp) did not listen nor pay attention to me,"
        declaration of Yahweh.
            ^{5}"Your (mp) ancestors, where are they?
            And the prophets, did they go on living forever?
            ^{6}The reality is, my words and my prescriptions which I commanded my servants, the prophets, did they not catch up with your (mp) ancestors?"'"
Then they (mp) returned and they (mp) said:
    "Just as Yahweh of Hosts planned to do to us, according to our ways and according to our deeds, so he has dealt with us."

Table 2: Rhetorical Levels in Zechariah 7:1–14

> Narrator (or Zechariah) describing actions of Zechariah and present generation
> > *Direct address of present generation*
> > > Direct address from Yahweh to Zechariah
> > > > *Zechariah's address to present generation*
> > > > > Yahweh's address to present generation (through Zechariah)
> > > > > > *Earlier prophets's address to ancestor generation*
> > > > > > > Yahweh's address to ancestor generation (through earlier prophets)

⁷:¹Now it came to pass in the fourth year of Darius the king, the word of Yahweh came to Zechariah, on the fourth of the ninth month, in Chislev. ²Bethel had sent Shar-ezer, the king's spokesman, and his men to seek the favor Yahweh, to say to the priests who were at the house of Yahweh of hosts, and to the prophets saying,

"Shall I weep in the fifth month, restricting myself, just as I have done these—how many years?"

⁴Then the word of Yahweh of hosts came to me, saying,

⁵"Say to all the people of the land and to the priests, saying,

'When you fasted, lamenting in the fifth and in the seventh month, these seventy years, did you really fast for me? ⁶And when you are eating and when you are drinking, are not only you the ones eating and only you the ones drinking?

⁷Are not these the words which Yahweh announced through the earlier prophets, when Jerusalem was inhabited and at ease and its cities were surrounding it, and the Negev and Shephelah were inhabited?'"

⁷:⁸Then the word of Yahweh came to Zechariah, saying,

⁹*"Thus has said Yahweh of hosts, saying,*

'Render true justice and practice covenant loyalty and mercy, each of you to one another. ¹⁰And do not exploit widow or orphan, sojourner or poor. Do not devise in your minds harm against one another.'

¹¹*Then they refused to listen attentively and they turned a rebellious shoulder and their ears they made unresponsive in order not to hear.* ¹²*And their heart they made into a diamond in order not to hear the law and the words which Yahweh of hosts sent by his Spirit through the former prophets. Then great wrath came from Yahweh of hosts.* ¹³*Then it came about that just as he called and they did not respond,*

so they are calling and I am not responding,

has said Yahweh of hosts.

¹⁴But I am blowing them away in a storm onto all the nations which they did not know.

And the land was desolated behind them in order to prevent passing over and returning. So they made a precious land uninhabited.

Table 3: Rhetorical Levels in Zechariah 8:14–23

Narrator (or Zechariah) describing actions of Zechariah and present generation
   Direct address of future generation
      Direct address from Yahweh to Zechariah
         Zechariah's address to present generation
            Yahweh's address to present generation (through Zechariah)
               Earlier prophets's address to ancestor generation
                  Yahweh's address to ancestor generation
                    (through earlier prophets)

      8:14For thus has said Yahweh of hosts,
         'Just as I have purposed to do harm to you, when your ancestors aroused me to anger,
      has said Yahweh of hosts,
         and have not relented, 15so I have turned and purposed in these days to do good to Jerusalem and the house of Judah. Do not fear.
         16These are the things which you should do: speak truth, each with his neighbor, judge with truth and with judgment which produces peace in your gates, and each of you, do not devise in your mind harm against your neighbor, and do not love a false oath because all these things are what I hate,'
      declaration of Yahweh."
18Then the word of Yahweh of hosts came to me, saying,
      19"Thus has said Yahweh of hosts,
         'The fast of the fourth, and the fast of the fifth and the fast of the seventh and the fast of the tenth will be turned for the house of Judah into jubilation, and gladness and merry festivals. Love truth and peace.'"
      20Thus has said Yahweh of hosts,
         "Again it will happen that peoples and leaders of many cities will come, 21 and leaders of one city will go to another city, saying, 'Let us surely go to entreat the face of Yahweh, that is, to seek Yahweh of hosts. I myself also am going.' 22Then many peoples and mighty nations will come in order to seek Yahweh of hosts in Jerusalem and to seek the favor of Yahweh."
      23Thus has said Yahweh of hosts,
         "In those days it will happen that ten men from all the languages of the nations will seize, they will seize on the hem of each Jewish person saying, 'We want to go with you for we have heard God is with you.'"

8
Freeing the Burden of Prophecy: מַשָּׂא and the Legitimacy of Prophecy in Zechariah 9–14[1]

While in the earlier chapters in this book I investigated Zech 1–8, I now shift my attention to Zech 9–14. I begin by analyzing the introductory formula (מַשָּׂא דבר יהוה) which structures the second half of the book of Zechariah, appearing at Zech 9:1; 12:1 (cf. Mal 1:1). I argue that this formula has been drawn from Jeremiah and signals the reemergence of authoritative prophecy in the Persian Period.

Zechariah 9, Zech 12, and Mal 1 all begin with the same grammatical construction: מַשָּׂא דבר יהוה. This phrase appears to serve as an editorial superscription introducing each of the sections which follow the construction: Zech 9:1a (Zech 9–11), Zech 12:1a (Zech 12–14), Mal 1:1a (Malachi), a theory that is bolstered by the thematic and stylistic integrity of each of these sections as well as by the use of the term מַשָּׂא to introduce prophetic pericopae and corpora elsewhere (Isa 13–23; Nahum; Habakkuk).

The purpose of this paper is to explore this term מַשָּׂא in order to ascertain its function as an editorial marker. Does it merely signal a new section of prophecy, does it function also as a form-critical designation identifying the subsequent section as a specific kind of prophecy, or does it function as a traditio-historical signal affirming the renewal of prophecy in the Persian period?

---

[1] Based on my original publication, Mark J. Boda, "Freeing the Burden of Prophecy: *Maśśā'* and the Legitimacy of Prophecy in Zech 9–14," *Bib* 87 (2006): 338–57. Slightly revised for inclusion in this volume.

משׂא IN THE HEBREW BIBLE: ETYMOLOGICAL DEFINITIONS

The lexeme משׂא occurs sixty-seven times in the Hebrew Bible. On four occasions it is a name of a person or region (Gen 25:14; 1 Chr 1:30; Prov 30:1; 31:1). Thirty-five times the word is used to describe something which is carried by another, either in the literal sense of carrying a heavy object or in the figurative sense of bearing a responsibility (compare Exod 23:5 and Num 11:11). This evidence suggests that this word is closely related to the Hebrew verbal root, נשׂא (to bear, carry). Important for our discussion, however, is the fact that on twenty-eight occasions, these same letters are used to describe or introduce prophetic speech,[2] and throughout the history of interpretation many have sought to determine the meaning and significance of these occurrences.

The most common route to determine this in the past has been through a lexical investigation of the etymological roots of the word. Most have concluded that the word is intimately related to the lexeme משׂא (burden, responsibility) either because it is an ominous prophecy,[3] because it was something carried by the prophet and laid upon an individual or nation,[4] or because it was part of the responsibility of the prophet.[5] Others, however, have not been convinced by this explanation and instead have located the origins of this word in the verbal root נשׂא. One view is that משׂא developed from the threatening gesture expressed by

---

[2] 2 Kgs 9:25; Isa 13:1; 14:28; 15:1; 17:1; 19:1; 21:1, 11, 13; 22:1; 23:1; 30:6; Jer 23:33²ˣ, 34, 35²ˣ, 38³ˣ; Ezek 12:10; Nah 1:1; Hab 1:1; Zech 9:1; 12:1; Mal 1:1; Lam 2:14; 2 Chr 24:27. There is some debate whether the appearances in Prov 30:1; 31:1 refer to a place or speech form.

[3] F. Stolz, "נשׂא," in *TLOT* 2:769–74; P. A. H. de Boer, "An Inquiry into the Meaning of the Term *maśśā'*," in *OtSt* 5 (1948), 197–214; G. Lambert, "'Mon joug est aisé et mon fardeau léger': Note d'exégèse," *NRTh* 77 (1955): 963–69; H. S. Gehman, "The Burden of the Prophets," *JQR* 31 (1940–41): 107–21; cf. Gen. Rab. 44:6 in which the rabbis note that prophecy went by ten names, the severest of which was משׂא. See recently, Peter D. Miscall, *Isaiah*, Readings: A New Biblical Commentary (Sheffield: JSOT Press, 1993), 46: "burden indicates that what follows weighs down on us; it is a nightmare."

[4] Gehman, "Burden"; similarly, Richard Weis, "A Definition of the Genre *Maśśā'* in the Hebrew Bible" (PhD diss., Claremont Graduate School, 1986), 353, although he does not approve of this view in the end; as J. A. Thompson, *The Book of Jeremiah*, NICOT (Grand Rapids: Eerdmans, 1980), 505: "an imposed burden, imposed by a master, an overlord, or a deity on beasts or men. Metaphorically it can mean a burden of leadership or of religious duty, and at times the heavy burden of God's judgment. Often in prophetic writings it suggests a judgment or catastrophe. The same word appears as a heading of prophetic oracles; but there it has acquired a technical sense, 'argument,' 'thesis,' even though the content of the passage that follows preserves the original sense of the term."

[5] Douglas R. Jones, *Jeremiah*, NCB (London: Marshall Pickering, 1992), 314: "the heavy responsibility of the prophetic word, like a burden on the shoulders of the prophet."

נשא (to lift) + יד (hand) (Deut 32:40–42; Ezek 36:7; cf. Rev 10:5, 6), thus, the משא is a "threatening oracle."⁶ Another view is that משא refers to the practice of "taking up" lots for divination.⁷ Many have linked משא to the collocation נשא (to raise) + קול (voice), arguing that משא is merely a prophetic utterance,⁸ a view bolstered by the fact that the word נשא is also used without the word קול (voice) to refer to uttering, speaking, reciting, and in the Balaam texts of Num 23–24 is used to introduce the utterances of a prophet (with משל, 23:7, 18; 24:3, 15, 20, 21, 23).⁹ One final view is that משא is related to another Hebrew noun: משאת which is used in Judg 20:38, 40; Jer 6:1 to designate a fire or smoke signal. In this way a משא is "the signal of YHWH's intentions received by the prophetic look-out."¹⁰

It is obvious from the review above that there are many ways to explain the lexical origins of the prophetic use of the term משא, testimony to the creativity and ingenuity of these many interpreters. However, using etymology to understand a word is a diachronic exercise, that is, reflection on the way a word developed through time. But such speculation is not always helpful for understanding the meaning of the word at the specific time, that is, its synchronic meaning. A review of the various prophetic passages in which the word משא appears establishes the following facts:

The word משא does not always introduce a negative prophecy and thus should not be translated as a "burden" or "threat" (cf. Jer 23:33–38; Zech 9–10).¹¹ It is used in conjunction with various means and types of prophecy: "word of Yahweh" (2 Kgs 9:25; cf. 1 Kgs 21:17–19; Zech 9:1; 12:1; Mal 1:1), something

---

[6] R. B. Y. Scott, "The Meaning of *maśśā'* as an Oracle Title," *JBL* 67 (1948): v–vi, who pointed to Isa 21:1–2, where משא is used in v. 1 and "a severe/harsh vision" is used in v. 2; cf. John D. W. Watts, *Isaiah 1–33*, WBC 24 (Waco, TX: Word, 1985), 190–91, who claims that in Isaiah it "means that which Yahweh signals (by hand or word) against someone or some group."

[7] See O. Procksch, *Jesaia I*, KAT 9 (Leipzig: Deichert, 1930), 184; see Weis, "Definition," 2 n. 1.

[8] E.g., Matitiahu Tsevat, "Alalakhiana," *HUCA* 29 (1958): 109–34 (119); Ronald E. Clements, *Isaiah 1–39*, NCB (Grand Rapids: Eerdmans, 1980), 132.

[9] See Hans Wildberger, *Isaiah 13–27*, trans. Thomas H. Trapp, CC (Minneapolis: Fortress, 1997); also Marvin A. Sweeney, *The Twelve Prophets*, 2 vols., Berit Olam (Collegeville, MN: Liturgical Press, 2000), 2:423.

[10] So Weis, "Definition," 353–55, who says of this view in relation to other views: "a mild preference at best."

[11] Contra then Barry Baruch Margulis, "Studies in the Oracles against the Nations" (PhD diss., Brandeis University, 1967), 202, 12 who states: "it would appear that maśśā' is the only prophetic term which is, by definition and without further qualification, an oracle of doom" and further "its meaning as a 'prophetic oracle'—especially an 'oracle of doom'—is beyond dispute and controversy."

"written in the annotations on the book of the kings" (2 Chr 24:27), answers to questions from people, possibly cult prophecy (Jer 23:33–38); something associated with, possibly juxtaposed to, "vision of your prophets" (Lam 2:14); a prophetic sign act (Ezek 12:10; cf. 12:1–16); something which Isaiah "saw" (Isa 13:1; cf. 1:1; 2:1, "vision"); a vision (Isa 21:1–2); the book of vision (Nah 1:1).

These observations have led some to a different type of analysis of משא, one which explores the various contexts in which משא appears. It is this exploration that has led a few to the conclusion that משא functions as more than just a signal of a new section of prophecy, but also as a genre tag that designates the material as a particular type of prophecy.[12]

משא AS FORM-CRITICAL TAG

This view that משא is a form-critical tag has been incorporated into recent commentary work on prophetic literature by Marvin Sweeney and Michael Floyd,[13] but their work assumes and relies upon the earlier and more extensive work of

---

[12] William L. Holladay, *Jeremiah 1: A Commentary on the Book of the Prophet Jeremiah, Chapters 1–25*, Hermeneia (Philadelphia: Fortress, 1986), 650, concludes from his study of משא in Jer 23 that this speech form was associated with the establishment in Jerusalem and their false prophets because it was never used of Jeremiah outside this passage. This does not account for the widespread use of the term in other prophetic books. Stolz, "נשא," 2:769–74, identified משא as a genre tag which as a rule indicated the oracles against the nations (Isa 13:1; 15:1; Nah 1:1; cf. Isa 14:28 etc.), but which could (probably secondarily) refer quite generally to prophetic address (Zech 9:1; 12:1; Mal 1:1) and can refer to a prophetic vision (Hab 1:1) and even a prophetic announcement of judgment to an individual (2 Kgs 9:25).

[13] Marvin A. Sweeney, *Isaiah 1–39, with an Introduction to Prophetic Literature*, FOTL 16 (Grand Rapids: Eerdmans, 1996), 213, 22, 534; Sweeney, *Twelve*; Michael H. Floyd, *Minor Prophets, Part 2*, FOTL 22 (Grand Rapids: Eerdmans, 2000); Michael H. Floyd, "The Maśśā' as a Type of Prophetic Book," *JBL* 121 (2002): 401–22. Sweeney sees the previous revelation in Zech 9–11 and 12–14 as that of Isaiah. Floyd uses 2 Kgs 9:25–26 as the basis for his construction of the genre and then limits himself to instances in the Book of the Twelve. He avoids the pitfalls of dubious theories of the final form of Haggai–Malachi which plagues Weis, but does not have to account for issues in Isaiah and Jeremiah. For him the previous revelation in Malachi is some form of the Torah; that of Zech 9–11 is Zech 1–8; and that of Zech 12–14 is Zech 1–11. See also the recent dissertation of Michael D. Woodcock, "Forms and Functions of Hope in Zechariah 9–14" (PhD diss., Fuller Theological Seminary, 2004), which assumes the results of Weis and Floyd.

Richard Weis.[14] Weis argued that משא is a genre tag denoting a prophetic explication of an earlier divine word. One key implication of Weis's work was that he concluded that the genre showed a shift in the history of prophetism, from a dynamic oral phenomenon to a fixed literary phenomenon. Since Weis represents the most extensive development of this stream of research and remains inaccessible to most scholars today, we will focus our attention on his work, offering a full description of his argument and evidence.[15]

WEIS AND משא

In his seminal work Weis followed three lines of enquiry.[16] First, he investigated the semantics of the term משא when it is related to prophets and prophetic texts and speeches. Secondly, after establishing the limits of each text introduced by משא, he researches the form and intention of the texts in themselves (that is, apart from their present canonical context). Finally, he researches the function of the texts in their literary contexts (that is, in their present canonical contexts).

1. Semantic

His semantic inquiry leads him to conclude that משא not only marks a definite prophetic speech or text unit, but is also a genre name.[17] It appears to be connected with revelatory experience, especially because of its use with the terms דבר (word) or חזון (vision). According to Weis a משא is not a דבר־יהוה (word of Yahweh), although it is probably based on and derived from a preexisting דבר־יהוה. It is closely related to concrete, human historical entities (nations, groups, individuals, Hebrew or foreign) and situations, which seem to be its topics. It may be oral or written and is preeminently a human composition which in some texts is attributable to or attributed to a prophet.

2. משא Texts apart from Their Literary Context

Weis's investigation of משא texts apart from their literary context leads him to the following conclusions grouped into Form and Intention.

---

[14] Weis, "Definition." Although this work was never published, Weis did provide a précis of his work in Richard Weis, "Oracle," in *ABD* 5:28–29.
[15] David L. Petersen, *Zechariah 9–14 and Malachi: A Commentary*, OTL (Louisville: Westminster John Knox, 1995), 2, 41–42, sees the term משא in Zech 9–14 and Malachi in terms of a prophetic redactional tradition in which oracles were presented in order: against the nations, concerning Israel, and on behalf of Israel.
[16] Weis, "Definition," 264.
[17] Ibid., 102.

In terms of form, there is an absence of prophetic messenger formula as well as the accusation + announcement of judgment pattern (except in occasional subordinate or peripheral roles). It is predominantly the speech of the prophet, although the speech of Yahweh is mixed in with this. Some texts contain specially highlighted citations of a revelation or a plan of Yahweh which are particularly bound up in the process of connecting Yahweh's acts and/or intentions with their manifestation in the human sphere. The addressee of the text is never Yahweh or the prophet, but rather the entity which is the topic or the prophet's own community. Texts are comprised of descriptive (report or announcement) and/or ordering (command or prohibition) genres. One group of eleven texts contains both descriptive and ordering and follows a pattern wherein the descriptive sections include reports and the descriptive materials motivate the ordering sections of the text. A second group of six texts contains only descriptive genres with announcements predominating. Taking both groups together, 75 percent of the time a Yahweh act is given with its human result. In the others the same connection is made but less explicitly. The commands fall into two groups according to the speaker, with a smaller group not spoken by the prophet but by Yahweh (one narratological level removed from the direct address to the readers), and with a larger group spoken by the prophet (on the primary narratological level to the readers). These commands fall into two subgroups: summons (jubilation or communal lamentation) and commands for a variety of concrete human actions.

Building on this formal analysis, Weis proceeds to Intention. He observes that the formal aspects "seem to point to a tendency to connect YHWH's acts and/or intentions (sometimes as communicated in a particular revelation) with events in the human sphere either for the purpose of providing direction (commands) or insight (announcements of future)."[18]

Weis notes that seven texts (Isa 13; 14:29; 15; 21; 23; Nah 1; Zech 9–11) instruct the audience in certain behavior through commands and/or prohibitions that are based on an explication of the way that some expression of the divine will or some act of Yahweh manifests itself in human affairs. Two other texts (Isa 22; Mal 1–3) follow this pattern, though not as explicitly. Five texts (Isa 19; 21; Ezek 12; Hab 1; Zech 12–14) do not give explicit instructions to the addressees, but explain certain events in human affairs as a manifestation of Yahweh's intention, declaration, or act(s) or expound how Yahweh's intention, declaration, or act(s) will be manifested in human affairs. This leads him to highlight the "common thread" in all these texts: "the explication of certain events in human affairs as manifesting the revealed will and/or act of YHWH".[19] In seven texts the explicated speech of Yahweh is actually quoted (Isa 14:29; 15; 21; 22; 23; Nah 1; Mal

---

[18] Ibid., 227.
[19] Ibid., 228.

1). In other texts that which is explicated is a vision (Isa 21; in Hab 1 a vision is clearly presupposed), Yahweh's plan (Isa 19; 23, although not quoted is explicitly cited), or a symbolic action (Ezek 12). Six other texts do not follow this pattern. Two of them lack an explicit quotation (Isa 13; Zech 12), while the four remaining (2 Kgs 9; Isa 17; 21; 30) do not constitute a serious deviation from this pattern. Isaiah 21 presupposes an absence of such a speech. Both Isa 30 and 2 Kgs 9 explicate points where the existing Yahweh speech is unclear or silent either within itself (Isa 30) or in relation to the human situation as well (2 Kgs 9).

For Weis, his investigation has suggested a common problem or situation to which the texts respond: "indeterminacy in respect to a piece of YHWH revelation whether within the revelation itself or between the revelation and human affairs and events."[20] Evidence for this is culled from Isa 14:29; 15; 21 which respond at least to some indeterminacy in the Yahweh revelation itself, Isa 17 which responds to indeterminacy within the Yahweh revelation, and Isa 22; Nah 1; Hab 1; Mal 1, all of which give clear evidence within themselves that they respond to a disjuncture, an indeterminacy, in the relation between the Yahweh revelation and human affairs and events.[21]

3. משא Texts in Their Present Literary Contexts

Weis's final stage is an evaluation of the משא texts in their present literary contexts. Here he finds similar evidence. The משא in 2 Kgs 9:26 connects a preexisting expression of divine intention with concrete human events. The משא texts in Isa 13–23 function within the book of Isaiah to explicate the relation between the existing expression of Yahweh's intention (found in Isa 2–4) and specific, concrete historical entities and events.[22] Isaiah 30:6–7 explicates the woe oracle found in Isa 30:1–5, while Ezek 12:11–16 explicates the sign act of Ezekiel 12:1–10. Habakkuk 1:2–2:20 presents a problem in the community's history and describes the historical manifestation of Yahweh's actions in response to that problem. Zechariah 9–11; 12–14; and Malachi are treated together because Weis proposes that they are a literary unit. Zechariah 9–11 responds to the expectations of Haggai and Zechariah (Hag 1:1–Zech 8:23). Zechariah 12–14 entails a reinterpretation based on the symbolic action of Zech 11:4–17. Finally, Malachi responds to Haggai–Zechariah as a whole, explicating why the community's history does not appear to manifest the intention of Yahweh.

---

[20] Ibid., 229.
[21] Ibid., 230.
[22] Ibid., 245.

4. Genre Definition

Near the end of his work, Weis synthesizes his analysis to provide a genre definition. In terms of the genre's constitution (that is, the oral origin of the genre), a משא is

> a prophetic speech or text unit, composed by a prophet in order to show how YHWH's acting or intention will or does manifest itself in human affairs. It does this for the purpose of providing insight into the future or direction for human action in the present or near future. The immediate topic of the משא will, in accord with this, always be some human historical entity whether or not that entity is actually addressed directly, or in apostrophe, by the text. The addressee of a משא is either its topic or the prophet's own community.[23]

In terms of the genre's use in the final form of the Hebrew Bible the definition of משא is more limited:

> Except for Nah 1:2–3:19, the exemplars of the genre משא that survive in the final form of the Hebrew Bible are used to expound the manifestation in human events and affairs of the divine plan/intention revealed in some _previously communicated_ expression of the divine will. This previously communicated revelation is always outside the משא. Except for Hab 1:2–2:20 this previously communicated [sic?] is always found in the literary context of the משא. This is true even if the משא itself communicates a revelation as described above. Moreover, this previous communication (be it speech, vision, drama, symbolic action) is presented as communication through a prophet and, at least in the final form, is written although, as with the genre משא itself, there are indications of oral delivery or performance. Finally, the problem addressed is still some question about the way YHWH's intention or acting will manifest itself in human affairs, but the points at which the question may arise are significantly restricted. The question may arise from an indeterminacy inherent in some revelation of YHWH"s intention (e.g., Isa 30:6b–7; Ezek 12:11–16). It may arise because the relation between some revelation of YHWH's intention and events in the human situation has not been played out in the expected way (e.g., Hab 1:2–2:20; Zech 9–11). It never seems to arise from some problem or question arising out of the human situation per se.[24]

In short the definition of the genre משא in terms of its use in oral contexts (its constitution) is "prophetic exposition of YHWH's revealed will or activity,"[25] while the definition of the genre משא in terms of its use in literary contexts is

---

[23] Ibid., 272.
[24] Ibid., 274–75. Underlining original to cited author.
[25] Ibid., 275–76.

"prophetic interpretation." Bridging these two definitions is the following expression: "prophetic exposition (of YHWH revelation)."

5. Tradition History

Weis also offers some reflection on the tradition history of the genre in order to take into account the temporal, societal, and geographical ranges of the works. He discovers that the genre endured among the prophetic tradition of Judah from the ninth/eighth until the fifth/fourth century BCE (in this he discounts 2 Kgs 9:25 which has a northern setting, because it has come through Dtr hands). Throughout this history, Weis discerns a few changes. First, in terms of the use of משא in titles for prophetic literature, the post-exilic examples (Zechariah, Malachi) distinguish carefully between משא and דבר־יהוה, while the pre-exilic examples in Isaiah make no distinction. Secondly, in terms of the citations of Yahweh revelation, the eighth-to-seventh-century examples all contained within themselves a quotation or report of the revelation, while the sixth-to-fifth-century examples (including also the function of the משא texts in their final literary context) all expound previously communicated Yahweh revelation that lies outside the משא text itself.

6. Semantics

At the end Weis returns to the etymological discussion and suggests three possible ways to understand the origins of the word משא: from נשא (utter, recite = prophetic expression of divine revelation), from נשא (bring, carry = the thing brought back to the inquirer from the prophet's encounter with the deity), from the same root as משאת (fire/smoke-signal = the signal of Yahweh's intention received by the prophetic lookout). Weis prefers the final option, but adds: "a mild preference at best."

7. History of Prophecy

Weis believes that his work contributes to our understanding of the history of prophecy in the Hebrew Bible:

> This suggests that, near its end, the prophetic movement had become fundamentally a movement of the tradents of the prophets. It further suggests that the locus of revelation had shifted from the living encounter of a prophet with YHWH to the recorded or remembered words of an earlier prophet who had had such an encounter—which words could, in some way or other, still be seen to have validity in human affairs. In this context the 'dying out' of the prophetic movement may not be due so much to the

'failure' of prophecy as to the fact that the locus of revelation was no longer living persons. We may do better to speak of a transformation of the movement.[26]

EVALUATING WEIS

At first sight, Weis's theory appears to have possibilities for the study of Zech 9–14. Over the past half century, scholars have struggled over the issue of the relationship between Zech 1–8 and 9–14, and Weis's theory offers form-critical evidence that Zech 9–14 is intimately related to at least Zech 1–8 and possibly also Hag 1–Zech 8. This conclusion echoes that of many who have worked on the book of the Twelve as a whole over the past decade.[27] Furthermore, scholars have often highlighted the density of inner biblical allusion in Zech 9–14, allusions not only to Zech 1–8, but also to most of the latter prophets. Weis's theory would establish that the intention of the writers of these texts was to explicate these earlier prophetic utterances in a time of crisis. But can this theory be exploited for the study of Zech 9–14? Is there any foundation to Weis's theory?

There is little question that Weis has provided the most intense study of the term משא and its attendant texts. His presentation of the history of debate is accurate and his analyses of the texts are sensitive to their diachronic and synchronic dimensions. But certain aspects of his argument do invite critical scrutiny.

In splendid fashion, Weis has undermined the enduring assumption that משא texts are negative prophecy, but as he replaces it with this new hypothesis that they are explicative prophecy, he seems to replicate similar problems. Consistently in his work on the genre's constitution (the משא texts apart from their final literary context) he must deal with exceptions to patterns he has highlighted for these משא texts. Thus, for example, on his way to concluding that the "norm" for these texts is that they are not a verbatim report of Yahweh speech, but rather the speech of the prophet, he must explain away exceptions in three texts.[28] In his search for formal elements of the genre, Weis must finally admit:

---

[26] Ibid., 365.
[27] Mark J. Boda, *Haggai and Zechariah Research: A Bibliographic Survey*, Tools for Biblical Study 5 (Leiden: Deo, 2003), 29–31; cf. Aaron Schart, "Reconstructing the Redaction History of the Twelve Prophets: Problems and Models," in *Reading and Hearing the Book of the Twelve*, ed. James D. Nogalski and Marvin A. Sweeney, SymS 15 (Atlanta: Society of Biblical Literature, 2000), 34–48; Paul L. Redditt, "The Formation of the Book of the Twelve: A Review of Research," in *Thematic Threads in the Book of the Twelve*, ed. Paul L. Redditt and Aaron Schart, BZAW 325 (Berlin: de Gruyter, 2003), 1–26.
[28] Weis, "Definition," 212–13.

Freeing the Burden of Prophecy 145

While we have been able to uncover some typical formal aspects of these texts, there remains among them a certain degree of formal diversity—especially of superstructural diversity. Various formal means—albeit falling within certain boundaries—are used to accomplish the same purpose. This suggests that intention may play a much more significant role as a unifying and characterizing aspect for משׂא texts as a genre than form does.[29]

The variety in the formal aspects of the texts should have been a signal to Weis that he may not be dealing with a form at all.[30] The appeal to "purpose" or "intention" appears to be a last ditch attempt to rescue his genre hypothesis. One

---

[29] Ibid., 227. Although focusing on the final literary rather than original oral level, Floyd says he follows Weis in identifying three formal elements of the משׂא genre, that is, (1) assertion about Yahweh's involvement in a particular situation; (2) allusion to previous prophecies whose status is clarified by the assertion; and (3) directives concerning an appropriate response to Yahweh's initiative based on this assertion; Floyd, "Maśśā'," 411. As with Weis, however, Floyd regularly admits inconsistency in the structure of his proposed genre (see comments on Habakkuk, p. 414, and on Malachi, p. 416). Additionally, for Floyd there is the problem of his identification of the proposed "previous revelation" (#2), especially the identification of Nah 1:11–14 and Hab 1:5–11, and for Malachi, the Torah. Such a claim is difficult to question as at many points in prophetic books there are allusions to earlier revelation, whether that is the Torah or the earlier prophets. Sweeney also is open to criticism on this point. In the case of Zech 9–11 and 12–14, Sweeney claims that the "previous revelation" is the book of Isaiah. Sweeney bases this on an allusive play he discerns between Zechariah ben Berechiah ben Iddo (Zech 1:1) and Zechariah ben Jeberechiah (Isa 8:2) and on his claim that "much of the material in Zechariah 9–11 and 12–14 appears to be heavily indebted to Isaiah"; Sweeney, *Twelve*, 2:657. The first basis is speculative and although the second may be true, Isaiah is certainly not the only prophet alluded to in Zech 9–14; cf. Mark J. Boda and Michael H. Floyd, eds., *Bringing out the Treasure: Inner Biblical Allusion and Zechariah 9–14*, JSOTSup 370 (Sheffield: Sheffield Academic, 2003). Note ironically Floyd, *Minor Prophets*, 547, whose criticism of Jeremias's work on "theophany" could have been directed at Weis's work: "He calls the theophany a *Gattung*, but he defines it in terms of formulaic themes and motifs that tend to cluster in the context of various compositional forms, without ever constituting an independent form of their own."

[30] In dealing with the term משׂא in the book of Isaiah, Sweeney speaks of "a consistent generic pattern known as the *maśśā'* or prophetic pronouncement" which he admits "has no fixed structure and may be composed of a number of diverse generic elements"; Sweeney, *Isaiah 1–39*, 227; so similarly in Sweeney's work on Habakkuk, Marvin A. Sweeney, "Structure, Genre, and Intent in the Book of Habakkuk," *VT* 41 (1991): 63–83 (65): "the genre is not constituted by a well-defined literary structure as examples of *maśśā'ôt* texts included a variety of literary elements." For similar remarks see Sweeney, *Twelve*, 2:423–25, 58–59; cf. Marvin A. Sweeney, "Concerning the Structure and Generic Character of the Book of Nahum.," *ZAW* 104 (1992): 364–77.

could say in response to Weis, that in prophetic speech one can speak (for instance) about the "intention" to express God's impending judgment, but this does not signal a form, since a variety of prophetic speech forms express this intention (woe oracles, dirges, laments, announcements of judgment, lawsuits), but do so with radically different forms.

Furthermore, when Weis treats the issue of "intention" again he finds a dominant intention, but then must admit that many texts do not fit this category. In the end, not only must he try to fit the many "deviations" into his hypothesis, but must generalize the intention to the point that it could describe many prophetic texts which are not משא. So when he concludes: "Perhaps we should think in terms of the genre responding to situations corresponding to one or the other of these two basic problems (indeterminacy connected with the revelation, indeterminacy connected with the human situation), or to some combination of both,"[31] the issue is that prophetic texts often speak to problems of indeterminacy in the human situation. This feature cannot be limited to משא.

When Weis investigates the genre's use (the משא texts as they function in their final literary context), he is limited in the number of texts which he can use and in each case must rely on contentious conclusions on the shape of the final form of the respective books, especially in the case of the משא texts in Isaiah and Zechariah–Malachi.

Finally, Weis treats the word משא as a genre tag very early on in his work, but this is far from certain. Such emic tags are very rare in the Hebrew Bible and when they do appear are usually more general than the precise tags that are used today in form criticism (see for instance Hab 3:1). No one would consider "the word of Yahweh" in Jer 46:1 and Ezek 1:3 as genre tags, no more than one would consider the "vision concerning Judah and Jerusalem" in Isa 1:1 as such.[32] It may be that Oswalt is on the right track when he notes how משא and דבר both are placed in the same syntactical spot prior to the phrase אשר חזה ישעיהו בן־אמוץ in both Isa 2:1 and 13:1, suggesting that they are synonyms.[33]

In summary, then, a focused evaluation of Weis reveals that this recent argument cannot be sustained. משא is no more a genre tag than phrases like "word of the Lord" or "vision of X prophet." As Goldingay, in his work on Isaiah, wisely notes: "To judge from the contents, *massa'* does not necessarily suggest an oracle in the narrow sense of an actual word from Yahweh. It can be (among other things) an imaginative picture, a lament, or a poem—in other words, any kind of prophetic

---

[31] Weis, "Definition," 230.
[32] Cf. Magne Sæbø, "Die deuterosacharjanische Frage: Eine forschungsgeschichtliche Studie," *ST* 23 (1969): 115–40 (140).
[33] John N. Oswalt, *The Book of Isaiah, Chapters 1–39*, NICOT (Grand Rapids: Eerdmans, 1986), 296 n. 1.

composition."[34] It appears to be a general tag denoting prophetic revelation and thus unhelpful for form-critical research, except for identifying in a general way the presence of prophetic literature. This also brings into question the tradition-historical argument that prophecy had shifted from oral to written and was no longer a dynamic movement. Nevertheless, this still leaves us with the quandary as to the significance of this editorial marker in the books of Zechariah and Malachi, and this significance is highlighted through a closer look at the traditio-historical relationship between the book of Jeremiah and Zech 9–14.

משא AS TRADITION-HISTORICAL MARKER

משא דבר־יהוה IN ZECHARIAH 9–14 AND MALACHI

In order to see this traditio-historical relationship let us introduce one aspect of Floyd's later work on משא.[35] Floyd notes in his work on Mal 1:1 that past scholarship has highlighted the close affinity between the superscription in Mal 1:1 and those in Zech 9:1 and 12:1, an affinity that has often forced people to presuppose a closer relationship between Zech 9–14 and Malachi than between Zech 9–14 and Zech 1–8. Floyd notes, however, that Mal 1:1 shares with Nahum and Habakkuk the common feature of a reference to a recipient of the prophetic message, a feature missing in Zech 9:1 and 12:1. Nevertheless, this feature is certainly not consistent in Nahum, Habakkuk, and Malachi as the following chart reveals. Additionally, Nahum at least is closely allied with the references in Isa 13–23 which place משא and the place name in construct relationship, and Habakkuk betrays a close relationship to Isa 13:1, which has a clause introduced by אשר followed by the verb חזה and the name of the prophet. In contrast to Nahum and Habakkuk, Malachi displays greater affinity with the two superscriptions in Zech 9–14, all three of which employ the phrase משא דבר־יהוה followed by a preposition. This collocation is not found in any other משא superscription in the Hebrew Bible.[36]

---

[34] John Goldingay, *Isaiah*, NIBCOT (Peabody, MA: Hendricksen, 2001), 91.

[35] Floyd, "Maśśā'," 401–22.

[36] For Margulis, "Oracles," 204–5, the features of similarity in Zechariah and Malachi, "suggests that the stereotyped [Oracle Against the Nations] usage is already in a process of stylistic break-down" for there is a shift to a focus on Israel. Interestingly, Margulis (206–11) believes that משא + place name is an apocopation of משא דבר־יהוה על + place name. Also he notes a similar apocopation process in the use of דבר־יהוה which is found alongside דבר־יהוה על + place name. Whereas משא is used in Isaiah, Nahum, and Habakkuk, in Jeremiah דבר is used in Oracles against the Nations (Jer 46:1; 47:1). Thus משא is a term related originally to the oracles against the nations. In the case of Zechariah and Malachi he surmises that one finds a "reversion back to the pre-apocopated forms of

Isa 13:1	משא בבל אשר חזה ישעיהו בן־אמוץ
Isa 14:28	בשנת־מות המלך אחז היה המשא הזה
Isa 15:1	משא מואב כי בליל שדד ער מואב נדמה כי בליל שדד קיר־מואב נדמה
Isa 17:1	משא דמשק הנה דמשק מוסר מעיר והיתה מעי מפלה
Isa 19:1	משא מצרים הנה יהוה רכב על־עב קל ובא מצרים ונעו אלילי מצרים מפניו ולבב מצרים ימס בקרבו
Isa 21:1	משא מדבר־ים כסופות בנגב לחלף ממדבר בא מארץ נוראה
Isa 21:11	משא דומה אלי קרא משעיר שמר מה־מלילה שמר מה־מליל
Isa 21:13	משא בערב ביער בערב תלינו ארחות דדנים
Isa 22:1	משא גיא חזיון מה־לך אפוא כי־עלית כלך לגגות
Isa 22:25	ונגדעה ונפלה ונכרת המשא אשר־עליה כי יהוה דבר
Isa 23:1	משא צר הילילו אניות תרשיש כי־שדד מבית מבוא מארץ כתים נגלה־למו
Isa 30:6	משא בהמות נגב
Ezek 12:10	אמר אליהם כה אמר אדני יהוה הנשיא המשא הזה בירושלם
Nah 1:1	משא נינוה ספר חזון נחום האלקשי
Hab 1:1	המשא אשר חזה חבקוק הנביא
Zech 9:1	משא דבר־יהוה בארץ חדרך ודמשק מנחתו כי ליהוה עין אדם וכל שבטי ישראל
Zech 12:1	משא דבר־יהוה על־ישראל נאם־יהוה נטה שמים ויסד ארץ ויצר רוח־אדם בקרבו
Mal 1:1	משא דבר־יהוה אל־ישראל ביד מלאכי

JEREMIAH 23:33–40 AND משא דבר־יהוה

The components of this superscription, which suggests affinity between Zech 9–14 and Malachi, however, are also found together in a key passage in the book of Jeremiah, 23:33–40, a passage that actually contains the greatest concentration of the word משא in the Hebrew Bible. This passage occurs in a larger literary context that is bringing serious attack on false prophets who are closely associated with the temple and priests (Jer 23:9–40). This passage was leveraged by David Petersen in his dissertation as evidence of a Persian period deutero-prophetic silencing of prophecy.[37]

Petersen argues that Jer 23:34–40 is not part of the Deuteronomic "C" layer of the book of Jeremiah, but rather is a "deutero-prophetic" text, "an exegesis of a wordplay [23:33] most probably going back to Jeremiah."[38] This redactional

---

these terms as evidenced by the use of the preposition," thus, משא + place name and דבר־יהוה > על יהוה־דבר משא + place name (see Jer 23:33–40).

[37] David L. Petersen, *Late Israelite Prophecy: Studies in Deutero-Prophetic Literature and in Chronicles*, SBLMS 23 (Missoula, MT: Scholars Press, 1977), 27–33.

[38] Ibid., 33; others echo this conclusion of Petersen. Cf. William McKane, *A Critical and Exegetical Commentary on Jeremiah*, ICC (Edinburgh: T&T Clark, 1986), 597–604; John Bright, *Jeremiah: Introduction, Translation, and Notes*, AB 21 (Garden City, NY:

Freeing the Burden of Prophecy 149

level was composed most likely in the Persian period, the purpose of which "was to prohibit new oracles in the classical prophetic style; apparently people were improperly claiming to have words from Yahweh."[39] Thus for those responsible for verses 34–40,

> Claiming to possess new oracles from Yahweh is no longer allowed (v. 34). A person could ask what Yahweh had spoken or answered (i.e. oracles spoken in the past) but he may no longer ask for a new word ... Therefore, the author has one objective—to prohibit the use of prophetic formulae and thereby to prohibit the prophetic enterprise as we know it from the classical prophets.[40]

Petersen's argument, however, needs to be carefully nuanced. There is no question that one key concern in the book of Jeremiah is the battle between true and false prophecy and Jer 23:9–40 brings focus on this issue. In the process of attacking opponents (called the "prophet and priest ... in my temple," v. 11; "prophets of Samaria," v. 13; "prophets of Jerusalem," vv. 14, 15), the one responsible for 23:9–40 attacks them for speaking "visions from their own minds" (v. 16) rather than "from the mouth of Yahweh" (v. 16). The concern is not particularly over the means of the prophecy, for even the legitimate prophet who stands in the "council of Yahweh" is identified as one who is able "to see or to hear his word" (v. 17). Rather, the concern is over the source of the prophecy: "their own minds" versus "Yahweh." In light of this, when verse 28 proclaims: "Let the prophet who has a dream tell his dream, but let the one who has my word speak it faithfully," the focus is not on the means (dream vs. word), but rather on the source (human vs. divine) and quality (false vs. true) of the revelation. This is made clear in verse 30 which points to false prophets as stealing from one another "words supposedly from me," and the dreams which are prophesied are explicitly identified as "false dreams."

Petersen makes a valid point. Jeremiah 23:34–40 does appear to prohibit asking for revelation from God using the terminology משׂא יהוה. It assumes a context in which מה־משׂא יהוה has become the stock way among the people of asking a prophet for a word of God on a certain issue. This section, then, does appear to move in a different direction than verse 33 and also go beyond the earlier sections which call the people to discern carefully the source of the prophetic message. It speaks to a particular crisis in the history of Israel in which the prophetic

---

Doubleday, 1965), 154; Robert P. Carroll, *Jeremiah: A Commentary*, OTL (Philadelphia: Westminster, 1986), 480; and recently Terence E. Fretheim, *Jeremiah*, SHBC (Macon, GA: Smith & Helwys, 2002), 340.
[39] Petersen, *Prophecy*, 33.
[40] Ibid., 28.

process is now curtailed from the side of the people: they are no longer to approach prophets for new revelation, for God has already provided revelation they have ignored.

This curtailing of the prophetic process, however, is not an anomaly in the Jeremianic tradition.[41] It can also be discerned in another key passage in Jeremiah, 14:1–15:4.[42] Lying behind this passage is the assumption of a prophetic liturgy in which the people cried out to God in lament and sent the prophet to enquire of God. There we find that the prophetic process is again curtailed, although this time the message is for the prophet rather than the people. The prophet is told not to intercede for the people. Interestingly, the issue is the same: false prophecy and idolatry related to messages that arise from their own minds. Just as Jer 23:33–40 prohibits the people from asking for an oracle from the prophet, so Jer 14:1–15:4 prohibits the prophet from asking for an oracle for the people. There is no reason then to identify Jer 23:34–40 as a much later deutero-prophetic insertion; it echoes themes found within what are considered earlier Jeremianic and Deuteronomic streams of tradition within the corpus.

Thus, the crisis of false prophecy related to idolatry in the closing moments of the kingdom of Judah's history leads to the judgment of God upon this disobedient generation. The judgment of God is first one of ceased revelation before it is one of fiery destruction. The mediation of true prophecy is cut off from the kingdom due to its penchant to follow idolatry and its attendant false prophecy. In the Jeremianic tradition this is closely related to the term מַשָּׂא, a term for prophecy. Asking for a prophetic מַשָּׂא is deemed inappropriate.

---

[41] Both Carroll, *Jeremiah: A Commentary*, 480 and Fretheim, *Jeremiah*, 340, follow Petersen in linking the expansion of vv. 34–40 to the same period as Zech 13:2–6, but Carroll admits that this "is quite likely, though not capable of demonstrable proof," and Fretheim shifts the focus ("more likely") to the tradition-history of the group responsible for the book of Jeremiah, who were defending the prophecy of Jeremiah "in the face of critical voices." Jones, *Jeremiah*, 315 sees it rather as the work of "either Jeremiah himself or a prophet in the tradition."

[42] Cf. Mark J. Boda, "From Complaint to Contrition: Peering through the Liturgical Window of Jer 14,1–15,4," *ZAW* 113 (2001): 186–97. Notice 23:10, where because of the wickedness of the land related to idolatry and prophecy, the land is parched. This resonates with Jer 14:1–15:4 which is echoed in Zech 10:1–3.

JEREMIAH, PROPHECY, AND ZECHARIAH 9–14

On one level there are points of similarity between this Jeremianic tradition of prophecy and Zech 9–14.[43] Many have noted clear echoes of the language of Jeremiah (14:1–15:4) in the account of the crisis over prophecy and idolatry in Zech 10:1–2.[44] There we read of false prophecy in the form of visionary divination linked to idolatry which offers comfort where there is no hope. Later in Zech 9–14, in 13:2–6, the text looks to a day when false prophets and their idols will be removed from the land. Petersen, followed by many others, has seen here, however, echoes of the rejection of prophecy as a means of new revelation, similar to Jer 23:33–40.[45] The language, however, used in Zech 13:2–6 is language associated with false prophecy ("told lies" [v. 3], "deceive" [v. 4]), punishments associated with false prophets ("his own parents will stab him" [v. 3]), and allusions to idolatry (v. 2).[46] Reference to "every prophet" who "will be ashamed of his prophetic vision" clearly indicates prophets who "put on a prophet's garment of hair *in order to deceive*" (v. 4). Similar vocabulary and connections also appear in the prophetic criticism of Zech 10:1–2: "deceit," "false," "in vain," "idols," "diviners," "vision," "dreams." In all of this, however, there is no indication that

---

[43] Of all the tradition streams that have had influence on the Zecharian tradition (Zech 1–14), the Jeremianic is clearly the strongest. I have argued this for Zech 1–8 as well as for Zech 9–14; see Mark J. Boda, "From Fasts to Feasts: The Literary Function of Zechariah 7–8," *CBQ* 65 (2003): 390–407 = *Exploring Zechariah*, volume 1, chapter 2; Mark J. Boda, "Zechariah: Master Mason or Penitential Prophet?," in *Yahwism after the Exile: Perspectives on Israelite Religion in the Persian Era*, ed. Bob Becking and Rainer Albertz, Studies in Theology and Religion 5 (Assen: Van Gorcum, 2003), 49–69 = chapter 6 in this present volume; Mark J. Boda and Stanley E. Porter, "Literature to the Third Degree: Prophecy in Zechariah 9–14 and the Passion of Christ," in *Traduire la Bible hébraïque: De la Septante à la Nouvelle Bible Segond = Translating the Hebrew Bible: From the Septuagint to the Nouvelle Bible Segond*, ed. Robert David and Manuel Jinbachian, Sciences Bibliques 15 (Montreal: Médiaspaul, 2005), 215–54 = chapter 10 in this present volume; Mark J. Boda, "Oil, Crowns and Thrones: Prophet, Priest and King in Zechariah 1:7–6:15," in *Perspectives on Hebrew Scriptures*, ed. Ehud Ben Zvi (Piscataway, NJ: Gorgias, 2006), 379–404 = chapter 4 in this present volume; Mark J. Boda, *"Hoy, Hoy*: The Prophetic Origins of the Babylonian Tradition in Zechariah 2:10–17," in *Tradition in Transition: Haggai and Zechariah 1–8 in the Trajectory of Hebrew Theology*, ed. Mark J. Boda and Michael H. Floyd, LHBOTS 475 (London: T&T Clark, 2008), 171–90 = chapter 3 in this present volume. A key and influential section of Jeremiah is the literary complex of Jer 22–25.

[44] Mark J. Boda, *Haggai/Zechariah*, NIVAC (Grand Rapids: Zondervan, 2004), 437–40 and literature cited there; see also Boda and Porter, "Third Degree."

[45] Petersen, *Prophecy*, 33–38; see more recently Petersen, *Zechariah 9–14*.

[46] Boda, *Haggai/Zechariah*, 490–94.

prophecy as a means of revelation has been eradicated; only that false prophecy linked to idolatry is the problem.

Zechariah 9–14 thus cannot be used to substantiate a continuance of the earlier Jeremianic tradition in which prophecy, in particular משא, has been silenced. As with Jeremiah there is deep concern over false prophecy and idolatry, a concern which in the days of the tradents of Jeremiah led to the curtailment of the prophetic process. But this should not be interpreted as a final rejection of prophecy, for there is no indication in Jer 23:33–40 that the restriction on משא would endure *ad infinitum* any more than that the destruction of Jerusalem and Judah was eternal. All we are told is that in the approach and wake of the exilic judgment, prophetic revelation was to cease. Furthermore, the term משא itself is used to introduce and structure the Zech 9–14 collection, but in what may be evidence of influence from the crisis reflected in Jer 23:33–40, these משאות are clearly defined as דבר־יהוה, strikingly similar to the concern over the claims for משא יהוה in Jer 23, which were shown to distort "the words of the living God, Yahweh Almighty" (Jer 23:36).

Zechariah 9:1, 12:1, and Mal 1:1 echo this vocabulary, making the claim now in the Persian period in the midst of the confusing cacophony of prophetic voices, that actually these prophetic texts are indeed an "oracle" which is the "the word of Yahweh." Rather than a curtailment of prophecy, as argued by Petersen, or even a transformation of prophecy, as argued by Weis, Zech 9–14 and Malachi represent a renewal of prophecy along the lines of earlier prophecy. This would explain the fact that the prophetic material in Zech 9–14 and Malachi not only utilizes language and forms echoing classic prophecy, but also expects the endurance of the prophetic line founded on Moses and which will endure even through an expected Elijah figure.

CONCLUSION

The prophetic word, denied in the closing phase of the kingdom of Judah, was now not only available but authoritative in the midst of the present prophetic crisis. Therefore, משא serves as an editorial marker that in the end bolsters the status of prophecy in the Persian period, rather than sounding its death knell.[47]

---

[47] The Zecharian tradition does celebrate earlier prophecy, citing it liberally and playing with earlier images and traditions. However, there is no indication that prophecy has come to an end. Clearly the imposing image of early prophecy is ever present, but this did not mean an end to new revelation. Zechariah 1–6 shows liberal use of earlier prophetic themes, language, and forms, but no more than prophets in the "earlier" era.

9
Zechariah 11:4–16 in Its Literary Contexts[1]

This chapter will build on the previous work of Rex Mason by analyzing Zech 11:4–16 both diachronically and synchronically. A diachronic analysis will identify connections between Zech 11:4–16 and two prophetic pericopae in the book of Ezekiel (chs. 34, 37) and interpret Zech 11:4–16 within its historical context in light of these connections. Then with synchronic sensibilities it will identify the way that this interpretation impacts the reading of Zech 9–14 as a whole.

ZECHARIAH 11:4–16

DELIMITATION OF TEXT

Although part of the larger literary complex of Zech 9–14, Zech 11:4–16 is a discrete unit. That it is a distinct unit from the preceding text unit in 11:1–3 is clear not only from our form critical analysis below which will highlight the sign-act form in 11:4–16, but also from the initial phrase of 11:4: "Thus says Yahweh my God" (כה אמר יהוה אלהי). Although it is possible that the subsequent textual unit, Zech 11:17, is merely the conclusion to the sign-acts,[2] two of its features

---

[1] Based on a portion of my original publication: Mark J. Boda, "Reading between the Lines: Zechariah 11:4–16 in Its Literary Contexts," in *Bringing out the Treasure: Inner Biblical Allusion and Zechariah 9–14*, ed. Mark J. Boda and Michael H. Floyd, JSOTSup 370 (Sheffield: Sheffield Academic, 2003), 277–91. Slightly revised for inclusion in this volume.
[2] So Rex A. Mason, "The Use of Earlier Biblical Material in Zechariah IX–XIV: A Study in Inner Biblical Exegesis" (PhD diss., University of London, 1973), 167; David L.

suggest that it is a separate unit.³ First of all, on the formal level 11:17 contrasts with verses 4–16 with its sign-act form by employing the woe oracle common in prophetic literature (see especially Isa 5). This form is the declaration of curse and judgement on those who have met the disapproval of God.⁴ Typically it includes three elements: the declaration "woe," the identification of the recipient of judgment, and then usually details of the judgment or accusation.⁵ Secondly, in terms of content 11:17 announces disaster for a shepherd, contrasting with verses 4–16 which has enacted judgment on the flock.

GENRE

Zechariah 11:4–16 contains the elements of a prophetic form displayed throughout the books of Jeremiah and Ezekiel, the prophetic sign-act.⁶ This form, also evident in Zech 6:9–15,⁷ has three basic elements: Exhortation, Execution, Explanation. God first commands the prophet to perform an action (exhortation) and

---

Petersen, *Zechariah 9–14 and Malachi: A Commentary*, OTL (Louisville: Westminster John Knox, 1995), 99. These scholars demonstrate from Ezek 24:1–14 that a "Woe" oracle can be inserted into a larger form unit. However, in this example the woe oracles are introduced by messenger formulae (לכן כה־אמר אדני יהוה), unlike Zech 11:17.

³ Many have treated 11:17 as part of 11:4–16, e.g., Stephen L. Cook, "The Metamorphosis of a Shepherd: The Tradition History of Zechariah 11:17 + 13:7–9," *CBQ* 55 (1993): 453–66; Paul L. Redditt, "The Two Shepherds in Zechariah 11:4–17," *CBQ* 55 (1993): 676–86. Others have tried to connect 11:17 to 13:7–9, even rearranging the text to accomplish this; e.g., Hinckley Gilbert Mitchell, John Merlin Powis Smith, and Julius August Brewer, *A Critical and Exegetical Commentary on Haggai, Zechariah, Malachi and Jonah*, ICC (Edinburgh: T&T Clark, 1912), 314–19. This is offensive to the redactor's purpose in Zech 9–14; see further below.

⁴ As opposed to the use of the "woe" as a cry of lamentation (see Ezek 2:10).

⁵ See Michael H. Floyd, *Minor Prophets, Part 2*, FOTL 22 (Grand Rapids: Eerdmans, 2000), 649.

⁶ So also ibid., 489–90. For the details of this form see Georg Fohrer, "Die Gattung der Berichte über symbolischen Handlungen der Propheten," *ZAW* 64 (1952): 101–20; Georg Fohrer, *Die symbolische Handlungen der Propheten*, 2nd ed., ATANT 54 (Zurich: Zwingli, 1968); W. D. Stacey, *Prophetic Drama in the Old Testament* (London: Epworth, 1990); Kelvin G. Friebel, *Jeremiah's and Ezekiel's Sign-Acts*, JSOTSup 283 (Sheffield: Sheffield Academic, 1999); Kelvin G. Friebel, "A Hermeneutical Paradigm for Interpreting Prophetic Sign-Actions," *Did* 12.2 (2001): 25–45.

⁷ See Mark J. Boda, "Oil, Crowns and Thrones: Prophet, Priest and King in Zechariah 1:7–6:15," *JHS* 3 (2001): Article 10 = chapter 4 in this present volume.

this action is reported by the prophet (execution) and interpreted by God (explanation). Although the exhortation is always the first element, the order of the others can vary, and sometimes one of these elements is absent.[8]

Zechariah 11:4–16 contains three sign acts introduced by the three exhortations: "Pasture the sheep/flock of slaughter" (רעה את־צאן ההרגה, 11:4), "Throw them to the metal worker" (השליכהו אל־היוצר, 11:13), "Take for yourself the equipment of a foolish/worthless shepherd" (קח־לך כלי רעה אולי, 11:15). The following chart lays out the basic elements of these sign acts:

Sign act 1	Sign act 2	Sign act 3
Exhortation: 4–5[9]		
Explanation: 6		
Execution: 7–12[10]		
	Exhortation: 13a[11]	
	Execution: 13b	
Execution: 14[12]		
		Exhortation: 15
		Explanation: 16

Although this does indicate three sign acts, it appears that the second sign-act is incorporated into the execution section of the first. The resulting structure indicates two basic sign-act reports, the one focused on a good shepherd and the other a foolish shepherd.[13]

---

[8] Thus, in Jer 13:1–11, some elements are repeated: Exhortation (1), Execution (2), Exhortation (3–4), Execution (5), Exhortation (6), Execution (7), Explanation (8–11). In Ezek 5, the execution is not reported: Exhortation (1–4), Explanation (5–17). Notice how in Ezek 5 the exhortation also contains some foreshadowing of the explanation (2b, 4b).

[9] Verse 5 extends the exhortation by building the picture almost in allegorical style.

[10] Verse 10b acts like an Explanation, although different than usual because the prophet is speaker, rather than God; verse 11 acts like a prophetic confirmation formula (knew it was the word of Yahweh).

[11] Prompted by the execution in v. 12 of Sign act 1.

[12] Verse 14b, like v. 10b, acts like an Explanation, although with prophet as speaker, rather than God.

[13] So, for example, Cook, "Metamorphosis," 456; Petersen, *Zechariah 9–14*, 100–1; contra Redditt, "The Two Shepherds in Zechariah 11:4–17," who sees both shepherds as evil/foolish. Redditt fails to see that the sign act is directed at the community, not at leadership, that the first shepherd pledges to care for the weak of the flock, and that he removes three shepherds as part of this protection.

Some have suggested that this passage represents an allegory or parable, rather than a sign-act.[14] Indeed, Zech 11:4–16 does transform and expand the sign-act form at points. In verse 5 the image introduced by the exhortation in verse 4 is expanded to include buyers, sellers, and shepherds. Although the exhortation is limited to the simple imperative: "Pasture the sheep/flock of slaughter" (רעה את־ צאן ההרגה), the execution is very detailed (taking two staffs) and includes the reaction of the flock to the fulfillment of the exhortation. The interpretation in verse 16 continues the shepherd motif introduced in the sign-act, rather than reveal its referent in reality (as v. 6). Finally, contrary to the earlier prophetic sign-acts, it is uncertain whether this sign-act was ever acted out by the prophet. These expansions and transformations in the form may be reason enough to conclude that here we find an allegorical use of the sign-act form.[15]

CONTENT

In typical sign-act fashion, the passage begins with an exhortation in the imperative mood as the prophet is to assume the role of a shepherd. Some have assumed this is a reference to the prophet as shepherd,[16] but roles laid on the prophet in sign-acts are usually not related to the vocation of a prophet, but rather merely function as a vehicle for communication. In this case, the prophet as shepherd is representing God's appointed leadership of his people.[17]

The first indication that this sign-act will not be positive for the people comes in the initial line as the flock is described as the flock of "slaughter" (הרגה). This slaughter is immediately linked to activities connected with the business of agriculture with people buying and selling sheep as the shepherds stand by. Slaugh-

---

[14] See discussion in Lester V. Meyer, "An Allegory Concerning the Monarchy: Zech 11:4–17; 13:7–9," in *Scripture in History and Theology: Essays in Honor of J. Coert Rylaarsdam*, ed. Arthur L. Merrill and Thomas W. Overholt (Pittsburgh: Pickwick, 1977), 225–40 (225–27); Petersen, *Zechariah 9–14*, 89; although Larkin stresses the allegorical/parabolic genre, she does note closeness stylistically to the prophetic sign act; Katrina J. Larkin, *The Eschatology of Second Zechariah: A Study of the Formation of a Mantological Wisdom Anthology*, CBET 6 (Kampen: Kok, 1994), 132–34.

[15] Nevertheless the suggestion by some that this is a prophetic commissioning is untenable considering the lack of elements from that genre; see Petersen, *Zechariah 9–14*, 89.

[16] E.g., Mason, "Use," 140; Larkin, *Eschatology*, 114.

[17] This need not refer to royal leadership exclusively. See the debate in Meyer, "Allegory"; Redditt, "The Two Shepherds in Zechariah 11:4–17"; Cook, "Metamorphosis." Marvin A. Sweeney, *The Twelve Prophets*, 2 vols., Berit Olam (Collegeville, MN: Liturgical Press, 2000), 2:678–79 has recently suggested that the shepherd here is a reference to a priest who had care for the temple flocks for sacrifice, but this does not fit the image of the shepherd who was to protect the sheep from slaughter.

tering sheep for food was obviously the purpose of raising sheep in ancient societies, but this purpose is not part of the positive form of this metaphor in the Hebrew Bible where good shepherds protect their sheep from destruction while bad shepherds neglect their duties by not caring for the injuries of the sheep and allowing them to be eaten.[18] In Zech 11, however, the indictment is not against the shepherds, but rather against the flock. Zechariah 11:6, which functions as the explanation in the sign-act form (here a foreshadowing), reveals that it is God who is responsible for this slaughter of "the inhabitants of the land" (יֹשְׁבֵי הָאָרֶץ). The people will be oppressed by their fellow human ("his neighbor," רֵעֵהוּ)[19] as well as by those over them ("his king," מַלְכּוֹ).

Zechariah 11:7–14 represents the execution of the first sign-act, signalled by the switch into autobiographical style. The shepherd is concerned for the "weak ones of the flock" (עֲנִיֵּי הַצֹּאן), a sign of good leadership in Israel, especially for the royal house which was commissioned to care for the oppressed (Ps 72:2, 4, 12).[20] Furthermore, the names of the two staffs ("Pleasantness/Delightfulness," נֹעַם and "Inheritance," חֹבְלִים) suggest a positive role for this shepherd.[21]

The positive picture of 11:7, however, is soon spoiled. The appointed shepherd must rid the flock of three shepherds. The verb "removed" (כחד *hiphil*) in verse 8 is used to speak of the annihilation of the Canaanites (Exod 23:23), of the house of Jeroboam (1 Kgs 13:34), of the Assyrian army (2 Chr 32:21), and of Israel as a nation (Ps 83:5), suggesting that the shepherd did more than just "fire"

---

[18] Contra Petersen, *Zechariah 9–14*, 91 who identifies the problem as the slaughter of the entire flock and Sweeney, *Twelve*, 2:678–79 who links the flock to temple sacrifice. The problem here is any slaughter.

[19] Some have repointed the vowels of the Hebrew term רֵעֵהוּ which translates "neighbor," in order to produce the reading "shepherd"; cf. Mitchell, Smith, and Brewer, *Haggai*, 304; Petersen, *Zechariah 9–14*, 87; Paul D. Hanson, *The Dawn of Apocalyptic: The Historical and Sociological Roots of Jewish Apocalyptic Eschatology*, rev. ed. (Philadelphia: Fortress, 1979), 340. Although possible, it appears that v. 6 has moved to the interpretation phase of the sign-act, thus leaving the shepherd motif.

[20] Redditt's textual emendation at this point is inappropriate; Redditt, "The Two Shepherds in Zechariah 11:4–17."

[21] There is some debate over the precise meaning of these two implements. The names associated with the two staffs in Zech 11 are נֹעַם and חֹבְלִים. The word נֹעַם which is linked to בְּרִיתִי אֲשֶׁר כָּרַתִּי אֶת־כָּל־הָעַמִּים (v. 10) is most likely a reference to God's use of the nations to bring blessing upon Israel, especially as seen in the Persian period with the restoration of the community in Yehud. The staff called חֹבְלִים which is linked to the הָאַחֲוָה בֵּין יְהוּדָה וּבֵין יִשְׂרָאֵל (v. 14) is most likely representative of the peaceful redistribution of the land in the restoration from exile (cf. Josh 17:5, 14; 19:9; Ezek 47:13). Cf. Mark J. Boda, *The Book of Zechariah*, NICOT (Grand Rapids: Eerdmans, 2016), 664–65.

the shepherds.²² Numbers are used here symbolically to refer to totality (three shepherds) and brevity (one month).²³ This removal of the shepherds is probably the cause of the tension that then arises between the shepherd and his flock. The phrase "my soul became impatient" (ותקצר נפשי) is used elsewhere to refer to one's inability to endure a particular state of affairs.²⁴ The shepherd's impatience is matched by the flock's disgust ("felt loathing," בחלה).

This mutual rejection has serious repercussions for both parties. The shepherd announces his intention to resign and describes the impact of this decision on the community as a whole (11:9). This verbal notice is followed by two symbolic gestures linked to the two staffs identified earlier. By breaking the first staff (11:10) the shepherd revokes his relationship with the "all the peoples/nations" (כל־העמים), a reference to the buyers and sellers of 11:5. Before breaking the second staff (11:14), the shepherd reports his request for payment of wages. The request for payment is addressed to the "peoples/nations" (העמים) at the end of 11:10. The shepherd, however, follows the command of God by throwing the payment into the temple, symbolizing his rejection of the payment while linking the payment of the nations to temple personnel.

With the payment the first symbolic gesture is completed, signalling the end of the covenant with the nations. In 11:14 the shepherd proceeds to break the second staff and with it shatter the hopes of a united kingdom.

Zechariah 11:15–16 represents the final sign-act and with it the complete fulfilment of the word of Yahweh in 11:6. The removal of the good shepherd in 11:9 represented the first instalment of the fulfillment of 11:6 ("I will deliver each person over to his neighbor," אנכי ממציא את־האדם איש ביד־רעהו). The prophet assuming the role of a foolish shepherd represents the fulfillment of the second warning: "and over to his king" (וביד מלכו).

The prophet is to take the equipment of a foolish shepherd. This equipment is not necessarily the staffs which were broken in the first sign-act, since the word "again" (עוד) does not modify the imperative "take" (קח), but rather the introductory statement ("then Yahweh said to me," ויאמר יהוה אלי).²⁵ The folly of

---

²² Of course, this is a metaphorical context, so even the use of a death motif does not necessarily mean that the appointed leader killed other leaders.

²³ For a review of the various attempts to identify these shepherds see Redditt, "The Two Shepherds in Zechariah 11:4–17"; recently Sweeney, *Twelve*, 2:678 suggests Cyrus, Cambyses, and Darius.

²⁴ The people's impatience in the wilderness (Num 21:4), Job's impatience over his sorry state (Job 21:4), Samson's inability to endure Delilah's nagging (Judg 16:16), and God's inability to endure Israel's misery (Judg 10:16).

²⁵ For this see the form in Isa 8:5 where clearly "again" (עוד) refers to God's speech; cf. Ezek 8:13; Hos 3:1. Notice in 2 Kgs 4:6 when "again" (עוד) refers to the exhortation it follows it.

this shepherd is detailed in 11:16 where, in contrast to the good shepherd (11:7), this shepherd refuses appropriate care for the vulnerable of the flock ("the missing ones, the young, the maimed ones, the exhausted ones," הנכחדות, הנער, הנשברת, הנצבה [26]) while devouring the healthy sheep.

These sign-acts in 11:4–16 speak of two situations involving two leaders within the community. The first situation involves the rejection of a leader appointed by God over the people, and the second the raising up of a replacement leader by God who would destroy the people. The first leader is appointed by God, although in covenant with the nations who are intimately related to temple personnel. He begins his commission with good intentions, equipped with the appropriate tools for leadership and with a sensitivity to his people. Due to tension between the leader and his people, however, the covenant with the nations is terminated. This rejection of the leader and demise of the covenant with the nations puts an end to hopes of the renewal of a unified people. The second leader is also appointed by God. The designation foolish is appropriate, for in contrast to the first leader he has ill intent for his people, insensitively forsaking his obligation to protect the vulnerable while abusing the community for his own benefit.

DIACHRONIC ANALYSIS: ZECHARIAH 11:4–16 AND EZEKIEL

CONNECTIONS

For those familiar with the book of Ezekiel, it is difficult to ignore several key links to this earlier prophet, in particular Ezek 34:1–31 and 37:15–28.[27] Ezekiel 34 contains a prophetic message to the leadership of Israel employing an extended metaphor of shepherd and flock imagery. God attacks the shepherds for feeding on the flock, promises to personally shepherd them, gathering them from the nations to their own land, appointing David as their "one shepherd" (רעה אחד,

---

[26] The fourth category, הנצבה, is a *niphal* participle from the root נצב ("to take one's stand, to stand"): thus, "ones which stand firm" or "healthy ones." If this is correct it would be a unique occurrence in the Hebrew Bible. Some have suggested another root which would render "exhausted ones" and fit the list better; see Petersen, *Zechariah 9–14*, 86; William L. Holladay, ed., *A Concise Hebrew and Aramaic Lexicon of the Old Testament* (Leiden: Brill; Grand Rapids: Eerdmans, 1988), 243.

[27] See Mason, "Use," 150–53; Meyer, "Allegory"; Hanson, *Dawn*, 228–40, 343–47; Rex A. Mason, "Prophets of the Restoration," in *Israel's Prophetic Tradition: Essays in Honour of Peter Ackroyd*, ed. Richard Coggins, Anthony Phillips, and Michael Knibb (Cambridge: Cambridge University Press, 1982), 137–54 (349); Douglas A. Witt, "Zechariah 12–14: Its Origins, Growth and Theological Significance" (PhD diss., Vanderbilt University, 1991), 60; Risto Nurmela, *Prophets in Dialogue: Inner-Biblical Allusions in Zechariah 1–8 and 9–14* (Åbo: Åbo Akademi University, 1996), 136–46.

34:23), and renewing covenant with the people (34:31). Ezekiel 37 contains a prophetic sign-act in which two sticks with names on them are fused, representing the promised union of Israel and Judah. As in Ezek 34 the focus is on gathering the people from the nations, returning them to their own land, appointing David as king over them as "one shepherd" (רועה אחד, 37:24), and renewing covenant with the people (37:23, 27).

Several elements in Zech 11:4–16 betray reliance on these two passages. First, on the formal level, 11:4–16 represents a fusion of allegorical and sign-act forms, probably due to reliance on Ezek 34 with its extended metaphor and Ezek 37 with its sign-act.

Secondly, and more importantly, on the rhetorical level, 11:4–16 employs similar imagery and vocabulary. The characteristics of the foolish shepherd in Zech 11:15–16 echo Ezekiel's description of shepherds in chapter 34. In Ezek 34:3–4 Ezekiel paints a dark portrait of the "shepherds of Israel" only to contrast it in 34:16 with that of God's compassionate care for the flock (cf. "fat" (בריה): Ezek 34:3; Zech 11:16; cf. Ezek 34:20; "eat" (אכל): Ezek 34:3; Zech 11:16; "heal" (רפא *piel*): Ezek 34:4; Zech 11:16; "raise up + shepherd" (קום *hiphil* + רעה): Ezek 34:23; Zech 11:16; "maimed" (הנשברת): Ezek 34:16; Zech 11:16; also cf. "seek" (דרש): Ezek 34:11, 16; "seek" (בקש): Zech 11:16).[28] Furthermore, both Ezek 37:13–23 and Zech 11:4–16 focus attention on the unity of the community by picturing two sticks connected to the northern and southern tribes which are given names.[29]

REUSE

Having first established these links between Zech 11:4–16 and these two prophecies in Ezekiel, we must now consider the way in which Zech 11 is reusing them in a new context. Ezekiel 34 declares judgement on the leadership of Israel who have not cared appropriately for their flock during the exile. God offers hope to the community by promising to assume this role himself and gather the scattered exiles. Ezekiel 37 also offers hope to the exiles, a hope that the scattered tribes will be reunited in the land of Israel.

Zechariah 11:4–16 reverses the hope expressed in these two Ezekiel passages.[30] Whereas Ezek 34 promises the judgment of the shepherds and care by God, Zech 11 promises God's judgment on the sheep through abandonment of the

---

[28] Mason, "Use," 167; Witt, "Zechariah 12–14," 60; Nurmela, *Prophets in Dialogue*, 136–46.

[29] Zechariah 11:4–16 creatively intertwines these two passages from Ezekiel by transforming the sticks into staffs. This forces the reader to reflect on both passages simultaneously.

[30] See Mason, "Use," 150–53: "here the meaning of the sign in Ezekiel is exactly reversed."

flock by the good shepherd and appointment of an inadequate evil shepherd. Whereas Ezek 37 promises the union of the tribes, Zech 11 promises disunity.

So far our analysis has been limited to points of contact between Zech 11:4–16 and Ezek 34 and 37. But a closer look at these two Ezekielian passages reveals points of contact that they share which should shape our reading of Zech 11:4–16.[31]

The points of contact that have been highlighted so far have been elements shared between Zech 11 and Ezek 34 exclusively from elements shared by Zech 11 and Ezek 37. The only point of contact shared by all three passages is the use of the motif of shepherd for human leadership. Zechariah 11 gives little indication as to the identity of the shepherds, but in light of the fact that it is reversing the expectations of Ezek 34 and 37, do these earlier prophecies offer any insight into the identity of the shepherds?[32]

---

[31] As per the encouragement of Richard L. Schultz, *The Search for Quotation: Verbal Parallels in the Prophets*, JSOTSup 180 (Sheffield: Sheffield Academic, 1999), 224: "a quotation is not intended to be self-contained or self-explanatory; rather a knowledge of the quoted context also is assumed by the speaker or author." Ziva Ben-Porat, "Intertextuality [Hebrew]," *HaSifrut* 34 (1985): 170–78 has noted this technique in her presentation of the fourth stage of allusion; cited in Benjamin D. Sommer, *A Prophet Reads Scripture: Allusion in Isaiah 40–66*, Contraversions Series (Stanford, CA: Stanford University Press, 1998), 12: "the reader activates the evoked text as a whole to form connections between it and the alluding text which are not based on the markers and marked items themselves:; earlier she had said: "the marker—regardless of the form its takes—is used for the activation of independent elements from the evoked text. Those are never referred to directly"; Ziva Ben-Porat, "The Poetics of Literary Allusion," *PTL: A Journal of Descriptive Poetics and Theory of Literature* 1 (1975): 105–28 (108–9). This has often been observed by New Testament scholars such as C. H. Dodd, *According to the Scriptures: The Sub-Structure of New Testament Theology* (London: Nisbet, 1952), 126 who notes the New Testament authors's technique in citing "particular verses or sentences ... as pointers to the whole context" so that "it is the *total context* that is in view, and is the basis of the argument." So also N. T. Wright, *Jesus and the Victory of God*, Christian Origins and the Question of God 2 (Minneapolis: Fortress, 1996), 584, who speaks of writers in Second Temple Judaism "conjuring up a world of discourse with a word or phrase." An excellent example of this is the work of Jane Schaberg, *The Illegitimacy of Jesus: A Feminist Theological Interpretation of the Infancy Narratives* (New York: Crossroad, 1990), 32–34 on the genealogy of Jesus in Matt 1, in which she shows how the allusions to the four women from the Old Testament are designed to prepare the reader for a fifth woman "who becomes a social misfit in some way; is wronged or thwarted; who is party to a sexual act that places her in great danger; and whose story has an outcome that repairs the social fabric and ensures the birth of the child who is legitimate or legitimated."

[32] This raises the question of the identity of the shepherds in the passage. Although Cook, "Metamorphosis"; Stephen L. Cook, *Prophecy and Apocalypticism: The Postexilic Social Setting* (Minneapolis: Fortress, 1995) argues for civil leaders, and Meyer, "Allegory," for

Although very different in genre and vocabulary, Ezek 34 and 37 intersect at two key points: 34:22–31 and 37:23–28. At these two points we find identical motifs and vocabulary: God will save his people (הוֹשַׁעְתִּי: 34:22; 37:23) and set his servant David over them as prince ("my servant David, the prince," עבדי דוד נשׂיא: 34:23–24; 37:24) who is called "one shepherd" (רעה אחד: 34:23; רועה אחד: 37:24). This is followed by a renewal of relationship as God makes a covenant of peace with them (כרתי להם ברית שלום; 34:25; 37:26) so that they will be his people and he their God (34:24, 31; 37:23). The good shepherd is identified as a Davidic descendant who will be "one shepherd" (רעה אחד), uniting the tribes of Israel once again.[33]

This evidence from the broader context of Ezek 34 and 37 suggests that the good shepherd in Zech 11:4–16 is a Davidic descendant. The foolish shepherd must then be someone from outside the Davidic line, evidence of the reversal of the promises of Ezek 34 and 37.

HISTORICAL CONTEXT

In light of this evidence from Ezek 34 and 37 the good shepherd in Zech 11:4–16 would be a Davidic descendant who led Yehud in the early Persian period. The primary candidate would be Zerubbabel who functioned as governor in the early part of Darius's reign.[34] Some have suggested that Sheshbazzar, who is called "governor" (פחה) in Ezra 5:14–16 and "prince of Judah" (הנשׂיא ליהודה) in Ezra 1:8, was of Davidic descent, but the evidence is not convincing.[35] The only

---

the royal house, many have considered this as a metaphor for the priestly establishment of the Persian period; see Hanson, *Dawn*; Paul L. Redditt, "Israel's Shepherds: Hope and Pessimism in Zechariah 9–14," *CBQ* 51 (1989): 631–42. Floyd, *Minor Prophets*, 487, suggests a "quasi official group," similar to the counselors to Joshua the High Priest (Zech 3:8) who in turn advised the governor (Zech 6:9–15). Petersen, *Zechariah 9–14*, 100–1, however, warns against such precision because the texts are "perspectival" rather than "particular," reporting "Yahweh's general response to and perspective on the international scene (as in the first report) and the Judean scene (the second report)."

[33] Although Ezek 34:22–31 does not explicitly discuss the issue of the unity of the tribes (as Ezek 37:23–28), the reference to "one shepherd" implies this theme.

[34] There is no reason to question Zerubbabel's Davidic lineage as, for example, Kenneth E. Pomykala, *The Davidic Dynasty Tradition in Early Judaism: Its History and Significance for Messianism*, EJL 7 (Atlanta: Scholars Press, 1995), 46. Haggai and Zechariah both use language closely associated with the Davidic line and action; cf. Boda, "Oil, Crowns and Thrones" = chapter 4 in this present volume.

[35] See Sara Japhet, "Sheshbazzar and Zerubbabel—Against the Background of the Historical and Religious Tendencies of Ezra–Nehemiah (Part One)," *ZAW* 94 (1982): 66–98; Johan Lust, "The Identification of Zerubbabel with Sheshbassar," *ETL* 63 (1987): 90–95; F. Bianchi, "Le rôle de Zorobabel et de la dynastie davidique en Judée du VIe siècle

other Davidide involved in leadership in Yehud was Zerubbabel's daughter Shelomith (1 Chr 3:19), who ruled in a co-regency with her husband Elnathan after the rule of Zerubbabel.³⁶ Although it is possible that Shelomith could be in view in Zech 11, it would be a stretch for an ancient community to connect a Davidic woman with the promises of Ezek 34 and 37, especially since she ruled in tandem with a non-Davidide. Most likely then Zech 11:4–16 reflects the transition of leadership at the end of Zerubbabel's tenure as governor. The fact that the good shepherd is paid by the owners and then throws this money into the temple precincts, not only reflects the accountability of the governor to the Persian overlords, but also possible collusion between the temple and the Persians in the demise of political influence for the Davidic line.

There have been many theories as to the fate of Zerubbabel. According to Haggai and Ezra 2–5 he was instrumental in the rebuilding of the temple precincts, but record of his participation is silent after the foundation laying ceremony of Hag 2:10–23 (reflected also in Ezra 3; Zech 4:6b–10a and 8:9–13). It may be significant that although he is mentioned in Ezra 5:2, once Tattenai, governor of Trans-Euphrates, enters the picture in 5:3, there are no more references to him. Is

---

au II siècle av. J.-C.," *Transeu* 7 (1994): 153–65. Berger has refuted attempts to equate Sheshbazzar with the Davidic Shenazzar (1 Chr 3:17); P.-R. Berger, "Zu den Namen שנאצר und ששבצר." *ZAW* 83 (1971): 98–100, while M. Ben-Yashar, "On the Problem of Sheshbazzar and Zerubbabel [Hebrew]," *Beth Mikra* 88 (1981): 46–56 undermines the attempt of A. Bartel, "Once Again—Who Was Sheshbazzar? (Heb.)," *Beth Mikra* 79 (1979): 357–69 to equate Sheshbazzar with Zerubbabel. H. G. M. Williamson, *Ezra, Nehemiah*, WBC (Waco, TX: Word, 1985), 17–18 has argued convincingly that the title "prince of Judah" (הנשיא ליהודה) used of Sheshbazzar in Ezra 1:8 is a traditio-historical allusion to the gifts of the "princes/leaders" (נשיאים) of the various tribes in Num 7.

³⁶ Cf. Eric M. Meyers, "The Shelomith Seal and Aspects of the Judean Restoration: Some Additional Reconsiderations," *ErIsr* 18 (1985): 33*–38*; Eric M. Meyers, "The Persian Period and the Judean Restoration: From Zerubbabel to Nehemiah," in *Ancient Israelite Religion: Essays in Honor of Frank Moore Cross*, ed. Patrick D. Miller, Paul D. Hanson, and S. Dean McBride (Philadelphia: Fortress, 1987), 509–21 (509–10); Carol L. Meyers and Eric M. Meyers, *Haggai, Zechariah 1–8: A New Translation with Introduction and Commentary*, AB 25B (Garden City, NY: Doubleday, 1987), xl, 12–13; H. G. M. Williamson, "The Governors of Judah under the Persians," *TynBul* 39 (1988): 59–82 (75–77); John Kessler, "The Second Year of Darius and the Prophet Haggai," *Transeu* 5 (1992): 63–84 (73); Charles E. Carter, *The Emergence of Yehud in the Persian Period*, JSOTSup 294 (Sheffield: Sheffield Academic, 1999), 50–52. See also Peter R. Ackroyd, "Archaeology, Politics and Religion: The Persian Period," *Iliff Review* 39 (1982): 5–24, for his evaluation of the debate over the order and names of governors in the early Persian period.

this absence significant?[37] Is it possible that Zerubbabel resigned from his post due to Persian policies in the wake of Babylonian and Egyptian revolts and Jewish political intrigue in the province of Yehud?[38]

In any case, in light of the great expectations afforded Zerubbabel within the Zecharian tradition,[39] it is not fantastic to suggest that the end of his tenure would spark debate over the Davidic promises. In light of Ezek 34 and 37, Zech 11:4–16 represents a prophetic interpretation designed to explain the waning influence of the Davidic line. The text traces this threat to the people's rejection of the Davidic shepherd and identifies the present inappropriate leadership as judgement from God: giving the people the kind of leadership they deserve.

SYNCHRONIC ANALYSIS: ZECHARIAH 11:4–16 WITHIN ZECHARIAH 9–14

Although a discrete unit within Zech 9–14, possessing unique origins, 11:4–16 has been placed into the larger complex of Zech 9–14 where it plays a significant role in our reading of its final form. Having read Zech 11:4–16 diachronically, our intention now is to allow these insights to influence our reading of the final form of Zech 9–14.

The complex of prophetic pericopae which constitute Zech 9–14 are distinguished from the remainder of the book of Zechariah by the absence of the superscription style used in Zech 1:1, 7; 7:1 and the appearance of the superscript: "Oracle, Word of Yahweh" (משא דבר־יהוה).[40] This superscription, which appears

---

[37] There is a reference to a "governor" in Ezra 6:7 alongside the "elders of the Jews," but Zerubbabel's name is not mentioned. This may be an intentional excision by the redactor of Ezra 1–6 who places greater focus on the elders, priests, and prophets and avoids Zerubbabel's Davidic connection.

[38] Many scholars have avoided this conclusion after the critique of Peter R. Ackroyd, "Two Old Testament Historical Problems of the Early Persian Period," *JNES* 17 (1958): 13–27 against Leroy Waterman, "The Camouflaged Purge of Three Messianic Conspirators," *JNES* 13 (1954): 73–78. However, see more recently Ephraim Stern, "The Persian Empire and the Political and Social History of Palestine in the Persian Period," in *The Cambridge History of Judaism, Volume One—Introduction: The Persian Period*, ed. W. D. Davies and Louis Finkelstein (Cambridge: Cambridge University Press, 1984), 70–87 (72). For an excellent review of dating questions related to this issue see Kessler, "Darius." In contrast to Waterman's theory, Zech 11:4–16 does not indicate a revolution led by Zerubbabel, but it may suggest a resignation due to frustration with certain elements within the Yehud community with links to Persian authority.

[39] Boda, "Oil, Crowns and Thrones" = chapter 4 in this present volume.

[40] This does not mean that Zech 9–14 are unrelated to Zech 1–8 as they represent the enduring tradition of Zechariah. See ibid. = chapter 4 in this present volume; Mark J. Boda, "From Fasts to Feasts: The Literary Function of Zechariah 7–8," *CBQ* 65 (2003): 390–407 = *Exploring Zechariah*, volume 1, chapter 2.

at 9:1 and 12:1, is a redactional marker which in the final form of the text signals rhetorical divisions.[41]

The first two major pericopae (9:1–17 and 10:3b–12) show affinity through their positive tone, concern for Judah and Ephraim, and focus on the return from exile. The first pericope depicts God as divine warrior recapturing his palace/sanctuary and then defending, saving, and prospering his people (9:1–8, 14–17).[42] In the midst of this depiction appears an address to Zion (placed strategically between vv. 8 and 14, in the transition between God's return to the sanctuary and his salvation of the people) which celebrates the arrival of the king[43] and the return of the exiles from Judah and Ephraim who will become God's weapons (9:9–13). The second pericope (10:3b–12) shows affinity with the qualities of chapter 9, both on a stylistic level (switching between first and third person), as well as on a thematic level (with reference to Judah, Ephraim, restoration). These two pericopae share key themes:

1. Restoration is inaugurated by the action of God who breaks into Israel's history to instigate and complete redemption (9:1–8, 14–17; 10:3b, 6, 8–10, 12)
2. Restoration is envisioned for both Judah and Ephraim as they are rescued from foreign bondage, although Judah has the leading role to play in this restoration (9:11–13, 16–17; 10:6–11)
3. The people are described as God's flock, a term emphasizing God's personal and caring leadership with the people (9:16; 10:3b)

These two sections in chapters 9–10 contrast with the two dominant pieces found in chapters 12–14. A key structural marker throughout the two oracles in 12:1–13:6 and 14:1–21 is the phrase "in that day" (ביום־ההוא) which appears at regular intervals (12:3, 4, 6, 8, 9, 11; 13:1, 4; 14:4, 6, 8, 9, 13, 20, 21). Rather than Judah-

---

[41] Although this section is focused on the rhetoric of the final form of Zech 9–14, I agree largely with the redactional sensibilities of Redditt, "Israel's Shepherds"; Paul L. Redditt, "Nehemiah's First Mission and the Date of Zechariah 9–14," *CBQ* 56 (1994): 664–78; Paul L. Redditt, *Haggai, Zechariah and Malachi*, NCB (London: Marshall Pickering, 1995).
[42] The switch between first and third person in 9:1–8, 14–17 is not odd; one can see this in 9:1–8 where there is a move from third person (9:1–4) to first person (9:6–8) and thus in (9:14–17) back to third person.
[43] The exact identity of this king here is difficult to discern: with God's statement of his arrival at his house and protection of it, one may surmise that this is thus an announcement to Zion of God's arrival as king. However, v. 10 seems to distinguish between the "I" (God) and "he" (the king). Thus, this is probably a reference to a royal figure in Jerusalem, which coupled with evidence of connections to the promise to Judah in Gen 49, suggests an allusion to the restoration of Davidic kingship. Contra Adrian Leske, "Context and Meaning of Zechariah 9:9," *CBQ* 62 (2000): 663–78.

Ephraim, chapters 12:1–13:6 and 14:1–21 focus on a different pair, Judah-Jerusalem with no mention of Ephraim (12:2, 4–5, 7–8, 10; 13:1; 14:14, 21). Whereas chapters 9–10 depict God's return to his sanctuary-city and subsequent rescue of his people from the nations, 12:1–13:6 and 14:1–21 picture the attack of Jerusalem by all the nations of the earth, a battle in which God intervenes on Jerusalem's behalf, defeats the nations, and makes Jerusalem a sanctified space (cleansed, holy).

Although each pericope has its unique internal logic and message, this study has highlighted clear affinities within 9–10 and 12–14. But to this point we have not discussed several smaller pieces within Zech 9–14: 10:1–3a, 11:1–3; 11:17; 13:7–9. Each of these stand out from the surrounding text by employing imperatival/attention vocabulary, using a negative tone, and presenting the shepherd motif. Each of them focuses on God's displeasure with shepherd leaders. There is a progression between the various pieces: from Yahweh's anger (10:1–3a), to the prophecy of destruction (11:1–3), to a curse (11:17), to the execution of judgment (13:7–9).

These smaller units which appear at regular intervals throughout Zech 9–14 display close affinity with the sign-acts of 11:4–16. Both use the shepherd motif, depict a frustrating leadership situation and highlight the impact of such leadership on the community as a whole. The difference between the two, however, is that while the smaller shepherd units direct judgment against the shepherds, 11:4–16 directs it against the flock.

In its central location in the rhetorical complex of Zech 9–14, 11:4–16 transitions the reader from chapters 9–10 to 12–14. This is displayed most vividly in the account of the breaking of two staffs. The breaking of the first staff signifies "breaking my covenant with all the nations" (להפיר את־בריתי אשר כרתי את־כל־העמים, 11:10). The breaking of the second staff signifies the "breaking of the brotherhood between Judah and Israel" (להפר את־האחוה בין יהודה ובין ישראל, 11:14). These two actions of breaking correspond to two key discontinuities between the oracles in chapters 9–10 and 12–14, especially seen in the focus on God's destruction of "all the nations" (העמים: 12:2, 3, 4, 6; 14:12, הגוים: 12:9; 14:2, 3, 14, 16, 18, 19), and the absence of reference to Israel in chapters 12–14.

Thus, Zech 11:4–16 serves a crucial role in its final position in Zech 9–14 by transitioning the reader from the expectations of chapters 9–10 to those of chapters 12–14. Hopes of reunification of the restored tribes under Davidic leadership are dashed because of the community's rejection of this leadership, and such rejection prompts God's promise of inappropriate leadership. God takes direct control of the leadership of the nation in chapters 12–14, even though a future hope for the Davidic line remains.

CONCLUSION

This study of Zech 11:4–16 has attempted to demonstrate a balanced intertextual approach. Such an approach flows from the diachronic to the synchronic. It demands careful delineation of the sources of ancient texts and interpretation of any transformation to these sources in their new context. It also, however, involves the description of the impact of such allusion on the reading of the final form of the text, especially within the broader context of the literary corpus in which it presently resides.

By honing diachronic and synchronic sensibilities the interpreter is able to "read between the lines" of the present text. Diachronic analysis brings into focus the various intertexts that inhabit the gaps "between the lines" of the ancient text.[44] As we have discovered, these intertexts are more than just the limited words or phrases that are shared between the passages, but extend to the larger context in which these words or phrases are embedded. But it is not enough to merely bring the various intertexts "between the lines" into focus, cataloguing their references and transformations. One must then reflect on the impact that such intertext has on the reading of the final form of the text embedded in its larger context.

---

[44] A complementary image is that of the palimpsest, in which ancient text appears in the background; cf. Gérard Genette, *Palimpsestes: La littérature au second degré* (Paris: Seuil, 1982); Gérard Genette, *Palimpsests: Literature in the Second Degree*, trans. Channa Newman and Claude Doubinsky (Lincoln: University of Nebraska Press, 1997), even if I do not embrace his approach to intertextuality.

10
Inner Biblical Allusions in the Shepherd Units of Zechariah 9–14[1]

Having analyzed the two introductory formulae in Zech 9:1 and 12:1 and the sign-act report that lies at the core of Zech 9–14, I now turn my attention to the other key elements of the redactional skeleton of Zech 9–14, the Shepherd Units which appear in 10:1–3; 11:1–3; 11:17; 13:7–9. Here we again see the influence of Jeremiah as well as Ezekiel.

It is rather ironic that the initial impetus for the critical study of Zech 9–14 arose from a desire to make sense of a New Testament citation of the Old Testament. It was 1664 when Joseph Mede pitted apostle against Masorete when he wrote: "And if one of the Apostles of our Lord play here [Matt 27:9–10] the Critick, it is no sin to follow him, say the masorites what they will."[2] Matthew 27:9–10 attributed Zech 11:13 to Jeremiah, suggesting to Mede that Zech 9–14 was written by the earlier prophet.

---

[1] Based on a portion of my original publication in: Mark J. Boda and Stanley E. Porter, "Literature to the Third Degree: Prophecy in Zechariah 9–14 and the Passion of Christ," in *Traduire la Bible hébraïque: De la Septante à la Nouvelle Bible Segond = Translating the Hebrew Bible: From the Septuagint to the Nouvelle Bible Segond*. Edited by Robert David and Manuel Jinbachian, Sciences Bibliques 15 (Montreal: Médiaspaul, 2005), 215–54. Slightly revised for inclusion in this volume.
[2] Joseph Mede, *The Works of Joseph Mede*, 2nd ed. (London: James Flesher, 1664), 963; cited in Paul D. Hanson, *The Dawn of Apocalyptic: The Historical and Sociological Roots of Jewish Apocalyptic Eschatology*, rev. ed. (Philadelphia: Fortress, 1979), 288; cf. Joseph

Medes's quandary brings into sharp focus the role that Zech 9–14 has played in the development of canonical traditions, one that relates both to the prophets that preceded this text and to the communities which would later embrace this text. In order to examine this dynamic we will investigate the intertextual character of this text.

The kind of analysis pursued below is one that defines "text" in the more limited sense of literary units (rather than any socio-cultural phenomena) and defines intertextual analysis as both a search for earlier literary texts that have influenced the creation of a later text (here, Zech 9–14) and also a consideration of the impact of these earlier texts (pre-texts) on the reading of the present form of the later text (post-text). Such definitions clearly distinguish us from post-structuralist fixation on the modern reader on the one side and historical-critical fixation on the pre-history of the text. In paying attention to the diachronic dimension of intertextuality before considering the synchronic dimension, we are taking our lead from the character of later biblical literature. Jewish and Christian literature which originated after the Babylonian period displays close attention to the vocabulary of earlier biblical material in the Torah and the Prophets, a trend that is most likely related to the process of canonization, that is, the recognition and identification of authoritative texts.[3] With such texts in hand, the community of writers had a powerful resource for bolstering the credibility of their message.

The goal of this study will be to identify the presence and impact of intertextuality in the texts in view.

Mede, *Dissertationum Dissertationum ecclesiasticarum triga: ... Quibus accedunt Fragmenta sacra.* (London: 1653).

[3] See for instance the treatment of Torah in the ceremonies of Neh 8 as well as the close attention to the vocabulary of Torah in the prayer of Neh 9 and other Persian period prayers; cf. Mark J. Boda, *Praying the Tradition: The Origin and Use of Tradition in Nehemiah 9*, BZAW 277 (Berlin: de Gruyter, 1999); Mark J. Boda, "Confession as Theological Expression: Ideological Origins of Penitential Prayer," in *Seeking the Favor of God: Volume 1—The Origin of Penitential Prayer in Second Temple Judaism*, ed. Mark J. Boda, Daniel K. Falk, and Rodney A. Werline, EJL 21 (Atlanta: Society of Biblical Literature, 2006), 21–50.

PAST RESEARCH

It is now long forgotten that the opening article in the inaugural issue of *ZAW* in 1881 was the first of three studies by then editor Bernhard Stade on Zech 9–14.[4] In these articles Stade would become the first modern scholar to bring sustained focus on the ways in which these enigmatic chapters depend upon earlier biblical materials, in particular earlier prophetic collections. Stade placed Deutero-Zechariah in a prophetic tradition which developed from Jeremiah through Ezekiel to Zech 9–14, displayed prominently in the expectation for the restoration of northern and southern tribes. Over seventy years later this issue would momentarily reappear in a treatment by Matthias Delcor in which he concluded that at least portions of Zech 9–14 rely mainly on Isaiah (Second and Third), Jeremiah, and Ezekiel, with a few references to Deuteronomy, Joel, and Zephaniah.[5] LaMarche took this study another step in his rhetorical analysis of Zech 9–14, especially drawing attention to the close association between Deutero-Zechariah and the servant passages of Deutero-Isaiah.[6] In the early 1970s both Rex Mason and Ina Willi-Plein mined these chapters for inner biblical allusion.[7] Mason confirmed Stade's conclusion that Deutero-Zechariah depends on earlier biblical material,

---

[4] Bernhard Stade, "Deuterosacharja: Eine kritische Studie I," *ZAW* 1 (1881): 1–96; Bernhard Stade, "Deuterosacharja: Eine kritische Studie II," *ZAW* 2 (1882): 151–72; Bernhard Stade, "Deuterosacharja: Eine kritische Studie III," *ZAW* 2 (1882): 275–309. For another review of intertextuality in Zech 9–14 and an exhaustive bibliography see Mark J. Boda, *Haggai and Zechariah Research: A Bibliographic Survey*, Tools for Biblical Study 5 (Leiden: Deo, 2003).

[5] Mathias Delcor, "Les sources du Deutero-Zacharie et ses procédés d'emprunt," *RB* 59 (1952): 385–411; cf. Mathias Delcor, "Zacharie (Chapitres IX–XIV)," in *Les petits prophètes*, ed. Alfons Deissler and Mathias Delcor, La Sainte Bible 8/1 (Paris: Letouzey & Ané, 1961).

[6] Paul LaMarche, *Zacharie IX–XIV: Structure littéraire et messianisme*, EBib (Paris: Librairie Lecoffre, 1961), 121–47.

[7] Rex A. Mason, "The Use of Earlier Biblical Material in Zechariah IX–XIV: A Study in Inner Biblical Exegesis" (PhD diss., University of London, 1973) = Rex A. Mason, "The Use of Earlier Biblical Material in Zechariah 9–14: A Study in Inner Biblical Exegesis," in *Bringing out the Treasure: Inner Biblical Allusion and Zechariah 9–14*, ed. Mark J. Boda and Michael H. Floyd, JSOTSup 370 (Sheffield: Sheffield Academic, 2003), 1–208; Rex A. Mason, "The Relation of Zech 9–14 to Proto-Zechariah," *ZAW* 88 (1976): 227–39; Rex A. Mason, "Some Examples of Inner Biblical Exegesis in Zech. IX–XIV," in *Studia Evangelica Vol. 7: Papers Presented to the 5th International Congress on Biblical Studies Held at Oxford, 1973*, ed. Elizabeth A. Livingstone, TUGAL 126 (Berlin: Akademie, 1982), 343–54; Rex A. Mason, "Inner Biblical Exegesis in Zech. 9–14," *Grace Theological Journal* 3 (1982): 51–65; Ina Willi-Plein, *Prophetie am Ende: Untersuchungen zu Sacharja 9–14*, BBB 42 (Köln: Hanstein, 1974).

rarely through "quotation," more often through "fluid and free adaptation of earlier material" which he calls "allusive word-play," which reinterpreted, reapplied, and at times reversed earlier materials.[8] These connections were drawn from a breadth of material including Psalms, Ezekiel, Amos, Second- and Trito-Isaiah and, finally, Proto-Zechariah. Willi-Plein concluded that the majority of allusions in Zech 9–14 could be traced back to the major prophetic books of Isaiah, Jeremiah, and Ezekiel and then lesser so to Hosea, with a few scattered allusions to Amos, Micah, Deuteronomy, the Tetrateuch and the Former Prophets.

After Mason and Willi-Plein it would then be two more decades before there was a monograph devoted to this subject, but when the subject reappeared there was a flurry of activity inaugurated by Schaeffer and then continued by Person, Larkin, Tai, and Nurmela.[9] Schaeffer focused on Zech 14 and argued that the composer depended on earlier parts of Zechariah (chs. 1–13), Jeremiah, Ezekiel, late parts of Isaiah, and possibly Joel. Person limited his attention to connections to Deuteronomic literature including Deuteronomy, the Deuteronomic History, and Jeremiah, concluding that Deutero-Zechariah was the product of an enduring Deuteronomic school in the Persian period and represented a fifth century BCE Deuteronomic reinterpretation of Zech 1–8. Larkin, building on an earlier suggestion of Fishbane,[10] identified in Zech 9–13 "mantological exegesis" of traditional prophetic, historical, and cultic traditions, with similar results to the conclusions

---

[8] Mason, "Use," 201–2.

[9] Konrad R. Schaefer, "Zechariah 14 and the Formation of the Book of Zechariah" (SSD diss., Ecole biblique et archéologique française, 1992); Konrad R. Schaefer, "Zechariah 14 and the Composition of the Book of Zechariah," *RB* 100 (1993): 368–98; Konrad R. Schaefer, "The Ending of the Book of Zechariah: A Commentary," *RB* 100 (1993): 165–238; Konrad R. Schaefer, "Zechariah 14: A Study in Allusion," *CBQ* 57 (1995): 66–91; Raymond F. Person, *Second Zechariah and the Deuteronomic School*, JSOTSup 167 (Sheffield: JSOT Press, 1993); Katrina J. Larkin, *The Eschatology of Second Zechariah: A Study of the Formation of a Mantological Wisdom Anthology*, CBET 6 (Kampen: Kok, 1994); Nicholas Ho Fai Tai, *Prophetie als Schriftauslegung in Sacharja 9–14: Traditions- und kompositionsgeschichtliche Studien*, Calwer Theologische Monographien 17 (Stuttgart: Calwer, 1996); Risto Nurmela, *Prophets in Dialogue: Inner-Biblical Allusions in Zechariah 1–8 and 9–14* (Åbo: Åbo Akademi University, 1996). We could also draw in the research of James Nogalski on inner-connections within the Book of the Twelve, although his agenda is slightly different; James D. Nogalski, *Literary Precursors to the Book of the Twelve*, BZAW 217 (Berlin: de Gruyter, 1993); James D. Nogalski, *Redactional Processes in the Book of the Twelve*, BZAW 218 (Berlin: de Gruyter, 1993). See now the collection of essays in Mark J. Boda and Michael H. Floyd, eds., *Bringing out the Treasure: Inner Biblical Allusion and Zechariah 9–14*, JSOTSup 370 (Sheffield: Sheffield Academic, 2003).

[10] Michael A. Fishbane, *Biblical Interpretation in Ancient Israel* (Oxford: Clarendon, 1985), 501–4, 520.

of Willi-Plein (Isaiah, Jeremiah, Ezekiel, Hosea, Amos, Genesis, Deuteronomy, Psalms). She claimed that the exegesis evident in Zech 9–14 was necessary to clarify, adapt, or revise earlier oral prophecy in new contexts. Tai combined redaction and tradition criticism to demonstrate that the first phase (9:1–11:3) drew on Jeremiah, the second phase (11:4–16) on Ezekiel, the third phase (12:1–13:9) on Ezekiel and Deuteronomic Hosea, and the final phase (14:1–21) on the prophetic motif of the Day of Yahweh. Finally, Nurmela concluded that Zech 9–14 depends heavily on Isaiah (1–11, 29–31), Jeremiah, and Ezekiel, besides Proto-Zechariah.

What this review reveals is the enduring conviction among researchers of Zech 9–14 that this corpus exhibits strong connections to other biblical materials. Consistent throughout these studies is the claim that Zech 9–14 draws upon earlier prophetic texts. While there is considerable debate over which part of Isaiah is connected, there is near unanimity that Jeremiah and Ezekiel are two crucial sources for those responsible for Zech 9–14.

A study of intertexts within all of Zech 9–14 is too ambitious a project for the present paper. The focus of an earlier study was on the report of a sign-act in 11:4–16, a pericope which plays a key literary role in the transition between the oracles in chapters 9–10 and those in chapters 12–14.[11] An intertextual analysis of this report of a sign-act revealed close affinities with the shepherd-flock tradition of the book of Ezekiel which is developed in 34:1–31 and 37:15–28.[12] Common to these Ezekielian passages is the enduring hope for a Davidic ruler, suggesting that the good shepherd here is a reference to someone from this royal line and that, in spite of the appearance of an abusive shepherd, there was an enduring hope for Davidic royal leadership.[13]

Building on this earlier work, this section of the paper will focus on a series of redactional links which lie at the seams between the major prophetic units in

---

[11] Mark J. Boda, "Reading between the Lines: Zechariah 11:4–16 in Its Literary Contexts," in *Bringing out the Treasure: Inner Biblical Allusion and Zechariah 9–14*, ed. Mark J. Boda and Michael H. Floyd, JSOTSup 370 (Sheffield: Sheffield Academic, 2003), 277–91 = chapter 9 in this present volume.

[12] Contra Person, *Second Zechariah and the Deuteronomic School*, 127, who links it to Jer 25:15–29. Nevertheless, one cannot deny one Jeremianic flourish in Zech 11:4–16: the use of הרגה in vv. 4, 7, a term restricted elsewhere to Jeremiah (7:32; 12:3; 19:6).

[13] See the argument for connections between Ezek 33–37 and the Gospel of John in Mary Katharine Deeley, "Ezekiel's Shepherd and John's Jesus: A Case Study in the Appropriation of Biblical Texts. Early Christian Interpretation of the Scriptures of Israel," in *Early Christian Interpretation of the Scriptures of Israel*, ed. Craig A. Evans and James A. Sanders, JSNTSup 148 (Sheffield: Sheffield Academic, 1997), 252–64; and between Ezek 34 and the Gospel of Matthew in John Paul Heil, "Ezekiel 34 and the Narrative Strategy of the Shepherd and Sheep Metaphor in Matthew," *CBQ* 55 (1993): 698–708.

174   *The Development and Role of Biblical Traditions in Zechariah*

Zech 9–14: 10:1–3; 11:1–3; 11:17; 13:7–9. Along with the report of a sign-act in 11:4–16, these links unite Zech 9–14 as a collection. They share common stylistic, lexical, and thematic features.[14] Each of them contain imperatival/attention vocabulary, a negative mood, and shepherd motifs. Each of them either promise or enact Yahweh's judgment against bad shepherds. This judgment progresses throughout the collection: from anger (10:1–3), to warning of destruction (11:1–3), to curse (11:17), to execution (13:7–9). The goal of this section of the paper will be to investigate the intertextual quality of these short redactional units and then consider the implications of this dimension of the text for interpretation and translation.

INTERTEXTUAL ANALYSIS OF THE SHEPHERD-FLOCK UNITS

ZECHARIAH 10:1–3

The first redactional unit in Zech 10:1–3 is regularly connected to Jer 14:1–15:4, first of all, due to a series of lexical affinities within 10:1–2a:[15] נתן and עשׂה (for giving/making rain; Jer 14:22; Zech 10:1); גשׁם (Jer 14:4; Zech 10:1); בשׂדה (Jer 14:5; Zech 10:1); עשׂב (Jer 14:6; Zech 10:1); דבר (*piel*; Jer 14:14; Zech 10:2); שׁקר (Jer 14:14; Zech 10:2); קסם/קסם (Jer 14:14; Zech 10:2); חזון/חזה (Jer 14:14; Zech 10:2). Secondly, both Jer 14:1–15:4 and Zech 10:1–2a bring together drought, idolatry, and false prophetic activity.[16] One, however, cannot ignore the close affinity between Zech 10:1–2a and Deut 11:11–17 where the following lexical links can be discerned:[17] מטר (Deut 11:11, 14, 17; Zech 10:1); עת (Deut

---

[14] The redactional character of these smaller units has been highlighted by Karl Elliger, *Das Buch der zwölf kleinen Propheten 2: Die Propheten Nahum, Habakuk, Zephanja, Haggai, Sacharja, Maleachi*, 7th ed., ATD 25.2 (Göttingen: Vandenhoeck & Ruprecht, 1975), 143–44; Paul L. Redditt, "Israel's Shepherds: Hope and Pessimism in Zechariah 9–14," *CBQ* 51 (1989): 631–42; and Larkin, *Eschatology*, passim, esp. 91. Elliger also includes 9:9–10 in the list. However, the shepherding motif does not occur in this piece as in the others.

[15] Mason, "Use," 64–69; Willi-Plein, *Prophetie*, 71–72, 93; Larkin, *Eschatology*, 87–88, 90; Tai, *Prophetie als Schriftauslegung*, 78–9, 83; Nurmela, *Prophets in Dialogue*, 114–19; and Eibert Tigchelaar, "Some Observations on the Relation between Zechariah 9–11 and Jeremiah," in *Bringing out the Treasure: Inner Biblical Allusion and Zechariah 9–14*, ed. Mark J. Boda and Michael H. Floyd, JSOTSup 370 (Sheffield: Sheffield Academic, 2003), 260–70 (267).

[16] For the character of Jer 14:1–15:4 and its relationship to the drought, see Mark J. Boda, "From Complaint to Contrition: Peering through the Liturgical Window of Jer 14,1–15,4," *ZAW* 113 (2001): 186–97.

[17] Willi-Plein, *Prophetie*, 72, 93; Larkin, *Eschatology*, 88–90; Tai, *Prophetie als Schriftauslegung*, 79–83; Nurmela, *Prophets in Dialogue*, 114–19.

11:14; Zech 10:1); מלקוש (Deut 11:14; Zech 10:1); עשב בשדה (Deut 11:15; Zech 10:1), all in a context where a connection is made between drought and idolatry. While most likely Jer 14:1–15:4 itself draws upon Deut 11:10–17 for its conceptual and lexical base[18] and that Zech 10:1–2a draws upon Jer 14:1–15:4, the appearance of three unique connections between Zech 10:1–2a and Deut 11:10–17 independent of Jer 14:1–15:4 suggests that Zech 10:1–2a is aware of both Jer 14:1–15:4 and Deut 11:10–17, even if the Jeremianic text is dominant.[19]

These connections to Jer 14:1–15:4 and Deut 11, however, are not related to the shepherd-flock imagery proper which is limited to verses 2b–3a. For this several scholars have noted an important link to Jer 23:1–3 where the verb פקד (*qal*) is used in a context speaking about shepherds (רעים; Jer 23:1, 2, 3) and sheep (צאן; Jer 23:1, 2) to refer both to caring for the flock and visiting punishment on the shepherds.[20] This is the only other place in the Hebrew Bible where this verb is used in both senses in the same context. The reference to the lack of a shepherd, אין רעה, occurs four other times in the Hebrew Bible (Num 27:17; 1 Kgs 22:17 // 2 Chr 18:16; Ezek 34:8; Zech 10:2). This may be merely a common idiom in Hebrew, but it should at least be noted that the only use in the latter prophets is in Ezek 34,[21] a passage that plays an important role in the development of the shepherd-flock tradition in Zech 11:4–16.

This analysis then suggests a close affinity between 10:1–2a and the Deuteronomic tradition and most likely Jer 14:1–15:4 and Deut 11:11–15 within this tradition. Zechariah 10:2b–3a evidences some affinity with the Jeremianic shepherd-flock tradition in Jer 23:1–3 and the Ezekielian shepherd-flock tradition in Ezek 34. This evidence alone, however, is not enough to establish a secure link.

ZECHARIAH 11:1–3

The connection to the Jeremianic shepherd-flock tradition, however, has often been noted for the next shepherding unit in 11:1–3. This time the source is Jer 25:34–38 where the following links are noteworthy:[22] ילל (*hiphil*; Jer 25:34; Zech 11:2); רעה (Jer 25:34; Zech 11:3); יללה (Jer 25:36; Zech 11:3); אדיר (Jer 25:34, 35, 36; Zech 11:2, 3); קול (Jer 25:36; Zech 11:3); שדד (Jer 25:36; Zech 11:2, 3);

---

[18] See Larkin, *Eschatology*, 88.
[19] This is further bolstered by Larkin's revelation that the sequence of thought from 9:17–10:3 appears to be based on Deut 11:13–17 (see footnote above).
[20] Willi-Plein, *Prophetie*, 72, 93; Larkin, *Eschatology*, 93; Tai, *Prophetie als Schriftauslegung*, 100–2; Nurmela, *Prophets in Dialogue*, 120–25.
[21] Willi-Plein, *Prophetie*, 72, 93.
[22] Mason, "Use," 74; Willi-Plein, *Prophetie*, 93; Person, *Second Zechariah and the Deuteronomic School*, 111–12, 124; Nurmela, *Prophets in Dialogue*; Tai, *Prophetie als Schriftauslegung*, 118–20.

כפיר (Jer 25:38; Zech 11:3). The extended imagery of the lion coming up from Jordan's thickets (מגאון הירדן) is restricted elsewhere in the Hebrew Bible to Jer 49:19 and 50:44. Zechariah 11:3 replaces the more common אריה with כפיר, most likely under the influence by Jer 25:38.

As in the previous unit of 10:1–3, shepherding vocabulary is fused with another type of imagery, this time botanical imagery. For this terminology some scholars have noted connections to Isa 2:13 with its common words: לבנון; ארז; בשן and אלון.[23] However, a stronger candidate is Jer 22 with its employment not only of the regularly associated words לבנון (Jer 22:6, 20, 23; Zech 11:1); ארז (Jer 22:7, 14, 15, 23; Zech 11:1, 2); בשן (Jer 22:20; Zech 11:2); but also אש (Jer 22:7; Zech 11:1); נפל (Jer 22:7; Zech 11:2); and רעה (Jer 22:22; Zech 11:3), three elements that are lacking in Isa 2:13.[24]

The number of lexical connections between Jer 22 and 25:34–38 and Zech 11:1–3 strongly suggests that there is an intertextual connection between these passages.

ZECHARIAH 11:17

On form-critical grounds Zech 11:17 is a self-contained unit, representing a "woe oracle." This distinguishes it from the preceding report of a sign-act in 11:4–16. There are only two other places in the Hebrew Bible where a woe oracle is directed against "shepherds": Jer 23:1–4 and Ezek 34.[25] In light of the influence of Ezek 34, especially in the final phase of the sign-act of Zech 11:4–16, one may assume that the Ezekielian tradition is to be credited as the source. However, we have already noted the possible fusion of Jeremianic and Ezekielian shepherd-flock traditions in 10:1–3, and there the two key texts were again Jer 23:1–4 and Ezek 34. Past scholarship also has recognized that the combination חרב על as marker of a sword-oracle is only found elsewhere in Jer 50:35–38, and in that case

---

[23] Willi-Plein, *Prophetie*, 72–73, 93; Larkin, *Eschatology*; Nurmela, *Prophets in Dialogue*, 133–36; Tai, *Prophetie als Schriftauslegung*, 118–20.

[24] The Lebanon-Bashan terms are a regular word pair in Biblical Hebrew (Isa 2:13; 33:9; 22:20; Ezek 27:5, 6; Nah 1:4; Ps 29:5–7; Judg 9:15) and in a couple of places one finds Lebanon-cedar-fire (Ps 29:5–7; Judg 9:15; Jer 22:6–7; Zech 11:1–3). However, only in Jer 22 and Zech 11:1–3 is there an intersection of Lebanon, Bashan, cedar, fire, falling, and shepherds.

[25] Person, *Second Zechariah and the Deuteronomic School*, 110, 126–27; Larkin, *Eschatology*, 137; Nurmela, *Prophets in Dialogue*, 136–40; Tai, *Prophetie als Schriftauslegung*, 144, 150–51, 155.

one also finds, as in Zech 11:17, the verb יבש (Jer 50:38; Zech 11:17).²⁶ It is important to note that Jer 50 was also mentioned in the analysis of Zech 11:1–3 above. Zechariah 11:17 displays close affinities with the shepherd-flock traditions in Jeremiah and Ezekiel.

ZECHARIAH 13:7–9

Zechariah 13:7 takes up the sword-oracle style seen already in Zech 11:17 (חרב על) and linked to the Jeremianic tradition found in Jer 50 (vv. 35–38). This sword oracle speaks of God's judgment of Babylon. Interestingly, shepherd-flock imagery is introduced in this same context (vv. 44–46, see our evaluation of 11:1–3 above). God (who compares himself to a lion coming up from the thickets of Jordan, cf. Zech 11:1–3), chases away oppressive Babylon and challenges any רעה to stand against him. His plan is to drag away צעירי הצאן. In Zech 13:7, the sword is awakened against רעה and when it strikes both הצאן and הצערים are deeply affected. Zechariah 13:7 and Jer 50:45 are the only two places in the Hebrew Bible where the root צער is used in reference to sheep. The vocabulary of scattering (פוץ) in reference to sheep is found elsewhere in 1 Kgs 22:17 // 2 Chr 18:16; Jer 10:21; 23:1, 2; Ezek 34:5, 6, 12, 21. The appearance of Jer 23 and Ezek 34 is not surprising in light of the above discussion. Some scholars have noted the influence here also of Isa 1:21–26²⁷ with its use of שוב + יד + על (Isa 1:25; Zech 13:7) followed by reference to refining in both word (צרף) and image (Isa 1:25; Zech 13:9). This is possible and if so would be the only clear reference to Isaiah in the shepherd-flock units.

But Jer 50 does not explain this entire pericope. The intersection of the image of the sword with that of punishment in three portions is only found elsewhere in the latter prophets in Ezek 5 where reference is made to burning a portion with fire and striking a portion with the sword as in Zech 13:7–9.²⁸ In this most severe of all the shepherd-flock units, there is an intertwining of Jeremianic and Ezekielian texts to accentuate purifying judgment. At the same time, however, this is the most hopeful of all the shepherd-flock units as it ends with a description of God and people in covenant intimacy.

---

[26] Willi-Plein, *Prophetie*, 76, 93; Larkin, *Eschatology*, 137; Person, *Second Zechariah and the Deuteronomic School*, 126–27, cf. Tigchelaar, "Some Observations," 267.
[27] Mason, "Use," 125–26; Tai, *Prophetie als Schriftauslegung*, 226; cf. Risto Nurmela, "The Growth of the Book of Isaiah Illustrated by Allusions in Zechariah," in *Bringing out the Treasure: Inner Biblical Allusion and Zechariah 9–14*, ed. Mark J. Boda and Michael H. Floyd, JSOTSup 370 (Sheffield: Sheffield Academic, 2003), 245–59 (256–57).
[28] Mason, "Use," 127; Willi-Plein, *Prophetie*, 78, 93; Larkin, *Eschatology*, 177—78; Tai, *Prophetie als Schriftauslegung*, 231–32.

CONCLUSION

The preceding analysis has showcased evidence for the influence of prophetic texts on the redactional shepherd-flock units in Zech 9–14. The shepherd-flock motif proper is most reliant on the Jeremianic tradition[29] with a few links to Ezekiel and one possible, though not secure, link to Isaiah.

This relationship to Jeremiah is not surprising since no prophetic tradition develops the shepherd-flock motif more than Jeremiah.[30] First, shepherd-flock imagery is used in Jeremiah to refer to foreign kings/generals as shepherds with their armies as flocks (Jer 6:34; 12:10; cf. 25:34–36).[31] Secondly and more commonly shepherd-flock imagery is used to refer to leaders of Israel/Judah over their people. In the majority of these cases the reference is to inappropriate leaders (10:21; 13:17, 20; 22:22; 23:1–4; 25:34–36; 50:6–7) whose idolatrous practices (3:15; 10:21, cf. vv. 7–8, 14; 13:20, cf. vv. 24–27; 23:1–4, cf. false prophecy in vv. 9–40) have led to judgment on the flock through punishment and exile (10:21; 12:3; 13:17, 20; 22:22; 23:1–4; 31:10; 50:17; cf. 49:19–20; 50:44–45) as well as judgment on the shepherds for their leadership (23:1–4). In a few cases, however, the reference is to future ideal leaders of Israel (3:15; 23:1–4; 31:10) who are connected to the gathering of the flock from exile (3:15; 23:1–4; 31:10). In two instances this future leadership is linked (at least redactionally) to the Davidic house (3:15; cf. 23:5–6), while in one it is connected to God (31:10).

The Jeremianic passages most influential on the shepherd-flock units in Zech 9–14 are those which use the shepherd-flock image to refer to leaders and flocks of Israel/Judah, both inappropriate present leadership and future ideal leadership. Such passages allude to punishment through exile as well as future restoration with Davidic leadership.

The strongest connections to the Jeremianic shepherd vocabulary appear to be found in Jer 22–25. This section of Jeremiah focuses attention on two key socio-functionary groups within pre-exilic Judah. First, there is an attack on the royal shepherds of the day, while affirming a future for the Davidic house (22:1–23:8; 24:1–10). This concern over the royal stream also is evidenced in the non-shepherd imagery of 11:1–2 which bears striking similarity to the imagery used of the royal line in Jer 22. Secondly, associated with this attack on the royal house are equally vicious attacks on false prophecy (23:9–40) and the lack of response to true prophecy (25:1–14) in Jer 22–25. Furthermore, the strong polemic against

---

[29] Similarly Tigchelaar, "Some Observations," 267, for 10:1–3, 11:1–3, 17.

[30] Our interest is in the way this motif is used in reference to leadership (shepherd) over people or nations (flock).

[31] One minor motif is that of Jeremiah the prophet as shepherd, which is mentioned once (Jer 17:16). This study will not examine all uses of the shepherd-flock imagery, but only those which point to leadership over people.

false prophecy in Jer 23:33–40, which contains the greatest concentration of the term משא (oracle) in the Hebrew Bible, may explain why this term was used by the redactor to introduce the two major collections in Zech 9–14.[32] It should also be noted that concerns over false prophecy and associated idolatry can also be discerned in the reliance of Zech 10:1–2 on Jer 14:1–15:4 which lies outside the Jer 22–25 complex but is closely related in terms of Jeremianic tradition. Thirdly, in Jer 22–25 the shepherd-flock imagery is expanded to include foreign nations (focusing on Babylon) who will experience a similar devastation to that of Judah and Jerusalem (25:12–38).

This intertwining of domestic and foreign shepherding with false prophecy and idolatry in the Jeremianic tradition is also demonstrated in another passage to which Zech 9–14 alludes: Jer 50, a passage that scholars often link to Jer 25 because of the order of the text in the (what is often deemed earlier) LXX, which has MT 46–51 in the middle of MT 25.[33] Jeremiah 50–51 represents a prophetic

---

[32] Weis and Floyd have identified this superscription as a genre tag, but this is not convincing. One should not miss that the phrase here is different from other uses of משא for it also contains דבר־יהוה. It is interesting that Jer 23:33–40 contains the most concentrated use of the term משא in the Hebrew Bible and that this section describes a crisis over the use of משא among false prophets, prophets who claimed to have the דבר־יהוה when they were only speaking their own words. In light of the close affinities with Jeremiah in Zech 9–14 and the references to false prophecy (see below), this superscription appears to be identifying what follows as a prophetic דבר־יהוה in contrast to the דבר of the false prophets. Cf. Richard Weis, "A Definition of the Genre *Maśśā'* in the Hebrew Bible" (PhD diss., Claremont Graduate School, 1986); Richard Weis, "Oracle," in *ABD* 5:28–29; Michael H. Floyd, "The Maśśā' as a Type of Prophetic Book," *JBL* 121 (2002): 401–22. See my critical review of this stream of research in chapter 7 above.

[33] The links between Zech 9–14 and Jeremiah in this article are based on a comparison of the two texts in MT. However, in each of these individual cases the LXX appears to be relying on a similar (if not identical) underlying Hebrew text (although cf. Jer 50:38 in MT יבש with LXX 27:38 καταισχύνω = בוש). Notice how Jer 50 is part of the larger complex of oracles against the nations that stretch in the MT text tradition from Jer 46–51. In the LXX text tradition, which is usually identified as earlier (see J. Gerald Janzen, *Studies in the Text of Jeremiah*, HSM 6 [Cambridge: Harvard University Press, 1973]; Emanuel Tov, "Some Aspects of the Textual and Literary History of the Book of Jeremiah," in *Le Livre de Jérémie: Le prophète et son milieu, les oracles et leur transmission*, ed. P.-M. Bogaert, BETL 54 [Louvain: University of Louvain Press, 1981], 145–67), this section follows Jer 25:13, showing that at an earlier point in the textual tradition, Jer 50 was closely related to Jer 22–25. In LXX, MT 25:35–38 closes off the oracles against the nations and MT 50 is placed at LXX 27. See James W. Watts, "Text and Redaction in Jeremiah's Oracles against the Nations," *CBQ* 54 (1992): 432–47; Robert P. Carroll, "Halfway through a Dark Wood: Reflections on Jeremiah 25," in *Troubling Jeremiah*, ed. A. R. Pete Diamond, Kathleen M. O'Connor, and Louis Stulman, JSOTSup 260 (Sheffield: Sheffield Academic, 1999), 73–86; and Anneli Aejmelaeus, "Jeremiah at the Turning-Point of History: The Function of

collection against Babylon, and here one finds echoes of the description of poor shepherding among Israel's leaders evident in Jer 22–25 (50:6–8, 17), but the focus is clearly on Babylon as a foreign power who will be punished.

One, however, cannot claim that the shepherd-flock units are drawing exclusively on Jeremianic traditions for there is possible evidence of Ezekielian influence in the reference to a lack of a shepherd in Zech 10:2 and the woe oracle in 11:17, and clear evidence of such influence in the tripartite punishment in 13:8–9. This Ezekielian connection is not surprising in light of the strong Ezekielian influence on the central shepherd prophetic sign-act in Zech 11:4–16. Furthermore, there may be a slight influence from Isa 1, but this is limited to 13:7–9.

In all of this, however, it should not be missed that Jeremiah is the dominant shaping *Vorlage* of these redactional shepherding units. What then is the impact of this intertextual backdrop on the reading of these shepherd-flock units? First, the Jeremianic source text expresses concern for Davidic leadership.[34] The negative stance towards the shepherds in both Jeremiah and Zech 9–14 shows that this Davidic stream is not above criticism. At the same time the Jeremianic backdrop affirms an enduring role for the Davidides, something that is assumed not only at the outset of Zech 9–14 (9:9–10), but also after the shepherd-flock crisis of Zech 11:4–16 in 12:1–13:6.[35] Jeremiah is a helpful prophetic text for a prophetic movement desirous to offer criticism without squelching optimism for a future royal

---

Jer. xxv 1–14 in the Book of Jeremiah," *VT* 52 (2002): 459–82, who argue that Jer 25:1–13 was originally an introduction to the oracles against the nations section; contra Martin Kessler, "The Function of Chapters 25 and 50–51 in the Book of Jeremiah," in *Troubling Jeremiah*, ed. A. R. Pete Diamond, Kathleen M. O'Connor, and Louis Stulman, JSOTSup 260 (Sheffield: Sheffield Academic, 1999), 64–72; Menahem Haran, "The Place of the Prophecies against the Nations in the Book of Jeremiah," in *Emanuel: Studies in Hebrew Bible, Septuagint, and Dead Sea Scrolls in Honor of Emanuel Tov*, ed. Shalom M. Paul et al., VTSup 94 (Leiden: Brill, 2003), 699–706; cf. Bernard Gosse, "The Masoretic Redaction of Jeremiah: An Explanation," *JSOT* 77 (1998): 75–80.

[34] See also Redditt, "Israel's Shepherds," 641. While many have identified the shepherds here as either leadership in general, priestly or prophetic, the Jeremianic intertexts suggest that the shepherds are civic leadership which included royal and imperial figures; cf. Stephen L. Cook, "The Metamorphosis of a Shepherd: The Tradition History of Zechariah 11:17 + 13:7–9," *CBQ* 55 (1993): 453–66 (453–66); contra Mason, "Use," 203; Redditt, "Israel's Shepherds," 641, Paul D. Hanson, *The Dawn of Apocalyptic: The Historical and Sociological Roots of Jewish Apocalyptic Eschatology* (Philadelphia: Fortress, 1975). Robert B. Crotty, "The Suffering Moses of Deutero-Zechariah," *Colloq* 14 (1982): 43–50, identified the shepherd figure as the "Suffering Moses," but there is no justification for this.

[35] See Mark J. Boda, "Figuring the Future: The Prophets and the Messiah," in *The Messiah in the Old and New Testaments*, ed. Stanley E. Porter, McMaster New Testament Studies (Grand Rapids: Eerdmans, 2007), 35–74 = *Exploring Zechariah*, volume 1, chapter 4,

role. As reading the central shepherd sign-act against the backdrop of Ezek 34–37 reveals positive and negative Davidic connections, so reading the redactional shepherd-flock units against the backdrop of Jeremiah and, in particular, Jer 22–25 reveals both positive and negative Davidic connections.

Secondly, the consistent link between royal-shepherds and false prophecy/idolatry in the Jeremianic tradition also isolates what must have been an enduring problem in the era when Zech 9–14 originated.[36] Again Zech 12:1–13:6 reveals that this was indeed the case as false prophecy linked with idolatry is singled out in 13:1–6. [37] Through intertextual allusions, the Zecharian tradents brought the Jeremianic textual tradition into view, texts which reminded them of the serious implications of such practices for the life of the people in the land.

Finally, the intertwining of domestic and foreign leadership through the shepherd-flock motif in Jeremiah does suggest that the crisis at hand involved both Jewish as well as foreign leaders. Evidence of foreign intrusion into domestic affairs can be discerned in the central sign-act of 11:4–16 as the good shepherd is called to rectify a situation in which owners and buyers are abusing the sheep and ultimately must break his covenant with the nations, an act that sets up the international crisis of Zech 12–14. The links to Babylon in Jer 25 and 50 may indicate

---

which highlights evidence for an enduring role for the Davidic line in 12:1–13:6; cf. Cook, "Metamorphosis," 460–63. There is a possibility that this role will be assumed by a different Davidic clan than the line of Solomon. Such a shift may reflect an appropriation of the rejection of Jehoiachin's line in Jer 22:24–30.

[36] There is debate over whether idolatrous practices continued into the Persian period. Morton Smith, "Jewish Religious Life in the Persian Period," in *The Cambridge History of Judaism, Volume One—Introduction: The Persian Period*, ed. W. D. Davies and Louis Finkelstein (Cambridge: Cambridge University Press, 1984), 219–78; Susan Ackerman, *Under Every Green Tree: Popular Religion in Sixth-Century Judah*, HSM 46 (Atlanta: Scholars Press, 1992); Herbert Niehr, "Religio-Historical Aspects of the 'Early Post-Exilic' Period," in *The Crisis of Israelite Religion: Transformation of Religious Tradition in Exilic and Post-Exilic Times*, ed. Bob Becking and Marjo C. A. Korpel, OtSt 42 (Leiden: Brill, 1999), 228–44 argue for enduring idolatrous practice. E. J. Bickerman, "The Diaspora: The Babylonian Captivity," in *The Cambridge History of Judaism, Volume One—Introduction: The Persian Period*, ed. W. D. Davies and Louis Finkelstein (Cambridge: Cambridge University Press, 1984), 162–88 suggests a transitional period until 480 BCE. Ephraim Stern, "Religion in Palestine in the Assyrian and Persian Periods," in *The Crisis of Israelite Religion: Transformation of Religious Tradition in Exilic and Post-Exilic Times*, ed. Bob Becking and Marjo C. A. Korpel, OtSt 42 (Leiden: Brill, 1999), 245–55 argues for radical discontinuity between Babylonian and Persian period practices.
[37] Boda, "Figuring" = *Exploring Zechariah*, volume 1, chapter 4.

concern over Babylon's enduring influence over Yehud at the beginning of Persian rule,[38] tension with a satrapal official in the heartland of the old Babylonian empire, or allusion to Babylon as image for the present reigning power (Persia).

---

[38] This is partly wrapped up with the context in which Zech 9–14 took shape. See Mark J. Boda, "Terrifying the Horns: Persia and Babylon in Zechariah 1:7–6:15," *CBQ* 67 (2005): 22–41 = chapter 2 in this present volume, for evidence of concern and delight in Babylon's demise in Zech 1–8. For the dating of the redaction of Zech 9–14, see Mark J. Boda, *The Book of Zechariah*, NICOT (Grand Rapids: Eerdmans, 2016), 31–37.

11
Reading Zechariah 9–14 with the Law and the Prophets: Sibling Rivalry and Prophetic Crisis[1]

In this final chapter I focus attention on the oracular core of Zech 9–14, identifying a common inner biblical strategy in the two major sections of Zech 9–10 and Zech 12–14. Analysis of 13:5–6 and 9:11 reveals influence from sibling rivalry texts in Genesis combined with prophetic crisis texts in 1 Kings, Amos, and Jeremiah. This interlinking of Torah and prophetic traditions suggest a canon consciousness for those responsible for Zech 9–14.

The study of the phenomenon of inner biblical allusion in Zech 9–14 has focused most attention on the influence of other prophetic books, especially Isaiah, Jeremiah, Ezekiel, and at times Zech 1–8.[2] Connections to the Torah have not been

---

[1] Based on my original publication, Mark J. Boda, "Reading Zechariah 9–14 with the Law and the Prophets: Sibling Rivalry and Prophetic Crisis," in *The Formation of the Pentateuch: Bridging the Academic Cultures of Europe, Israel, and North America*, ed. Jan C. Gertz et al., FAT (Tübingen: Mohr Siebeck, 2016), 979–90. Slightly revised for inclusion in this volume.

[2] For example, Bernhard Stade, "Deuterosacharja: Eine kritische Studie I," *ZAW* 1 (1881): 1–96; Bernhard Stade, "Deuterosacharja: Eine kritische Studie II," *ZAW* 2 (1882): 151–72; Bernhard Stade, "Deuterosacharja: Eine kritische Studie III," *ZAW* 2 (1882): 275–309, focused on the prophetic traditions of Jeremiah and Ezekiel; Mathias Delcor, "Les sources du Deutero-Zacharie et ses procédés d'emprunt," *RB* 59 (1952): 385–411, on Ezekiel, Jeremiah, Trito-Isaiah, Job, and Joel; Rex A. Mason, "The Use of Earlier Biblical Material in Zechariah 9–14: A Study in Inner Biblical Exegesis," in *Bringing out the Treasure: Inner Biblical Allusion and Zechariah 9–14*, ed. Mark J. Boda and Michael H. Floyd,

prominent in this area of research, except for some championing of the influence of Deuteronomy.³

The present paper focuses attention on two places in Zech 9–14 (Zech 9:11 and 13:4–5) which suggest reliance on a similar motif within the book of Genesis, the sibling rivalry tradition. Accompanying these uses of the sibling rivalry tradition of Genesis, and bolstering their status as a common strategy, is a parallel employment of prophetic traditions drawn from what are now called the former and latter prophets, with attention given to a ninth-century (Elijah), eighth-century (Amos), and seventh-sixth-century (Jeremiah) prophet. After laying out the evidence of employment of these earlier traditions, the paper will look at the appropriateness of this allusion within the literary horizon of the source (Genesis, Prophets) as well as host (Zech 9–14) text.

INNER BIBLICAL ALLUSION IN ZECHARIAH 13:4–5 AND 9:11

ZECHARIAH 13:4–5

והיה ביום ההוא יבשו הנביאים איש מחזינו בהנבאתו
ולא ילבשו אדרת שער למען כחש:
ואמר לא נביא אנכי איש־עבד אדמה אנכי כי אדם הקנני מנעורי:

And it will happen on that day that the prophets will be ashamed, each of his vision when he prophesies, and they will not put on a garment of hair in order to deceive.

JSOTSup 370 (Sheffield: Sheffield Academic, 2003), 1–208, on the major prophets especially Second and Third Isaiah and Zech 1–8; Ina Willi-Plein, *Prophetie am Ende: Untersuchungen zu Sacharja 9–14*, BBB 42 (Köln: Hanstein, 1974), on the major prophets and Hosea; Konrad R. Schaefer, "Zechariah 14 and the Formation of the Book of Zechariah" (SSD diss., Ecole biblique et archéologique française, 1992), analyzing Zech 14, on Zech 1–13, Jeremiah, and Ezekiel; Raymond F. Person, *Second Zechariah and the Deuteronomic School*, JSOTSup 167 (Sheffield: JSOT Press, 1993), on Deuteronomic literature; Nicholas Ho Fai Tai, *Prophetie als Schriftauslegung in Sacharja 9–14: Traditions- und kompositionsgeschichtliche Studien*, Calwer Theologische Monographien 17 (Stuttgart: Calwer, 1996), on Jeremiah, Ezekiel, Deuteronomic literature, and Hosea; Risto Nurmela, *Prophets in Dialogue: Inner-Biblical Allusions in Zechariah 1–8 and 9–14* (Åbo: Åbo Akademi University, 1996), mostly on Isaiah (1–11, 29–31, not 40–55), Jeremiah, Ezekiel, and Zech 1–8.

³ For connections to Deuteronomy see especially Person, *Second Zechariah and the Deuteronomic School*. Those that have placed more emphasis on Genesis are Katrina J. Larkin, *The Eschatology of Second Zechariah: A Study of the Formation of a Mantological Wisdom Anthology*, CBET 6 (Kampen: Kok, 1994) and Suk Yee Lee, *An Intertextual Analysis of Zechariah 9–10: The Earlier Restoration Expectations of Second Zechariah*, LHBOTS 599 (London: Bloomsbury, 2015).

And he will say, "I am not a prophet. I am a man who works the ground because a man has begotten/acquired me since the time of my youth."[4]

Zechariah 9–14 has traditionally been divided into two major sections, each introduced by the phrase מַשָּׂא דְבַר־יְהוָה followed by a preposition which appears at 9:1 and 12:1.[5] The second of these sections encompassing chapters 12–14 is usually divided into two major oracular units (12:2–13:6; 14:1–21) between which lies the pericope 13:7–9. Unlike 13:7–9, the two major oracular units share in common the general theme of battles at Jerusalem resulting in submission of people and renewal of holiness and a similar discourse style which punctuates the material at regular intervals with the phrase בַּיּוֹם־הַהוּא. There appears to be some evidence of redactional layers lying behind the two major oracular units, relating to developments in the sociology of post-exilic Yehud and especially the shifting relationship between Jerusalem and the outlying Judean regions.[6] The first oracular unit in 12:2–13:6 ends with an emphasis on the cleansing of the land in 13:1–6, one that begins with the provision of a cleansing fountain for sin and impurity in 13:1 followed by a removal of idols, prophets, and the unclean spirit in 13:2. Zechariah 13:3–6 focuses attention on the removal of illicit prophets from the land. The section begins by calling for the eradication of false prophets from the land as parents turn on their child who dares to prophesy falsely (13:3).

Such a situation orients the reader to the scenarios described in 13:4–6, each of which reveals false prophets seeking to hide their prophetic activity or identity due to what is called "shame" in verse 4. According to this verse this means those

---

[4] For this translation with accompanying notes see Mark J. Boda, *The Book of Zechariah*, NICOT (Grand Rapids: Eerdmans, 2016), 721–22.
[5] See further Mark J. Boda, "Reading between the Lines: Zechariah 11:4–16 in Its Literary Contexts," in *Bringing out the Treasure: Inner Biblical Allusion and Zechariah 9–14*, ed. Mark J. Boda and Michael H. Floyd, JSOTSup 370 (Sheffield: Sheffield Academic, 2003), 277–91 = chapter 9 in this present volume; Mark J. Boda, "Freeing the Burden of Prophecy: Maśśā' and the Legitimacy of Prophecy in Zech 9–14," *Bib* 87 (2006): 338–57 = chapter 8 in this present volume.
[6] Paul L. Redditt, "Israel's Shepherds: Hope and Pessimism in Zechariah 9–14," *CBQ* 51 (1989): 631–42; Robert Rhea, "Attack on Prophecy: Zechariah 13,1–6," *ZAW* 107 (1995): 288–93.

who had identified as prophets will no longer don אדרת שער. These words appear within the Elijah biblical traditions.[7] אדרת is used in 1 Kgs 19:13 in a passage where the prophet encounters Yahweh on Horeb.[8] שער is employed again in reference to Elijah in 2 Kgs 1:8 within the idiom איש בעל שער which most likely means that he regularly dressed in clothing made from animal hide.[9] Most have concluded that Elijah's apparel was used to gain legitimacy for later prophets among the community.

Interestingly, however, while the individual words used in 13:4 appear in the Elijah traditions, the construct used in 13:4, אדרת שער, only occurs in one other place in the Hebrew Bible, that is, in Gen 25:25 in reference to Esau's hairy body at the time of his birth.[10] Rebekah and Jacob will later have to imitate this hairy condition in order to extract the firstborn blessing from Isaac (Gen 27). The importance of deceitfulness to the אדרת שער tradition in Genesis suggests a relationship to Zech 13:4 where the אדרת שער is used למען כחש.[11]

Zechariah 13:5 goes on to say that these false prophets will not only stop dressing like prophets, but also will verbally deny their prophetic status while pretending to be just common laborers who work the ground (עבד אדמה) and have done so from their youth (אדם הקנני מנעורי). Again one can discern the use of earlier biblical traditions in this strategy for concealing the identity of a false prophet. First, Amos 7:14 bears striking resemblance to Zech 13:5:[12]

---

[7] Carol L. Meyers and Eric M. Meyers, *Zechariah 9–14: A New Translation with Introduction and Commentary*, AB 25C (New York: Doubleday, 1993), 379; Larkin, *Eschatology*, 171; Judith Gärtner, *Jesaja 66 und Sacharja 14 als Summe der Prophetie: Eine traditions- und redaktionsgeschichtliche Untersuchung zum Abschluss des Jesaja- und des Zwölfprophetenbuches*, WMANT 114 (Neukirchen-Vluyn: Neukirchener, 2006), 296; Marvin A. Sweeney, *The Twelve Prophets*, 2 vols., Berit Olam (Collegeville, MN: Liturgical Press, 2000), 2:694; Paul L. Redditt, *Zechariah 9–14*, IECOT (Stuttgart: Kohlhammer, 2012), 117; cf. Henning Graf Reventlow, *Die Propheten Haggai, Sacharja und Maleachi*, ATD 25.2 (Göttingen: Vandenhoeck & Ruprecht, 1993), 120; contra David L. Petersen, *Zechariah 9–14 and Malachi: A Commentary*, OTL (Louisville: Westminster John Knox, 1995), 127.
[8] See also 1 Kgs 19:19; 2 Kgs 2:2, 8.
[9] Although it is possible that it means he was hairy, as suggested by Gen 25:25.
[10] Meyers and Meyers, *Zechariah 9–14*, 379; Petersen, *Zechariah 9–14*, 127; Paul L. Redditt, *Haggai, Zechariah and Malachi*, NCB (London: M. Pickering/Harper Collins, 1995), 135; Edgar W. Conrad, *Zechariah*, Readings: A New Biblical Commentary (Sheffield: Sheffield Academic, 1999), 187; Michael H. Floyd, *Minor Prophets, Part 2*, FOTL 22 (Grand Rapids: Eerdmans, 2000), 532; Sweeney, *Twelve*, 2:694.
[11] Meyers and Meyers, *Zechariah 9–14*, 379.
[12] Mason, "Use," 171; Meyers and Meyers, *Zechariah 9–14*, 380; Reventlow, *Die Propheten Haggai, Sacharja und Maleachi*, 120; Larkin, *Eschatology*, 171; Gärtner, *Jesaja 66 und Sacharja 14*, 296; Sweeney, *Twelve*, 2:694; James D. Nogalski, *The Book of the*

לא־נביא אנכי ולא בן־נביא אנכי כי־בוקר אנכי ובולס שקמים (Amos 7:14)
לא נביא אנכי איש־עבד אדמה אנכי כי אדם הקנני מנעורי (Zech 13:5)

In both passages the speaker begins by denying their prophetic status using the exact same words לא־נביא אנכי, followed by reference to agricultural activity using different vocabulary. This difference in wording highlights a second allusion in this verse to earlier biblical traditions. The phrase עבד אדמה in Zech 13:5 also appears in Gen 4:2 in reference to Cain.[13] In the previous verse in Gen 4, one finds Adam (האדם) impregnating Eve and producing their firstborn son Cain. This is followed by the declaration of Eve: קניתי איש את־יהוה, a phrase that is echoed in the declaration of the one hiding his prophetic status: אדם הקנני מנעורי. Once again we see a tradition connected with the legitimacy of a prophetic figure is intertwined with a sibling rivalry tradition in Genesis.

This evidence strongly suggests that Zech 13:4 and 13:5 employ a common strategy in their allusion to earlier biblical traditions.[14] Both allude to an earlier prophetic tradition related to the calling of a prophet whose commission is to attack pagan religion in the northern kingdom of Israel (Elijah/Elisha donning their cloak; Amos defending his call). At the same time both allude to an earlier Genesis sibling tradition which involves deceit. Interestingly in the case of both Esau/Jacob and Cain/Abel, a deception leads to the deceiver roaming the earth in fear of others.

ZECHARIAH 9:11

גם־את בדם־בריתך שלחתי אסיריך מבור אין מים בו:

Also you, because of the blood of the covenant which you made,
I have set free your prisoners from the cistern in which there is no water.[15]

Most scholars have noted the presence of two major parallel oracular units as well within the first משא unit in Zech 9–14, the units now encompassing 9:1b–17 and 10:4–12. As with chapters 12–14, a short pericope lies between these two units

---

Twelve: Micah–Malachi, SHBC (Macon, GA: Smyth & Helwys, 2011), 962; Redditt, *Zechariah 9–14*, 117; Al Wolters, *Zechariah*, HCOT 19 (Leuven: Peeters, 2014), 429.

[13] Floyd, *Minor Prophets*, 533; Redditt, *Zechariah 9–14*, 118. Sweeney, *Twelve*, 2:694, notes this, but misses the connection to Eve's statement, instead linking it back to Zech 11:5 for which there is little justification. Sweeney also considers this connection between false prophecy and Cain as farmer as a prelude to the slaying of a shepherd (like Abel) in 13:7–9. Meyers and Meyers, *Zechariah 9–14*, 381, note a connection to Gen 4 but then suggest an emendation that distances it from this passage.

[14] For similar connections see Rhea, "Attack," 291–92.

[15] For this translation with accompanying notes see Boda, *The Book of Zechariah*, 574–75.

(10:1–3). Chapter 11 is distinguished from chapters 9–10, and serves as a central pericope comprised of three units which lie between the two משא units. As with chapters 12–14 there is some evidence of redactional layering within chapters 9–10, marked possibly by the modulation of prophetic and divine voices throughout the oracles. The two main oracular units in 9:1b–17 and 10:4–12, however, share some key elements in common, both highlighting God's plan to enact restoration for his people by restoring royal rule at Jerusalem, releasing both southern (Judah) and northern (Ephraim, Joseph) tribes from captivity, defeating the nations by using these released captives, and renewing the prosperity of the land.

In the opening chapter, after defeating the nations and encamping at Jerusalem in 9:1–8, Yahweh addresses the Daughter of Zion/Jerusalem, introducing first her king to her (in vv. 9–10) before announcing the release of her inhabitants from captivity (v. 11). These same inhabitants are then addressed in verse 12, invited to return to Jerusalem and identified in verse 13 as Judah and Ephraim who are Zion's sons.

Zechariah 9:11 contains a strikingly similar biblical allusion to what was observed in 13:4–5. The location from which Yahweh promises to set free (שלח piel) the prisoners related to Zion is: בור אין מים בו. The word בור is used in relation to imprisonment several other times in the Hebrew Bible: Gen 37:20, 22, 24, 28–29; 40:15; 41:14; Isa 24:22; Jer 38:6–7, 9–11, 13; Lam 3:53. The designation for a prison in Exod 12:29 and Jer 37:16 is בית הבור. The combination of the verb שלח piel with the phrase בור אין מים also occurs in Jer 38:6 where Jeremiah is imprisoned in a cistern lacking water (... וישלכו אתו אל־הבור וישלחו את־ירמיהו בחבלים ובבור אין־מים).[16] One element in the phrase in Zech 9:11, however, does not occur in Jer 38:6, the prepositional morpheme בו. Interestingly the only other place, besides Zech 9:11 and Jer 38:6, in the Hebrew Bible where the combination בור אין מים occurs is in Gen 37:24 which describes Joseph being thrown into a cistern by his brothers.[17] The term בור appears elsewhere in the Joseph narrative to describe his prison in Egypt (Gen 40:15; 41:14). Interestingly, the Joseph narrative refers to Joseph as a אסיר (prisoner, 39:20Q, 22; cf. 40:3, 5) the same term that appears in Zech 9:11 to refer to those who are

---

[16] Mason, "Use," 49–50; Meyers and Meyers, *Zechariah 9–14*, 142; Redditt, *Haggai, Zechariah and Malachi*, 54; Person, *Second Zechariah and the Deuteronomic School*, 118; Larkin, *Eschatology*, 80; Tai, *Prophetie Als Schriftauslegung*, 55; Wolters, *Zechariah*, 284.

[17] Magne Sæbø, *Sacharja 9–14: Untersuchungen von Text und Form*, WMANT 34 (Neukirchen-Vluyn: Neukirchener, 1969), 190; Mason, "Use," 49–50; Meyers and Meyers, *Zechariah 9–14*, 142; Petersen, *Zechariah 9–14*, 60; Reventlow, *Die Propheten Haggai, Sacharja und Maleachi*, 98; Redditt, *Haggai, Zechariah and Malachi*, 54; Larkin, *Eschatology*, 80; Tai, *Prophetie als Schriftauslegung*, 55; Wolters, *Zechariah*, 284; Lee, *An Intertextual Analysis*. Contra Sweeney, *Twelve*, 2:665, who links the reference to prisoners in a waterless pit to Isa 24.

in the waterless pit. Thus Zech 9:11 contains elements that betray influence from both of these passages.

It appears then that once again inner biblical allusions can be discerned which intertwine an earlier sibling rivalry tradition from the book of Genesis (Joseph and his brothers) with an earlier prophetic crisis tradition, this time, related to the prophet Jeremiah.[18] In the context of chapters 9–10, 9:11 is seeking to communicate the message of salvation to the audience, focusing especially on the restoration of the community from captivity to Jerusalem.

INNER BIBLICAL ALLUSION AND THE SOURCE AND HOST TEXT

To this point we have noted the presence of inner biblical allusions within Zech 9–14 which intertwine earlier sibling rivalry traditions from the book of Genesis with earlier prophetic crisis traditions. Such a pattern could be understood as an example of what Michael Stead has identified as "Sustained Allusion," that is, "multiple scattered references to another text," or in this case multiple scattered references to similar types of texts.[19] It is one thing to identify an inner biblical allusion, but it is another to identify the reason for this inner biblical allusion. This section of the article will build a foundation for reflection on the rhetorical strategy which underlies these allusions by first considering the source texts (Genesis and Prophets) and then the host text (Zech 9–14). Consideration of both is important since as Ben-Porat noted long ago the purpose of inner biblical connections like this is "the simultaneous activation of two texts."[20]

---

[18] As Meyers and Meyers, *Zechariah 9–14*, 141–42, also see here "an attempt to draw a connection between this passage and the Joseph and Jeremiah stories (Gen 37:24; Jer 38:6)"; similarly Mason, "Use," 49–50.

[19] Michael R. Stead, "Sustained Allusion in Zechariah 1–2," in *Tradition in Transition: Haggai and Zechariah 1–8 in the Trajectory of Hebrew Theology*, ed. Mark J. Boda and Michael H. Floyd, LHBOTS 475 (New York: T&T Clark, 2008), 144–70 (145); cf. Michael R. Stead, *The Intertextuality of Zechariah 1–8*, LHBOTS 506 (London: T&T Clark, 2009).

[20] Ziva Ben-Porat, "The Poetics of Literary Allusion," *PTL: A Journal of Descriptive Poetics and Theory of Literature* 1 (1976): 105–28 (107); cf. Ziva Ben-Porat, "Intertextuality [Hebrew]," *Ha-Sifrut* 34 (1985): 170–78; with thanks to Stead, "Sustained Allusion," 154. See a further example of this approach in Boda, "Zechariah 11:4–16 in Its Literary Contexts" = chapter 9 in this present volume.

APPROPRIATENESS OF THIS LITERARY ALLUSION WITHIN THE SOURCE TEXTS:
GENESIS AND PROPHETS

1. Genesis

There is little question that the term תולדת plays a significant function within the book of Genesis, whether as a structural signal at key intervals within the book or simply a consistent lexical motif.[21] This term sets the tone for the book as a whole which consistently emphasizes the origins and growth of the Abrahamic clan. This theme appears early in the book with the introduction of the theme of seed and multiplication of seed in Gen 1 and 9 and then in the covenantal and promissory scenes in relation to Abraham, Isaac, and Jacob. This theme is articulated through certain leitmotifs and/or type scenes which appear throughout the book, including those related to female characters: the threat to the seedbearer scenes (Abraham/Sarah, Isaac/Rebekah), barrenness scenes (Eve, Sarah, Rachel), maidservants used for bearing seed (Sarah/Hagar, Leah/Rachel/Bilhah/Zilpah).[22]

Alongside these scenes related to female characters is a series of scenes related to male figures, all of which focus on sibling rivalry dynamics: Cain/Abel, Shem/Ham/Japhet, Abram/Lot, Isaac/Ishmael, Jacob/Esau, Ephraim/Manasseh, Jacob's sons.[23] These are key stories that drive the narrative of Genesis along, accentuating the key theme of תולדת, but doing so through crisis which threatens the life of the promised seed. It is then not surprising that the one(s) responsible for Zech 9–14 have leveraged three of these stories from Genesis where they play

---

[21] See recently, Matthew A. Thomas, *These Are the Generations: Identity, Covenant, and the Toledot Formula*, LHBOTS 551 (New York: T&T Clark, 2011); Jason S. DeRouchie, "The Blessing-Commission, the Promised Offspring, and the Toledot Structure of Genesis," *JETS* 56 (2013): 219–47; and for bibliography see Carol M. Kaminski, *Was Noah Good? Finding Favour in the Flood Narrative*, LHBOTS 563 (New York: Bloomsbury, 2014), 41–42.

[22] On these female rivalry traditions see Ilana Pardes, *Countertraditions in the Bible: A Feminist Approach* (Cambridge: Harvard University Press, 1992), 63. Alter's classic treatment of type scenes draws on the female rival traditions, Robert Alter, "Biblical Type-Scenes and the Uses of Conventions," *Critical Inquiry* 5 (1978): 355–68.

[23] On sibling rivalry see Mark J. Boda, "Sibling Rivalry," in *Dictionary of Biblical Imagery*, ed. Leland Ryken, James C. Wilhoit, and Tremper Longman III (Downers Grove, IL: InterVarsity Press, 1997), 789, and Kathleen W. Stuebing, "Sibling Rivalry," in *The IVP Women's Bible Commentary*, ed. Catherine Clark Kroeger and Mary J. Evans (Downers Grove, IL: InterVarsity, 2002), 17–18. It may be that the reason only Cain/Abel, Jacob/Esau, Joseph/brothers were chosen in Zech 9–14 was because they are the most similar, with Shem/Ham/Japheth involving a father figure, Abram/Lot involving an uncle/nephew relationship, and Isaac/Ishmael reflecting a wife rivalry tradition. The only other story that is similar is the Ephraim/Manasseh story.

a key role in the final form of the book. The stories, however, are not all the same, and one can discern a development in the type scene/motif among the stories which have been chosen in Zech 9–14. The Cain/Abel story is the most severe in outcome without positive resolution to the sibling rivalry as Abel is killed. This emphasis on death is also apparent in the story of Jacob/Esau, as Jacob must flee from his brother lest he be killed (Gen 27:41–42; 32:11). However, Esau does not carry this out, and in the end there is a scene of reconciliation (ch. 33), admittedly with some ambiguity since Jacob never does fulfil his promise to meet Esau at Seir (33:14, see 33:17–20). In the Joseph/brothers story the brothers discuss killing their brother and even fake his death by spilling blood on his coat, but in the end there is resolution to this sibling rivalry story in light of the discussion between Joseph and his brothers in 50:15–21 and the reuniting of the families in Egypt.

2. Prophetic Crisis Traditions

Among the Hebrew canonical section called the Prophets, Former and Latter, the three stories that are alluded to in Zech 9–14 are the three most intensely focused on the legitimacy of true prophecy. Within the Former Prophets it is the Elijah/Elisha complex which highlights the problem of and defeat of false prophetic sources, showcased especially in Elijah's defeat of the prophets of Baal in 1 Kgs 18. Amos's encounter with the priest Amaziah in Amos 7 highlights the challenge that prophet experienced from the religious hierarchy. Jeremiah regularly expresses concern over false prophecy, showcased especially in his attack on those prophets at both Samaria and Jerusalem who speak a vision from their own imagination rather than from having stood in the council of Yahweh (ch. 23). Of all the prophets it is not surprising that these three were chosen in that they share in common a serious crisis in prophecy. Furthermore, these prophets have been plucked from three different eras of the history of Israel (Elijah in the ninth century, Amos in the eighth century, and Jeremiah in the seventh-sixth century BCE), and each represent a different configuration of north/south prophet-audience relations (Elijah: northern prophet to north; Amos: southern prophet to north; Jeremiah: southern prophet to south).

3. Summary

This analysis shows that those responsible for Zech 9–14 are drawing on key motifs within at least one literary unit (Genesis) and possibly another (Prophets). The repeated use of these source texts within Zech 9–14 brings into the background these larger literary traditions and their associated themes which in turn affects our reading of Zech 9–14.

APPROPRIATENESS OF THIS LITERARY ALLUSION WITHIN THE HOST TEXT: ZECHARIAH 9–14

While these two passages in Zech 9–14 employ a similar combination of earlier biblical traditions, their respective contexts are quite different. How then do these instances of inner biblical allusion function within their respective sections?

1. Orientation to the Redactional Structure of Zechariah 9–14

As already noted, Zech 9–14 is comprised of two major oracular sections, distinguished by the employment of the phrase משא דבר־יהוה at the outset of Zech 9 and 12.[24] These two sections are each dominated by a particular literary style (historical/eschatological), prophetic tone (positive/negative), and sociological projection (Judah-Ephraim/Judah-Jerusalem) displayed in the major oracular material in 9:1–17; 10:4–12 in the first section and 12:1–13:6; 14:1–21 in the second. Throughout these contrasting oracular sections is a series of smaller negative prophetic units which all share in common shepherd-flock imagery and imperatival expressions (10:1–3; 11:1–3; 11:17; 13:7–9).[25]

    משא דבר־יהוה (9:1a)
        Oracle for Jerusalem, Judah, and Ephraim (9:1b–17)
            Shepherd-flock unit: with Vegetation imagery (10:1–3)
        Oracle for Judah and Ephraim (10:4–12)
            Shepherd-flock unit: with Vegetation imagery (11:1–3)
                Shepherd-flock unit: Prophetic Sign-act Report (11:4–16)
            Shepherd-flock unit: with Sword imagery (11:17)
    משא דבר־יהוה (12:1a)
        Oracle for Jerusalem, Judah, House of David, and Nations (12:2–13:6)
            Shepherd-flock unit: with Sword imagery (13:7–9)
        Oracle for Jerusalem, Judah, and Nations (14:1–21)[26]

At the center of this complex lies the Report of a Prophetic Sign-Act in Zech 11:4–16 which also employs shepherd-flock imagery and imperatival expressions. The depiction in this Sign-Act of the dissolution of the relationship between the shepherd and the nations and between Israel and Judah signals the shift in literary style,

---

[24] For further argumentation see Boda, "Zechariah 11:4–16 in Its Literary Contexts" = chapter 9 in this present volume.
[25] Note Ernst R. Wendland, *The Discourse Analysis of Hebrew Prophetic Literature: Determining the Larger Textual Units of Hosea and Joel*, Mellen Biblical Press Series 40 (Lewiston, NY: Mellen Biblical Press, 1995), 42, who speaks of the use of forceful expression as a key discourse marker.
[26] Cf. Boda, *The Book of Zechariah*, 520–21.

prophetic tone, and sociological projection between the two major oracular sections in Zech 9–14. The four short shepherd-flock units in 10:1–3; 11:1–3; 11:17; 13:7–9 divide the two major oracular sections each into two smaller sections but are lexically and imagistically related to their surrounding sections and thus were created with those in view.

2. Zechariah 9:11 within Zechariah 9–10

In light of the above discussion it is apparent that the use of the sibling rivalry/prophetic crisis traditions in Zech 9:11 comes in a section dominated by prophetic promise, focusing on the repopulation of Jerusalem by a community comprised of Judah and Ephraim.

The allusion to Joseph's experience of imprisonment in 9:11 is important in the context of Zech 9–10 which envisions salvation for the house of Joseph/Ephraim (9:13; 10:6, 7; cf. 9:10). In Gen 37–50, it is Judah who saves the life of Joseph by suggesting that the brothers sell him to the Ishmaelites. Later in the Joseph story Judah will play a key role in ensuring the survival of Jacob's family, assuming the role of spokesperson for the brothers as they dialogue first with Jacob and then with Joseph (Gen 43:3, 8–9; 44:14, 16, 18–34; cf. 46:28). By bringing the Joseph story into view, Zech 9:11 provides a precedence for Judah's role in relationship to Joseph and Ephraim. As the one who sold his brother into slavery, he now will play a role in releasing him from imprisonment in exile (see 10:6). As mentioned in the review of Genesis above, the Joseph sibling rivalry story is the most positive of the various stories, and thus it is not surprising that an allusion to this story would appear in Zech 9–10 which speaks mostly positively about a restoration which would include both northern and southern tribal entities.

As for the role that the allusion to the Jeremianic prophetic crisis tradition plays in 9:11, there are a couple of possibilities. First, it may be that Jeremiah's experience is treated as an ironic foreshadowing of what would happen to the Judeans who refused to listen to his message (cf. Jer 18:19–23). In Zech 9:11 this would serve to remind the audience of the source of the captivity of the Judeans whose release is now announced. Second, it may be that this allusion to the prophetic crisis is subtly connected to the redactional strategy of the Shepherd units, especially to the issue raised in the first Shepherd unit at the center of chapters 9–10 which focuses on false prophecy, citing Jeremianic tradition (see esp. 10:1; cf. Jer 14:1–15:4).[27] This could serve as a subtle reminder that what caused the captivity in the first place was concern over the relationship between people and

---

[27] See Mark J. Boda, "Freeing the Burden of Prophecy," 338–57 (355) = chapter 8 in this present volume.

prophecy and this was an enduring issue within the present community which threatened the success of the restoration (see further below).

3. Zechariah 13:4–5 within Zechariah 12–14

In contrast to Zech 9:11, the sibling rivalry/prophetic crisis traditions in Zech 13:4–5 appear in a section dominated by prophetic judgment, focusing on the eradication of false prophecy from a community comprised of Jerusalem and Judah. While in the case of Zech 9:11 it was the sibling rivalry tradition that seemed to fit most comfortably within the broader context, here it is the prophetic crisis tradition that better suits the context since Zech 13:1–6 focuses considerable attention on the cleansing of the community. By alluding to these earlier traditions the one(s) responsible for Zech 13:1–6 highlight Yahweh's rejection of the idolatrous stream highlighted in Zech 13:2 and also developed within the Shepherd units throughout Zech 9–14.[28]

The role that the sibling rivalry traditions of Zech 13:4–5 play in Zech 12–14 is not as clear. As noted in the review of Genesis above, the sibling rivalry traditions used in Zech 13:4–5 (Cain/Abel, Jacob/Esau) are not fully resolved as is the sibling rivalry tradition (Joseph/brothers) used in Zech 9:11. In the rhetorical flow of Zech 9–14 it is then not odd that these unresolved sibling rivalry traditions are used in a text after the dissolution of the covenant between Israel and Judah in the Shepherd unit of Zech 11:4–16.[29] In addition, the use of the earlier Cain/Abel and Jacob/Esau traditions here in Zech 13 rather than Joseph/brothers with its focus on the various tribes of Israel may reflect the focus of Zech 12–14 on a more limited definition of the community (Judah). One other possibility is that the allusion to the sibling rivalry traditions alongside prophetic crisis traditions focused on the north may be a subtle way of pointing to the source of the post-exilic prophetic crisis: that is, figures in the province of Samaria who according to the sociological worldview of Zech 12–14 are not even within the orbit of Jerusalem.

CONCLUSION

While there is no question that the prophetic biblical traditions and Deuteronomy exerted the most influence on the one(s) responsible for the texts now found in Zech 9–14, one can discern within both major oracular sections the influence of

---

[28] Notice also the similar use of the language and diction of Deuteronomy and Jeremiah in both Zech 10:1–2 (which may explain prophetic crisis tradition use in 9:11) and Zech 13:3. Thus the development of what we see in Zech 13:1–6 or a portion of it may be related to the stage when the Shepherd units were used to draw together the collection.

[29] See Boda, "Zechariah 11:4–16 in Its Literary Contexts" = chapter 9 in this present volume.

the opening book of the Torah. In Genesis the one(s) responsible for Zech 9–14 found a narrative which echoed some of their own hopes and fears: an initial hope of estranged brothers saving one another in order to return to the land only to be followed by later fear of an estrangement necessary due to threats to the very life of one brother. Intertwined, however, with these connections to the sibling rivalry traditions of Genesis are prophetic crisis traditions which are part of the section of the Hebrew canon known today as the Prophets.

If this strategy of intertwining biblical traditions from Genesis and the Prophets can be sustained, then this may suggest the role Zech 9–14 and possibly the Twelve as a collection played in an emerging canon consciousness. This has been suggested for the final verses of the book of Malachi, which intertwine Moses (Torah) and Elijah (Prophets),[30] as well as for Zech 1–8 which refers at three places explicitly to the "earlier prophets" (Zech 1:3; 7:7, 12).[31] The substantial inner biblical allusion found in Zech 9–14 (beyond what has been discussed in this article) also heightens the possibility that this intertwining of Torah and Prophets biblical traditions reflects consciousness of a collection that includes Torah-Prophets.

These literary signals of a possible larger collection if not canonical consciousness suggest another important direction of research on the Torah which is possibly in danger of being overlooked or drowned out by other legitimate and helpful approaches which either focus on the Torah alone or on underlying developmental layers within the Torah. To read the Torah in its final form and in connection with the Prophets not only provides keys to interpreting a text like Zech 9–14, but possibly also the Torah itself.

---

[30] James D. Nogalski, *Redactional Processes in the Book of the Twelve*, BZAW 218 (Berlin: de Gruyter, 1993), 185; Barry Alan Jones, *The Formation of the Book of the Twelve: A Study in Text and Canon*, SBLDS 149 (Atlanta: Scholars, 1995), 236–37; Stephen G. Dempster, "An 'Extraordinary Fact': Torah and Temple and the Contours of the Hebrew Canon," *TynBul* 48 (1997): 23–56; Aaron Schart, *Die Entstehung des Zwölfprophetenbuchs*, BZAW 260 (Berlin: de Gruyter, 1998), 302–3; Stephen B. Chapman, *The Law and the Prophets: A Study in Old Testament Canon Formation*, Fat 27 (Tübingen: Mohr Siebeck, 2000), 112; Stephen G. Dempster, "The Prophets, the Canon and a Canonical Approach," in *Canon and Biblical Interpretation*, ed. Craig G. Bartholomew, Scott Hahn, Robin Parry, Christopher Seitz, and Al Wolters, The Scripture and Hermeneutics Series 7 (Grand Rapids: Zondervan, 2006), 293–325.

[31] See Boda, *The Book of Zechariah*, 39–41.

12
Afterword

In this volume I have provided the results of my reflection on the impact of other biblical traditions on the Book of Zechariah. In my broader work on Zechariah I have highlighted the impact of the Torah, Former Prophets, and the Writings on Zechariah, but it is the great prophetic corpora in the Hebrew Bible, Isaiah, Jeremiah, Ezekiel, and the Twelve, which are most prominent. This particular volume focuses most attention on the influence of these collections, an influence that is not surprising in light of the explicit claims of the impact of the earlier prophets in Zech 1 and 7. Among these prophets it is Jeremiah that is most prominently featured in my studies, although Isaiah, Ezekiel, and the prophets within the Twelve do play a significant role, too. In the end, evidence in Zech 9–14 points to an intertwining of material within the canonical divisions of the Torah and the Prophets, which along with the oft cited evidence from the closing three verses of Malachi, point to a possible canonical consciousness and to a possible role for Zechariah and Haggai–Malachi within the formation of the Hebrew canon.

There is plenty of room for further study on inner biblical allusion in Zechariah. Earlier studies focused most attention on culling Zechariah for evidence of allusion, identifying the presence of allusions. Later studies have sought to build on this base by providing deeper reflection on what constitutes an allusion and by shifting attention to the impact of these allusions on the reading of the host text. It is this second exercise that needs to be refined in the days ahead. At the same time, however, there is an opportunity to reflect more deeply on what it means to reread even the earlier texts in light of a later text like Zechariah. While such rereading of earlier texts has often been motivated by the placement of Zechariah in the canon of later believing communities, evidence of canon consciousness within Zechariah itself only strengthens the case for such a reading strategy. If Zechariah is key to the final stages of the development of the canon, how does it shape the reading of the Torah, Prophets, and Writings? While my first volume highlighted the impact of Zechariah on the legacy of the Book of the Twelve, this second volume has extended this impact beyond the Twelve to the Prophets in general as well as the canon. Hopefully, this evidence will compel others to take up the exploration of Zechariah as a key to unlock the meaning of the Hebrew Bible.

BIBLIOGRAPHY

Achtemeier, Elizabeth. *Nahum—Malachi*. IBC. Atlanta: Westminster John Knox, 1986.
Ackerman, Susan. *Under Every Green Tree: Popular Religion in Sixth-Century Judah*. HSM 46. Atlanta: Scholars Press, 1992.
Ackroyd, Peter R. "Archaeology, Politics and Religion: The Persian Period." *Iliff Review* 39 (1982): 5–24.
———. *Exile and Restoration: A Study of Hebrew Thought of the Sixth Century B.C.* OTL. Philadelphia: Westminster, 1968.
———. "Historical Problems of the Early Achaemenian Period." *Orient* 20 (1984): 1–15.
———. "Some Historical Problems of the Early Achaemenian Period." Pages 37–53 in *Proceedings, Eastern Great Lakes and Midwest Biblical Societies*. Edited by Philip Sigal. Proceedings, Eastern Great Lakes and Midwest Biblical Societies 4. Grand Rapids: Eastern Great Lakes Biblical Society, 1984.
———. "Studies in the Book of Haggai (Part One)." *JJS* 2 (1951): 163–76.
———. "Studies in the Book of Haggai (Part Two)." *JJS* 3 (1952): 1–13.
———. "Two Old Testament Historical Problems of the Early Persian Period." *JNES* 17 (1958): 13–27.
Aejmelaeus, Anneli. "Jeremiah at the Turning-Point of History: The Function of Jer. xxv 1–14 in the Book of Jeremiah." *VT* 52 (2002): 459–82.
Ahlström, G. W. *Joel and the Temple Cult of Jerusalem*. VTSup 21. Leiden: Brill, 1971.
Albertz, Rainer. "Darius in Place of Cyrus: The First Edition of Deutero-Isaiah (Isaiah 40.1–52.12) in 521 B.C.E." *JSOT* 27 (2003): 371–88.

Alter, Robert. "Biblical Type-Scenes and the Uses of Conventions." *Critical Inquiry* 5 (1978): 355–68.
Amsler, S. "La parole visionnaire des prophètes." *VT* 31 (1981): 359–63.
Andersen, Francis I. *Habakkuk*. AB 25. New York: Doubleday, 2001.
Andreasen, Niels-Erik A. "The Role of the Queen Mother in Israelite Society." *CBQ* 45 (1983): 179–94.
Applegate, John. "Jeremiah and the Seventy Years in the Hebrew Bible." Pages 91–110 in *The Book of Jeremiah and Its Reception: Le Livre de Jérémie et sa réception*. Edited by Adrian H. W. Curtis and Thomas C. Römer. BETL 128. Leuven: Peeters, 1997.
Baldwin, Joyce G. *Haggai, Zechariah, Malachi: An Introduction and Commentary*. TOTC. Downers Grove, IL: InterVarsity Press, 1972.
———. "Tsemach as a Technical Term in the Prophets." *VT* 14 (1964): 93–97.
Barker, Margaret. "The Evil in Zechariah." *HeyJ* 19 (1978): 12–27.
———. "The Two Figures in Zechariah." *HeyJ* 18 (1977): 33–46.
Barnes, William Emery. *Haggai, Zechariah and Malachi: With Notes and Introduction*. 2nd ed. Cambridge Bible for Schools and Colleges 38. Cambridge: Cambridge University Press, 1934.
Bartel, A. "Once Again—Who Was Sheshbazzar? (Heb.)." *Beth Mikra* 79 (1979): 357–69.
Bautch, Richard J. *Developments in Genre between Post-Exilic Penitential Prayers and the Psalms of Communal Lament*. AcBib 7. Atlanta: Society of Biblical Literature, 2003.
Beale, G. K. "Questions of Authorial Intent, Epistemology, and Presuppositions and Their Bearing on the Study of the Old Testament in the New: A Rejoinder to Steve Moyise." *IBS* 21 (1999): 152–80.
———. "A Response to Jon Paulien on the Use of the Old Testament in Revelation." *AUSS* 39 (2001): 23–34.
Bedford, Peter R. "Early Achaemenid Monarchs and Indigenous Cults: Towards the Definition of Imperial Policy." Pages 17–39 in *Religion in the Ancient World: New Themes and Approaches*. Edited by Matthew Dillon. Amsterdam: Hakkert, 1996.
———. *Temple Restoration in Early Achaemenid Judah*. Supplements to the JSJ 65. Leiden: Brill, 2001.
Begg, Christopher T. "Babylon in the Book of Isaiah." Pages 121–25 in *The Book of Isaiah—Le Livre d'Isaïe: Les oracles et leurs relectures. Unité et complexité de l'ouvrage*. Edited by J. Vermeylen. BETL 81. Leuven: Peeters, 1989.
Behrens, Achim. *Prophetische Visionsschilderungen im Alten Testament: Sprachliche Eigenarten, Funktion und Geschichte einer Gattung*. AOAT 292. Münster: Ugarit-Verlag, 2002.

Bellinger, W. H., Jr. *Psalmody and Prophecy.* JSOTSup 27. Sheffield: JSOT Press, 1984.
Bellis, Alice Ogden. "The Structure and Composition of Jeremiah 50:2–51:58." PhD diss., Catholic University of America, 1986.
Ben-Porat, Ziva. "The Poetics of Literary Allusion." *PTL: A Journal of Descriptive Poetics and Theory of Literature* 1 (1976): 105–28.
———. "Intertextuality [Hebrew]." *HaSifrut* 34 (1985): 170–78.
Ben-Yashar, M. "On the Problem of Sheshbazzar and Zerubbabel [Hebrew]." *Beth Mikra* 88 (1981): 46–56.
Ben Zvi, Ehud. *Micah.* FOTL 21B. Grand Rapids: Eerdmans, 2000.
Berger, P.-R. "Zu den Namen שנאצר und ששבצר." *ZAW* 83 (1971): 98–100.
Berlin, Adele. *Lamentations: A Commentary.* OTL. Louisville: Westminster John Knox, 2002.
———. *Zephaniah: A New Translation with Introduction and Commentary.* AB 25A. New York: Doubleday, 1994.
Berquist, Jon L. *Judaism in Persia's Shadow: A Social and Cultural Approach.* Philadelphia: Fortress, 1995.
Beuken, Wim A. M. *Haggai–Sacharja 1–8: Studien zur Überlieferungsgeschichte der frühnachexilischen Prophetie.* SSN 10. Assen: Van Gorcum, 1967.
Bianchi, F. "Le rôle de Zorobabel et de la dynastie davidique en Judée du VIe siècle au II siècle av. J.-C." *Transeu* 7 (1994): 153–65.
Bič, Miloš. *Die Nachtgesichte des Sacharja: Eine Auslegung von Sacharja 1–6.* BibS(N) 42. Neukirchen-Vluyn: Neukirchener, 1964.
Bickerman, E. J. "The Diaspora: The Babylonian Captivity." Pages 162–88 in *The Cambridge History of Judaism, Volume One—Introduction: The Persian Period.* Edited by W. D. Davies and Louis Finkelstein. Cambridge: Cambridge University Press, 1984.
———. "En marge de l'écriture II: La seconde année de Darius." *RB* 88 (1981): 23–28.
Biddle, Mark. "The Figure of Lady Jerusalem: Identification, Deification, and Personification of Cities in the Ancient Near East." Pages 173–94 in *The Biblical Canon in Comparative Perspective.* Edited by William W. Hallo. Lewiston, NY: Mellen, 1991.
Blenkinsopp, Joseph. *Ezra–Nehemiah: A Commentary.* OTL. Philadelphia: Westminster, 1988.
Block, Daniel I. *The Book of Ezekiel: Chapters 1–24.* NICOT. Grand Rapids: Eerdmans, 1997.
———. *The Book of Ezekiel: Chapters 25–48.* NICOT. Grand Rapids: Eerdmans, 1998.
Boda, Mark J. "Babylon in the Book of the Twelve." *HBAI* 3 (2014): 225–48.

———. *The Book of Zechariah*. NICOT. Grand Rapids: Eerdmans, 2016.
———. "Confession as Theological Expression: Ideological Origins of Penitential Prayer." Pages 21–50 in *Seeking the Favor of God: Volume 1—The Origin of Penitential Prayer in Second Temple Judaism*. Edited by Mark J. Boda, Daniel K. Falk, and Rodney A. Werline. EJL 21. Atlanta: Society of Biblical Literature, 2006.
———. "Figuring the Future: The Prophets and the Messiah." Pages 35–74 in *The Messiah in the Old and New Testaments*. Edited by Stanley E. Porter. McMaster New Testament Studies. Grand Rapids: Eerdmans, 2007.
———. "Freeing the Burden of Prophecy: *Maśśā'* and the Legitimacy of Prophecy in Zech 9–14." *Bib* 87 (2006): 338–57.
———. "From Complaint to Contrition: Peering through the Liturgical Window of Jer 14,1–15,4." *ZAW* 113 (2001): 186–97.
———. "From Dystopia to Myopia: Utopian (Re)Visions in Haggai and Zechariah 1–8." Pages 211–49 in *Utopia and Dystopia in Prophetic Literature*. Edited by Ehud Ben Zvi. Publications of the Finnish Exegetical Society 92. Helsinki: Finnish Exegetical Society; Göttingen: Vandenhoeck & Ruprecht, 2006.
———. "From Fasts to Feasts: The Literary Function of Zechariah 7–8." *CBQ* 65 (2003): 390–407.
———. "Haggai: Master Rhetorician." *TynBul* 51 (2000): 295–304.
———. *Haggai and Zechariah Research: A Bibliographic Survey*. Tools for Biblical Study 5. Leiden: Deo, 2003.
———. *Haggai/Zechariah*. NIVAC. Grand Rapids: Zondervan, 2004.
———. "*Hoy, Hoy*: The Prophetic Origins of the Babylonian Tradition in Zechariah 2:10–17." Pages 171–90 in *Tradition in Transition: Haggai and Zechariah 1–8 in the Trajectory of Hebrew Theology*. Edited by Mark J. Boda and Michael H. Floyd. LHBOTS 475. London: T&T Clark, 2008.
———. "Majoring on the Minors: Recent Research on Haggai and Zechariah." *CurBR* 2 (2003): 33–68.
———. "Oil, Crowns and Thrones: Prophet, Priest and King in Zechariah 1:7–6:15." *JHS* 3 (2001): Article 10.
———. "Oil, Crowns and Thrones: Prophet, Priest and King in Zechariah 1:7–6:15." Pages 379–404 in *Perspectives on Hebrew Scriptures*. Edited by Ehud Ben Zvi. Piscataway, NJ: Gorgias, 2006.
———. *Praying the Tradition: The Origin and Use of Tradition in Nehemiah 9*. BZAW 277. Berlin: de Gruyter, 1999.
———. "Quotation, Allusion." Pages 298–300 in *Dictionary of Biblical Criticism and Interpretation*. Edited by Stanley E. Porter. New York: Routledge, 2006.

———. "Reading between the Lines: Zechariah 11:4–16 in Its Literary Contexts." Pages 277–91 in *Bringing out the Treasure: Inner Biblical Allusion and Zechariah 9–14*. Edited by Mark J. Boda and Michael H. Floyd. JSOTSup 370. Sheffield: Sheffield Academic, 2003.

———. "Reading Zechariah 9–14 with the Law and the Prophets: Sibling Rivalry and Prophetic Crisis." Pages 979–90 in *The Formation of the Pentateuch: Bridging the Academic Cultures of Europe, Israel, and North America*. Edited by Jan C. Gertz, Bernard M. Levinson, Dalit Rom-Shiloni, and Konrad Schmid. FAT. Tübingen: Mohr Siebeck, 2016.

———. "Review of Edelman: *The Origins of the 'Second' Temple: Persian Imperial Policy and the Rebuilding of Jerusalem* (2005)." *JHS* (2006).

———. "Sibling Rivalry." Pages 789 in *Dictionary of Biblical Imagery*. Edited by Leland Ryken, James C. Wilhoit, and Tremper Longman III. Downers Grove, IL: InterVarsity Press, 1997.

———. "Terrifying the Horns: Persia and Babylon in Zechariah 1:7–6:15." *CBQ* 67 (2005): 22–41.

———. "When God's Voice Breaks Through: Shifts in Revelatory Rhetoric in Zechariah 1–8." Pages 169–86 in *History, Memory, Hebrew Scriptures: A Festschrift for Ehud Ben Zvi*. Edited by Diana Edelman and Ian Wilson. Winona Lake, IN: Eisenbrauns, 2015.

———. "Writing the Vision: Zechariah within the Visionary Traditions of the Hebrew Bible." Pages 101–18 in *'I Lifted My Eyes and Saw': Reading Dream and Vision Reports in the Hebrew Bible*. Edited by Elizabeth R. Hayes and Lena-Sofia Tiemeyer. T&T Clark Library of Biblical Studies. LHBOTS 584. London: Bloomsbury, 2014.

———. "Zechariah: Master Mason or Penitential Prophet?" Pages 49–69 in *Yahwism after the Exile: Perspectives on Israelite Religion in the Persian Era*. Edited by Bob Becking and Rainer Albertz. Studies in Theology and Religion 5. Assen: Van Gorcum, 2003.

Boda, Mark J., and Jamie R. Novotny. *From the Foundations to the Crenellations: Essays on Temple Building in the Ancient Near East and Hebrew Bible*. AOAT 366. Münster: Ugarit-Verlag, 2010.

Boda, Mark J., and Michael H. Floyd, eds. *Bringing out the Treasure: Inner Biblical Allusion and Zechariah 9–14*. JSOTSup 370. Sheffield: Sheffield Academic, 2003.

Boda, Mark J., Michael H. Floyd, and Colin M. Toffelmire, eds. *The Book of the Twelve and the New Form Criticism*. ANEM 10. Atlanta: SBL Press, 2015.

Boda, Mark J., and Stanley E. Porter. "Literature to the Third Degree: Prophecy in Zechariah 9–14 and the Passion of Christ." Pages 215–54 in *Traduire* la Bible hébraïque: De la Septante à la Nouvelle Bible Segond = Translating the Hebrew Bible: From the Septuagint to the Nouvelle Bible Segond. Edited by Robert David and Manuel Jinbachian. Sciences Bibliques 15. Montreal: Médiaspaul, 2005.

Boehmer, J. "Wer ist Gog von Magog? Ein Beitrag zur Auslegung des Buches Ezechiel." *ZWT* 40 (1897): 321–55.

Boer, P. A. H. de. "An Inquiry into the Meaning of the Term *maśśā'*." *OtSt* 5 (1948): 197–214.

Bosshard-Nepustil, Erich. *Rezeptionen von Jesaja 1–39 im Zwölfprophetenbuch: Untersuchungen zur literarischen Verbindung von Prophetenbüchern in babylonischer und persischer Zeit.* OBO 154. Göttingen: Vandenhoeck & Ruprecht, 1997.

Braun, Roddy L. *1 Chronicles.* WBC 14. Waco, TX: Word, 1986.

———. "Message of Chronicles: Rally 'Round the Temple." *CTM* 42 (1971): 502–14.

Brewer, D. I. *Techniques and Assumptions in Jewish Exegesis before 70 C.E.* Tübingen: Mohr Siebeck, 1992.

Briant, Pierre. "La date des révoltes babyloniennes contre Xerxès." *Studia Iranica* 21.1 (1992): 7–20.

———. *From Cyrus to Alexander: A History of the Persian Empire.* Translated by Peter T. Daniels. Winona Lake, IN: Eisenbrauns, 2002.

Bright, John. *Jeremiah: Introduction, Translation, and Notes.* AB 21. Garden City, NY: Doubleday, 1965.

Bruce, F. F. "The Book of Zechariah and the Passion Narrative." *BJRL* 43 (1960–61): 167–90.

Brueggemann, Walter. *A Commentary on Jeremiah: Exile and Homecoming.* Grand Rapids: Eerdmans, 1998.

Butterworth, Mike. *Structure and the Book of Zechariah.* JSOTSup 130. Sheffield: Sheffield Academic, 1992.

Carroll, Robert P. "The Book of J: Intertextuality and Ideological Criticism." Pages 220–43 in *Troubling Jeremiah.* Edited by A. R. Pete Diamond, Kathleen M. O'Connor, and Louis Stulman. JSOTSup 260. Sheffield: Sheffield Academic, 1999.

———. *From Chaos to Covenant: Prophecy in the Book of Jeremiah.* New York: Crossroad, 1981.

———. "Halfway through a Dark Wood: Reflections on Jeremiah 25." Pages 73–86 in *Troubling Jeremiah.* Edited by A. R. Pete Diamond, Kathleen M. O'Connor, and Louis Stulman. JSOTSup 260. Sheffield: Sheffield Academic, 1999.

———. *Jeremiah: A Commentary.* OTL. Philadelphia: Westminster, 1986.

———. *Jeremiah.* OTG. Sheffield: JSOT Press, 1989.

Carter, Charles E. *The Emergence of Yehud in the Persian Period.* JSOTSup 294. Sheffield: Sheffield Academic, 1999.
Chandler, Daniel. *Semiotics: The Basics.* London: Routledge, 2002.
Chapman, Stephen B. *The Law and the Prophets: A Study in Old Testament Canon Formation.* FAT 27. Tübingen: Mohr Siebeck, 2000.
Childs, Brevard S. *Isaiah.* OTL. Louisville: Westminster John Knox, 2001.
Clark, David J. "The Case of the Vanishing Angel." *BT* 33 (1982): 213–18.
———. "Discourse Structure in Zechariah 7:1–8:23." *BT* 36 (1985): 328–35.
Clements, Ronald E. *Isaiah 1–39.* NCB. Grand Rapids: Eerdmans, 1980.
Coggins, R. J. *The First and Second Books of the Chronicles.* CBC. Cambridge: Cambridge University Press, 1976.
———. *Haggai, Zechariah, Malachi.* OTG. Sheffield: JSOT Press, 1987.
Colless, Brian E. "Cyrus the Persian as Darius the Mede in the Book of Daniel." *JSOT* 56 (1992): 113–26.
Conrad, Edgar W. "Messengers in Isaiah and the Twelve: Implications for Reading Prophetic Books." *JSOT* 91 (2000): 83–97.
———. *Zechariah.* Readings: A New Biblical Commentary. Sheffield: Sheffield Academic, 1999.
Cook, J. M.. *The Persian Empire.* New York: Barnes & Noble, 1983.
———. "The Rise of the Achaemenids and Establishment of Their Empire." Pages 200–91 in *The Cambridge History of Iran. Volume 2—the Median and Achaemenian Periods.* Edited by Ilya Gershevitch. Cambridge: Cambridge University Press, 1985.
Cook, Stephen L. "The Metamorphosis of a Shepherd: The Tradition History of Zechariah 11:17 + 13:7–9." *CBQ* 55 (1993): 453–66.
———. *Prophecy and Apocalypticism: The Postexilic Social Setting.* Minneapolis: Fortress, 1995.
Crotty, Robert B. "The Suffering Moses of Deutero-Zechariah." *Colloq* 14 (1982): 43–50.
Crüsemann, Frank. *Studien zur Formgeschichte von Hymnus und Danklied in Israel.* WMANT 32. Neukirchen-Vluyn: Neukirchener, 1969.
Dandamaev, Muhammad A. *Iranians in Achaemenid Babylonia.* Columbia Lectures on Iranian Studies 6. Costa Mesa, CA: Mazda/Bibliotheca Persica, 1992.
———. "Xerxes and the Esagila Temple in Babylon." Pages 326–34 in vol. 3 of *Encyclopaedia Iranica.* Edited by Ehsan Yarshater. New York: Encyclopaedia Iranica Foundation/Columbia University, 1993.
Dandamaev, Muhammad A., and Vladimir G. Lukonin. *The Culture and Social Institutions of Ancient Iran.* Translated by Philip L. Kohl and D. J. Dadson. Cambridge: Cambridge University Press, 1989.
Deeley, Mary Katharine. "Ezekiel's Shepherd and John's Jesus: A Case Study in

the Appropriation of Biblical Texts. Early Christian Interpretation of the Scriptures of Israel." Pages 252–64 in *Early Christian Interpretation of the Scriptures of Israel.* Edited by Craig A. Evans and James A. Sanders. JSNTSup 148. Sheffield: Sheffield Academic, 1997.

Delcor, Mathias. "Les sources du Deutero-Zacharie et ses procédés d'emprunt." *RB* 59 (1952): 385–411.

———. "Zacharie (Chapitres IX–XIV)." in *Les petits prophètes.* Edited by Alfons Deissler and Mathias Delcor. La Sainte Bible 8/1. Paris: Letouzey & Ané, 1961.

Delkurt, Holger. *Sacharjas Nachtgesichte: Zur Aufnahme und Abwandlung prophetischer Traditionen.* BZAW 302. Berlin: de Gruyter, 2000.

———. "Sacharja und der Kult." Pages 27–39 in *Verbindungslinien: Festschrift für Werner H. Schmidt zum 65. Geburtstag.* Edited by Axel Graupner, Holger Delkurt, and Alexander B. Ernst. Neukirchen-Vluyn: Neukirchener, 2000.

Dempster, Stephen G. "An 'Extraordinary Fact': Torah and Temple and the Contours of the Hebrew Canon." *TynBul* 48 (1997): 23–56.

———. "The Prophets, the Canon and a Canonical Approach." Pages 293–325 in *Canon and Biblical Interpretation.* Edited by Craig G. Bartholomew, Scott Hahn, Robin Parry, Christopher Seitz, and Al Wolters. Scripture and Hermeneutics Series 7. Grand Rapids: Zondervan, 2006.

DeRouchie, Jason S. "The Blessing-Commission, the Promised Offspring, and the Toledot Structure of Genesis." *JETS* 56 (2013): 219–47.

Dobbs-Allsopp, F. W. "The Syntagma of *bat* Followed by a Geographical Name in the Hebrew Bible. A Reconsideration of Its Meaning and Grammar." *CBQ* 57 (1995): 45–70.

Dodd, C. H. *According to the Scriptures: The Sub-Structure of New Testament Theology.* London: Nisbet, 1952.

Draisma, Sipke, ed. *Intertextuality in Biblical Writings: Essays in Honour of Bas van Iersel.* Kampen: Kok, 1989.

Edelman, Diana. *The Origins of the Second Temple: Persian Imperial Policy and the Rebuilding of Jerusalem.* London: Equinox, 2005.

———. "Proving Yahweh Killed His Wife (Zechariah 5:5–11)." *BibInt* 11 (2003): 335–44.

Elliger, Karl. *Das Buch der zwölf kleinen Propheten 2: Die Propheten Nahum, Habakuk, Zephanja, Haggai, Sacharja, Maleachi.* 7th ed. ATD 25.2. Göttingen: Vandenhoeck & Ruprecht, 1975.

Eph'al, Israel. "Changes in Palestine During the Persian Period in Light of Epigraphic Sources." *IEJ* 48 (1998): 106–19.

Erlandsson, Seth. *The Burden of Babylon: A Study of Isaiah 13:2–14:23.* ConBOT 4. Lund: Gleerup, 1970.

Eskenazi, Tamara Cohn. *In an Age of Prose: A Literary Approach to Ezra–Nehemiah*. SBLMS 36. Atlanta: Scholars Press, 1988.

Eslinger, Lyle. "Inner-Biblical Exegesis and Inner-Biblical Allusion: The Question of Category." *VT* 42 (1992): 47–58.

Evans, Craig A. "Did Jesus Predict His Death and Resurrection?" Pages 82–97 in *Resurrection*. Edited by Stanley E. Porter, Michael A. Hayes and David Tombs. JSNTSup 186. Sheffield: Sheffield Academic, 1999.

———. "Jesus and Zechariah's Messianic Hope." Pages 373–88 in *Authenticating the Activities of Jesus*. Edited by Bruce Chilton and Craig A. Evans. NTTS 28.2. Leiden: Brill, 1998.

———. "'The Two Sons of Oil': Early Evidence of Messianic Interpretation of Zechariah 4:14 in 4Q254 4 2." Pages 566–75 in *The Provo International Conference on the Dead Sea Scrolls: Technological Innovations, New Texts, and Reformulated Issues*. Edited by Donald W. Parry and Eugene Ulrich. STDJ 30. Leiden: Brill, 1999.

Fewell, Danna Nolan. *Reading between Texts: Intertextuality and the Hebrew Bible*. Literary Currents in Biblical Interpretation. Louisville: Westminster John Knox, 1992.

Finitsis, Antonios. *Visions and Eschatology: A Socio-Historical Analysis of Zechariah 1–6*. LSTS 79. London: T&T Clark, 2011.

Fishbane, Michael A. *Biblical Interpretation in Ancient Israel*. Oxford: Clarendon, 1985.

———. "Inner-Biblical Exegesis." Pages 33–48 in *Hebrew Bible/Old Testament: The History of Its Interpretation—I: From the Beginnings to the Middle Ages (until 1300). Part I: Antiquity*. Edited by Magne Sæbø. Göttingen: Vandenhoeck & Ruprecht, 1996.

Floyd, Michael H. "The Maśśā' as a Type of Prophetic Book." *JBL* 121 (2002): 401–22.

———. *Minor Prophets, Part 2*. FOTL 22. Grand Rapids: Eerdmans, 2000.

Fohrer, Georg. "Die Gattung der Berichte über symbolische Handlungen der Propheten." *ZAW* 64 (1952): 101–20.

———. *Die symbolische Handlungen der Propheten* 2nd ed. ATANT 54. Zurich: Zwingli, 1968.

Follis, Elaine R. "The Holy City as Daughter." Pages 173–84 in *Directions in Biblical Hebrew Poetry*. Edited by Elaine R. Follis. JSOTSup 40. Sheffield: Sheffield Academic, 1987.

———. "Zion, Daughter of." Pages 1103 in vol. 6 of *ABD*.

Franke, Chris A. "Reversals of Fortune in the Ancient Near East: A Study of the Babylon Oracles in the Book of Isaiah." Pages 104–23 in *New Visions of Isaiah*. Edited by Roy F. Melugin and Marvin A. Sweeney. JSOTSup 214. Sheffield: Sheffield Academic, 1996.

Franzmann, Majella. "The City as Woman: The Case of Babylon in Isaiah 47." *ABR* 43 (1995): 1–9.
Fretheim, Terence E. *Jeremiah*. SHBC. Macon, GA: Smith & Helwys, 2002.
Friebel, Kelvin G. "A Hermeneutical Paradigm for Interpreting Prophetic Sign-Actions." *Did* 12.2 (2001): 25–45.
———. *Jeremiah's and Ezekiel's Sign-Acts*. JSOTSup 283. Sheffield: Sheffield Academic, 1999.
Fried, Lisbeth S. "Cyrus the Messiah? The Historical Background of Isaiah 45:1." *HTR* 95 (2002): 373–93.
———. *The Priest and the Great King: Temple-Palace Relations in the Persian Empire*. BJSUCSD 10. Winona Lake, IN: Eisenbrauns, 2004.
Galling, Kurt. "Die Exilswende in der Sicht des Propheten Sacharja." *VT* 2 (1952): 18–36.
Gärtner, Judith. *Jesaja 66 und Sacharja 14 als Summe der Prophetie: Eine traditions- und redaktionsgeschichtliche Untersuchung zum Abschluss des Jesaja- und des Zwölfprophetenbuches*. WMANT 114. Neukirchen-Vluyn: Neukirchener, 2006.
Gehman, H. S. "The Burden of the Prophets." *JQR* 31 (1940–41): 107–21.
Genette, Gérard. *Palimpsestes: La littérature au second degré*. Paris: Seuil, 1982.
———. *Palimpsests: Literature in the Second Degree*. Translated by Channa Newman and Claude Doubinsky. Lincoln: University of Nebraska Press, 1997.
Goldingay, John. *Isaiah*. NIBCOT. Peabody, MA: Hendrickson, 2001.
Good, Robert M. "Zechariah's Second Night Vision (Zech 2, 1–4)." *Bib* 63 (1982): 56–59.
Gosse, Bernard. *Isaïe 13,1–14,23: Dans la tradition littéraire du livre d'Isaèie et dans la tradition des oracles contre les nations—Étude de la transformation du genre littéraire*. OBO 78. Freiburg, Schweiz: Universitätsverlag; Göttingen: Vandenhoeck & Ruprecht, 1988.
———. "The Masoretic Redaction of Jeremiah: An Explanation." *JSOT* 77 (1998): 75–80.
Grabbe, Lester L. "Another Look at the Gestalt of 'Darius the Mede'." *CBQ* 50 (1988): 198–213.
———. *Priests, Prophets, Diviners, Sages: A Socio-Historical Study of Religious Specialists in Ancient Israel*. Valley Forge, PA: Trinity Press International, 1995.
Grothe, Jonathan F. "An Argument for the Textual Genuineness of Jeremiah 33:14–26 (Massoretic Text)." *CJ* 7 (1981): 188–91.
Gunkel, Hermann, and Joachim Begrich. *Einleitung in die Psalmen: Die Gattungen der religiösen Lyrik Israels*. 2nd ed. Göttingen: Vandenhoeck & Ruprecht, 1933.

Haerinck, E. "Babylonia under Achaemenid Rule." Pages 26–34 in *Mesopotamia and Iran in the Persian Period: Conquest and Imperialism 539–331 B.C. (Proceedings of a Seminar in Memory of Vladimir G. Lukonin)*. Edited by John Curtis. London: British Museum, 1997.

Hallaschka, Martin. "Zechariah's Angels: Their Role in the Night Visions and in the Redaction History of Zech 1,7–6,8." *SJOT* 24 (2010): 13–27.

Halpern, Baruch. "The Ritual Background of Zechariah's Temple Song." *CBQ* 40 (1978): 167–90.

Hanson, Paul D. *The Dawn of Apocalyptic: The Historical and Sociological Roots of Jewish Apocalyptic Eschatology*. Revised ed. Philadelphia: Fortress, 1979.

———. "Israelite Religion in the Early Postexilic Period." Pages 485–508 in *Ancient Israelite Religion: Essays in Honor of Frank Moore Cross*. Edited by Patrick D. Miller, Paul D. Hanson, and S. Dean McBride. Philadelphia: Fortress, 1987.

———. "Zechariah, Book of." Pages 982–83 of *IDBSup*.

Haran, Menahem. "The Place of the Prophecies against the Nations in the Book of Jeremiah." Pages 699–706 in *Emanuel: Studies in Hebrew Bible, Septuagint, and Dead Sea Scrolls in Honor of Emanuel Tov*. Edited by Shalom M. Paul, Robert A. Kraft, Lawrence H. Schiffman, and Weston W. Fields. VTSup 94. Leiden: Brill, 2003.

Harrelson, Walter. "Messianic Expectations at the Time of Jesus." *Saint Luke's Journal of Theology* 32 (1988): 28–42.

Hatim, Basil, and Ian Mason. *Discourse and the Translator*. London: Longman, 1990.

———. *The Translator as Communicator*. London: Routledge, 1997.

Hatina, Thomas R. "Intertextuality and Historical Criticism in New Testament Studies: Is There a Relationship?" *BibInt* 7 (1999): 28–43.

Hays, Richard B., and Joel B. Green. "The Use of the Old Testament by New Testament Writers." Pages 224–38 in *Hearing the New Testament: Strategies for Interpretation*. Edited by Joel B. Green. Grand Rapids: Eerdmans, 1995.

Heil, John Paul. "Ezekiel 34 and the Narrative Strategy of the Shepherd and Sheep Metaphor in Matthew." *CBQ* 55 (1993): 698–703.

Heltzer, Michael. "A Recently Published Babylonian Tablet and the Province of Judah after 516 B.C.E." *Transeu* 5 (1992): 57–61.

Hepner, Gershon. "Verbal Resonances in the Bible and Intertextuality." *JSOT* 96 (2001): 3–27.

Hiebert, Theodore. *God of My Victory: The Ancient Hymn in Habakkuk 3*. HSM 38. Atlanta: Scholars Press, 1986.

Hoglund, Kenneth G. *Achaemenid Imperial Administration in Syria-Palestine* and the Mission of Ezra and Nehemiah. SBLDS 125. Atlanta: Scholars Press, 1992.

Holladay, William L. *Jeremiah 1: A Commentary on the Book of the Prophet Jeremiah, Chapters 1–25*. Hermeneia. Philadelphia: Fortress, 1986.

———. *Jeremiah 2: A Commentary on the Book of the Prophet Jeremiah, Chapters 26–52*. Hermeneia. Minneapolis: Fortress, 1989.

Holladay, William L., ed. *A Concise Hebrew and Aramaic Lexicon of the Old Testament*. Leiden: Brill; Grand Rapids: Eerdmans, 1988.

Horst, Friedrich. "Die Visionsschilderungen der alttestamentlichen Propheten." *EvT* 20 (1960): 193–205.

———. *Die zwölf kleinen Propheten*. 2nd ed. HAT 14. Tübingen: Mohr Siebeck, 1964.

Janzen, J. Gerald. *Studies in the Text of Jeremiah*. HSM 6. Cambridge: Harvard University Press, 1973.

Japhet, Sara. *I and II Chronicles: A Commentary*. OTL. Louisville: Westminster John Knox, 1993.

———. "Sheshbazzar and Zerubbabel—Against the Background of the Historical and Religious Tendencies of Ezra–Nehemiah (Part One)." *ZAW* 94 (1982): 66–98.

Jeppesen, Knud. "The *maśśā'* Babel in Isaiah 13–14." *PIBA* 9 (1985): 63–80.

Jeremias, Christian. *Die Nachtgesichte des Sacharja: Untersuchungen zu ihrer Stellung im Zusammenhang der Visionsberichte im Alten Testament und zu ihrem Bildmaterial*. FRLANT 117. Göttingen: Vandehoeck & Ruprecht, 1977.

———. "Sacharja und die prophetische Tradition, untersucht im Zusammenhang der Exodus-, Zion-, und Davidüberlieferung." PhD diss., University of Göttingen, 1966.

Johnson, Aubrey R. *The Cultic Prophet and Israel's Psalmody*. Cardiff: University of Wales Press, 1979.

———. *The Cultic Prophet in Ancient Israel*. 2nd ed. Cardiff: University of Wales Press, 1962.

Jones, Barry Alan. *The Formation of the Book of the Twelve: A Study in Text and Canon*. SBLDS 149. Atlanta: Scholars Press, 1995.

Jones, Douglas R. *Jeremiah*. NCB. London: Marshall Pickering, 1992.

Kaminski, Carol M. *Was Noah Good? Finding Favour in the Flood Narrative*. LHBOTS 563. New York: Bloomsbury, 2014.

Kessler, John. *The Book of Haggai: Prophecy and Society in Early Persian Yehud*. VTSup 91. Leiden: Brill, 2002.

———. "The Second Year of Darius and the Prophet Haggai." *Transeu* 5 (1992): 63–84.

Kessler, Martin. "The Function of Chapters 25 and 50–51 in the Book of Jeremiah." Pages 64–72 in *Troubling Jeremiah*. Edited by A. R. Pete Diamond, Kathleen M. O'Connor and Louis Stulman. JSOTSup 260. Sheffield: Sheffield Academic, 1999.

———. *Battle of the Gods: The God of Israel Versus Marduk of Babylon. A Literary/Theological Interpretation of Jeremiah 50–51*. SSN 42. Assen: Van Gorcum, 2003.

Kim, Hyukki. "The Interpretation of בַּת־צִיּוֹן (Daughter Zion): An Approach of Cognitive Theories of Metaphor." MA thesis, McMaster Divinity College, 2006.

Kim, Seyoon. "Jesus—the Son of God, the Stone, Son of Man, and the Servant: The Role of Zechariah in the Self-Identification of Jesus." Pages 134–48 in *Tradition and Interpretation in the New Testament*. Edited by Gerald F. Hawthorne and Otto Betz. Grand Rapids: Eerdmans, 1987.

Kline, Meredith G. "By My Spirit." *Kerux* 9.1 (1994): 3–15.

Kloos, Carola J. L. "Zech. II 12: Really a Crux Interpretum?" *VT* 25 (1975): 729–36.

Knierim, Rolf P. "Old Testament Form Criticism Reconsidered." *Int* 27 (1973): 435–68.

Knight, Douglas A. *Rediscovering the Traditions of Israel: The Development of the Traditio-Historical Research of the Old Testament, with Special Consideration of Scandinavian Contributions*. Revised ed. SBLDS 9. Missoula, MT: Scholars Press, 1975.

———. "Tradition History." Pages 633–38 in vol. 6 of *ABD*.

Koldewey, Robert. *The Excavations at Babylon*. London: Macmillan, 1914.

Kuhrt, Amélie. "Babylonia from Cyrus to Xerxes." Pages 112–38 in *The Cambridge Ancient History—Volume IV: Persia, Greece and the Western Mediterranean c. 525 to 479 B.C.* Edited by John Boardman, N. G. L. Hammond, D. M. Lewis, and M. Ostwald. Cambridge: Cambridge University Press, 1988.

Kuhrt, Amélie, and S. Sherwin-White. "Xerxes' Destruction of Babylonian Temples." Pages 69–78 in *The Greek Sources: Proceedings of the Groningen 1984 Achaemenid History Workshop*. Edited by H. Sancisi-Weerdenburg and Amélie Kuhrt. Achaemenid History 2. Leiden: Nederlands Instituut voor het Nabije Oosten, 1987.

Laato, Antti. *A Star Is Rising: The Historical Development of the Old Testament Royal Ideology and the Rise of the Jewish Messianic Expectations*. USFISFCJ 5. Atlanta: Scholars Press, 1997.

LaMarche, Paul. *Zacharie IX–XIV: Structure littéraire et messianisme*. EBib. Paris: Librairie Lecoffre, 1961.

Lambert, G. "'Mon joug est aisé et mon fardeau léger': Note d'exégèse." *NRTh*

77 (1955): 963–69.

Larkin, Katrina J. *The Eschatology of Second Zechariah: A Study of the Formation of a Mantological Wisdom Anthology.* CBET 6. Kampen: Kok, 1994.

Lee, Suk Yee. *An Intertextual Analysis of Zechariah 9–10: The Earlier Restoration Expectations of Second Zechariah.* LHBOTS 599. London: Bloomsbury, 2015.

Leske, Adrian. "Context and Meaning of Zechariah 9:9." *CBQ* 62 (2000): 663–78.

Lichtenberger, Hermann. "Messianic Expectations and Messianic Figures in the Second Temple Period." Pages 9–20 in *Qumran-Messianism: Studies on the Messianic Expectations in the Dead Sea Scrolls.* Edited by James H. Charlesworth, Hermann Lichtenberger, and Gerbern S. Oegema. Tübingen: Mohr Siebeck, 1998.

Lindblom, Johannes. *Prophecy in Ancient Israel.* Philadelphia: Fortress, 1962.

Lipinski, E. *La liturgie pénitentielle dans la Bible.* LD 52. Paris: Cerf, 1969.

Litwak, Kenneth D. "Echoes of Scripture? A Critical Survey of Recent Works on Paul's Use of the Old Testament." *CurBS* 6 (1998): 260–88.

Lohfink, N. "Die Gattung der 'historischen Kurzgeschichte' in den letzten Jahren von Juda und in der Zeit des babylonischen Exils." *ZAW* 90 (1978): 319–47.

Long, Burke O. "Reports of Visions among the Prophets." *JBL* 95 (1976): 353–65.

Lust, Johan. "The Identification of Zerubbabel with Sheshbassar." *ETL* 63 (1987): 90–95.

Lutz, Hanns-Martin. *Jahwe, Jerusalem und die Völker: Zur Vorgeschichte von Sach. 12, 1–8, und 14, 1–5.* WMANT 27. Neukirchen-Vluyn: Neukirchener, 1968.

Machinist, Peter. "Assyria and Its Image in the First Isaiah." *JAOS* 103 (1983): 719–37.

Mallowan, Max. "Cyrus the Great." Pages 392–419 in *The Cambridge History of Iran: Volume 2—the Median and Achaemenian Periods.* Edited by Ilya Gershevitch. Cambridge: Cambridge University Press, 1985.

Marguerat, Daniel, and Adrian Curtis, eds. *Intertextualités: La Bible en échos.* Le Monde de la Bible 40. Geneva: Labor et Fides, 2000.

Margulis, Barry Baruch. "Studies in the Oracles against the Nations." PhD diss., Brandeis University, 1967.

Martens, Elmer. "Reaching for a Biblical Theology of the Whole Bible." Pages 83–101 in *Reclaiming the Old Testament: Essays in Honour of Waldemar Janzen.* Edited by Gordon Zerbe. Winnipeg, MB: CMBC Publications, 2001.

Mason, Rex A. *The Books of Haggai, Zechariah and Malachi*. CBC. Cambridge: Cambridge University Press, 1977.

———. "Inner-Biblical Exegesis." Pages 312–14 in *A Dictionary of Biblical Interpretation*. Edited by R. J. Coggins and J. L. Houlden. London: SCM, 1990.

———. "Inner Biblical Exegesis in Zech. 9–14." *Grace Theological Journal* 3 (1982): 51–65.

———. "The Messiah in the Postexilic Old Testament Literature." Pages 338–64 in *King and Messiah in Israel and the Ancient Near East: Proceedings of the Oxford Old Testament Seminar*. Edited by John Day. JSOTSup 270. Sheffield: Sheffield University Press, 1998.

———. *Preaching the Tradition: Homily and Hermeneutics after the Exile*. Cambridge: Cambridge University Press, 1990.

———. "Prophets of the Restoration." Pages 137–54 in *Israel's Prophetic Tradition: Essays in Honour of Peter Ackroyd*. Edited by Richard Coggins, Anthony Phillips, and Michael Knibb. Cambridge: Cambridge University Press, 1982.

———. "The Purpose of the 'Editorial Framework' of the Book of Haggai." *VT* 27 (1977): 413–21.

———. "The Relation of Zech 9–14 to Proto-Zechariah." *ZAW* 88 (1976): 227–39.

———. "Some Examples of Inner Biblical Exegesis in Zech. IX–XIV." Pages 343–54 in *Studia Evangelica Vol. 7: Papers Presented to the 5th International Congress on Biblical Studies Held at Oxford, 1973*. Edited by Elizabeth A. Livingstone. TUGAL 126. Berlin: Akademie, 1982.

———. "The Use of Earlier Biblical Material in Zechariah IX–XIV: A Study in Inner Biblical Exegesis." PhD diss., University of London, 1973.

———. "The Use of Earlier Biblical Material in Zechariah 9–14: A Study in Inner Biblical Exegesis." Pages 1–208 in *Bringing out the Treasure: Inner Biblical Allusion and Zechariah 9–14*. Edited by Mark J. Boda and Michael H. Floyd. JSOTSup 370. Sheffield: Sheffield Academic, 2003.

———. *Zephaniah, Habakkuk, Joel*. OTG. Sheffield: Sheffield Academic, 1994.

Mastin, Brian A. "A Note on Zechariah VI 13." *VT* 26 (1976): 113–16.

McHardy, W. D. "The Horses in Zechariah." Pages 174–79 in *In Memoriam: Paul Kahle*. Edited by Matthew Black and Georg Fohrer. BZAW 103. Berlin: Töpelmann, 1968.

McKane, William. *A Critical and Exegetical Commentary on Jeremiah*. ICC. Edinburgh: T&T Clark, 1986.

Mede, Joseph. *Dissertationum ecclesiasticarum triga: ... Quibus accedunt Fragmenta sacra*. London: 1653.

———. *The Works of Joseph Mede*. 2nd ed. London: James Flesher, 1664.

Melvin, David P. *The Interpreting Angel Motif in Prophetic and Apocalyptic Literature.* Emerging Scholars. Minneapolis: Fortress, 2013.
Merrill, Eugene H. *Haggai, Zechariah, Malachi: An Exegetical Commentary.* Chicago: Moody Press, 1994.
Meuleau, Maurice. "Mesopotamia under Persian Rule." Pages 354–85 in *The Greeks and the Persians from the Sixth to the Fourth Centuries.* Edited by H. Bengston. Delacorte World History 5. New York: Delacorte, 1968.
Meyer, Lester V. "An Allegory Concerning the Monarchy: Zech 11:4–17; 13:7–9." Pages 225–40 in *Scripture in History and Theology: Essays in Honor of J. Coert Rylaarsdam.* Edited by Arthur L. Merrill and Thomas W. Overholt. Pittsburgh: Pickwick, 1977.
Meyers, Carol L., and Eric M. Meyers. *Haggai, Zechariah 1–8: A New Translation with Introduction and Commentary.* AB 25B. Garden City: Doubleday, 1987.
———. *Zechariah 9–14: A New Translation with Introduction and Commentary.* AB 25C. New York: Doubleday, 1993.
Meyers, Eric M. "The Persian Period and the Judean Restoration: From Zerubbabel to Nehemiah." Pages 509–21 in *Ancient Israelite Religion: Essays in Honor of Frank Moore Cross.* Edited by Patrick D. Miller, Paul D. Hanson, and S. Dean McBride. Philadelphia: Fortress, 1987.
———. "The Shelomith Seal and Aspects of the Judean Restoration: Some Additional Reconsiderations." *ErIsr* 18 (1985): 33*–38*.
Miscall, Peter D. *Isaiah.* Readings: A New Biblical Commentary. Sheffield: JSOT Press, 1993.
Mitchell, Hinckley Gilbert, John Merlin Powis Smith, and Julius August Brewer. *A Critical and Exegetical Commentary on Haggai, Zechariah, Malachi and Jonah.* ICC. Edinburgh: T&T Clark, 1912.
Morgenstern, J. "A Chapter in the History of the High-Priesthood." *AJSL* 55 (1938): 1–24, 183–97, 366–77.
Moyise, Steve. "Intertextuality and the Study of the Old Testament in the New." Pages 14–41 in *The Old Testament in the New Testament: Essays in Honour of J. L. North.* Edited by Steve Moyise. JSNTSup 189. Sheffield: Sheffield Academic, 2000.
———. "The Language of the Old Testament in the Apocalypse." *JSNT* 76 (1999): 97–113.
Moyise, Steve, ed. *The Old Testament in the New Testament: Essays in Honour of J. L. North.* JSNTSup 189. Sheffield: Sheffield Academic, 2000.
Muilenburg, James. "Form Criticism and Beyond." *JBL* 88 (1969): 1–18.
Newman, Judith H. *Praying by the Book: The Scripturalization of Prayer in Second Temple Judaism.* EJL 14. Atlanta: Scholars Press, 1999.
Nicholson, Ernest Wilson. *Preaching to the Exiles: A Study of the Prose Tradition*

in the Book of Jeremiah. New York: Schocken, 1971.
Niditch, Susan. *The Symbolic Vision in Biblical Tradition*. Chico, CA: Scholars Press, 1983.
Niehr, Herbert. "Religio-Historical Aspects of the 'Early Post-Exilic' Period." Pages 228–44 in *The Crisis of Israelite Religion: Transformation of Religious Tradition in Exilic and Post-Exilic Times*. Edited by Bob Becking and Marjo C. A. Korpel. OtSt 42. Leiden: Brill, 1999.
Nielsen, Kirsten. "Intertextuality and Biblical Scholarship." *SJOT* 2 (1990): 89–95.
Nogalski, James D. *The Book of the Twelve: Micah–Malachi*. SHBC. Macon, GA: Smyth & Helwys, 2011.
———. *Literary Precursors to the Book of the Twelve*. BZAW 217. Berlin: de Gruyter, 1993.
———. *Redactional Processes in the Book of the Twelve*. BZAW 218. Berlin: de Gruyter, 1993.
Nurmela, Risto. "The Growth of the Book of Isaiah Illustrated by Allusions in Zechariah." Pages 245–59 in *Bringing out the Treasure: Inner Biblical Allusion and Zechariah 9–14*. Edited by Mark J Boda and Michael H. Floyd. JSOTSup 370. Sheffield: Sheffield Academic, 2003.
———. *Prophets in Dialogue: Inner-Biblical Allusions in Zechariah 1–8 and 9–14*. Åbo: Åbo Akademi University, 1996.
Odell, Margaret S. *Ezekiel*. SHBC. Macon, GA: Smyth & Helwys, 2006.
———. "'The Wall Is No More': Architectural and Ritual Reform in Ezekiel 43:8,." Pages 339–56 in *From the Foundations to the Crenellations: Essays on Temple Building in the Ancient Near East and Hebrew Bible*. Edited by Mark J. Boda and Jamie R. Novotny. AOAT 366. Münster: Ugarit-Verlag, 2010.
Olmstead, A. T. *History of the Persian Empire*. Chicago: University of Chicago Press, 1948.
Oppenheim, A. L. "The Babylonian Evidence of Achaemenian Rule in Mesopotamia." Pages 529–87 in *The Cambridge History of Iran: Volume 2—the Median and Achaemenian Periods*. Edited by Ilya Gershevitch. Cambridge: Cambridge University Press, 1985.
Orr, Avigdor. "The Seventy Years of Babylon." *VT* 6 (1956): 304–6.
Oswalt, John N. *The Book of Isaiah, Chapters 1–39*. NICOT. Grand Rapids: Eerdmans, 1986.
Pardes, Ilana. *Countertraditions in the Bible: A Feminist Approach*. Cambridge: Harvard University Press, 1992.
Patterson, Richard D. *Nahum, Habakkuk, Zephaniah*. Wycliffe Exegetical Commentary. Chicago: Moody Press, 1991.
Paulien, Jon. "Dreading the Whirlwind: Intertextuality and the Use of the Old

Testament in Revelation." *AUSS* 39 (2001): 5–22.
Perdue, Leo G., and Brian W. Kovacs, eds. *A Prophet to the Nations: Essays in Jeremiah Studies*. Winona Lake, IN: Eisenbrauns, 1984.
Person, Raymond F. *The Deuteronomic School: History, Social Setting, and Literature*. SBLMS 2. Atlanta: Society of Biblical Literature, 2002.
———. *Second Zechariah and the Deuteronomic School*. JSOTSup 167. Sheffield: JSOT Press, 1993.
Petersen, David L. *Haggai and Zechariah 1–8: A Commentary*. OTL. Philadelphia: Westminster, 1984.
———. *Late Israelite Prophecy: Studies in Deutero-Prophetic Literature and in Chronicles*. SBLMS 23. Missoula, MT: Scholars Press, 1977.
———. *Zechariah 9–14 and Malachi: A Commentary*. OTL. Louisville: Westminster John Knox, 1995.
———. "Zechariah's Visions: A Theological Perspective." *VT* 34 (1984): 195–206.
Petitjean, Albert. *Les oracles du proto-Zacharie: Un programme de restauration pour la communauté juive après l'exil*. Paris: Librairie Lecoffre, 1969.
Phinney, D. Nathan. "Life Writing in Ezekiel and First Zechariah." Pages 83–103 in *Tradition in Transition: Haggai and Zechariah 1–8 in the Trajectory of Hebrew Theology*. Edited by Mark J. Boda and Michael H. Floyd. LHBOTS 475. London: T&T Clark, 2008.
———. "Portraying Prophetic Experience and Tradition in Ezekiel." Pages 234–43 in *Thus Says the Lord: Essays on the Former and Latter Prophets in Honor of Robert R. Wilson*. Edited by John J. Ahn and Stephen L. Cook. LHBOTS 502. New York: T&T Clark, 2009.
Pierce, Ronald W. "Literary Connectors and a Haggai – Zechariah – Malachi Corpus." *JETS* 27 (1984): 277–89.
———. "A Thematic Development of the Haggai – Zechariah – Malachi Corpus." *JETS* 27 (1984): 401–11.
Pola, Thomas. "Form and Meaning in Zechariah 3." Pages 156–67 in *Yahwism after the Exile: Perspectives on Israelite Religion in the Persian Era*. Edited by Bob Becking and Rainer Albertz. Studies in Theology and Religion 5. Assen: Van Gorcum, 2003.
Pomykala, Kenneth E. *The Davidic Dynasty Tradition in Early Judaism: Its History and Significance for Messianism*. EJL 7. Atlanta: Scholars Press, 1995.
Porter, Stanley E. "The Use of the Old Testament in the New Testament: A Brief Comment on Method and Terminology." Pages 79–96 in *Early Christian Interpretation of the Scriptures of Israel: Investigations and Proposals*. Edited by Craig A. Evans and James A. Sanders. JSNTSup 148. Sheffield: Sheffield Academic, 1997.

Pröbstl, Volker. *Nehemia 9, Psalm 106 und Psalms 136 und die Rezeption des Pentateuchs*. Göttingen: Cuvillier, 1997.
Procksch, O. *Jesaia I*. KAT 9. Leipzig: Deichert, 1930.
Rast, Walter E. *Tradition History and the Old Testament*. Philadelphia: Fortress, 1971.
Redditt, Paul L. "The Formation of the Book of the Twelve: A Review of Research." Pages 1–26 in *Thematic Threads in the Book of the Twelve*. Edited by Paul L. Redditt and Aaron Schart. BZAW 325. Berlin: de Gruyter, 2003.
———. *Haggai, Zechariah and Malachi*. NCB. London: Marshall Pickering, 1995.
———. "Israel's Shepherds: Hope and Pessimism in Zechariah 9–14." *CBQ* 51 (1989): 631–42.
———. "Nehemiah's First Mission and the Date of Zechariah 9–14." *CBQ* 56 (1994): 664–78.
———. "The Two Shepherds in Zechariah 11:4–17." *CBQ* 55 (1993): 676–86.
———. *Zechariah 9–14*. IECOT. Stuttgart: Kohlhammer, 2012.
———. "Zerubbabel, Joshua, and the Night Visions of Zechariah." *CBQ* 54 (1992): 249–59.
Reimer, David J. *The Oracles against Babylon in Jeremiah 50–51: A Horror among the Nations*. San Francisco: Mellen Research University Press, 1993.
Reventlow, Henning Graf. *Die Propheten Haggai, Sacharja und Maleachi*. ATD 25.2. Göttingen: Vandenhoeck & Ruprecht, 1993.
Rhea, Robert. "Attack on Prophecy: Zechariah 13,1–6." *ZAW* 107 (1995): 288–93.
Roberts, J. J. M. *Nahum, Habakkuk, and Zephaniah: A Commentary*. OTL. Louisville: Westminster John Knox, 1991.
Rooke, Deborah W. "Kingship as Priesthood: The Relationship between the High Priesthood and the Monarchy." Pages 187–208 in *King and Messiah in Israel and the Ancient Near East: Proceedings of the Oxford Old Testament Seminar*. Edited by John Day. JSOTSup 270. Sheffield: Sheffield Academic, 1998.
———. *Zadok's Heirs: The Role and Development of the High Priesthood in Ancient Israel*. Oxford Theological Monographs. Oxford: Oxford University Press, 2000.
Rose, Wolter H. *Zemah and Zerubbabel: Messianic Expectations in the Early Postexilic Period*. JSOTSup 304. Sheffield: Sheffield Academic, 2000.
Rudman, Dominic. "Zechariah 5 and the Priestly Law." *SJOT* 14 (2000): 194–206.
Rudolph, Wilhelm. *Haggai, Sacharja 1–8, Sacharja 9–14, Maleachi*. KAT 13.

Gütersloh: Mohn, 1976.

———. *Jeremia*. 3rd ed. HAT 12. Tübingen: Mohr Siebeck, 1968.

Sæbø, Magne. "Die deuterosacharjanische Frage: Eine forschungsgeschichtliche Studie." *ST* 23 (1969): 115–40.

———. *Sacharja 9–14: Untersuchungen von Text und Form*. WMANT 34. Neukirchen-Vluyn: Neukirchener, 1969.

Schaberg, Jane. *The Illegitimacy of Jesus: A Feminist Theological Interpretation of the Infancy Narratives*. New York: Crossroad, 1990.

Schaefer, Konrad R. "The Ending of the Book of Zechariah: A Commentary." *RB* 100 (1993): 165–238.

———. "Zechariah 14 and the Composition of the Book of Zechariah." *RB* 100 (1993): 368–98.

———. "Zechariah 14 and the Formation of the Book of Zechariah." SSD diss., Ecole biblique et archéologique française, 1992.

———. "Zechariah 14: A Study in Allusion." *CBQ* 57 (1995): 66–91.

Schart, Aaron. *Die Entstehung des Zwölfprophetenbuchs*. BZAW 260. Berlin: de Gruyter, 1998.

———. "Reconstructing the Redaction History of the Twelve Prophets: Problems and Models." Pages 34–48 in *Reading and Hearing the Book of the Twelve*. Edited by James D. Nogalski and Marvin A. Sweeney. SymS 15. Atlanta: Society of Biblical Literature, 2000.

———. "Redactional Models: Comparisons, Contrasts, Agreements, Disagreements." Pages 893–908 in *Society of Biblical Literature 1998 Seminar Papers ... Part Two*. SBLSP 37. Atlanta: Scholars Press, 1998.

Schearing, Linda S. "Queen." Pages 583–86 in vol. 5 of *ABD*. Edited by David Noel Freedman. New York: Doubleday, 1992.

Schmid, Konrad, and Odil Hannes Steck. "Restoration Expectations in the Prophetic Tradition of the Old Testament." Pages 41–82 in *Restoration: Old Testament, Jewish and Christian Conceptions*. Edited by James M. Scott. Supplements to the JSJ 72. Leiden: Brill, 2001.

Schöpflin, Karin. "God's Interpreter: The Interpreting Angel in Post-Exilic Prophetic Visions of the Old Testament." Pages 189–203 in *Angels: The Concept of Celestial Beings—Origins, Development and Reception*. Edited by Friedrich V. Reiterer, Tobias Nicklas, and Karin Schöpflin. Deuterocanonical and Cognate Literature Yearbook 2007. Berlin: de Gruyter, 2007.

Schultz, Richard L. *The Search for Quotation: Verbal Parallels in the Prophets*. JSOTSup 180. Sheffield: Sheffield Academic, 1999.

Scott, R. B. Y. "The Meaning of *maśśā'* as an Oracle Title." *JBL* 67 (1948): v–vi.

Seitz, Christopher R. *Word without End: The Old Testament as Abiding Theological Witness*. Grand Rapids: Eerdmans, 1998.

Seybold, Klaus. *Bilder zum Tempelbau: Die Visionen des Propheten Sacharja*. Stuttgart: KBW, 1974.
Siebeneck, Robert T. "Messianism of Aggeus and Proto-Zacharias." *CBQ* 19 (1957): 312–28.
Sinclair, Lawrence A. "Redaction of Zechariah 1–8." *BR* 20 (1975): 36–47.
Sister, Moses. "Die Typen der Prophetischen Visionen in der Bibel." *Monatsschrift für Geschichte und Wissenschaft des Judentums* 78 (1934): 399–430.
Smelik, Klaas A. D. "The Function of Jeremiah 50 and 51 in the Book of Jeremiah." Pages 87–98 in *Reading the Book of Jeremiah: A Search for Coherence*. Edited by Martin Kessler. Winona Lake, IN: Eisenbrauns, 2004.
Smith, Morton. "Jewish Religious Life in the Persian Period." Pages 219–78 in *The Cambridge History of Judaism, Volume One—Introduction: The Persian Period*. Edited by W. D. Davies and Louis Finkelstein. Cambridge: Cambridge University Press, 1984.
Snyman, Gerrie. "Who Is Speaking? Intertextuality and Textual Influence." *Neot* 30 (1996): 427–49.
Sommer, Benjamin D. "Exegesis, Allusion and Intertextuality in the Hebrew Bible: A Response to Lyle Eslinger." *VT* 46 (1996): 479–89.
———. *A Prophet Reads Scripture: Allusion in Isaiah 40–66*. Contraversions Series. Stanford, CA: Stanford University Press, 1998.
Sowers, Sidney G. "Did Xerxes Wage War on Jerusalem?" *HUCA* 67 (1997): 43–53.
Stacey, W. D. *Prophetic Drama in the Old Testament*. London: Epworth, 1990.
Stade, Bernhard. "Deuterosacharja: Eine kritische Studie I." *ZAW* 1 (1881): 1–96.
———. "Deuterosacharja: Eine kritische Studie II." *ZAW* 2 (1882): 151–72.
———. "Deuterosacharja: Eine kritische Studie III." *ZAW* 2 (1882): 275–309.
Stead, Michael R. *The Intertextuality of Zechariah 1–8*. LHBOTS 506. London: T&T Clark, 2009.
———. "Sustained Allusion in Zechariah 1–2." Pages 144–70 in *Tradition in Transition: Haggai and Zechariah 1–8 in the Trajectory of Hebrew Theology*. Edited by Mark J. Boda and Michael H. Floyd. LHBOTS 475. New York: T&T Clark, 2008.
———. "Visions, Prophetic." Pages 818–26 in *Dictionary of the Old Testament: Prophets*. Edited by Mark J. Boda and J. Gordon McConville. Downers Grove, IL: IVP Academic, 2012.
Stern, Ephraim. "The Persian Empire and the Political and Social History of Palestine in the Persian Period." Pages 70–87 in *The Cambridge History of Judaism, Volume One—Introduction: The Persian Period*. Edited by W. D. Davies and Louis Finkelstein. Cambridge: Cambridge University

Press, 1984.

———. "Religion in Palestine in the Assyrian and Persian Periods." Pages 245–55 in *The Crisis of Israelite Religion: Transformation of Religious Tradition in Exilic and Post-Exilic Times*. Edited by Bob Becking and Marjo C. A. Korpel. OtSt 42. Leiden: Brill, 1999.

Stinespring, W. F. "No Daughter of Zion: A Study of the Appositional Genitive in Hebrew Grammar." *Enc* 26 (1965): 133–41.

Stökl, Daniel. "Yom Kippur in the Apocalyptic Imaginaire and the Roots of Jesus' High Priesthood: Yom Kippur in Zechariah 3, 1 Enoch 10, 11QMelkizedeq, Hebrews and the Apocalypse of Abraham 13." Pages 349–66 in *Transformations of the Inner Self in Ancient Religions*. Edited by Jan Assmann and Guy G. Stroumsa. SHR 83. Leiden: Brill, 1999.

Stolper, Matthew W. "The Governor of Babylon and Across-the-River in 486 B.C." *JNES* 48 (1989): 283–305.

Stolz, F. "נשא." Pages 769–74 in vol. 2 of *TLOT*.

Strand, Kenneth A. "The Two Olive Trees of Zechariah 4 and Revelation 11." *AUSS* 20 (1982): 257–61.

Stuart, Douglas K. "The Prophetic Ideal of Government in the Restoration Era." Pages 283–92 in *Israel's Apostasy and Restoration: Essays in Honor of Roland K. Harrison*. Edited by Abraham Gileadi. Grand Rapids: Baker, 1988.

Stuebing, Kathleen W. "Sibling Rivalry." Pages 17–18 in *The IVP Women's Bible Commentary*. Edited by Catherine Clark Kroeger and Mary J. Evans. Downers Grove, IL: InterVarsity Press, 2002.

Stuhlmueller, Carroll. *Rebuilding with Hope. A Commentary on the Books of Haggai and Zechariah*. ITC. Grand Rapids: Eerdmans, 1988.

Stulman, Louis. *The Prose Sermons of the Book of Jeremiah: A Redescription of the Correspondences with Deuteronomistic Literature in the Light of Recent Text-Critical Research*. SBLDS 83. Atlanta: Scholars Press, 1987.

Süring, Margit L. *The Horn-Motif in the Hebrew Bible and Related Ancient Near Eastern Literature and Iconography*. Andrews University Seminary Dissertation Series 4. Berrien Springs, MI: Andrews University Press, 1980.

Sweeney, Marvin A. "Concerning the Structure and Generic Character of the Book of Nahum." *ZAW* 104 (1992): 364–77.

———. *Isaiah 1–39, with an Introduction to Prophetic Literature*. FOTL 16. Grand Rapids: Eerdmans, 1996.

———. "Structure, Genre, and Intent in the Book of Habakkuk." *VT* 41 (1991): 63–83.

———. *The Twelve Prophets*. 2 vols. Berit Olam. Collegeville, MN: Liturgical Press, 2000.

———. "Zechariah's Debate with Isaiah." Pages 335–50 in *The Changing Face*

of Form Criticism for the Twenty-First Century. Edited by Marvin A. Sweeney and Ehud Ben Zvi. Grand Rapids: Eerdmans, 2003.
Tai, Nicholas Ho Fai. *Prophetie als Schriftauslegung in Sacharja 9–14: Traditions- und kompositionsgeschichtliche Studien.* Calwer Theologische Monographien 17. Stuttgart: Calwer, 1996.
Thomas, Matthew A. *These Are the Generations: Identity, Covenant, and the* toledot *Formula.* LHBOTS 551. New York: T&T Clark, 2011.
Thompson, David L. "Ezekiel." Pages 1–284 in *Ezekiel, Daniel.* Edited by David L. Thompson and Eugene E. Carpenter. Cornerstone Biblical Commentary. Carol Stream, IL: Tyndale House, 2010.
Thompson, J. A. *The Book of Jeremiah.* NICOT. Grand Rapids: Eerdmans, 1980.
———. *1, 2 Chronicles.* NAC 9. Nashville: Broadman & Holman, 1994.
Tidwell, N. L. A. "*Wā'ōmar* (Zech 3:5) and the Genre of Zechariah's Fourth Vision." *JBL* 94 (1975): 343–55.
Tiemeyer, Lena-Sofia. "Through a Glass Darkly: Zechariah's Unprocessed Visionary Experience." *VT* 58 (2008): 573–94.
Tigchelaar, Eibert. "Some Observations on the Relation between Zechariah 9–11 and Jeremiah." Pages 260–70 in *Bringing out the Treasure: Inner Biblical Allusion and Zechariah 9–14.* Edited by Mark J. Boda and Michael H. Floyd. JSOTSup 370. Sheffield: Sheffield Academic, 2003.
Toffelmire, Colin M. "Form Criticism." Pages 257–71 in *Dictionary of the Old Testament: Prophets.* Edited by Mark J. Boda and J. Gordon McConville. Downers Grove, IL: IVP Academic, 2012.
Tollington, Janet E. "Readings in Haggai: From the Prophet to the Completed Book, a Changing Message in Changing Times." Pages 194–208 in *The Crisis of Israelite Religion: Transformation of Religious Tradition in Exilic and Post-Exilic Times.* Edited by Bob Becking and Marjo C. A. Korpel. OtSt 42. Leiden: Brill, 1999.
———. *Tradition and Innovation in Haggai and Zechariah 1–8.* JSOTSup 150. Sheffield: JSOT Press, 1993.
Tournay, Raymond Jacques. *Seeing and Hearing God with the Psalms: The Prophetic Liturgy of the Second Temple in Jerusalem.* Translated by J. Edward Crowley. JSOTSup 118. Sheffield: JSOT Press, 1991.
Tov, Emanuel. "Some Aspects of the Textual and Literary History of the Book of Jeremiah." Pages 145–67 in *Le Livre de Jérémie: Le prophète et son milieu, les oracles et leur transmission.* Edited by P.-M. Bogaert. BETL 54. Louvain: University of Louvain Press, 1981.
Tsevat, Matitiahu. "Alalakhiana." *HUCA* 29 (1958): 109–34.
Tuell, Steven Shawn. *Ezekiel.* NIBCOT 15. Peabody, MA: Hendrickson; Milton Keynes, UK: Paternoster, 2009.
Unger, Merrill F. *Zechariah: Prophet of Messiah's Glory.* Grand Rapids:

Zondervan, 1970.
Vanderhooft, David S. *The Neo-Babylonian Empire and Babylon in the Latter Prophets*. HSM 59. Atlanta: Scholars Press, 2000.
VanderKam, James C. "Joshua the High Priest and the Interpretation of Zechariah 3." *CBQ* 53 (1991): 553–70.
Vaux, Roland de. *Ancient Israel: Its Life and Institutions*. Translated by John McHugh. New York: McGraw-Hill, 1961.
Vermeylen, J. *Du prophète Isaïe à l'apocalyptique: Isaïe, I–XXXV, miroir d'un demi-millénaire d'expérience religieuse en Israël*. EBib 1. Paris: Gabalda, 1977.
Vriezen, T. C. "Two Old Cruces." *OtSt* 5 (1948): 80–91.
Waterman, Leroy. "The Camouflaged Purge of Three Messianic Conspirators." *JNES* 13 (1954): 73–78.
Waters, M. M. "Darius and the Achaemenid Line." *Ancient History Bulletin* 10 (1996): 11–18.
Watts, James W. "Text and Redaction in Jeremiah's Oracles against the Nations." *CBQ* 54 (1992): 432–47.
Watts, James W., and Paul R. House, eds. *Forming Prophetic Literature: Essays on Isaiah and the Twelve in Honor of John D. W. Watts*. JSOTSup 235. Sheffield: Academic, 1996.
Watts, John D. W. *Isaiah 1–33*. WBC 24. Waco, TX: Word, 1985.
———. "Zechariah." Pages 308–65 in vol. 7 of *The Broadman Bible Commentary, Volume 7: Hosea–Malachi*. Edited by C. J. Allen. London: Marshall, Morgan & Scott, 1972.
Weinfeld, Moshe. *Deuteronomy and the Deuteronomic School*. Oxford: Clarendon, 1972.
Weis, Richard. "A Definition of the Genre *Maśśā'* in the Hebrew Bible." PhD diss., Claremont Graduate School, 1986.
———. "Oracle." Pages 28–29 in vol. 5 of *ABD*.
Wendland, Ernst R. *The Discourse Analysis of Hebrew Prophetic Literature: Determining the Larger Textual Units of Hosea and Joel*. Mellen Biblical Press Series 40. Lewiston, NY: Mellen Biblical Press, 1995.
Werline, Rodney A. *Penitential Prayer in Second Temple Judaism: The Development of a Religious Institution*. EJL 13. Atlanta: Scholars Press, 1998.
Whitley, C. F. "The Seventy Years Desolation—a Rejoinder." *VT* 7 (1957): 416–18.
———. "The Term Seventy Years Captivity." *VT* 4 (1954): 60–72.
Wildberger, Hans. *Isaiah 13–27*. Translated by Thomas H. Trapp. CC. Minneapolis: Fortress, 1997.
Willi-Plein, Ina. *Prophetie am Ende: Untersuchungen zu Sacharja 9–14*. BBB 42. Köln: Hanstein, 1974.

Williamson, H. G. M. *1 and 2 Chronicles*. NCB. Grand Rapids: Eerdmans, 1982.
―――. *The Book Called Isaiah: Deutero-Isaiah's Role in Composition and Redaction*. Oxford: Oxford University Press; New York: Clarendon, 1994.
―――. *Ezra, Nehemiah*. WBC. Waco, TX: Word, 1985.
―――. "The Governors of Judah under the Persians." *TynBul* 39 (1988): 59–82.
―――. "Structure and Historiography in Nehemiah 9." Pages 117–32 in *Proceedings of the Ninth World Congress of Jewish Studies (Panel Sessions: Bible Studies and Ancient Near East, Jerusalem 1988)*. Edited by M. Goshen-Gottstein. Jerusalem: Magnes, 1988.
Wilson, Robert R. *Prophecy and Society in Ancient Israel*. Philadelphia: Fortress, 1980.
Winkle, Ross E. "Jeremiah's Seventy Years for Babylon: A Re-Assessment (Part I: The Scriptural Data)." *AUSS* 25 (1987): 201–14.
Witt, Douglas A. "Zechariah 12–14: Its Origins, Growth and Theological Significance." PhD diss., Vanderbilt University, 1991.
Wöhrle, Jakob. "The Formation and Intention of the Haggai–Zechariah Corpus." *JHS* 6 (2006): Article 10.
―――. *Die frühen Sammlungen des Zwölfprophetenbuches: Entstehung und Komposition*. BZAW 360. Berlin: de Gruyter, 2006.
Wolde, Ellen van. "Trendy Intertextuality?" Pages 43–49 in *Intertextuality in Biblical Writings: Essays in Honour of Bas van Iersel*. Edited by Sipke Draisma. Kampen: Kok, 1989.
Wolters, Al. *Zechariah*. HCOT 19. Leuven: Peeters, 2014.
Woodcock, Michael D. "Forms and Functions of Hope in Zechariah 9–14." PhD diss., Fuller Theological Seminary, 2004.
Woude, Adam S. van der. "Die beiden Söhne des Öls (Sach 4:14): Messianische Gestalten?" Pages 262–68 in *Travels in the World of the Old Testament: Studies Presented to M. A. Beek*. Edited by M. S H. G. Heerma van Vos, Ph. H. Houwink ten Cate, and N. A. van Uchelen. Assen: Van Gorcum, 1974.
―――. "Zion as Primeval Stone in Zechariah 3 and 4." Pages 237–48 in *Text and Context: Old Testament and Semitic Studies for F. C. Fensham*. Edited by W. Claassen. JSOTSup 48. Sheffield: Sheffield Academic, 1988.
Wright, N. T. *Jesus and the Victory of God*. Christian Origins and the Question of God 2. Minneapolis: Fortress, 1996.
Yamauchi, Edwin M. *Persia and the Bible*. Grand Rapids: Baker, 1990.
Yarchin, William, ed. *History of Biblical Interpretation: A Reader*. Peabody, MA: Hendrickson, 2004.
Young, T. Cuyler. "The Consolidation of the Empire and Its Limits of Growth under Darius and Xerxes." Pages 53–111 in *The Cambridge Ancient History—Volume IV: Persia, Greece and the Western Mediterranean c. 525*

to 479 B.C. Edited by John Boardman, N. G. L. Hammond, D. M. Lewis, and M. Ostwald. Cambridge: Cambridge University Press, 1988.

———. "The Early History of the Medes and the Persians and the Achaemenid Empire to the Death of Cambyses." Pages 1–52 in *The Cambridge Ancient History—Volume IV: Persia, Greece and the Western Mediterranean c. 525 to 479 B.C.* Edited by John Boardman, N. G. L. Hammond, D. M. Lewis, and M. Ostwald. Cambridge: Cambridge University Press, 1988.

Zapff, Burkard M. *Redaktionsgeschichtliche Studien zum Michabuch im Kontext des Dodekapropheton.* BZAW 256. Berlin: de Gruyter, 1997.

Zimmerli, Walther. *Ezekiel: A Commentary on the Book of the Prophet Ezekiel.* Hermeneia. Philadelphia: Fortress, 1979.

Ancient Sources Index

Old Testament

Genesis

1	190
2:9	76
2:25	75
3:7	75
4	187
4:2	187
7:17	20
7:23	24
9	190
9:23	75
10:8–12	21
10:10	23
11:1–9	30
13:14	96
13:16	65
18:2	96
18:8	72
19:20	42
22:4	96
22:11–13	96
24:63	96
24:64	96
25:14	136
25:25	186
27	186
27:41–42	191
29:34	46
31:11–13	96
32:11	191
33	191
33:1	96
33:14	191
33:17–30	191
33:5	96
36:33–39	76
37–50	193
37:20	188
37:22	188
37:24	188–89
37:25	96
37:28–29	188
39:20	188
39:22	188
40:3	188
40:5	188
40:15	188
41:14	188
43:3	193
43:8–9	193
43:29	96
43:33	68
44:14	193
44:16	193
44:18–34	193

46:28	193	Leviticus	
49	165		
50:15–21	191	6:15	76
		8	5
Exodus		8:9	67, 79
		8:10	71
3:13	44	8:12	71
3:14	44	16	5
3:15	44	16:4	79
6:18	71	26:33	21
6:21	71	26:39–40	118
7:3	67	26:39–45	116
7:16	44		
8:17	65	Numbers	
10:5	76		
11–12	6	3:19	71
12:29	188	7	163
18:23	65	7:13	75
22:10	75	8:4	96
23:5	136	11:11	136
23:23	157	16:1	71
24:17	79	18:2	46
24:23	79	18:4	46
25	6	20:26–28	67
25–27	5	21:4	158
25:9	96	22:6	24
25:40	96	22:13	108
26:30	96	22:14	108
27:8	96	23–24	137
28–29	5	23:3	96
28:24	79	23:7	137
28:37	79	23:18	137
28:39	79	24:2	96
28:40	79	24:3	137
29:6	67, 79	24:7	20
29:7	71	24:15	137
29:9	79	24:20	137
29:30	76	24:21	137
30:23–33	71	24:23	137
32:9	114	27:17	175
33:18	96		
39:28	79	Deuteronomy	
39:30	79		
39:31	79	2:12	76
		2:21–23	76

3:27	96	17:14	157
4:19	96	19:9	157
9:6	114		
9:13	114	Judges	
9:27	114		
11	175	3:19	47
11:10–17	175	5:12	42
11:11	174	8:3	25
11:11–15	175	9:15	176
11:11–17	174	10:16	158
11:13–17	175	16:16	158
11:14	174, 175	19:17	96
11:15	175		
11:17	174	1 Samuel	
11:24	24		
13:1	67	1:9	79
13:3	109	2:1	20
17:8–11	65	2:10	20
17:9	69	4:13	79
17:18	69	4:18	79
18	5	6:13	96
18:1	69	8:19	108
24:8	69	9:6	75
26:15	47	9:17	75–76
27:9	69	16:13	71
28–30	6	19:10	42
28:2	110	30:17	42
28:15	110		
28:26	21	2 Samuel	
28:33	109		
28:45	110	1:10	79
29	6	5:3	24
29:27	109	6–7	60
32:40–42	137	7	6
33:17	20	7:5	24
34:2	24	7:7	24
		7:13	24
Joshua		7:27	24
		11:3	80
1:8	123	12:24	80
2:2	75	12:30	78
3:3	69	13:34	96
5:13	96	16:7	42
8:33	69	18:24	96
17:6	157	20:16	42

1 Kings

1–2	80
1:39	71
1:46	77
2:19	74, 79–80
3:1	24
7:27	24
7:29	24
8:46–53	116, 118
11:26	80
13:1	75
13:34	157
14:18	107
14:21	80
15:2	80
15:10	80
15:11–13	80
15:13	80
16:7	107
16:11	77, 79
16:12	107
16:31	80
18	191
18–19	80
19:13	186
19:19	186
20:20	42
20:39	75
21:17–19	137
22	94
22:10	79
22:11	20
22:17	85, 175, 177
22:17–22	84
22:19	72, 85, 96
22:19–21	12
22:42	80

2 Kings

1:8	186
2:2	186
2:8	186
2:11	75
3:2	80
3:27	109
4:6	158
4:38	68
6:1	68
6:16	24
6:17	96
8:9	44
8:13	96
8:26	80
9	141
9:7	107
9:18–19	24
9:22	80
9:25	136–138, 143
9:25–26	138
9:26	141
11	60
11:1	80
11:12	79
12:1	80
14:2	80
14:25	107
15:2	80
15:33	80
17:13	2, 107
17:14	114
17:23	107
18:2	80
19:22	20
20	30
21:1	80
21:10	107
21:19	80
22:1	80
23:31	80
23:36	80
24–25	30
24:2	107
24:8	80
24:18	80
25:1	115
25:2	107
25:3–7	115

25:8–12	115	3	163
25:13	24	3:3	24
25:16	24	5–6	102
25:25–26	115	5:1–2	72
		5:1–3	102
1 Chronicles		5:1–6:15	37
		5:2	163
1:30	136	5:3	163
3:17	163	5:12	30
3:19	163	5:14–16	162
5:28	71	6:7	164
6:3	71	6:14	37, 72, 102
6:23	71	8:24–32	74
9:2	69	8:33–34	74
9:24	43	9	115, 120
20:2	78	9:6–7	116
21:16	96	9:7	116
23:12	71	9:10	116
23:18	71	9:10–11	116
		9:11	116
2 Chronicles		9:11–12	120
		9:14	116
5:5	69	9:15	116
10:15	107	10:6	69
18:10	20		
18:16	175, 177	Nehemiah	
18:18	72, 96		
23:11	79	1	115, 120
23:18	69	1:4	115
24:27	136, 138	1:6	116
29:25	107	1:6–7	116
30:27	47, 69	1:7	116
32:21	157	1:8–9	120
32:31	30	2:6	66
33:11	30	8	170
33:36	30	8–10	115
36	37	8:11	47
36:21	19, 112	9	113–17, 120, 170
		9:1	115
Ezra		9:1–4	115
		9:2	116
1–6	37, 80, 101–2, 164	9:5–37	115
1:8	163	9:9	116
2–5	163	9:16	116
2–6	71	9:17	114

9:26	116	68:6	47
9:29	114, 116	72:2	157
9:30	114, 116–17	72:4	157
9:32	60	72:12	157
9:33	116	74	115
9:34	114, 116	75:5–6	20
9:35	113	75:11	20
9:36	116	79	115, 119
10	114	83:5	157
10:29	69	83:9	46
10:35	69	85:12	76
11:20	69	89	115
		89:6–7	72
Esther		89:18	20
		89:25	20
1:11	79	89:40	79
2:17	79	90:10	19
2:18	74	92:1	20
6:8	79	102:11	109
8:15	79	106	109, 115
9:27	46	106:6	116
		106:7	116
Job		106:23	116
		106:24	109
1–2	12	106:29	116
5:6	76	106:32	116
8:19	76	106:40	116
15:8	72	110:2	80
19:9	78	110:4	80
21:4	158	112:9	20
29:14	67, 79	132:18	79
31:36	78	137:7	42
		137:8	42
Psalms		148:14	20
2:2	80	Proverbs	
2:6–8	80		
21:3	78	1:20	78
21:5	77	4:9	79
24	12	9:1	78
29:5–7	176	12:4	79
45:4	77	14:1	78
47:7	42	14:24	79
48	51	16:31	79
48:3	51	16:32	25

Ancient Sources Index 231

17:6	79	5	5, 12, 154
17:15	75	5:1	71
20:10	75	6	5, 72, 84–85, 94
20:12	75	6:1	17, 20, 96
27:3	75	6:1–2	72
27:24	79	6:1–13	12
29:11	25	6:9	124
30:1	136	8:1–4	40
30:13	20	8:2	145
30:15	42	8:5	158
31:1	136	8:18	68
		9:2	41
Ecclesiastes		10:20–11:16	56
		11	115
4:3	75	11–12	56
4:15	66	11:1	56, 68
8:15	46	11:10	56
		11:11	23
Song of Songs		11:15	41, 44
		12–14	13, 39, 46–47, 57
3:11	78	12:1	41, 56
7:1	42	12:1–6	56
		12:4–6	45
Isaiah		12:6	41, 46, 56
		13	55–56, 140–41
1–11	5, 173, 184	13–14	46, 55–56
1–39	47	13–23	55–56, 135, 141
1:1	138, 146	13:1	136, 138, 146–48
1:10–17	128	13:1–22	55
1:21–26	177	13:1–14:23	30, 55
1:25	177	13:2	20, 44, 45
1:31	75	13:3–4	55
2–4	141	13:17	55
2:1	138, 146	13:17–18	31
2:1–4	41	13:19	55
2:2–4	41	13:19–22	56
2:3	6	14:1	46
2:6–21	41	14:1–2	46, 55–56
2:10–17	28	14:1–4	55
2:12–14	20	14:2	44, 46, 56
2:13	176	14:3–23	56
3:20	79	14:4–21	21, 55
3:23	67, 79	14:13	52
3:25–4:1	41	14:28	17, 136, 138, 148
4:2	69	14:29	140–41

14:31	12	34:2	109
15	140–41	35:2	41
15:1	136, 138, 148	35:6	41
17	141	35:10	110
17:1	136, 148	39	30
17:2	21	40–48	31
19	140–41	40–55	5, 47, 184
19:1	136, 148	40–66	9, 42
19:16	41, 44	40:1	42
20:3	67	40:9	43
20:6	42	40:26	96
21	55, 140–41	41:15	21
21:1	136–37, 148	41:27	43
21:1–2	137–38	42:1–9	41
21:1–10	30, 84	42:11	41
21:2	31, 84, 137	43:10	44
21:7	84	43:14	30
21:9	55	44–45	6
21:11	136, 148	44:22	108
21:13	136, 148	44:23	41
22	140–41	44:28	31
22:1	136, 148	45:1	31
22:20	176	45:3	44
22:25	148	45:9–14	41
23	140–41	45:13	31
23:1	136, 148	46:13	43
23:15–18	19	47	41
24	188	47:1	42
24:14	41	47:1–15	30
24:22	188	47:5–7	28
25:6–10	41	47:6	109
26:2	12	48	28
26:19	41	48–51	5
28:1	78	48:14–15	30–31
28:3	78	48:20	31, 41, 43
28:5	78	49:1–26	41
29–31	5, 173, 184	49:8–13	41
29:6	109	49:13	41
30	141	49:14	43
30–31	5	49:18	41, 96
30–33	5	49:22	20
30:1–5	141	49:23	44
30:6	136, 148	50–51	28
30:6–7	141–42	51:1–11	41
33:9	176	51:3	43, 110

Ancient Sources Index

51:9	42	65:7	108
51:9–11	41	65:12	109
51:11	43, 110	65:24	109
51:16	41, 43	66:4	109
51:17	42	66:8	43
52:1	42–43	66:10	41
52:1–2	41	66:18–24	41
52:2	43		
52:7	43	Jeremiah	
52:8	41, 43		
52:9	41	1	12, 90–91
52:11	42	1:11	90, 94
52:11–12	41	1:11–14	85
52:13	20	1:12	19, 94
54	5, 41	1:13	90, 94
54:1	41, 45	1:14	19
54:8	109	1:14–19	94
54:9	109	1:15	79, 91
55:1	22	1:16	19
56:1–8	41	1:17	19
56:6–7	46	1:19	91
56:3	46	2:15	108
56:6	46	3:1	108
56:6–7	41	3:2	96
56:7	41	3:7	108
57:15	20	3:10	108
57:16	109	3:12	124
57:17	109	3:14	43
59:9–15	115	3:15	178
59:20	43	3:18	22, 25, 42, 108
60–62	41	3:19	109
60:4	96	4:1	108
60:10	109	4:2	94
60:14	43	4:6	43
60:16	44	4:7	109
61:3	43, 79, 110	4:13–28	110
61:7	41	4:23–28	94
62:1	43	4:28	110
62:3	67, 78–79	4:31	43
62:10	42	5:2	94
62:11	43	5:3	108
63:7–64:11	115	5:28	108
64:4	109	6:2	43
64:8	109	6:22	25, 42, 52
64:9	43	6:23	43

6:26	12	13:5	155
6:34	178	13:6	155
7	6, 111	13:7	155
7:1–8:3	107	13:8–11	155
7:2	109	13:10	108
7:5–6	108, 113	13:17	178
7:9	5, 109	13:18	78, 80
7:11–12	108	13:20	96, 178
7:13	109	14	119
7:14	108	14:1–15:4	150–51, 174–75, 179, 193
7:22	108	14:2–3	175
7:24–26	108	14:4	174
7:25	107–8	14:5	174
7:26	114	14:6	174
7:27	109	14:14	174
7:32	173	14:19	43
7:33	21	14:22	174
7:34	110	15:7	21
8:5	108	15:14	109
8:19	43	15:19	5
9:18	43	16	12
9:23	108	16:9	110
10:1–3	178	16:11	108
10:10	109	16:12	108
10:21	177–78	16:13	108–9
10:22	25, 42	16:15	22, 25, 42
11:1–2	178	17:4	109
11:1–5	107	17:16	178
11:1–13	108, 178	17:22	108
11:4	108	18:1–12	107
11:5	108	18:11	107
11:6	109	18:16	109
11:7	108	19	12
11:9–14	107	19:1–2	107
11:10	108	19:6	173
11:11	109	19:8	109
11:14	109	19:10–11	107
11:17	178	19:14–20:6	107
12:3	173	20–39	30
12:10	178	20:16	110
13	12	21:1–10	107
13:1	155	21:5	109
13:1–11	155	22	6, 77, 176, 178
13:2	155	22–25	178–81
13:3–4	155		

Ancient Sources Index 235

22:1–23:8	178	23:35	136
22:3	108	23:36	152
22:6	176	23:38	136
22:6–7	176	24	12, 90–91
22:7	176	24:1	85, 90, 94, 96
22:14	176	24:1–2	90, 94
22:15	176	24:3	90, 94
22:18	77	24:4–10	91, 94, 178
22:20	176	24:5	91
22:20–23	109	24:7	108
22:22	176, 178	24:8	91
22:23	176	24:13	90
22:24–30	181	24:14–19	91
22:28	109	25	13, 30, 39, 47, 49–
23	177, 191		51, 57, 179, 181
23:1	175, 177	25:1	17
23:1–3	175	25:1–11	51, 107
23:1–4	176, 178	25:1–13	49–50, 180
23:2	175, 177	25:1–14	178
23:3	175	25:1–32:38	49
23:5–6	178	25:4	107
23:19	109	25:5	107
23:22	107	25:9	109
22:30	77	25:10	110
23	6, 77, 138, 152	25:11	19, 46, 112
23:3	77	25:11–12	19, 30
23:5–6	68–69, 77	25:12	19, 111
23:8	22, 25, 42, 77	25:12–14	51
23:9–40	148–49, 178	25:12–38	179
23:10	150	25:13	179
23:11	149	25:15–29	173
23:13	149	25:15–38	49–50
23:14	149	25:18	51
23:15	149	25:19–26	51
23:16	149	25:25	31
23:16–22	72	25:26	30–31, 50, 52
23:17	149	25:28	50–51
23:18	65, 79	25:29	50–51
23:28	149	25:29–38	51
23:30	149	25:30–31	47, 50
23:33	136, 148–49	25:31	51
23:33–38	137–38	25:32	109
23:33–40	148, 150–52, 179	25:34	175
23:34	136	25:34–36	178
23:34–40	148–50	25:34–38	175–76

25:35	175	33:18	69
25:36	175	33:21	69
25:38	176	34:1–7	107
26	12, 110–11	34:8–22	107
26–44	107	34:13	108
26:5	107	34:14	108
26:18	43	35	12
26:19	111	35:1–19	107
27–28	12	35:15	107
27:19	24	35:17	109
27:38 (LXX)	179	36	5, 12, 110
28:1	17	36:1	111
29:1–7	19	36:2–3	111
29:10	19, 30, 46, 112	36:3	118
29:12	109	36:6	111
29:19	107	36:7	111, 118
30–31	6	36:9	111
30:17	43	36:22	111
30:23	109	36:32	111
31:6	43	37	60
31:8	22, 25, 42, 52	37–41	12, 110
31:10	21, 178	37:2	107
31:12	43	37:3	60
31:36	65	38:6	188–89
31:37	65	38:6–7	188
32	12	38:9–11	188
32:1–2	107	38:13	188
32:6–16	107	38:14	51
32:15–38 (LXX)	49–50	38:20–23	94
32:17–25	115	38:21	96
32:18	108	38:21–23	94
32:24–44	107	39:1	115
32:37	109	39:2	51
33	6, 69–70, 77	39:4	51
33:7	69	40–41	60
33:7–9	77	41:1–3	115
33:7–13	77	41:4–5	115
33:8	69	42:21	44
33:9	69	43	12
33:10–11	110	44:1–14	107
33:14–16	69	44:3	108
33:14–26	69	44:9	108
33:15–16	68–69, 77	44:10	108
33:17–18	69	44:21	108
33:17–26	77	46–50	43

Ancient Sources Index

46–51	42–43, 179	50:42	42–43
46:1	146–47	50:44	176
46:2–25	49	50:44–46	177
46:6	42	50:45	177
46:10	25, 42	51	12, 48
46:19	43	51:1	31, 52
46:27–28	49	51:1–2	30
47:1	147	51:1–64	49
47:1–7	49	51:6	42–43, 49
48:1–45	49	51:7	43
48:6	42	51:10	43
48:18	43	51:11	30, 48–49
48:19	42	51:12	110
48:25	20	51:19	47
49:1–5	49	51:24	43
49:19	176	51:25–26	49
49:23	49	51:27	48
49:27	49	51:28	30, 48
49:33–38	49	51:29	109
49:34–39	49	51:32	49
49:36	25, 43	51:33	42–43
49:36–37	25	51:35	43
50	47–48, 177, 179, 181	51:36	49
		51:41	31, 52
50–51	13, 30, 39, 42–43, 47–49, 57, 179	51:45	42–43
		51:48	42
50:1	107	51:50	42
50:1–46	49	51:59–64	48
50:3	42	52:12–16	115
50:5	43, 46–47	52:17	24
50:6–7	178	53:20	24
50:6–8	180		
50:8	30, 43	Lamentations	
50:8–13	30		
50:9	25, 42	2	5
50:10	44	2:14	136, 138
50:13	109	2:17	20, 110
50:14	21	2:20	60
50:15	49	3:53	21, 188
50:17	21, 180	4:15	42
50:17–18	21	4:21	45
50:28	43, 48–49	5:16	79
50:35–38	12, 176–77	5:22	109
50:38	177, 179		
50:41	42, 52		

Ezekiel		8–11	5, 84–85
		8:1	17, 68
1	12, 92–93	8:2	92, 95
1–3	5, 72, 85	8:2–4	92
1–11	6	8:5	92, 95–96
1:2	17	8:6	92, 95
1:3	146	8:7	92, 95
1:4	92, 95	8:8–9	93, 95
1:4–14	92	8:9	92
1:4–2:8	85	8:9–10	92
1:15	95	8:10	95
1:24	95	8:12	92, 95
1:28	95, 97	8:13	158
2	12, 92–93	8:14	95
2:1–2	93, 95	8:15	92, 95
2:1–8	97	8:16	95
2:2	95	8:17	92, 95
2:9	95	8:18	109
2:9–3:9	85	9–10	95
2:10	154	9:2–4	95
2:15	92	9:11	95
2:15–28	92	10	12, 92–93
3	12	10:1	92, 95
3:1	42	10:2	95
3:1–2	97	10:6	95
3:1–11	93, 95	10:7	95
3:7	67	10:9	92, 95
3:12	95	10:9–22	92
3:14	25	10:10	92
3:15	66	10:10–11	92
3:23	95	10:16	20
4–5	12	10:20	95
5	155	11:10	44
5:1–4	155	11:12	44
5:2	155	11:25	96
5:4	155	12	12, 140–41
5:5–17	155	12:1–10	141
5:13	25	12:1–16	138, 142
6	12	12:6	67–68
6:7	44	12:10	136, 138, 148
6:13	44, 79	12:11	67–68
7:4	44	12:11–16	141
7:9	44	12:20	44
8	6, 12, 92–93, 95	13:9	44
8–10	95	13:13	25

13:14	44	33	12, 52
13:21	44	33–37	173
13:23	44	33:11	42
14:1	68	33:31	68
14:8	44	34	153, 159–64, 173, 175–77
15:7	44		
16:12	74, 78	34–37	181
16:23	42	34:1–31	14, 159, 173
16:42	25	34:3	160
16:49	109	34:3–4	160
16:62	44	34:4	160
17–32	30	34:5	177
17:21	44	34:6	177
20:1	17, 68	34:8	175
20:18	108	34:11	160
20:27	108	34:12	177
20:30	108	34:16	160
20:36	108	34:20	160
20:38	44	34:21	177
20:42	44, 108	34:22	162
20:44	44	34:22–31	162
21:24	75	34:23	160
21:26	67, 78–79	34:23–24	162
21:31	67, 79	34:25	162
22:16	44	34:31	160, 162
22:22	44	35:4	44
22:30	66	35:9	44
23:42	78	35:12	44
23:49	44	36:7	137
24	12	36:11	44
24:1–14	154	36:24	52
24:13	25	36:26–27	52
24:14	110	36:33–36	109
24:17	79	36:37–38	52
24:23	79	37	12, 52, 92–93, 153, 160–64
24:24	44, 67–68		
24:27	67–68	37:1–2	95
25–32	52	37:3	95
25–48	53	37:6	44
25:3	109	37:8	92, 95
25:5	44	37:9	25, 43
25:7	44	37:9–10	93, 95
26:1–14	19	37:12–14	52
27:5	176	37:13	44
27:6	176	37:13–23	160

37:14	44	43:5	95
37:15–28	14, 159, 173	43:15	20
37:22–25	52	43:19	69
37:23	160, 162	44	5, 12, 68, 92–93
37:23–28	162	44:4	92, 95
37:24	160, 162	44:5–31	93, 95
37:26	52	44:15	69
37:26–28	52	44:18	79
37:27	52, 160	46:19	95
37:28	52	46:21	95
38–39	5, 13, 31, 39, 45, 47, 51–53, 57	47:1	95
		47:2	95
38:6	51	47:7	95
38:8	51	47:13	157
38:11	53	47:14	108
38:11–12	51		
38:15	51	Daniel	
38:16	44, 51		
38:17	107	1:2	23
38:17–39:20	51	3:25	66
38:23	44, 51	3:26–45 (LXX)	115
39:2	51	4:34	66
39:6	44	8	84
39:7	44	8:8	43
39:7–8	51	9	115–16, 120
39:10	44, 51	9:1	19
39:13	51	9:2	112
39:21	51	9:3	115
39:21–24	51	9:5	116
39:21–29	44	9:6	116
39:22	44	9:10	116
39:23–29	51	9:10–11	116
39:25	51	9:14	116
39:28	44	9:16	116
40	5	9:24	112
40–42	53	10:5	75
40–48	5, 52–53, 95	11:14	43
40:3	75, 95	11:34	46
40:4	95–96		
40:17	95	Hosea	
40:24	95		
42:4	66	1:1	17
42:13	95	1:9	5
42:15	95	2:10	5
43	53	3:1	158

5:1	60	8:2	90–91, 94
8:6	5	8:2–3	91, 94
9:1	45	8:3	47
9:10	108	8:4–14	5
11:5	108	9	12
12:11	107	9:1	42, 96
13:2	5	9:1–4	85
14:7	5		
14:10	123	Obadiah	

Joel

		1	17
1:2	108		
1:2–14	12	Jonah	
2	5		
2:12	108	3:3	66
2:20	24	3:3–4	66
2:21–24	45		
		Micah	

Amos

		1:1	17
		4:10	21
1:1	17	4:13	20
1:14	109	7:18–20	5
3:7	72		
3:14	20	Nahum	
4	5		
4:11	5	1	140–41
6:10	47	1:1	136, 138, 148
7:1	90, 94	1:2–3:19	142
7	12, 90–91, 191	1:4	176
7–8	85	1:11–14	145
7:1	90	2:9	42
7:1–3	84, 97		
7:2–3	91, 94	Habakkuk	
7:4	90, 94		
7:4–6	97	1	140–41
7:5–6	91, 94	1–2	54–55
7:7	90, 94	1:1	136, 138, 148
7:7–8	84	1:2–2:1	54
7:8	90, 94	1:2–2:20	141–42
7:8–9	91, 94	1:3	96
7:14	186–87	1:5	42
8	6, 90–91	1:5–11	31, 53, 145
8:1	90, 94	2	13, 39, 47, 57
8:1–2	84	2:2	55

2:2-20	31, 54	1-14	18, 151
2:4	54	1:1	26, 102, 126, 145, 164
2:6-20	54		
2:8	44, 54	1:1-6	1, 11-14, 57, 82, 101, 104-6, 112, 118, 121-23, 125-28, 130-31
2:9-11	5		
2:20	47, 53-55		
3	55		
3:1	146	1:2	109, 116, 118, 122-25, 128
3:2-15	54		
3:12-14	54-55	1:2-6	117, 124-25
3:14	109	1:3	106-8, 118-19, 122-25, 195
3:16-19	54		
		1:4	2, 15, 105-8, 113-14, 116, 118, 122, 124-25
Zephaniah			
1:1	17	1:4-6	57, 124
1:7	47	1:5	1, 108, 116, 118
3:14	45-46	1:5-6	106, 122, 125
		1:6	2, 107-8, 110, 116, 118-19, 124-25
Haggai			
		1:6-17	19
1-2	71-72	1:7	26, 36, 102, 164
1:1	61	1:7-17	6, 12, 18, 22, 25, 61, 122
1:12-14	61		
2:1-2	61	1:7-6:15	12-13, 17-18, 22, 26, 28-29, 36-37, 39, 41, 57, 59, 61-63, 73, 81, 83, 85-86, 94, 96, 99, 105, 122, 126
2:4	61		
2:6-9	104		
2:10-23	104, 163		
2:21	61		
2:21-22	104		
2:23	61	1:8	24, 75, 86, 88, 90, 92
Zechariah		1:8-17	28, 37, 84, 87-89
		1:8-6:15	28-29, 88, 90-93
1	27, 119, 197	1:9	87-90, 92, 98
1-2	5, 84	1:10	87, 89, 91, 93
1-6	5, 20, 44, 152	1:11	24, 99
1-8	x, 2-6, 13, 18, 26, 37, 39, 58, 68-69, 73, 82, 101-6, 113, 117, 119, 121, 135, 138, 144, 147, 151, 172, 182-84, 195	1:11-13	87, 89, 91, 93, 98-99
		1:12	19, 46, 118-19
		1:12-13	99
		1:14	22, 105, 118, 122
		1:14-17	87, 89, 91, 93, 99
1-11	138	1:15	19, 25, 54, 104, 118, 122
1-13	4, 172		

1:16	102, 104–5, 118–19, 122	3:1	65, 72, 86–88, 90, 92, 94, 97
1:16–17	19	3:1–10	61, 73, 87–89, 105
1:17	22, 105	3:2–6	87, 89, 91, 93, 98
2:1	20, 86, 88, 90, 92	3:3	65
2:1–4	20–21, 61, 88–89	3:4	65, 69
2:1–5	53	3:5	24, 64–66, 79, 97
2:2	87–93	3:6	65
2:2–4	26	3:6–7	68
2:2–5	105	3:7	64–66
2:3	86, 88, 90, 92, 94, 97	3:7–10	87, 89, 91, 93
		3:8	56, 64, 68, 70, 76, 162
2:3–4	99		
2:4	20, 22, 87, 88–93, 104	3:8–10	68, 73
		3:9	69
2:5	75, 86, 88, 90, 92, 104	4	5, 23, 59, 61–62, 70–71, 73, 86, 98, 105
2:5–9	22, 53, 87		
2:5–17	61, 88–89	4:1–2	88
2:6	87–93	4:1–6	73
2:7–8	87, 89, 91, 93, 98–99	4:1–14	12, 61, 73, 84, 88–89
2:9	87, 89, 91, 93, 99	4:2	86, 88, 90, 92, 97
2:9–11	26	4:2–3	88
2:10	22, 25, 42–43	4:4	87–88, 90, 92
2:10–11	42–44, 46	4:5	87, 89, 98
2:10–17	13, 22, 25, 30, 39–41, 43, 46–49, 53–58, 87, 89, 91, 93, 104–5	4:6	73, 87, 89, 91, 93, 122
		4:6–10	13, 49, 73, 80, 87, 89, 91, 93, 102, 104, 163
2:10–3:10	56		
2:11	22, 41–43	4:9	44, 112
2:12	44, 54	4:10	87, 89, 91, 93
2:12–13	22, 43–45, 51	4:10–14	73
2:13	22, 44, 112	4:11	87, 90, 92
2:14	12, 41, 45–46, 56	4:13	87, 89, 98
2:14–16	45	4:14	70–72, 87, 89, 91, 93
2:15	41, 44, 46, 104, 112		
2:15–16	46, 55	5	103, 119
2:16	46	5:1	86, 88, 90, 92
2:17	47, 53–54	5:1–4	6, 23, 61, 84, 86–89, 104
3	5, 12, 23, 59, 61–65, 68, 70, 73, 77, 86, 119	5:2	86, 88, 90, 92, 97
		5:3	22, 87, 89, 91, 93
3–4	12	5:4	87, 89, 91, 93

5:5	86, 88, 90, 92	7:1–14	2, 106, 121–22, 128, 130, 132
5:5–6	23		
5:5–11	6, 23, 61, 87–89	7:1–8:23	12–14, 57, 82, 101, 104–6, 112, 121–22
5:6	87–93		
5:7	86, 88, 90, 92	7:2	111
5:7–8	23, 87	7:2–3	126
5:8	87, 89, 91, 93, 98, 99	7:3	66, 115, 129
		7:4	106, 118
5:9	86, 90, 92	7:5	82, 111, 115, 119
5:9–11	23	7:5–6	106, 122, 126–27
5:10	87, 90, 92	7:5–14	127
5:11	26, 87–88, 91, 93	7:7	2, 15, 57, 106, 109, 116, 126, 128, 195
6	59, 62, 77		
6:1	86, 88, 90, 92	7:7–10	106, 122
6:1–3	88, 90, 92	7:7–14	128
6:1–8	6, 12, 24–25, 61, 84, 87	7:8	106, 128
		7:8–10	104, 118
6:1–15	88–89	7:8–14	127
6:2	24	7:9	107
6:4	87–88, 90, 92	7:9–10	2, 107, 113, 127–28
6:5	43	7:9–12	128
6:5–6	87, 89, 91, 93	7:11	108, 114
6:6	24, 42	7:11–12	106, 108, 122, 128
6:6–7	24	7:11–14	127
6:7	24, 87, 89, 91, 93, 98–99	7:12	15, 57, 106, 109, 114, 116–17, 128, 195
6:8	42, 87, 89, 91, 93, 99		
		7:12–14	106, 122
6:9	25, 88	7:13	109, 128–29
6:9–15	6, 12, 25, 61, 73–74, 76–78, 81, 87, 89, 91, 93, 102, 105, 154, 162	7:13–14	128
		7:14	109, 127–29
		8	6
		8:1	106
6:10	74, 88	8:1–7	105
6:11	75, 78, 80, 89	8:1–8	12
6:12	75, 77	8:1–13	106
6:12–13	69, 76	8:2	116
6:13	75–78, 80	8:9–13	12, 72, 102, 104, 163
6:14	78		
6:15	44, 81, 104, 112	8:14	106, 108–10, 116, 127
7	6, 128–29, 197		
7–8	ix, 105, 111, 116–18, 126, 128, 130	8:14–15	110, 112
		8:14–22	106
7:1	26, 73, 102, 106, 126, 164	8:14–23	106, 133
		8:16–17	104, 118

Ancient Sources Index

8:18	106	10:1–2	151, 174–75, 179, 194
8:18–19	119		
8:19	115	10:1–3	14, 150, 166, 169, 174, 176, 188, 192–93
8:20–23	104		
8:23	141		
8:24–32	74	10:2	174–75, 180
8:33–34	74	10:2–3	175
9	x, 135, 165, 192	10:3	165
9–10	6, 137, 165–66, 173, 183, 188–89, 193	10:3–12	165
		10:4–12	187–88, 192
		10:6	193
9–11	138, 140–42, 145	10:6–11	165
9–13	172	10:7	193
9–14	x, 2, 4–6, 11–12, 14, 57–58, 82, 102, 123, 130, 135, 139, 144, 147–48, 151–53, 164, 166, 169–74, 178–85, 187, 189–92, 195, 197	11	157, 160–61, 163, 188
		11:1	12, 176
		11:1–3	14, 153, 166, 169, 174, 176–77, 192–93
		11:2	12, 175–76
9:1	12, 14, 102, 135–38, 147–48, 152, 165, 169, 185	11:3	175–76
		11:4	153, 155–56, 173
		11:4–5	155
9:1–4	165	11:4–16	5, 12, 14, 153–56, 159–64, 166–67, 173–76, 180–81, 192, 194
9:1–8	165, 188		
9:1–17	165, 187–88, 192		
9:1–11:3	4, 14, 173		
9:6–8	165	11:4–17	141
9:8	165	11:5	155–56, 158, 187
9:8–10	165	11:6	155–58
9:9	12, 45–46	11:7	173
9:9–10	174, 180, 188	11:7–12	155
9:9–13	165	11:7–14	157
9:10	165, 193	11:9	158
9:11	183–84, 187–88, 189, 193–94	11:10	155, 157–58, 166
		11:11	155
9:11–13	165	11:12	155
9:12	165	11:13	155, 169
9:13	188, 193	11:14	155, 157, 166
9:14	165	11:15	155
9:14–17	165	11:15–16	158
9:16	79, 165	11:16	155–56, 159–60
9:16–17	165	11:17	12, 14, 153–54, 166, 169, 174, 176–77, 180, 192–93
9:17–10:3	175		
10:1	174–75, 193		

12	135, 141, 192	14:4	165
12–14	14, 135, 138, 140–41, 145, 165–66, 173, 181, 183, 185, 187–88, 194	14:8	24, 165
		14:9	165
		14:12	166
		14:13	165
12:1	12, 14, 102, 135–38, 147–48, 152, 165, 169, 185, 192	14:14	166
		14:16	166
		14:18	166
12:1–13:6	165–66, 180–81, 192	14:19	166
		14:20	165
12:1–13:9	5, 173	14:21	165–66
12:2	166		
12:2–13:6	185, 192	Malachi	
12:3	165–66		
12:4	165–66	1:1	14, 135–38, 141, 147–48, 152
12:4–5	166		
12:6	165–66	2:2	65
12:7–8	166	3:7	108
12:8	165		
12:9	165–66	**Ancient Near Eastern Texts**	
12:10	166		
12:11	165	Cyrus Cylinder	32
13:1	165–66, 185		
13:1–6	181, 185, 194	Darius I's Bisitun Inscription	
13:1–9	5		
13:2	151, 185, 194	*DB Bab.* 19	44
13:2–6	150–51		
13:3	151, 185, 194	*Nabonidus Chronicle*	32
13:3–6	185		
13:4	151, 165, 185–86, 187	**Deuterocanonical Books**	
13:4–5	184, 188, 194	Baruch	
13:4–6	185		
13:5	186–87	1–3	120
13:5–6	183	1:15–3:8	115
13:7	177		
13:7–9	12, 14, 154, 166, 169, 174, 177, 180, 185, 187, 192–93	1 Enoch	
		10	81
13:8–9	180		
14	4, 11, 172	Sirach	
14:1–21	5, 165–66, 173, 185, 192	38:34–39:3	123
14:2	166		
14:3	166		

Ancient Sources Index

Dead Sea Scrolls

1QS 1:18–3:12	115
4Q254 4:2	72
4Q393	115
4Q504–506	115
11QMelkizedeq	81

New Testament

Matthew

1	161
27:9–10	169

Hebrews

5:1–10	80
7:1–25	80

Revelation

10:5	137
10:6	137
11	72
19:12	78

Rabbinic Works

Genesis Rabbah

44:6	136

Early Christian Writings

Augustine

Epistle 143.2	xi

Greco-Roman Literature

Herodotus, *Histories*

1.178–200	34–35
1.188–91	32
3.150–59	34
3.159	34

Xenophon, *Cyropaedia*

7.5.7–32	32
7.58	32

Modern Authors Index

Achtemeier, Elizabeth Rice 107
Ackerman, Susan 181
Ackroyd, Peter R. 23, 27, 36–37, 68, 71, 73, 80, 102–3, 115, 163–64
Aejmelaeus, Anneli 50, 179–80
Ahlström, G. W. 60
Albertz, Rainer 17
Alter, Robert 190
Amsler, S. 84
Andersen, Francis I. 54
Andreasen, Niels-Erik A. 80
Applegate, John 19
Bakhtin, Mikhail 8
Baldwin, Joyce G. 20, 29, 70–73, 76, 80, 107, 117
Barker, Margaret 23, 62, 69–70
Barnes, William Emery 21
Bartel, A. 163
Barthes, Roland 8
Bautch, Richard J. 116
Beale, G. K. 10
Bedford, Peter R. 33, 37
Begg, Christopher T. 30, 56
Begrich, Joachim 115
Behrens, Achim 85
Bellinger, W. H., Jr. 60
Bellis, Alice Ogden 48–49
Ben-Porat, Ziva 161, 189

Ben-Yashar, M. 163
Ben Zvi, Ehud 121, 123
Berger, P.-R. 163
Berlin, Adele 45, 54
Berquist, Jon L. 34
Beuken, Wim A. M. 2–3, 66, 79, 102–3, 109, 113, 128
Bianchi, F. 162
Bič, Miloš 62, 64
Bickerman, E. J. 26, 181
Biddle, Mark 22
Blenkinsopp, Joseph 102
Block, Daniel I. 31, 52, 95–96
Boda, Mark J. 1, 3, 7, 13, 17–18, 22, 27–28, 39, 45–46, 49, 57–61, 74, 82–83, 85, 101, 104, 106–8, 111–16, 118–22, 126–27, 130, 135, 144–45, 150–51, 153–54, 157, 162, 164, 169–74, 180–83, 185, 187, 189–90, 192–95
Boehmer, J. 31, 52
Boer, P. A. H. de 136
Bosshard-Nepustil, Erich 103

- 249 -

Braun, Roddy L. 102
Brewer, D. I. 6
Brewer, Julius August 29, 124–25, 154, 157
Briant, Pierre 32–34, 36, 38
Bright, John 48, 148
Bruce, F. F. 81
Brueggemann, Walter 107
Butterworth, Mike 122
Calvin, Jean xi
Carroll, Robert P. 8, 48–50, 69, 107, 149–50, 179
Carter, Charles E. 163
Chandler, Daniel 8
Chapman, Stephen B. 195
Childs, Brevard S. 55–56
Clark, David J. 19, 106
Clements, Ronald E. 55, 137
Coggins, R. J. 62, 64, 101–2,
Colless, Brian E. 38
Conrad, Edgar W. 18, 64, 186
Cook, J. M. 32, 34, 36, 38
Cook, Stephen L. 63, 154–56, 161, 180–81
Cowley, Arthur E. 45, 78
Crotty, Robert B. 180
Crüsemann, Frank 45
Curtis, Adrian 10
Dandamaev, Muhammad A. 32–36
Deeley, Mary Katharine 173
Delcor, Mathias 2, 171, 183
Delkurt, Holger 3, 5
Dempster, Stephen G. 195
DeRouchie, Jason S. 190
Dobbs-Allsopp, F. W. 45
Dodd, C. H. 161
Draisma, Sipke 9
Edelman, Diana 23, 27
Ehrlich, A. B. 24
Elliger, Karl 174
Eph'al, Israel 35
Erlandsson, Seth 55
Eskenazi, Tamara Cohn 102
Eslinger, Lyle 10
Evans, Craig A. 72, 81

Fewell, Danna Nolan 9
Finitsis, Antonios 84, 97
Fishbane, Michael A. 7, 19, 69, 83, 172
Floyd, Michael H. v, x–xi, 3, 5, 14, 23, 37, 62, 66, 85, 123–24, 138, 145, 147, 154, 162, 172, 179, 186–87
Fohrer, Georg 67, 154
Follis, Elaine R. 22
Foucault, Michel 8
Franke, Chris A. 30
Franzmann, Majella 30
Fretheim, Terence E. 48, 149–50
Friebel, Kelvin G. 67, 154
Fried, Lisbeth S. 17, 31, 33
Galling, Kurt 37
Gärtner, Judith 186
Gehman, H. S. 136
Genette, Gérard 167
Gesenius, Wilhelm 45, 78
Goldingay, John 55, 146–47
Good, Robert M. 21
Gosse, Bernard 43, 50, 56, 180
Grabbe, Lester L. 38, 59, 60
Green, Joel B. 10
Grothe, Jonathan F. 69
Gunkel, Hermann 115
Haerinck, E. 32–33, 36
Hallaschka, Martin 86
Halpern, Baruch 20, 24, 71, 104
Hanson, Paul D. 61–62, 103, 157, 159, 162, 169, 180
Haran, Menahem 50, 180
Harrelson, Walter 81
Hatim, Basil 8, 11
Hatina, Thomas R. 9
Hays, Richard B. 10
Heil, John Paul 173
Heltzer, Michael 35
Hepner, Gershon 6
Hiebert, Theodore 54
Hoglund, Kenneth G. 35
Holladay, William L. 48, 138, 159

Horst, Friedrich	84, 124	Mallowan, Max	32
House, Paul R.	103	Marguerat, Daniel	10
Janzen, J. Gerald	50, 179	Margulis, Barry Baruch	137, 147
Japhet, Sara	102, 162	Martens, Elmer	8
Jeppesen, Knud	47	Mason, Ian	8, 11
Jeremias, Christian	2, 23, 63, 65, 71, 84, 145	Mason, Rex A.	2–3, 7, 23, 28, 54, 62, 64–65, 71, 102–4, 107–9, 116–17, 153, 156, 159–60, 171–72, 174–75, 177, 180, 183, 186, 188–89
Johnson, Aubrey R.	60		
Jones, Barry Alan	195		
Jones, Douglas R.	48, 107, 136, 150		
Joüon, Paul	45		
Kaminski, Carol M.	190		
Kautzsch, Emil	45, 78	Mastin, Brian A.	79
Kessler, John	3, 17, 27, 163–64	McHardy, W. D.	25
Kessler, Martin	48, 50, 180	McKane, William	107, 148
Kim, Hyukki	45	Mede, Joseph	169, 170
Kim, Seyoon	81	Melvin, David P.	98
Kline, Meredith G.	72	Merrill, Eugene M.	23, 71, 80
Kloos, Carola J. L.	22	Meuleau, Maurice	35
Knierim, Rolf P.	85	Meyer, Lester V.	156, 159, 161
Knight, Douglas A.	7	Meyers, Carol L.	ix, 3, 18, 20–21, 23–24, 29, 43–44, 62, 64, 78, 103, 105–6, 111, 118, 122, 127, 163, 186–89
Koldewey, Robert	34		
Kovacs, Brian W.	107		
Kristeva, Julia	8		
Kuhrt, Amélie	32–36		
Laato, Antti	62, 64, 69–70, 74, 76		
		Meyers, Eric M.	ix, 3, 18, 20–21, 23–24, 29, 43–44, 62, 64, 78, 103, 105–6, 111, 118, 122, 127, 163, 186–89
LaMarche, Paul	171		
Lambert, G.	136		
Larkin, Katrina J.	4, 45, 130, 156, 172, 174–77, 184, 186, 188		
		Miscall, Peter D.	9, 136
Lee, Suk Yee	6, 130, 184, 188	Mitchell, Hinckley Gilbert	29, 124–25, 154, 157
Lenzi, Alan	xi		
Leske, Adrian	165	Morgenstern, J.	70, 71
Lichtenberger, Hermann	81	Moyise, Steve	8–10
Lindblom, Johannes	84	Muilenburg, James	85
Lipinski, E.	115	Muraoka, Takamitsu	45
Litwak, Kenneth D.	10	Newman, Judith H.	120
Lohfink, N.	110	Nicholson, Ernest Wilson	107
Long, Burke O.	22, 84	Niditch, Susan	71–72, 84–85, 97
Lukonin, Vladimir G.	32–36	Niehr, Herbert	60, 62, 181
Lust, Johan	162	Nielsen, Kirsten	8
Lutz, Hanns-Martin	2		
Machinist, Peter	21		

Nogalski, James D.   3, 103, 172, 186–87, 195
Novotny, Jamie R.   49
Nurmela, Risto   3, 5, 43, 46–47, 127, 130, 159–60, 172–77, 184
O'Connor, M.   24
Odell, Margaret S.   52–53, 95
Olmstead, A. T.   26, 36
Oppenheim, A. L.   32
Orr, Avigdor   19
Oswalt, John N.   146
Pardes, Ilana   190
Patrick, Frank Y.   3
Patterson, Richard D.   54
Paulien, Jon   10
Perdue, Leo G.   107
Person, Raymond F.   3–4, 130, 172–73, 175–77, 184, 188
Petersen, David L.   ix, 3, 18, 20, 22–25, 28–29, 39–41, 43, 46, 62, 64, 67, 71, 76, 84, 107, 109–10, 112–13, 117–18, 125, 127–28, 139, 148–57, 159, 162, 186, 188
Petitjean, Albert   2, 40, 78, 113, 117, 128
Phinney, D. Nathan   3, 95, 97
Pierce, Ronald W.   103
Pola, Thomas   3, 67
Pomykala, Kenneth E.   162
Porter, Stanley E.   1, 9, 58, 151, 169
Pröbstl, Volker   115
Procksch, O.   137
Rast, Walter E.   7
Redditt, Paul L.   3, 23, 28, 71, 78, 103, 117, 127, 144, 154–58, 162, 165, 174, 180, 185–88
Reimer, A.   59
Reimer, David J.   22, 30, 36, 42–44, 46–47, 49

Reventlow, Henning Graf   186, 188
Rhea, Robert   185, 187
Roberts, J. J. M.   54–55
Rooke, Deborah W.   61–64, 71, 74–75, 79
Rose, Wolter H.   61, 63, 65–66, 68, 72, 74, 78–80
Rudman, Dominic   3, 23
Rudolph, Wilhelm   24, 48, 71, 76, 105
Sæbø, Magne   146, 188
Schaberg, Jane   161
Schaefer, Konrad R.   4, 11, 172, 184
Schart, Aaron   3, 103, 144, 195
Schearing, Linda S.   80
Schmid, Konrad   37
Schnocks, Johannes   3
Schöpflin, Karin   97–98
Schultz, Richard L.   10–11, 161
Scott, James M.   37
Scott, R. B. Y.   137
Seitz, Christopher R.   8
Seybold, Klaus   104
Sherwin-White, S.   36
Siebeneck, Robert T.   70, 74
Sinclair, Lawrence A.   107, 109–10, 112
Sister, Moses   84
Smelik, Klaas A. D.   48
Smith, John Merlin Powis   29, 124–25, 154, 157
Smith, Morton   181
Snyman, Gerrie   9
Sommer, Benjamin D.   9–10, 161
Sowers, Sidney G.   26
Stacey, W. D.   67, 154
Stade, Bernhard   2, 171, 183
Stead, Michael R.   3, 5, 83, 96, 122, 127–28, 189
Steck, Odil Hannes   37
Stern, Ephraim   35, 164, 181
Stewart, Alexander C.   xi
Stinespring, W. F.   45
Stökl, Daniel   81
Stolper, Matthew W.   35
Stolz, F.   136, 138

Modern Authors Index

Strand, Kenneth A. 71–72, 81
Stuart, Douglas K. 69
Stuebing, Kathleen W. 190
Stuhlmueller, Carroll 23
Stulman, Louis 107
Süring, Margit L. 20–21
Sweeney, Marvin A. 3, 14, 20, 31, 40–41, 55, 125, 128, 137–38, 145, 156–58, 186–88
Tai, Nicholas Ho Fai 4, 130, 172, 174–77, 184, 188
Thomas, Matthew A. 190
Thompson, David L. 95
Thompson, J. A. 102, 107, 136
Tidwell, N. L. A. 24, 67
Tiemeyer, Lena-Sofia 3, 98
Tigchelaar, Eibert 3, 174, 177–78
Tilford, Nicole xi
Toffelmire, Colin M. 85
Tollington, Janet E. 3–4, 21, 26, 29, 44, 47, 61–62, 64–65, 67–69, 71, 77, 80, 84, 96–97, 103–4, 106–10, 112, 119
Tournay, Raymond Jacques 60
Tov, Emanuel 50, 179
Tsevat, Matitiahu 137
Tuell, Steven Shawn 96
Unger, Merrill F. 21
Vanderhooft, David S. 17, 21, 30, 32, 49, 55–56
VanderKam, James C. 64, 66–67
Vaux, Roland de 59
Vermeylen, J. 56
Vriezen, T. C. 22
Waltke, Bruce K. 24
Waterman, Leroy 26, 36, 164
Waters, M. M. 34, 38
Watts, James W. 50, 103, 179
Watts, John D. W. 55, 128, 137
Weinfeld, Moshe 107, 109, 116

Weis, Richard 14, 136–46, 152, 179
Wendland, Ernst R. 192
Werline, Rodney A. 115, 120
Whitley, C. F. 19
Wildberger, Hans 55–56, 137
Williamson, H. G. M. 46–47, 56, 101–2, 117, 163
Willi-Plein, Ina 2, 130, 171–77, 184
Wilson, Robert R. 60
Winkle, Ross E. 19
Witt, Douglas A. 159–60
Wöhrle, Jakob 122
Wolde, Ellen van 9, 11
Wolters, Al 3, 187–88
Woodcock, Michael D. 138
Woude, Adam S. van der 22, 71, 74
Wright, N. T. 161
Yamauchi, Edwin M. 34–35
Yarchin, William 6
Young, T. Cuyler 32, 34, 36
Zapff, Burkard M. 103
Zimmerli, Walther 95–96

www.ingramcontent.com/pod-product-compliance
Lightning Source LLC
Chambersburg PA
CBHW021659230426
43668CB00008B/673